Acclaim for THE *JESUS* DRIVEN LIFE

"I scarcely know how to find words to do justice to this brilliant study. *The Jesus Driven Life* is nothing less than a magisterial synthesis of much that can be known about Jesus and the early centuries of Christianity and their continuing relevance for today."

Walter Wink,

United States Institute of Peace, Recipient: Martin Luther King, Jr. Peace Prize, author of the award winning *Engaging the Powers* and *The Human Being*

"There are so many books about finding meaning and fulfillment, secret formulas for success and prosperity. *The Jesus Driven Life* reminds us that we must be careful amidst all the narcissistic, self-centered prosperity preaching lest we lose the simple secret at the heart of Jesus -- if you want to find your life... you have to give it away. This is an invitation to take a closer look at the Pearl that is so precious it is worth leaving everything in the world to pursue."

Shane Claiborne,

Activist, recovering sinner and co-author of *Jesus for President*

"The Jesus Driven Life emerges out of Hardin's life struggles on his journey toward and into Jesus, reshaping his view of God and transforming the wayward self. His journey encompasses a wide range of biblical scholarship to help us understand God, Jesus, and believers united in redemptive solidarity (John 17:20-24). Our journeys may differ within this broad landscape of generous orthodoxy, but we profit from hearing Hardin's, whose synthesis of biblical, historical, and practical Christian wisdom is engaging."

Willard Swartley,

Author of *Covenant of Peace* and *Send Forth Your Light: A Vision for Peace, Mission, and Worship*, Emeritus Associated Mennonite Biblical Seminary

"There is extraordinary value in *The Jesus Driven Life* for any reader who is hungry for a realistic, intelligent, and peaceful version of the Christian faith. Michael Hardin faces directly those Christians who imagine the Bible as "a divine telegram from a retributive God," and offers a more compelling alternative. Hardin is a public theologian who writes with clarity and panache. By putting Jesus, rather than some ideologically driven "purposes" at the center, Hardin points us toward a nonviolent way of trusting in grace and forging more just civil societies."

Jon Pahl,

The Lutheran Theological Seminary, Philadelphia, author of *Empire of Sacrifice*

"Michael Hardin asks a simple question in this passionate, pastoral, and peaceable book — what would it mean for our life in the world were we truly to place the Jesus of the Gospels at the center? And Hardin's answer is pretty simple, too — it would mean a revolution of reconciliation and healing. Hardin challenges the reader head on. Here's Jesus. Here's his message. And here's what Jesus wants from us — trust, love responding to love, life that reflects the mercy of God seen in Jesus."

Ted Grimsrud,

Eastern Mennonite University, author of *God's Healing Strategy* and *Embodying the Way of Jesus*

"*The Jesus Driven Life* is a great and much needed book. Hardin takes an earth-shattering idea that has always been vaguely at back of our collective consciousness and puts it out front and center: we need to read the bible in principle and practice beginning from the gospel narrative of Jesus and the radically new thing he brings to the human situation. Jesus does not fit any current schemes of biblical interpretation, biblical literalist, literary critical or dispensationalist, which make the text more important than Jesus himself and thus neutralizes the revolution of his teaching. Rather we should see that Jesus has brought a transforming possibility of nonviolence and forgiveness to our way of being human, and all biblical interpretation, including the pathways of revelation in the Old Testament, flows from that. Hardin has given essential Christian reading for our time, a book that will overturn conventional hermeneutics to date."

Tony Bartlett,

Author of *Cross Purposes* and *Virtually Christian,* founder of Wood Hath Hope

"Michael Hardin's *The Jesus Driven Life* is a great new resource in the Christian Adventure. It bears a wonderful witness to the impact of Rene Girard's thought in enabling us to recover a fecund, fresh, basic Christian orthodoxy that is thoroughly ecumenical in its scope, richly biblical in its sourcing and gloriously Christ-centered in its excitement about God. Here is another push forward in the great paradigm shift that is reshaping Christianity from within."

James Alison,

Catholic priest, theologian and author of *Faith Beyond Resentment* and *The Joy of Being Wrong*

"Unlike most popular and scholarly books which contain few ideas and insights and many illustrations and evidences, this text flashes with insight and coruscates like a Roman candle. We're given a detailed restatement of Synoptic, Pauline, Johannine and Patristic theology and interpretation. A convincing demonstration of the power of Girard's "mimetic realism" that shows how deftly the Christian story reveals the human world (anthropology) and how elegantly it deploys its therapeutic resource (forgiveness) at the precise point of infection (vengeance). Hardin deploys Girard's realism masterfully against the contagion of violence we also call 'sin.'"

Robert Hamerton-Kelly,

Co-founder of Imitatio Inc, Emeritus, Stanford University, author of *The Gospel and the Sacred* and *Sacred Violence.*

"In this wonderful book Michael Hardin argues that the church and its official theology domesticated Jesus and eviscerated the Bible. Taken alone both were too dangerous, too powerful, to be tolerated. Loaded with qualifications and philosophical encrustations Jesus and the Bible ceased to unveil the world's violence. They were, in fact, called upon to sustain the violence of the powerful—the very violence they intended to reveal, critique, and destroy. *The Jesus Driven Life* presents a Jesus who refuses to be silenced, even by the theologians, and a Bible that pulls back every shroud to reveal the marks of death upon the victims of injustice and scapegoating."

John E. Phelan, Jr.

President and Dean, North Park Theological Seminary

"More and more followers of Jesus are waking up to the extent to which western Christianity is steeped in the idolatrous values of western (especially American) culture. In this comprehensive, insightful, scholarly, yet very readable work, Michael Hardin presents a clear and compelling vision of the original *Christ*-driven (not "purpose-driven") Gospel and demonstrates how it contrasts with the dominant Christianity of our day. This religion too often amounts to little more than a "Christianized" version of the nationalism, consumerism, individualism, militarism and triumphalism of the pagan empire we find ourselves in. Because of this, the Christianity most of us are familiar with is radically different from the humble, servant-like, non-violent, self-sacrificial movement Jesus came to establish, a movement he called "the reign of God." For all who sense that there's something profoundly off with the westernized Gospel they've been given, *The Jesus Driven Life* is a 'must read'! And for all who don't yet sense what's wrong with the Gospel they've been given, it's even more of a 'must read'!"

Gregory Boyd

Pastor Woodland Hills Church, Founder, Christus Victor Ministries, author of *The Myth of a Christian Nation* and *The Jesus Legend*

"For those of us feeling dissatisfied with the Christianity we grew up with or whose only knowledge of the Bible and the story of Jesus is that they are a collection of silly superstitions that must either be accepted as solid fact or rejected as irrelevant, this is the book to read. In his engaging, conversational style, Michael Hardin offers a different way of looking at Jesus that shows he was far more concerned with compassion than with vengeance. *The Jesus Driven Life* is highly intellectual yet very accessible, and presents a new way of looking at our humanity through the Bible in a way that is relevant in the modern world."

Tyler Horst

High School Senior, Lancaster PA

"We have been told that we should imitate Jesus. I thought I did as a Christian until I read *The Jesus Driven Life*. Read this refreshing book with friends and I guarantee that Jesus' teachings in Scripture will inspire you to serve and love others like never before."

Jim Wiegner

Director of Development American Baptist International Ministries, Former Missionary

THE *JESUS* DRIVEN LIFE

Also By Michael Hardin

Stricken by God?
Nonviolent Identification and the Victory of Christ
Essays on the Nonviolent Atonement
Edited by Brad Jersak and Michael Hardin

Peace Be With You:
Christ's Benediction Amid Violent Empires
Essays on the Church at Peace in a World at War
Edited by Sharon Baker and Michael Hardin

Compassionate Eschatology
Essays on Apocalyptic Realism and Hope and
the Coming of the Peaceable Kingdom
Edited by Michael Hardin and Ted Grimsrud

Michael Hardin

THE *JESUS* DRIVEN LIFE

Reconnecting Humanity With Jesus

THE *JESUS* DRIVEN LIFE

This title is also available as a Preaching Peace DVD series that can be used for group study and discussion.

For book or DVD orders go to: www.preachingpeace.org or www.thejesusdrivenlife.com

---

Published in the United States of America by
JDL Press
Lancaster, PA 17602

ISBN 978-1-4507-0945-3

Cover design and interior layout by Lorri Hardin

Printed in the United States of America

Dedicated to the memory of

Derrion Albert 1993-2009

Who, innocent like Jesus,
Died at the hands of an unjust Chicago mob
While this book was being written.

"There's a time and the time is now and it's right for me
It's right for me, and the time is now.
There's a word and the word is love and it's right for me
It's right for me and the word is love."
-Jon Anderson & Yes

"Greatest of all Jesus is"
- Hillsong London

"Explaining belief has always been difficult. How do you explain a love and logic at the heart of the universe when the world is so out of whack?"
- Bono

Thanks to all who over the years have been my friends:

My Beloved, Lorri Lyn Hardin
My family: Galadriel, Arwen, Melian, Quelebrian and Laurelin
All of our brothers and sisters from Church in the Park
Rene and Martha Girard
Kim and Jane Kerchal
Mark and Carol Sullivan
Edwin A. Hallsten, Susan Bonfiglio
My friends in the Colloquium on Violence and Religion
Karsten Johnson
James P. Smollon, Jeffrey H. Krantz
Jonathan and Brenda Sauder
Dick and Phyl Leaman
John Kleist, Bryce Rich, John Stoner and Ron Vogt

And in Memory of Friends:

George Eldon Ladd
Eddie "Doc" Sivertsen
Bernard Ramm
F. Burton Nelson
Wolf Dieter Zimmermann
Raymund Schwager S.J.
Grandfather (Stalking Wolf)

I have learned so much from all of you. Thank you.

May Jesus always be your light!

Table of Contents

Foreword by Brian McLaren

Michael Hardin is an interesting guy. He's hard to categorize, but not hard to get to know. When you meet him, you might think he runs an organic food store or maybe leads a nonprofit that helps the homeless; you don't expect him to be the graduate of a respected Evangelical seminary. Maybe it's the ponytail, the sandals or that unmistakable aura of the 60's-70's counterculture -- you aren't surprised when you find out he's an old rock-and-roller who's a big fan of the classic rock band Yes. But you are surprised when you find out he's a serious independent scholar engaging with some of the most important theological issues of the day.

Michael exemplifies the generous orthodoxy that has won the hearts of many of us. He combines the zeal and activism of an Evangelical with the sensitivity to ecumenical history and scholarship that are more characteristic of Mainliners.

Reading *The Jesus Driven Life* is like joining Michael for a road trip. As you drive along, you get in a series of important and deep conversations, but you never feel that you're sitting in a lecture hall: you feel that you're talking with a wise friend.

As I read *The Jesus Driven Life*, I was especially intrigued by five themes that Michael returns to again and again. First, of course, is Jesus. As a committed Christian, I am enthralled whenever someone can help me better understand the One I believe, love, and seek to follow. In chapter after chapter, I felt I was getting a fresh understanding of this story from the gospels, of that parable on Jesus' lips, of this teaching he gave, of that action or interaction. For this theme alone, I was amply rewarded as a reader.

Second, I appreciated Michael's approach to Scripture. Whether he was reflecting on Genesis, the Psalms, or the writings of Paul, he would point out things that were obviously there all along, but I had been well trained not to notice. The Bible has been used to justify some pretty terrible things through the years, so much so that some people would be happy if it stayed in a museum somewhere. But Michael shows us how the Bible can be used for peaceable purposes.

Third, Michael addresses a particularly contentious and important theological issue, namely, atonement theory. Evangelical communities in particular are grappling afresh with atonement theology in recent years, sometimes with an inquisitor's fury. Michael understands better than most why this issue is so important, and he brings a fresh approach to the subject, getting to deeper levels of the issue that have powerful ramifications not just upon what we believe, but upon how we live.

Fourth, Michael realizes that in the twenty-first century, Christianity - along with all world religions - must develop a more mature, robust, and ethically responsible theology of violence and peacemaking. It was one thing for our ancestors to use God's name to legitimize violence inflicted with swords and spears; it was another thing when more recent ancestors sought to justify violence with guns and artillery. But for us and our children, living in a world of nuclear bombs, biological and chemical weapons, and as-yet unimagined terrorist adaptations of these weapons of mass destruction; the issue of God and violence takes on unprecedented importance.

Whether spoken in English or Arabic, the word "God" itself can seem like a dangerous weapon so far in the twenty-first century, a source of destruction rather than salvation. That's why it matters so much that Michael grapples with this issue head-on. He brings the important work of Rene Girard to bear on the subject, along with a range of needed resources from biblical studies and many other fields as well. Again, for this theme alone, the book rewards the readers' time and effort.

Finally, these four themes raise the question of our vision of God's character. What kind of God do we believe in? Is God violent? Or is God selectively violent to some, and kind to others, or kind for a while, but violent in the end - or vice versa? Does God practice torture? Does God suffer from an inability to forgive without inflicting pain on someone? Is God best seen as a warrior planning to defeat and eternally punish his opposition, or is God a God of peace who will not be satisfied until every prodigal is welcomed home? Michael courageously faces these kinds of questions, and he helps us do the same.

As you read, I hope you'll keep your attention especially focused on Michael's treatment of these five issues: Jesus, the Bible, atonement, violence, and God's character. No subjects could be more important - not only for Christians seeking to live a Jesus-driven life, but also for the future of the human race. After all, we woke up this morning on a planet where over half the population (Christian and Muslim) revere Jesus either as Son of God or a great prophet of God, yet these very same people are playing out old scripts that repeatedly have driven them to violence and counter-violence. If we don't want to stay stuck in these old cycles of violence, we need to listen to people like Michael Hardin ... and we need to read books like *The Jesus Driven Life*.

Brian D. McLaren
December 2009

Preface

This book has been written with two diverse types of readers in mind: readers of Rick Warren's *The Purpose Driven Life* or William Young's *The Shack*. I share certain affinities with both writers and their audiences. These points of juxtaposition might seem to cancel one another out but such is not the case, there is value in both conservative and progressive Christian theology in America today. I do not seek to find a *via media* between the two but to offer a third way, a new paradigm that incorporates the best (from my perspective) insights of both traditions. Warren's audience might think I am no longer orthodox; Young's audience might find me too orthodox. I have simply tried in this book to reframe orthodoxy in its most generous fashion (to paraphrase Brian McLaren). It seems to me that conversations in both Mainline and Emergent communities require this. Christianity is changing and there is nothing we can do to stop it. It is changing because it is finally being recognized that some theological paradigms handed down to us for centuries or millennia don't really work and are being given up.

Who specifically, is the audience for *The Jesus Driven Life*? Actually, it is multiple audiences. The text of the book is written for educated laity, those with an interest in theological matters, but perhaps with little or no formal training. I do my very best to explain things as I go along. Another audience will be served by the endnotes. They will desire to know more about why I say what I do, and hopefully, will also explore further these developing themes. *The Jesus Driven Life* proposes a radically new way of thinking from that which has dominated so much church life this past 2,000 years. Yet it is not new; it is as old as human history and as radical as the thought and life of Jesus of Nazareth.

A word about the title: I intentionally played off of Pastor Warren's title because I was not satisfied with the assumption that a 'purpose' should push me from behind, as though discipleship was to be a Type-A personality experience. There are certain Augustinian/Calvinist assumptions here worth questioning. I use the word 'Driven' in the more modest sense of traveling with Jesus, journeying through life with him as our chauffeur, if you will. Discipleship seems to me to become a walk of friends side-by-side (John 15:15).

This book grew out of talks given around the United States in 2007-2009. Everywhere I went people asked for more. So for those of you who pleaded, begged and cajoled me, here it is. My hope is that Christians in America would turn to Jesus. In so doing, perhaps, we might find ourselves no longer on the precipice of an apocalypse but standing at the horizon of a new adventure.

Thanks to Judy Yoder, Lorri Hardin and John Stoner for their careful reading of the manuscript; their hundreds of corrections have improved it immensely. I also thank other readers who took the time to offer suggestions: Jonathan and Brenda Sauder, James Alison, Tony Bartlett and Walter Wink. My deep gratitude goes to Bob and Susan Hurst who threw a wonderful party for me on the completion of the manuscript. To all who attended these talks at Akron Mennonite Church in 2008-2009, thank you for our conversations, your questions and your courage. My students in the Monday night classes at Landisville Mennonite Church continually inspire me.

I also thank the dozens of readers of the manuscript for their feedback: doctors, farmers, administrators, homemakers, teens and seniors, high school and college students, pastors and professors and real people from all walks of life and many different Christian backgrounds. Their enthusiasm for *The Jesus Driven Life* is encouraging and contagious.

To all of my friends and colleagues in the academy: please keep up your diligent efforts. I have done my best to interpret your work for a broader audience. I am certain that none of you will be completely satisfied with all of it, but I hope you take solace in the fact that I have done my best, as a lay theologian, to work at the same problems you do, and that I have learned from so many of you. I love your books!

Thanks especially to Walter and June Wink for their encouragement and friendship. Walter's research has had a salutary influence on me, particularly the way he engages Rene Girard and the mimetic theory. Rarely do New Testament scholars cross disciplines with the courage Walter has; nor do they pay the price Walter has paid. I encourage my readers to buy and read his *Engaging the Powers*.

Also, heartfelt thanks to Rene Girard, Robert Hamerton-Kelly, Peter Thiel, Lindy Fishburne and the Board of Imitatio Inc. for their generous support without which this project could not have come to fruition.

Although I am the author of record for this book, it was actually co-authored with my wife, Lorri. I write, she edits, thus making a tortured text readable. We have had thousands of conversations and experiences over the years around the various biblical and theological themes explored here. I cannot imagine life without her. Her story is much more interesting than mine because she actually lives *The Jesus Driven Life*; I just stumble along behind her.

My prayer is that this book will help all Christians to reconsider Jesus, truly Human, truly God, as the "one Word we are called to obey in life and in death" (*The Barmen Declaration*). I am grateful that God's mercies are new every morning. Like most of the nation I was stunned by the mob beating and consequent death of Derrion Albert this past autumn in Chicago. Such a promising life snuffed out for no reason at all. I did not know Derrion Albert. Yet, in his death I somehow felt the presence of the crucified Christ. I dedicate this book to him *in memoriam*. I pray that such violence never again erupts on our streets. May the peace of God prevail in our time.

Lent 2010
Lancaster, PA

Introduction

"Who is Jesus Christ for us today?" This was the question that haunted Dietrich Bonhoeffer in his Tegel Prison cell just a year before the Gestapo executed him in 1945. It is, in all reality, the question facing the church from the beginning and which each new Christian generation must ask itself. It is the question already present in the ministry of Jesus when, just after the mob would make him king, he retreats and asks his innermost circle of followers, "Who do you say I am?"

My friend Tony Bartlett observes, "Jesus has brought something 'startlingly new' to human history and to 'get it' you have to pay attention exclusively to him, as the master interpreter. Once this is established everything falls into place, postmodern confusion, the failure of the grid, the subversive presence of Christ in culture, the babble of New Testament criticism and the Bible's irreducible Jewish and Jesus core." The question we must ask today is "Do we get Jesus?" or have we substituted false portraits of him in our theology?

It is said of Albert Schweitzer that when he wrote his history of the 19th century Life-of-Jesus research, his study consisted of piles and piles of books everywhere. It takes great effort to try and stay abreast of the many and varied "Jesus's" that pop up on the current scene today. This is not only the case within the academic community but also in the churches, both as denominational institutions and on the congregational level. Jesus has many faces today.

This book is a contribution to this plethora of Jesus portraits available on the market. But it stands alone calling into question many of the deep assumptions shared by other portraits. In the long run, what really is the difference between Schweitzer's Jesus and the Jesus of Fundamentalist Dispensationalism? What differentiates either of these from the zealot- like Jesus of Reimarus and Brandon?[i] What is the difference between these and the triumphal Jesus of contemporary American Christianity?

Sadly, while there have been substantial contributions to Jesus research over the last century, little of it has filtered down to the level of the local church. Pastors are not equipped to deal with the complex relation of disciplines necessary to engage in this task. This void has been filled somewhat more recently, thanks to the work of the members of the Jesus Seminar, but even here there is great disparity among the portraits of Jesus produced by members of this group.

Over the years I have sought to immerse myself in studying the life and teaching of Jesus. The real difficulty was trying to hold together so many different claims and ways to warrant those claims. Rather than engage in debate with those in the Jesus guild, I decided to use their work to paint my portrait of Jesus, much like a painter uses paints to compose a masterpiece. These authors include both Jews and Christians. As disparate as they may seem at times, I have learned much from Samuel Sandmel, Geza Vermes, David Flusser, Harvey Falk, Sandor Goodhart, Jacob Neusner, Simone Weil, and Joachim Jeremias, Martin Hengel, Walter Wink, Marcus Borg, Richard Bauckham, N.T. Wright, Bruce Chilton, James Charlesworth, Raymund Schwager and Ben Witherington III as well as the older scholarship of T.W. Manson, Nils Dahl, Oscar Cullmann, Matthew Black, Gustaf Dalman, John A.T. Robinson, Gunther Bornkamm, George Eldon Ladd and C.H. Dodd. I even appreciated (much to my surprise) the portrait of Jesus composed by Pope Benedict XVI. I would be remiss and unkind if I did not acknowledge a debt to those from whom I learned much though I could not follow them to their conclusions including Rudolf Bultmann, John Dominic Crossan, Robert Funk, Burton Mack, Helmut Koester and James M. Robinson. There are hundreds of other names that I should include here. Walter Wink told me to "get rid of all the footnotes, they won't get you into heaven." I decided to keep them but turn them into endnotes so they are not distracting.

There is one seminal book that influences everything for me. I still recall October 1987, when in my last year of seminary, I purchased Father Raymund Schwager's *Must There Be Scapegoats?*[ii] It is the one book that I can say absolutely changed my course heading. Those privileged to know Father Schwager before his sad and untimely death in 2004 know his significance for anything that is written here. This book owes everything it has in it to others.[iii] I am not one to claim original ideas. I am only too well aware that we learn by imitating. I do think, though, that the way the insights of others are put together here is original.

I am not attempting to prove an academic hypothesis, which would require a more critical approach that the one being taken. This book is meant as a work of constructive theology; I am painting a portrait, writing from my own subjectivity. But I am writing about the Jesus I see in the Gospels. A way of describing the relationship I see between Jesus and the Gospels has been put forth by Richard Burridge who observes that some scholars look at the Gospels as a window through which one can see the 'historical Jesus.' Here the Gospel writers, communities and theologies are bypassed to get to the real Jesus. Another way to view the relation is to argue that the gospels are less like windows and more like mirrors, what we see in them is but a reflection of our own projection, we cannot get back to the author/s as such. Burridge's solution to this dilemma is to view the gospels like stained glass; yes, they can be peered through but "the main point about stained glass is the picture *within* the glass."[iv] The historical Jesus and the Gospel portraits of Jesus are both necessary for a complete understanding of Jesus.[v]

My friend John Stoner thought I should tell you, "In a culture which oversizes everything but thought and compassion, this is a big book. In that sense it is goes where most have not gone. The reader would have to think that a paradigm shift is worth some effort." I think that Christianity has reached a point in her self-understanding that we are ready and willing to accept a paradigm shift that rings true to Jesus as the New Testament writers share him. I try to refer to the Bible as much as possible in this book, for what is ultimately being proposed is a theological shift that could affect American Christianity at its core. And American Christianity is nothing if not biblical (or so its adherents insist). I offer this way of thinking not as a challenge to duel but as an invitation to an authentic conversation over the Bible and the ways we interpret the life of Jesus. American Christianity must answer the question "Who do you say I am?"

Is he the triumphalist white Jesus sold in many Bible bookstores? Is he the divine avenging super-hero that one encounters on the radio while driving across America? Is he the Billionaire in the Sky with promises of financial wealth? Is he the Militant Jesus sold on Christian TV with it's dangerous cocktail of American civil religion, 19th century revivalism, and an inerrant faith in an inerrant book? Where is Jesus to be found? Is he the victim of our religious zeal, cast out, temporalized in a dispensation, or frozen in dogmatic precision?

Is Jesus simply the purveyor of Good Morals, Good Citizenship and Good Ideals? Is he to be found as the Wandering Sage dispensing platitudes that may be separated from his mission? Isn't he the Nice Guy who failed? If his teaching didn't work for him (because it got him killed), then why bother with it today? Is he to be found in this kind of cynicism? Is he to be found as the Enlightened Mystic Redeemer of Gnostics, ancient and modern?

It is as if the time has come for us to play *'Will the Real Jesus Please Stand Up?'* It is important because it is apparent we do not all follow the same Jesus. Why is that? I intend to show you that certain philosophical and theological assumptions, structuring principles and interpretive grids, blind us from seeing what is right there in front of our eyes. Or rather, *who* is right there.

This brings me directly to a core conviction I have, namely, that Scripture does not make sense until we see Jesus in the context of his culture. There is a superficial approach to biblical culture in the Christian churches. Old reference works are still the norm. Those who use them are completely unaware of the reassessment ancient Judaism (and Christianity) has undergone (and continues to undergo) since the 1950's. They have no idea that discoveries both archeological and textual have influenced this regeneration of ancient Jewish studies. Perhaps the most important element in bringing about this new approach was the Shoah, the genocide of the Jews under Nazi rule and then the growing and profitable Jewish-Christian dialogues, particularly amongst biblical scholars. A key consequence of this new interpretation was that as we understood the groups in Jesus' culture differently, we also understood Jesus differently. He became clearer as they became clearer. It is no longer Jesus and Christians Vs. Judaism. We have learned to know Jesus the Jew.[vi]

The church has had a tendency to de-Judaize Jesus. When this happens, Jesus is understood as the perfect sacrifice sent from God to redeem us from our sin. His life doesn't count except as a preparation for sacrifice; the emphasis shifts from how Jesus lived as a model for our discipleship to how Jesus kept God's law perfectly so he could be a perfect/sinless sacrifice. De-Judaizing Jesus removes a key lens when interpreting Jesus' relationships to the peoples of his time. Paul gives us a clue that this is very important in Galatians 4:4 when he said that Jesus was born at the right time, born of a woman and born under Torah. The interpretive background of Jesus is the many different interpretive strategies of Torah and how they played out amongst the peoples. How did others interpret Torah and what did Jesus bring to the table when he interpreted Torah, and then lived out his interpretation? This, to me, is the heart of the matter I have been wrestling with for over thirty years.

Karl Barth was the first one to teach me how to keep the gospel message separate from the way that some in the church misinterpret or fail to live it. This has always given me hope for the discipline of Christian theology. No matter how bad the church mangles it, the message manages to get through from generation to generation.

From Dietrich Bonhoeffer I learned that the great theological questions were those with consequences for everyday life. The gospel was not cheap grace, it did not divorce spirituality and ethics, being and action; it was costly grace because the gospel bids us "Come and die." He also taught me how to read the Bible from the perspective of those below. These two have been my primary theological 'mentors' for over thirty years.

Jacques Ellul showed me the importance of applying the gospel to modern technological society as a critique and a balm. His work paved the way for me to understand how Rene Girard interprets the effects of the gospel on western civilization, effects that both deconstruct and reconstruct our way of thinking and relating.[vii] I mention this because my goal is to lead you through both the deconstruction and the reconstruction at the same time. I also follow Dietrich Ritschl and "will try to replace the question of how to make biblical texts relevant to modern situations, with the opposite question of how to make the modern situation relevant to the biblical texts."[viii]

It is imperative to see that every error begins with an honest but misguided question. We do not realize the extent or depth of the virtually invisible grids we use to interpret our reality. If we do not ask questions about the ideas that are assumed or presupposed in these founding grids, then our beliefs contain within themselves the acceptance of these assumptions. From this mislaid foundation any chance for dialogue will be lost as we descend into the absurd, the heretical, the error of unexamined assumptions that come from we know not where.

The same questions asked from within the same philosophical and theological assumptions, but asked differently by each generation, are all answered within this assumed grid of understanding. Very little changes, the core is identified as the orthodox 'faith of our fathers', and one becomes locked into a God who is bound by tradition not necessarily the revelation of Jesus. We must change the way we see and thus ask questions.

Sad as it is to say, Christianity has lost her vision. As the third common millennium opens, the Christian faith has been officially declared *persona non grata* (unwelcome) on the intellectual playground. Modern culture is post-Christian we are told. Yet, the blurring of the lines between the gospel and American culture is growing exponentially. Many are the ways the church has assimilated to culture, many are the ways American culture has its own internal religious structure.

We see that clearly now.

Now this is not necessarily a bad thing because what is being rejected is not the gospel (the good news), but the interpretation of that gospel which included slavery, colonialism, capitalism, holy war, pogrom, Inquisition and Holocaust as well as hierarchy, greed and an insatiable lust for power, wealth and control. In a nutshell, it is Constantinian Christianity that is being rejected, the alignment of religion and politics, of God and Caesar. Interpretations of the Bible that somehow justify the subjection of women, holy war or crusade, the increase of poverty and injustice, racism or discrimination of any sort have all been roundly criticized and rejected. But as Christendom Christianity (as Kierkegaard might call it) is rejected, the gospel of the Prince of Peace shines forth in the darkness.[ix]

There is a dawning breath of radicalism beginning to run through American Christianity, especially among its youth. One thinks of the New Monastic movement or the radical spirituality of Shane Claiborne's *The Simple Way* in Philadelphia, PA, or *Reba Place Fellowship* in Evanston, IL. There is a quiet growing movement that is most exciting. It is as Brian McLaren says, "a deep shift occurring." It transcends denominational and racial lines. In tens of thousands of groups around the country the question is being asked, "What does it really mean to follow Jesus?"

We have new questions, questions asked from outside the box of religious certainty. An inerrant text, inerrant church institutions and congregations, inerrant or guaranteed interpretation from On High are not real for us. We know our propensity for self-deception and making God in our own image, after our own likeness. The real world is not inerrant. It is full of accidents, unanticipated incidents, startling revelations and surprises. Why, even our description of the world in terms of quantum mechanics would by definition include contingency or chance. We live in a world beyond foundations, as we have known them.

Our questions revolve around the interpretation of the Bible, but our questions begin with this presupposition: *a crucial component in understanding Jesus is following him*. Not a slavish or blind following, but the willingness to take the risk that he meant what he said, that he had a spiritual path that if followed would bring light and healing to the world. I believe that Jesus does love the little children, all the little children of the world, and that he does care for the poor and the needy and I believe we are called and empowered to find ways to effectively serve *all* others.

We also hear the cry of the Earth. Without her, we do not survive as a species. We have stripped, raped and murdered her as we have each other. Our questions begin from a new framework of understanding the Creator to the Creation. We have believed in the old Watchmaker theory for about as long as we believed in Santa. I believe that first and foremost, God is love and that that love became incarnate in Jesus who shared his life in order to free us from our misconceptions, remove our sin, and become the most excellent example of what true humanness can be. The highest way for us to express our humanity is by learning Jesus' story and by the grace of the Spirit, participating in that story as much as possible. The four gospels are the narrative world the Christian inhabits. And as a rabbi might say with regard to Torah, all else is commentary.

Getting the Most from This Book

This book is intended to take you on a journey of discovering how the entire Bible can be profitable for preaching, teaching, catechesis and worship while no longer being tied to certain assumptions that have for a long time dominated Christian thinking (inside the box). Friends and students frequently ask me if there is a big picture to all of the work I do. For years I have been content to write for my website as well as essays for presentation and publication; I have edited a few books I thought brought this cutting-edge work to the pastor. *The Jesus Driven Life*, however, is written for the regular person *who has some interest in Christian theology and the Bible* but may not have any formal training.

The Jesus Driven Life is structured as a thirty-two week study. It has eight chapters with four sections each. It can also be read at one sitting (although that is not recommended; it is good to take time to absorb, ponder, think, reference and discuss). To supplement this book there is a DVD series with a thirty-minute talk on each section. This book and the DVD series overlap by about 30% in terms of information that is presented; they are truly meant as supplements for each other. *The Jesus Driven Life* DVD's are available from Preaching Peace (www.preachingpeace.org).

The first, second and third chapters concern Jesus, his rightful place as our interpretive lens by which we know anything about God, the pinnacle of his teaching and how his teaching spoke very clearly to the problem of human violence and sacrificial mentalities.[x] The fourth chapter highlights the early church from the second to the fourth centuries to see how they understood Scripture, for good and for ill. It is important to recognize that there is not a straight line from Jesus to the early church and then from the early church to us. It is a crooked and often broken line. We are still living with both the gains and the mistakes of the early church. A key thesis will be that we have to go back and learn from Jesus how to read our Bibles all over again.

After discussing Jesus and early Christian understandings of him I will bring in an important tool for understanding the human condition, Rene Girard's mimetic realism. The implications of a mimetic anthropology, which are congruent with the biblical anthropology, are nothing short of breath taking and full of "A-ha!" moments. We will then turn to broad discussions of how to interpret key texts from the Jewish Scriptures (Genesis, Job, Psalms, Isaiah, and the Wisdom of Solomon).

Isaiah was the book of the Jewish canon that Jesus most frequently quoted or alluded to. I owe a huge debt of gratitude to Tony Bartlett[xi] for allowing me to include an abridged portion of his Bible Study on Second Isaiah for it is a coherent, comprehensive and deeply insightful commentary. It has had a profound impact on my interpretation of Isaiah. In this book I only reproduce Tony's commentary on Isaiah 53. Readers that would like a more thorough analysis of Isaiah from this perspective can read and download the entire document at www.preachingpeace.org. It will require more brainpower to read than other sections of this book, but the interpretation of Isaiah 53 is crucial to understanding both the Jewish and the Christian 'canons.'

We will conclude *The Jesus Driven Life* by using this frame of interpretation with the two great thinkers of the New Testament, Paul and the writer of the Fourth Gospel. The only omission to this book that I would have liked to include is an exploration of the Epistle to the Hebrews, particularly in the area of atonement. Interested readers may wish to consult my essay "Sacrificial Language in Hebrews" in *Violence Renounced* edited by Willard Swartley (Pandora Press, 2000). Having read this book I think it will be clear that Christians do not need to be fearful of God, nor Jesus, and it will be clearer, I hope, that neither does anyone else. I will have done my best to anticipate key points at stake in the conversation. But most of all I hope this will encourage others to ask questions when they are not satisfied with the religious status quo and to join in the quest of Jesus, for he truly is the Living and Truthful Way (John 14:6).

Numbers in parentheses with a dot (5.1) indicate a chapter and section of this book, thus, 5.1 refers to "What Does it Mean to Be Human?" Numbers in parentheses with a colon (1:2 or 22:14) refer to the biblical text under discussion.

In order to avoid as much supercessionist language as possible, I use the terms Old Testament, Older Testament, Jewish Scriptures, Hebrew Bible and Jewish Canon interchangeably. Torah can refer to the first five books of the Bible, Genesis through Deuteronomy; it can also refer to the entirety of Jewish scriptural teaching depending on the context.

A Theological Autobiography

I was raised Roman Catholic and experienced both pre-Vatican II and post Vatican II church life. I loved the Mass (and from a distance, still do). At 18 I was 'born again' into Christian Dispensationalist Fundamentalism. Fortunately, I was discipled by a family that really sought to love each other and Jesus with all their hearts and minds. I remember reading voraciously in my new Scofield Thompson Chain Reference Bible and authors like Ray Stedman, Francis Schaeffer, Josh McDowell and Watchman Nee. Puritans like Jonathan Edwards and John Owens were the rage in the circles in which I traveled.

By the grace of God I began attending a very small Bible school in a nearby town. The instructors (blessed be their memory) first introduced me to thinking about the Scriptures outside the framework I had been given by introducing me to critical thinking. I still remember those days so full of the joy of discovery and the despair at thinking that I was losing my salvation if my theology changed. I began to live in two worlds: that of the church and that of the intellect and the two no longer matched up. What I saw in Scripture, particularly as I studied the life of Jesus, and what I saw lived out in Christianity (and my own life) were two really different things. I tried my hand at being a pastor for a while and this split wrenched me apart in the ministry. I was hit by both mid-life crisis and pastoral burnout at the same time. I turned my life into a train wreck, as they say.

In the years that followed I packed up my books and left them in boxes in the attic and stopped going to church. I gave up on my loves, theology and the church. The things I write about have come at a very great cost to others because of my sin. My wife Lorri, however, angel that she is, chose to model Jesus' forgiveness to me. I began to interpret my life not in terms of loss but in terms of gain: the gain that God had to at least be as good as my wife who, in her own quiet way, showed me the way back to Jesus. When I write about *The Jesus Driven Life* it is not because I live it but because I have seen it lived. There is an apostolic succession in the church; only it is more than formal. That succession occurs whenever anyone is completely sold out to Jesus and chooses Him as their exemplar of what it means to be fully and truly human, beloved by God and in love with God and the world that God so loves.

In 2000, I serendipitously met an Episcopal priest, Fr. Jeff Krantz, who took this theological Humpty-Dumpty and helped me begin to piece my experience together with what I had learned from my studies. Jeff took the time with me to create the first years of Preaching Peace. As I began again to get excited about theology, I also began to wonder if the time would ever come where Lorri and I could enjoy church again. Would we ever find a church that wanted to do nothing else besides take Jesus seriously in every way possible without being religious? We are still on that quest.

I began writing for the Preaching Peace website in fall of 2002. Jeff and Lorri became my two crutches. They believed in me, when I had given up all faith in myself. They loved me back to spiritual health. That's when I began to see that, yes, Jesus was still present and active on the planet by His Spirit. More so, I heard the voice of Jesus calling me back to follow Him as his messenger.

It has been almost a decade since I really began this healing process. I travel a lot in Historic Peace Church orbits these days, particularly among the Mennonites. But I had already worked my way to a peace position apart from the Anabaptist tradition. The 'peace' influence began with our friendship with Pam and Phil Franklin back in the late 70's when we shared in a beautiful part of the Jesus Movement called Church in the Park. Today our friends Jonathan and Brenda Sauder are inspirations for us on what *The Jesus Driven Life* looks like.

Even as I write this I know I am still in the recovery process, healing and getting better as time flows by. So, when I say 'you' in this book, it is 'me' now that is speaking to 'you' now, but I have been the 'you' in this book. Perhaps I am writing it for myself. If so, welcome to the conversation.

Chapter 1 The Christian Life

1.1 Beginning with Jesus

It might seem strange to suggest that when we Christians interpret the Scriptures we begin with Jesus. In some circles, a prevailing "flat view" of Scripture requires us to acknowledge that Jesus has been displaced as the interpretive center of the Bible by something else. That something else calls itself Jesus but it is not. Jesus, Yeshua of Nazareth, whose mother was Miriam, who came with a defined mission and message, has been papered over and painted over so much that 2,000 years later we can no longer recognize him.

In other circles, the gospels are not trustworthy, and Jesus cannot be known. We are told that the real geniuses behind the gospel story were folks in the early church. A vaguely defined, historically docetic, oral tradition handed on by anonymous communities dramatically changed or invented much of what Jesus says in the Gospels. Jesus is papered over in this way of thinking too. Making him an algebraic variable, impossible to get a grip on, this type of thinking has dispensed with Jesus.[xii] Yet, in spite of this befuddling, it is clear that some have known Jesus and have lived their lives modeled on his Jewish life.

Ever since the second century, the church has been out of touch with her parent, Judaism. Paul's vision of a reconciled Jewish and Gentile world has yet to be realized. I will venture to guess that close to 100% of my readers will not be Jewish. They will be "Christians" already. They will most likely come from one of the two circles mentioned above. They are reading this book because they are searching for Jesus, for a way to understand Jesus that is not just the same old tripe served up week in and week out. A good number of these sojourners have felt like they were driving in circles in a dead end cul-de-sac. The French have a word for this, it is *ennui*.

There is a reason for the *ennui* gripping theology and church today. One might point to the fact that Christianity is postmodern, part of a world without foundations or absolutes. Parts of Christendom have transitioned to this; a larger part has yet to acknowledge this. Another reason is the stunning displacement of Christian ecumenical dialogue with religious inter-faith conversations. We Christians are having an identity crisis. Revolt against this *ennui* can be seen in communities springing up engaged in following Jesus in an authentic and radical way, who see and understand Jesus in a vital, new and refreshing way. This Jesus feels real. He doesn't feel plastic, boxed or fake.

Jesus was Jewish. This is an indisputable fact. Therefore, we cannot understand Jesus apart from the religion into which he was born and raised. The earliest Christians, like Jesus, were all Jewish. The story of this specific people and their God is the matrix apart from which we cannot understand Jesus. And that story is contained in the canonical literature Christians call the Old Testament.[xiii]

The author of the letter to the Hebrews (1:1-3) says explicitly, "In the past God spoke to our forefathers through the prophets at many times and in diverse ways, but in these last days he has spoken to us by His Son." There is an explicit contrast between the way God spoke 'in the past' and the way 'God has spoken' in Jesus Christ. The Gospel of John also shares this contrast. In John 1:1-18 (8.1) the grace and truth that have come through Jesus are contrasted with the 'Instruction' (Torah) that came through Moses. Similarly, the apostle Paul contrasts the revelation of the covenant in the Old Testament with that covenant inaugurated in Jesus in 2 Cor. 3:7-18 (7.1).

In all three of these writers, it is never assumed that the Old Testament was so inspired as to be perfect, dropped from heaven. This *was* a view of the Jewish Bible held by certain traditions within Jesus' Judaism but is foreign to the apostolic witness. Rather, there is an implicit awareness that something startlingly new had occurred in Jesus; so new, so different, that it demanded a complete revaluation of all their theology, interpretive grids and sacred texts. The apostolic church read the Scriptures in the light of Jesus before they read Jesus in the light of the Scriptures.

Luke records for us that after his resurrection Jesus traveled along the road with two of his followers (Luke 24:13-33). Jesus had to do Bible Study with them to explain *how* to read the Scriptures. These were not men who were ignorant of their Scripture. What they lacked, and what is frequently missing in Christian interpretation of Scripture today, is *how* to interpret the Old Testament. The resurrected Jesus begins by turning their attention to the problem of violence. It is violence done to an innocent victim that is the key for interpreting the Bible. Jesus begins by asking them a question about suffering, specifically the Jewish scriptural possibility of the suffering of God's Anointed.

I suspect that what may have astonished them the most was that the emphasis placed by Jesus on the meaning of his suffering and death did not result in some kind of retribution from God. It was the forgiveness expressed by God in the resurrected Jesus that collapsed all of their previous theological ideas and assumptions. Their theologies dictated a violent or retributive response on the part of God. That never happened; instead peace, reconciliation, forgiveness and love were announced! The speeches of the earliest Christian preaching in Acts (2:22-39, 3:17-26) reflect this corporate human murder of another human, who by virtue of the resurrection was recognized as truly Human. And as the truly Human One filled to the fullness with the Divine (Col. 2:9), Jesus forgives us our sin. This is the trajectory of the New Testament when referring to the Older Testament.

Reading the Gospels

Christianity today needs to learn how to read its Bible from this perspective, the perspective of Jesus. There is a singularity of perspective in the New Testament, especially the Gospel tradition, which is easily overlooked by those of us who begin our biblical interpretation from a privileged social perspective. More and more we are seeing the value of the death of Jesus as this singular place by which to interpret Scripture. There is a cruciform center, a place to begin our interpretation of both Bible and culture. That center is the violence done by humans to the innocent Jesus; it is the passion, the story of the cross. It is reflected in our movies, literature and art and can be found in the great philosophers of the 19th and 20th centuries. The problem of violence, its origin, manifestations and cure are at the front and center of human culture and public discourse as well. Just read a newspaper.

Today the more the relationship between religion and culture is exposed, the more clearly the violent history of Christianity is named and indicted as well. My friend Tony Bartlett observes that our contemporary cultural crisis has been brought about because violence is finally being exposed for what it truly is: demonic, satanic. It is the gospel of Jesus Christ that is bringing about this cultural destabilization for it is the perspective of the Crucified and Risen Lord.

Later in this book, we will look at some passages from the Gospels that demonstrate that Jesus was deconstructing the religion he was raised in, Judaism. In the same way, the gospel deconstructs violent Christianity as well. The gospel has so penetrated our human consciousness that what has previously worked in maintaining social order and church structure, hierarchy and institution, is no longer viable.

When I come to the gospels, I read them through several lenses all at the same time. My training has been to read the Bible as literature. I can appreciate all of the work that form, redaction, tradition, rhetorical, literary and social criticism bring to bear on the text. But the field of gospel studies is littered with hypotheses and speculations; it is by no means an exact science. There is significant debate on hundreds and hundreds of issues. So, I hold these various scientific guesses in a 'suspended state.'[xiv]

The four canonical Gospels are more than just important literature, although they are that. The Gospels tell us how the early church told the story of Jesus in four different contexts. While the Gospels *can* tell us about the early church, they *do* tell us about Jesus. It is neither possible nor desirable to separate Jesus from his followers. He has chosen to make himself known through those who follow him. In this sense there can be no scientific, objective, historical Jesus *as such*, only Jesus as the church has faithfully borne witness to (and this includes the *historical*) and proclaimed him.

One of the saddest things about all of the criticism of the Gospels for the past several hundred years is that they have removed Jesus from the gospels, hidden him behind so much rationalist baggage. In my travels I constantly encounter people who have quit reading their Bible because they no longer trust it. They have been inundated with the so-called 'assured results' (sic) of biblical scholarship. These results ultimately suggest that the writers of Scripture are biased, that they write from the top down, and that they cannot be trusted.[xv]

I also meet people who have marginalized the person and teaching of Jesus by allocating him to a certain dispensation as though "Jesus Christ [was not] the same yesterday, today and forever (Heb. 13:8)." These folks believe that every word of the Bible comes from God and they begin their interpretive task with a defining concept, whether it is covenant, revelation, reason, history or even 'God' (a word that you can load with a lot of unexamined baggage).

In short, the Bible is being misused in the churches today whether those churches are conservative or liberal. More to the point, the Bible is being used in all kinds of circles to justify cultural mores and imperatives. The Bible is no longer a dangerous book. The story of the Bible is no longer a challenge to culture grounded in violence. It is treated as an antiquated relic or worse as a divine telegram from a retributive god.

When we look back to the earliest Christian communities who wrote the texts we now have in our New Testament, we see that they did not preach a view of the inspiration and authority of Scripture, they preached Jesus. Jesus, his life, death and resurrection and ascension were the beginning, middle and end of all they thought and taught.

One can see the centrality of Jesus in early Christian hymns.[xvi] We know from the book of Acts that the early church was a singing church (Acts 2:47). Many of the key texts in the New Testament that refer to the crucified/exalted Lord are fragments or verses of hymns. Colossians 1:15-20, John 1:1-18 (8.1), Philippians 2:5-11 (7.4) and Hebrews 1:1-3 have all been recognized as such (Eph 1:3-14 comes close to being hymnic).[xvii] This is to say nothing of the hymns and liturgy in the Revelation of John.

In each of these hymns, Jesus is front and center. Martin Luther said, "We cannot vex the devil more than by teaching, singing, preaching, or talking of Jesus."[xviii] Today you can go to church and wait 20 or 30 minutes before you hear the name of Jesus. There is a lot of talk about God, but little mention of Jesus. Why is this? Because Jesus is particular, God is generic. It is easy to follow a generic God because you can fill the term God with any presupposition you please; it is difficult to follow Jesus, because then you have to take seriously his teachings on discipleship, on what exactly following him entails. Karl Barth rightly saw that Christian theology begins with the particular rather than with the general.[xix] Christian theology has its particular beginning with the person Jesus of Nazareth.

Misreading Scripture

A major flaw of so much theology is that it begins with abstract notions of God, filling out divinity with metaphysical terminology. One can see an example of this in the Westminster Confession (1647) where God is described, not with reference to saving acts in history, but as a series of adjectives and nouns:

> "There is but one only living and true God, who is infinite in being and perfection, a most pure spirit, invisible, without body, parts or passions, immutable, immense, eternal, incomprehensible, almighty, most wise, most holy, most free, most absolute, working all things according to the counsel of his own immutable and most righteous will, for his own glory; most loving, gracious, merciful, long suffering, abundant in goodness and truth, forgiving iniquity, transgression and sin; the rewarder of them that diligently seek him; and with all most just and terrible in his judgments, hating all sin, and who will by no means clear the guilty."

So abstract has God become that in describing God there is no mention of the specific, final, authoritative revelation of God's character in Jesus. Lest one think that the centuries old Westminster Confession has lost its influence, Rick Warren in his best selling *The Purpose Driven Life* suggests the same thing.[xx] By contrast, the Bible does not begin with an abstract God in relation to an abstract humanity, it begins with the relation of a specific God (Creator of all that is) to a specific person, Abram, and then to a specific people, Israel, and finally to a specific person, Jesus.

Now this is not to say that all of the above quote from Westminster might not be true but it misses the biblical trajectory of history and narrative. That is, it doesn't tell the story of how God has acted. It fails to observe that God's being is revealed in God's acts, most notably the act of the incarnation, life, death, resurrection and ascension of Jesus.

One of the key aspects of contemporary work on Jesus is the recognition that there is a deep connection between character and behavior. To experience a person, how they act toward you is to know them. We know whom Jesus *is* by *how* he acted. Moreover, the early Christians made the bold claim that God has acted (thus revealing God's self) definitively in Jesus (8.2).

What then, is the relationship between what the Old Testament asserts about God and what we know about God from the teachings of Jesus? Many in the early church not only made this distinction; it was made again at the time of the Reformation by many Anabaptist leaders and again in the Enlightenment by those who could not seem to reconcile the violence of God in the Old Testament with the nonviolence of Jesus. At times they over exaggerated the difference, but their instincts were correct. They rejected any view of the Bible that saw all the words about the character and acts of God in the Jewish Scriptures, as equal with the Word of God fully revealed in the life of Jesus.

It is at this juncture that we must take an important step to deal with what is called a 'flat' view of Scripture. Some are taught that just as Jesus is the Word of God (John 1:1) so also the Bible is the Word of God. In many places the Bible is simply referred to as 'The Word.' These Christians invoke the Christology of Nicaea and Chalcedon when they say that just as Jesus is truly God and truly human so also the Bible is truly divine and truly human. It is certainly possible to use these categories for by them one recognizes that the Scriptures share in a dual reality. The next leap they make, however, is the troublesome one. For they assert just as Jesus is sinless, so the Bible is free from error, that is, the human aspect of Scripture is so superintended by God in its inspiration that so-called errors or contradictions cannot be attributed to God. Where there are differences one must not assume that one text is to be preferred over another but that all texts can be harmonized.

What this type of theology seeks to affirm is that the Scripture has something to say that is revelatory and that revelation comes from God. Unlike the progressive, the conservative goes to the Bible to hear a divine message (much like the Orthodox Jew uses Torah or the Muslim uses the Qur'an). The solution lies in defining the locus or place of this revelation. For the conservative, the revelation is the very words themselves. God gave the words of the Bible to their respective authors and because God is perfect, the Bible too is perfect. This way of thinking is in complete contradiction to what I will be saying throughout this book, namely, that something new occurred in the revelation process with Jesus, that Jesus is the final 'word of God' to humans.

To identify or equate Jesus the Living Word with the Bible as The Written Word is to miss the interpretive direction of the apostolic church. It relativizes Jesus in relation to the Bible rather than seeing the Bible in relation to Jesus. The proof in the pudding lies in the virtual dismissal of the teaching of Jesus in the conservative churches. Dispensationalism, a sectarian view of periods of history popular in conservative churches relegates Jesus' teachings to his temporal life or to the coming Kingdom of God. Jesus' teachings then are moralized or spiritualized so that their social, or here and now effect, is muted.

The conservative has no choice but to manufacture an alternative method for reading the New Testament in relation to the Old. This method, as we shall see in later chapters, is grounded largely in pagan concepts of religion, but for now it is important to ask whether this method employed by the conservative does not have something to say to the progressive. At the very least, the conservative is willing to come to the Bible believing that it has something to say. That is, they know that when reading Scripture they are *encountering the strange new world within the Bible* as Karl Barth put it.

The progressive, on the other hand, has given up on hearing God through Scripture. To be sure, the progressive finds inspiration in the Bible, but it is usually reduced to 'general ethics.' Some progressive Christians are activists and see themselves as prophets against empire. I suppose some of them are. But too often their understanding of Jesus is just as preprogrammed as the conservative. What passes for hypotheses in the academy are accepted as 'assured results' by many progressives, including various forms of a militant Jesus.[xxi]

The "third way" of Christian thinking in the 21st century must begin by acknowledging Jesus the Peacemaker, the Just Reconciler, as Lord (for there are other lords out there, false lords that may have his name but have nothing to do with Him). We must begin with Jesus, the full and final revelation of God, as did the early Christians, or we will not end with Him.

1.2 The Great Commandment

One of the striking things about religions, Christianity in particular, is the number of manifestations that they take. The splits, splinters, and sects number in the tens of thousands. Each one has a different understanding as to what constitutes the center or heart of the Christian faith. All of this is well known and does not have to be documented. The Judaism of Jesus' day was only slightly different. There were various groups, and groups within groups, that held to different understandings as to what comprised knowing and doing God's will (2.3). Just as Christianity is not a monolith, neither was Judaism. Therefore, when a scribe comes to Jesus and desires to get his opinion on what constitutes the greatest commandment, we need not see him coming with guile.[xxii] The story is found in all three Synoptic Gospels (Mark 12:28-34, Matthew 22:34-40 and Luke 10:25-37). We shall use Luke's text as the basis for this discussion.

In Luke Jesus answers the question "who is my neighbor?" with a parable, a *mashal* or a riddle. It is meant to puzzle the hearer. The Samaritan is an unlikely hero. It would be like saying a TV preacher and a priest walked by a wounded Christian, but an Islamic terrorist stopped to aid him. This parable has shock value, or it should. The problem is that it is so familiar and we think we know what it means!

It is important to know that for Jews of Jesus' day, obeying God's commandments did not earn salvation. Obedience was the rightful due of the (male) Jew who had taken on himself the yoke of the Torah and who participated in the covenant community. Obedience was not the way to heaven, but the way by which the witness of God's work among the Jewish people took form.

So we should not be surprised that some sought to discern what might be the key commandments to keep, after all, no one chooses to strain at gnats while swallowing camels. Jesus' response has four connecting parts, all of which are essential, 1) the confession of Faith (the Shema), 2) the command to love God and 3) the command to love our neighbor. The fourth part is, as we shall see, the radical part.

What we have here is a balanced ethical spirituality, that is, the recognition that spirituality is to be lived out in all relationships. Jesus' recognition of these two parts, spirituality, or a relationship with God, and human ethics, or our relationships with others, are one and the same thing. How we behave toward 'others' is an indication of how we behave toward God and vice versa.

Conservative Christianity in the United States has criticized liberal Christianity because it is focused on the second part of the great commandment. Liberal Christianity critiques conservative Christianity because it is focused on the first part of the command and is so heavenly bound it is no earthly good. Both sides have a point. Authentic imitation of Jesus involves us in both a journey inward and a journey outward.

Interpreting the Great Commandment

Jesus' way begins with the confession that God is one. This should already alert us to the fact that we do not have to do here with two commands but one command expressed in terms of our two most significant relations, God and others. The confession that God is one also indicates that God is not dualistic. God is not a mixture of yin and yang, good and evil, terror and love. God is consistent with God's self. The gods of our theologies might be mixed up, but the One who made the heavens and the earth is and always will be the One we are called to love because God is Love.

Those who fear God also fear others. Some might say that the Old Testament states, "The fear of the Lord is the beginning of wisdom," but only a retributive God need be feared. More so, Jesus is God's Wisdom incarnate (6.4), and Jesus says, "Don't be afraid." The great command is not to fear the Lord, but to love the Lord and "perfect love casts out fear" (I John 4:18; cf Romans 8:15).

The call to love God is not simply an assent to commands and prohibitions, nor can it be equated with promotion of an ethical ideology. This would be to introduce fear back into the equation. When Paul in 2 Cor. 3:6 and the writer to the Hebrews (chapters 8 and 10) speak of the New Covenant, the covenant inaugurated on the last night of Jesus' life, they both understand that obedience is not compelled, coerced or compulsory. Obedience as love is the willingness to offer oneself to God as God has offered God's self to us.

Loving God is not an abstract category anymore than loving our neighbor. Most of us know what love is because someone at some time or another has loved us. Even so we only love God because God loved us first (I John 4:8). If our neighbor or friend should love us with conditions and qualifications, expectations and judgments, would we call that love? It is certainly not the free radical grace-overflowing love of God. Our obedience knows no fear for we know that God is not Janus-faced (or two faced, like the Greek mask of tragedy and comedy).[xxiii]

Our love of God as obedience is not, however, to be construed as conformity to an external ideal. The law of the new covenant is "written in our hearts and minds." In reality, however, Christians exhibit two types of external laws. These laws can be doctrinal or ethical. An example of the former would be the ten fundamentals of Fundamentalism. Here certain interpretations of the Bible are held to be inviolable. To disbelieve any of the fundamentals amounts to apostasy. An example of the latter can be found in almost any sectarian group where 'holiness codes' function as an external marker, e.g., one can clearly see this in the Old Order Mennonites and the Amish. Either way, obedience while internal (the necessity of a 'born again' experience), is proven or demonstrated externally by conformity to an outward standard. In the time of the Puritans it was called *experiential predestinarianism*. Today it might be called moral conformity; either way it is self-justification, it is not love.

It is clear from the gospels that Jesus did not fit in with established cultural and religious conventions and mores. His critique of the Sabbath laws (Mark 2:23-27), kosher (Mark 7:1-23), and his use of Torah against Torah

(Mark 10:1-9), not to mention the antitheses of the Sermon on the Mount (Matt. 5:21-48) all point to Jesus making his own independent interpretive decisions when it came to the Jewish tradition including Torah.[xxiv]

Thus love of God for Jesus is more than 'just keeping the Law.' Love for God found expression in Jesus' life in the way he interpreted what keeping Torah meant. And for Jesus, love trumped everything including sacrifice (Hosea 6:6), empire, and cultural religion based upon hatred, resentment and vengeance. Love of God was for Jesus, as for many Jews of his time (e.g., Hillel), expressed as compassion, mercy, generosity and forgiveness. People knew the value of helping each other back then (we only need recall the strong emphasis on hospitality in Middle Eastern culture), just as they do now.

But for Jesus, love for God is expressed as love of neighbor and one other thing – which is the kicker!

Who was the neighbor? The bad guy was the neighbor; the enemy was the neighbor. Love of God is expressed as love of neighbor both to those who are part of our world/community and those with whom we are at odds. Love your enemy! Did Jesus teach love of enemy elsewhere? Sure he did, many times, e.g., Matthew 5:43-48. Does not Paul also say in Romans 5:8 that when we considered even God to be the enemy, God demonstrated his love toward us by sending Jesus to show us the way out? Enemy love is the flip side of the coin of neighbor love. The reality is that love of God is expressed fully as love of both friend and enemy. It recognizes in everyone the image of God. Love is all-inclusive. Love knows no boundaries or limits. Love God, love your neighbor, love your enemy, this is the Greatest Commandment.

What is this love of neighbor? Jacques Ellul has pointed out that while Scripture says God loved the world, we are enjoined to love our neighbor, the one close to us. The slogan 'think globally, act locally' reflects this. Yet, in this era of global awareness, our neighbor includes all 7+ billion people on the planet. Love of God, for Jesus, expressed as love of neighbor is going to be expressed as compassion for those 'less fortunate'; it is going to be actively involved in seeing to it that the members of the community are adequately cared for; it actively forgives others' sins and is a peacemaking reconciler. Love of God, expressed as love of neighbor, also challenges and emerges victorious over the principalities and powers of people's lives; it does not lord it over with moral authority but rather serves the broken, the broken-hearted, those who have no possibility of reciprocation. Jesus was all of these things and more to the morally suspect in his world.

Love of God and love of neighbor, and enemy, thus have a standard, the person of Jesus. To love God is to love as Jesus loved. The gospels are a shining witness to this. Today, rational concepts of morality, holiness, principles and perfection dominate common discourse on what love of God expressed as love of neighbor looks like. There is a standard we can use. For the Christian this standard is not an abstract concept of law or right and wrong, or morality or ethics, but the concrete person of Jesus. In a later chapter we will look at how Jesus both challenged and changed this kind of legalistic thinking using the notion of 'social-religious codes.' For now, it is crucial to establish that the greatest commandment is, from Jesus' perspective, to love God and to love all persons, neighbor and enemy.

The Great Commandment as Jesus' Interpretive Lens

But there is one more interesting aspect of this text that is of great value. Notice that what prompts the whole conversation is a question of interpretive method. At stake in this conversation is how one interprets the Jewish Scriptures and how one lives out that interpretation. In short, we have a dialogue on hermeneutics (the art and science of interpretation).

When we look at the Gospel of Mark this comes home in an even clearer fashion. In Mark 12:34, the response of the man causes Jesus to say to him, and only to him, "you are not far from the kingdom of God." The man's response was to recognize that love of God and neighbor was "more important than all burnt offerings and sacrifices." The man articulated a view of God apart from religion, *sacrificially* oriented religion. Jesus, I'm sure, was delighted. Here was someone who saw things the same way he did; well, almost.

It is Matthew 22 that gives us an explicit clue and once again, Lo and Behold!, the greatest commandment is couched in a hermeneutical context. In this case, it is about how to interpret the Old Testament. Matthew records that this *hermeneutic* (method of interpretation) was made explicit by Jesus himself when he says "all the Law and the Prophets hang on these two commandments." Each gospel may express this differently, but they are all related to the question of the relationship between the greatest commandment and the interpretation of the Torah. Why is this important?

We live out in our everyday relationships what we believe about God. That is, there is a direct connection between what one believes and how one lives. What Jesus is pointing out is that we live our interpretation of this literature. It can be lived out in many different ways and was and has been and still is! For Jesus, there is a way into this literature that speaks clearly to him. When Jesus read or heard his Bible, he had a lens, a grid, a method of interpreting it. We not only want to know how he interpreted his people's writings, but also how we can follow him in interpreting these Scriptures.

For many in the churches, hermeneutics falls under the category of revelation or language. Much time can be spent profitably discussing these things. But for Jesus, as for any Jew of his time, covenantal obedience was everything and Jesus subsumes hermeneutics under obedience or discipleship in the story of the greatest commandment. One 16th century Anabaptist, Hans Denck, put it this way, "No man can truly know Christ except he follow him in life; and no man can follow him except he first know him." I am saying that only a dim shadow of Jesus can be known rationally, logically or scientifically. Jesus is best known and fully known in radical obedience to him. Not only does this kind of discipleship radicalize our method of bible interpretation, it also changes the paradigm of our epistemology, the way we think, how we know what we know. Obedience to Jesus is our active participation in interpreting the Old Testament.

Jesus saw around him a plethora of ways of living out Torah. The Judaism of his time was multi-flowered, some prettier than others. It was a very diverse faith tradition with many and varied ways of living out that faith. Jesus could have chosen any number of traditions and become a disciple. He comes closest when he chooses the radical preacher John the Baptizer. But even then, as we will see later, this way of understanding the relation between the greatest commandment and the interpretation of the Jewish Scriptures already helped Jesus to begin to take a different path from that of John.

In 1.1 we observed that the apostolic witness begins with God's work in Jesus, not God's work in us. God's work in us is only possible because of God's work in Jesus. It is a consequence of God's primary work and revelation in Jesus. I believe that this focus was intentionally taught to his followers following his resurrection. Luke-Acts and the Fourth Gospel certainly imply as much (Luke 24:13-25, John 20:19-23). It is *the* hot topic on the road to Emmaus. It's all about how we interpret this collection of sacred literature.

Now there are many who claim to have a *Christological* (Christ-centered) approach to the Old Testament. They are right, they do, only it is not 'the Christology of Jesus' as Ben Witherington III puts it. It is a Christology apart from Jesus. If Jesus, the Jesus of the gospels, is going to be our primary interpretive matrix, and if for Jesus the three-pronged greatest commandment was the lens by which we interpret the Bible, and if Jesus is a living example of how that interpretation was to be lived, then anything that did not look like the Jesus of the Gospels, any behavior that could not be attributed to Jesus, would be that of a false Jesus, a theological construct called a Christology.

The writer to the Fourth Gospel puts it this way, "I am the Way, the Truth and the Life." The time has come to stop relating to Christologies and to begin relating to Jesus. Then we will know how to truly love God, each other and those with whom we need to be reconciled.

1.3 Jesus' Abba

It is hard for some to recognize that Jesus' teaching on God is really different and really, really radical. That's because most of us think we know what we mean by the term God. When we come to the Gospels we find the God we already believe in and think we know, we only hear texts through certain straitjacketed grids.

We have a two thousand year history of the Father, Son and Holy Ghost. For about 1870 of those years, we have tended to make God out to be a Eurocentric male with all of its patriarchal delusions.[xxv] Father became a term of power, might, authority and fear. The God of western Christendom was conceived in terms of raw power. Metaphors, sermons, catechisms, doctrines, theological disputes, dogmas all took as their starting point the unlimited capacity of God to do anything God wants because God is God. This may well be true but only as an adjunct to the God revealed in the life and death of Jesus. Really, strange as it may seem, it is not power that best describes God, but powerlessness, the powerlessness of God dying on the cross.

Protestant Christians laud Luther's discovery of *grace alone and faith alone* and highly esteem the doctrine of justification by faith. What is missed though is Luther's more central tenet when doing theology, namely, beginning with the powerlessness of God in the death of Jesus. This principle is known as a *theology of the cross.*[xxvi] It means that if we begin our discussion of the character of God anywhere but in the dying Jesus we will miss the starting point around which God's character has been revealed. This was Luther's great protest against the glorified, majestic, all-powerful Christ of the Holy Roman Empire.

The Protestant principle is a principle of protest. It speaks out against any attempt to describe God other than that found in the life of Jesus. If Jesus is forgiving, can God be any less so? If Jesus heals the sick, does God do any less? If Jesus battles the principalities and powers, which imprison souls and minds, can less be said of God? If Jesus and God are one, and if to know Jesus is to know God (John 8:19), then any conception of God that doesn't look like Jesus is an idol.

This then is the third principle when interpreting the Bible. The first was that Christians must interpret their Bible with Jesus as their lens (1.1). The second was that Jesus lived out the interpretation of his Scriptures in the light of love (1.2). The third principle is that God is revealed in Jesus' life, death and resurrection as a loving God, one whose judgment is grounded in mercy and tempered liberally with forgiveness. In both Luke and the Fourth Gospel, as Jesus dies he calls upon God as his *Abba*. Who is this God upon whom Jesus calls?

Jesus' *Abba* Is Not Two-Faced

Jesus' favorite designation for God is *Abba*. But before we assume we know what an *abba* is, or try to use analogies compared to an earthly parent we should note that Jesus observes that even our understanding of 'father' must change. He says in Luke 11:11-13,

> "Which of you *abbas*, if your son asks for a fish will give him a snake instead? Or if he asks for an egg will give him a scorpion? If you then, though you are evil, know how to give good gifts to your children, how much more will your *Abba* in heaven give good gifts to those who ask him?"

Jesus is saying that God is not arbitrary or malicious and that we human fathers (who can be both arbitrary and malicious) even when we are at our best, cannot be compared to God who is the giver of all good gifts and only good gifts. More importantly is that in Matthew's Gospel (7:12), this giving of God is tied into the 'Golden Rule.' To do unto others as we would have them to do us reflects a way of life oriented to forgiveness, peace, reconciliation and healing. If this is what God requires of us and if in so doing we are following Jesus, then a new definition of God the Father is in the making in the teaching of Jesus.

In our time, when 'bad' fathers are in the news all too frequently for harming or killing their children, to call upon God as Father might seem uncouth to some. As we have noted earlier, patriarchal connotations have caused many to see God as a power figure, whose authority must be absolutely obeyed or dire consequences will follow. 'Father', as a term for God can carry extremely negative connotations for many whose earthly parents were abusive, emotionally unavailable or tyrannical. Some prefer to jettison the term 'father' and call God 'mother.' Yet even here, not all mothers are equal and the same principle applies to earthly mothers as to fathers, neither being a direct analogue for God.

Whether one calls God father or mother is not the issue. What is at stake is our willingness to recognize that God, as our spiritual parent, is not like us. Nor can we fruitfully apply analogies from our own parental relationships to the divine except to say that if we do our best to love, care and nurture our children, how much more does God love, care for and nurture God's children?

I suggested earlier that we begin with the cross of Jesus as the place to begin our thinking about the fatherhood of God, as Jesus understood it. In so doing, we are brought face to face with one of the most complicated issues in Christian thought: what is the relation of God to Jesus as he is dying? For many, God is in heaven as Jesus dies on earth and God is pouring wrath or anger out on Jesus. God must do this because God has placed our sins on Jesus and God deals with sin by exercising wrath. Some point out that even Jesus believed this when he quotes Psalm 22 from the cross "My God, my God, why have you forsaken me?" God could only forsake Jesus if he had turned his back on our sin (or so the logic goes).

Jesus' quotation of Psalm 22 is the only time in the gospels where Jesus does not refer to God as Father, so we must ask what is occurring here. Most of us are familiar with Psalm 23 and could recite it by heart. It brings us comfort in times of distress. But perhaps we are not so familiar with Psalm 22.

Psalm 22 is a cry of dereliction. It is a psalm about the experience of being the victim of an unjust accusation and of being prosecuted. In short, it is a psalm about being a scapegoat. Many of us have had experience with this, where we have been part of a group that has generated rumors about us that we knew were not true. One by one our friends took the side of the group against us until we were standing alone and no longer part of the group. It is a horrible experience.

When Jesus quotes Psalm 22, he is seeking to bring to the mind of his executioners that they are playing the role of the scapegoating community.[xxvii] If someone were to quote the opening line of Psalm 23 "The Lord is my shepherd" most of us could go on and recite a good portion of that psalm. By quoting the opening line of Psalm 22, Jesus is not saying that God has abandoned him; he is bringing to mind the entire context of the psalm. One might object that this is not necessarily the case but it is important to note that breathing was very difficult on a cross and extended conversations and dialogues would have been both very painful and virtually impossible.[xxviii]

But that is not all. Psalm 22 is a psalm of vindication. At the end the psalmist knows that "God is not far off" and that "God has not hidden his face." The Psalmist knows that God has neither "despised nor disdained the suffering of the afflicted one." Ultimately Psalm 22 is a cry of hope. The Jews who heard Jesus cry the first words of Psalm 22 from the cross heard not only the sense of abandonment, but also the hope, because they knew that Psalm! This hope is reflected in all of the passion predictions of Jesus who, knowing he will suffer at the hands of an angry mob still believes, in spite of everything to the contrary in his circumstances, that God will deliver him by vindicating his innocence. For Jesus, as for the psalmist, God is not some far off angry deity. It is the crowd who is angry, who requires sacrifice of the innocent. God is caring and present with the victim.

A final point of the recitation of Psalm 22 from the crucified Jesus is a theological one: unlike the belief of the mob and the Jewish leaders that they are doing God a favor in getting rid of the troublemaker Jesus, the use of Psalm 22 is an indication that God does not authorize humanity's sacrifice of Christ. God is not seen as the actor who sacrifices His Son; rather, this sacrificial death is one that God rejects. Thus God is 'absent', not 'present', in our sacrificial processes. We shall have more to say about this in 3.3, the section on atonement.

So far I have sought to head off at the pass two major objections to a wide spread misunderstanding of God as Father. The first is that Father is to be perceived in power terms and the second is that God was angry with Jesus as he hung dying. I have also suggested that by beginning with the cross of Jesus in our understanding of God we can see that God's relationship to Jesus must be conceived in terms other than those we have been given in our dominant theological traditions.

When, at his baptism (Mark 1:9-11), God says to Jesus that "You are my beloved son", we should not suppose that anything ever changed in Jesus' relationship to his *Abba*. If there is one constant we can rely on in our theology it is that the relationship between Jesus and God never changed. This is why (and it can get complicated) it is so important to begin our Christian understanding of the Trinitarian God from the perspective of the cross. If God is two-faced, if he is both loving, evidenced at Jesus' baptism and transfiguration, and later at the point of the cross, angry with Jesus, we have a pagan, and therefore idolatrous, view of God. The gods of paganism were a blend of human characteristics both good and bad. Some say that we must hold things like God's love and wrath, or God's mercy and holiness in tension. If God is Janus-faced this is true. Janus is the god of the double face. But an authentic understanding of the relationship of the Father to the Son does away with any tension. If our god is tense maybe he needs to see a psychiatrist!

Jesus on Judgment and Hell

If we read the teaching of Jesus about God through the inherited lens of the metaphysical god of western Christendom, we will find there the double-faced god. The term God is like luggage, you can fill it with just about anything you want. The metaphysical god is the god who is the highest we can conceive. So we say God is the greatest good or the highest beauty or the most righteous One. We take our known categories of value and simply raise them to the nth power and Poof!, we have God. This is what Greek philosophy did and as we shall see (4.3), this way of thinking has had a tremendous impact on Christian doctrines of God.

But God is more than our highest thoughts. When God says in Isaiah (55:8), "My ways are not your ways, my thoughts are not your thoughts" it is because God is not like that which we perceive about divinity. If God is simply the best value raised to an exponential level, then God can be described as a series of adjectives such as we find in so many Confessions and catechisms. But what if God is different than that which we can think or imagine?

No doubt some will say Jesus taught that God is angry with sinners and God will punish those who reject him. Some turn to the parables of Jesus to demonstrate this (3.4). So, for example in the parable of the tenants (Matthew 21:33-44), the king in the parable takes away the vineyard from the tenants who abused the messengers and killed the son. But does this parable mean that God is punishing the tenants or that God is angry? Let us look closely at some of these 'parables of judgment.'

Matthew 22:1-14 contains a parable about a king who invited many to a wedding banquet to be thrown in honor of his son. Some mistreat and kill the heralds and so the enraged king destroys their city. Our first inclination is to assume that the king is analogous to God. The king of the parable then fills the banquet hall with folks from the byways. Does this sound like the *Abba* of Jesus or is something else going on?

We are easily fooled because the parable begins "the kingdom of heaven is like" and so we assume that the parable is referring to God as the King. As I see it part of the problem can be traced to how we translate the words used when Jesus says "the Kingdom of God is as if" and "How shall we liken the kingdom of God?" (Mark 4:26, 30) If we translate the phrases "To what shall we liken the kingdom of God?" or "The kingdom of God is like" we are presumptively looking for analogies, similarities, likenesses, analogs, anything where a = b. But if we translate this phrase, "To what shall I compare the kingdom?" and "the kingdom of God can be compared to" then the possibility is open that one could see similarities but that one might also see dissimilarities. In some parables it is the contrast between God's kingdom and earthly kingdoms, in others it is the similarities. Part of being parabled is to discern this difference.

The king of this parable is like an earthly king who handles scorn with retribution. This king brooks no dissent. In fact, this king sounds like a tyrant. Political figures that act this way in the modern world are put on trial before a United Nations tribunal. Saddam Hussein was executed for acting this way. If the king represents God why then do we condemn figures like Idi Amin or Robert Mugabe or Joseph Stalin? If the king is within his rights to kill those who irk him, why do we suppose that political leaders today who kill their people are unjust?

The king in the parable is not God. Luke's version of the parable (Luke 14:15-23) contains no such retributive activity with regard to the king. In Luke's version of the parable, there is no introductory formula "the kingdom of heaven is like." Why then this difference and is it really important? The difference arises from the use of the parable in the early church. It is Matthew's gospel that portrays kings in parables as harsh taskmasters, so we must ask why Matthew has included this section on the king destroying the city of those who rejected his invitation. The same could be said for the master of the parable of the talents (Matthew 25:14-29). In both of these parables, Matthew concludes the parables with the king/master casting out those who rejected him "outside in the darkness where there will be weeping and gnashing of teeth." The 'king' in the parables in Matthew has an analogue to earthly rulers not to God. In Matthew parables about kings function subversively by arguing that the *Basileia Theou* (the reign of God) is fundamentally different or other than supposed.

It is commonplace to refer these parables to the invitation to salvation offered by Jesus, and this is partially correct. What is missed is the fact that these parables are addressed to the religious, the faithful, those who believe in a God who inflicts retribution. By rejecting Jesus, parables are a way of communicating that you get the god you believe in.[xxix] You will only be able to interpret your life in terms of a Janus-faced god, and that was a horrid prospect for Jesus. We have heard many sermons preached on this parable and in the end, it is 'sinners' (the morally corrupt and bankrupt of society) who are cast out for rejecting the salvation message. Those of us on the inside are saved; those on the outside are damned. Yet the point of the parable is that the reverse is true; those outside are saved, while those inside who think they have the truth and are saved *but who reject the message of Jesus* will find themselves outside.[xxx]

Why is this so? Because for Jesus, God is inclusive and reaches out to those whom the religious had consigned to an eternity of being roasted over a devilish fire like marshmallows. Those who consign others to hell will, in the end, get the god they have believed in. The parable then does not say that sinners are going to hell while Christians are going to heaven. Quite the contrary, the parable in its Matthean context asserts that if you are like the king and engage in the violence of the king (by mistreating and murder), you will find yourself on the outside looking in. The parables are subversive of our views of God.

Some will point out that Jesus talks about hell. Jesus, so they say, saves believers and rejects unbelievers by sending them to hell. Mark 9:42-48 says:

> 42And if anyone causes one of these little ones who believe in me to sin, it would be better for him to be thrown into the sea with a large millstone tied around his neck. 43If your hand causes you to sin, cut it off. It is better for you to enter life maimed than with two hands to go into hell, where the fire never goes out.[a] 45And if your foot causes you to sin, cut it off. It is better for you to enter life crippled than to have two feet and be thrown into hell.47And if your eye causes you to sin, pluck it out. It is better for you to enter the kingdom of God with one eye than to have two eyes and be thrown into hell.

Sadly, some have read this text literally and cut off hands or cut out eyes. They turn Jesus into Jigsaw (from the movie series *Saw*). If one is not to read it literally then Jesus must have been talking about choices we make in this life about our eternal destiny. The proper choice, so some say, is the choice for holiness in this life and the putting away of all sin which is pollution of the soul. Not even close. Neither interpretation is really satisfactory because neither have a context for the saying. Read it again. The Gospel's audience is the disciples, but originally I think it was directed to another type of person.[xxxi]

I want to propose a possible Setting in the Life of Jesus (*Sitz-im-Leben*) for this pericope. What possible audience might such sayings a) apply to and b) be understood by the implied audience? Cutting off of hands and feet. Blinding eyes. Maiming is what it is. Self-maiming. Now what group would loathe the idea of being maimed? Priests who served in the Temple. If they were maimed or blemished in any fashion they could not serve, whether they were full time local priests or part of the rotating courses of priests that served the Temple on a bi-weekly basis. These men, and they were all males, would never hope to be maimed, let alone self-maimed.

Jesus is saying to the priests: "Look at what you do. You can be an unmaimed priest in this Temple or a maimed priest in the kingdom but you can't have both." This interpretation is congruent with how I understand the Temple episode (2.3). Jesus is not being pro-sacrificial in this saying, just the opposite. Jesus connects the sacrificial process of the Temple with Gehenna, the garbage dump in the valley of Hinnom near the Temple. It had a bad reputation as the place where pagan human sacrifice had taken place, fit now only for carcasses. Sacrificial logic leads straight to Gehenna. These are folks who know Gehenna; some of them could be tasked with making the dumps of Temple 'trash.' Jesus is saying to them, "You guys know how bad Gehenna is; and how it is used as a metaphor for the place of the damned in your theology. Look at what you do. You can follow your sacrificial logic straight to hell or let it go and enter the kingdom of God."[xxxii]

What is important to observe is that the sayings of Jesus about hell are not directed to those who are labeled sinners by others, but to those who consider themselves holy, righteous and pious. If we only worship a God who casts other people into hell, we can be assured that when the time comes we might find ourselves amongst that group.

At stake in our discussion is the character of God as seen in the teaching of Jesus. The religious of Jesus' time rejected his message because they could not accept the God Jesus introduced. If Jesus taught that God was retributive, that God would send bad people to hell, that God would punish evildoers, then there would have been no need to reject his message. Jesus would have been saying the same things about God that many others had been saying for hundreds of years. But Jesus was saying something different, very different and it is this difference that will create the crisis for his hearers. They could either believe what they had been taught and what had "always been believed, everywhere by all" (Vincent of Lerins) or they could believe in the gracious life-giving God that Jesus announced.

In the Sermon on the Mount (Matthew 7:21-23) a warning is given to those who say they follow Jesus but do not follow his teachings, "Not everyone who says to me Lord, Lord will enter into the kingdom of heaven." This warning is given to those who say they are Christians and look at what they do! They do miracles, prophesy and cast out demons, the very hallmarks of Jesus' own ministry. They look a lot like Jesus, but he rejects them. Why? Because they have failed to observe that the God who is spoken of in the Sermon is a compassionate, forgiving, reconciling God. They continue to harbor grudges, destroy relationships, insist on retribution and fail to love their enemies. By not being like God, who does not discriminate (Matthew 5:45), they have failed to be "perfect or whole" as God is perfect (Matthew 5:48).

The God of the Lowly

Who then is this God who is perfect, non-discriminatory and inclusive? Once again let us turn to the parables of Jesus remembering that the parables are given to those who think they are inside but who, by their judgments, are really outside (Mark 4:11).

We will begin with the well-known parable of the Pharisee and the Tax Collector (Luke 18:9-14). In order to capture the power of this little vignette I want to offer two contemporary "translations."

> "Two men went to church to worship. The first, a respected elder prayed thus, 'Lord I thank you that I am not like so many Christians or this drug addled pimp. I am faithful in attending church, Bible study and council meetings; I tithe on my gross income and do daily devotions. I oppose abortion and will not let homosexuals in my church.' The pimp sat in the back pew softly crying and prayed, 'God be merciful to me, a sinner.'"
>
> "Two women went to church to worship. The first, an associate pastor prayed thus, 'Lord I thank you I am not like other pastors or that baby killer. I am an excellent exegete, spend quality time with church members and dutifully fulfill my responsibilities. I attend protest rallies, seek justice and recycle.' The solider in the back pew lifted her eyes to heaven and simply said, 'Lord, be merciful to me a sinner.'"

We would normally not find anything wrong with either the elder or the pastor but would have a lot to criticize about the pimp or the solider (depending on our perspective). Yet in our retelling of the parable, it is in fact the "oppressive" pimp and the "baby killing" soldier that go home right with God. How can this be? There is apparently nothing wrong with the elder and the pastor and a lot wrong with the pimp and the solider. Jesus turns on its head all of our notions of what counts as being right with God! Those who counted themselves on the inside are outside and those who were judged by others to be outside and rue their condition are inside.

This business of who was in and who was out was a major theme in Jesus' teaching about God. There are many occasions when Jesus is criticized by the 'holy' people of his time about those with whom he spent his time, people who had been marginalized by the holiness codes (2.3) of his time (e.g., tax collectors and prostitutes). Similar situations prevail in many if not most churches today. Those whom we are not like, those whom we are over against, those whom we do not think fit our perception of what a good Christian is form our identities. Yet, God does not look at people and accept them in the same manner we religious humans do.

Luke 15 records three parables that all reiterate this theme, the parables of the faithful Shepherd, the diligent Widow and the Waiting Father. The context for these parables is precisely the scandal caused by Jesus including those whom others would exclude. If Jesus proclaims the kingdom of God and an essential aspect of that proclamation is the inclusion of the socially unacceptable this can only mean that Jesus reflects God's concern for everyone, not just those we or others think should belong. This is made clear in a saying from Matthew (5:45) that God does not discriminate when it comes to blessing us; good and evil people alike find their place within the grace of God.

This grace is manifest in the term Jesus used for God, the Aramaic word '*abba*.' The term *abba* reflects both intimacy as well as respect. It is the one of the first words a child learns along with '*imma*' (mommy). It can also be used for elders or respected and venerated men of the village. The fact that the gospels, composed in Greek, should retain this Aramaic term indicates that it was in use not only within the Jewish context of early Christianity but also the Gentile one as well. Like a few other well-known Aramaic terms used by Jesus (*mammon, gehenna*), *abba* retains its place in the Jesus tradition because it was obviously a favorite of Jesus himself.

God as *abba* means this: God is the one whom we respect, listen to and obey, yet God is also the one with whom we can cuddle, trust unconditionally and turn to for any and all of our needs just like little children. This is the point of the passage about God clothing the lilies of the field and feeding the sparrows (Matthew 6:25-32). God, our *abba*, is portrayed in Jesus' teaching with language of nurture not power. Jesus' God is not the god of Plato and Greek philosophy. His God is the One to whom he turns again and again in good times and in challenging times: he believes unequivocally that God will care for the lost, the despairing, the outcast, the rejected, the lonely, the impoverished and conversely that God cannot but turn away from the rich, the snobbish, the exclusive and those who would consign others to a fate worse than death.

If we are going to call God our heavenly *abba*, as Jesus did, if the Spirit poured out in our hearts cries "*abba*, daddy" (Romans 8:15, Galatians 4:6), then it is to One who has the best interests of everyone in mind, not just those who call themselves righteous or holy. This is the good news, for all of us have "fallen short of the glory of God" (Romans 3:23) and among us "there is not one righteous among us, not even one" (Romans 3:10). When we think we have a claim on God we are deceived, but when we cast ourselves upon the mercy of God, our *Abba's* arms are wide open to accept us and embrace us as God does everyone else. When it comes to God as our '*abba*' we are all 'Children of the Heavenly Father.'[xxxiii]

1.4 The Life of the Kingdom of God

There have been countless descriptions of what it means to be a Christian over the last two thousand years. In America, it usually means some sort of 'born again' experience or personal relationship with Jesus. It often includes a list of vices to be avoided and virtues to be inculcated. It can be as extreme as sectarianism or as bland as a state church where all the citizens of a given country are "Christian."

Countless thousands of books have been written on what it means to be a Christian. For some it is as minimal as faith and baptism, for others as maximal as complete and total obedience to church authority on everything from dress, to food and sex taboos. In all these cases Christian groups tend to define themselves over against their fellow Christians each accusing the other of compromise with the world.

It is not as complicated as all that. The Christian life looks like Jesus. It is that simple. There is certain wisdom in the saying "What would Jesus do?" It is striking that in the Gospels Jesus nowhere tells his followers that they should be more obedient than they are. Even Matthew's gospel, which has a tendency to portray Jesus as an obedient Jew, does not simply assume that all commands in the Jewish Scriptures are to be followed in a legalistic manner. Some have interpreted Matthew 5:17-20 in such a way but this is an incorrect reading.

Interpreting the Sermon on the Mount

In 5:17-20 we have a series of utterances by Jesus that have been brought together by Matthew. Many say this passage indicates that the Law (which for some means the truthfulness of everything in the Old Testament) will always remain valid. If this were the case it is hard to figure out why Jesus then goes on to make explicit contrasts between what is commanded in the Scriptures and what his rule of life looks like. It is also difficult to understand how and why Jesus could break with some of the most significant commandments that marked Judaism from the Gentile world, e.g., keeping kosher and Sabbath laws. Jesus could have said, "Keep the whole Torah" or "Keep the moral and spiritual components of the Law" and "ignore the cultic and ritual ones" but he didn't.

There have been many ways that the Sermon on the Mount has been interpreted. To keep things simple, I have arranged them in four major categories although there may well be others. Each interpretation has both its debits and its assets. These four categories are the legalistic, the dispensational, the academic, and the idealistic. After a quick review of these four I will propose a fifth category that I think makes more sense in our modern world and is closer to the intention of Matthew's Gospel.

First are those who contend that Jesus meant everything in the Sermon to be followed literally or legalistically. We don't see much of this anymore except in certain conservative traditions of the Historic Peace Church and Old Order churches (e.g., the Amish). In this way of thinking, the Sermon is a new Law on the order of the Law given to Moses at Sinai, to be obeyed without question. When these admonitions and injunctions are interpreted in this fashion they tend to become legalistic rules for the Christian life. The downside is that the grace and blessing found in the Sermon, the compassionate character of God and the concern for others as real people is missed. The asset is that these followers of Jesus believe that real obedience is not only possible but essential to Christian faith and life.

Second are those who see in the Sermon on the Mount an authentic way of living but it is not for this world, it is for the world to come. It has some common characteristics with the fourth category (the idealistic). Dispensationalism suggests that Jesus offered the kingdom to Israel and as part of that kingdom came the way of life found in the Sermon, but since Israel rejected Jesus' offer, the Sermon is then relegated to the distant future when the Kingdom comes. The downside to this view is that the essential components of Christian peacemaking, love of enemy, etc., are no longer to be seen as a way of life for the Christian and are to be modified by other passages in the Bible. The clear disjunction created by the antitheses ("you have heard it said...but I say unto you") is muted. The benefit of this way of understanding the Sermon is that there is a clear connection between the teaching of Jesus and the kingdom of God or God's reign, although it is relegated to another time.

The third way of reading the Sermon can be found primarily in academic literature. Here, scholars parse the Sermon into its various forms and show how Matthew has edited the Sermon from Jesus' utterances. The downside to this way of reading the Sermon is less fraught with difficulties than the first two but one has to be an expert in biblical studies to make sense of what is being said and for this reason most of what is written in academia that would lead to better understanding about the Sermon rarely finds its way into the pulpit. The upside of this reading is that scholars have been able to clarify a great many otherwise strange details that can only be illumined by placing the Sermon back into a first century Palestinian context.

The fourth way to read the Sermon is to conceive of it as a high ideal, but not very realistic. Some scholars, like Albert Schweitzer and Reinhold Niebuhr would call the Sermon an 'impossible ethic,' nice but neither real nor practicable for our complex world. In the Middle Ages, the idealism of the Sermon was such that it was intended to be followed only by the religious (monks and nuns) and clergy; the laity was exempt, as it really had nothing to do with the day-to-day work of their mundane lives.

Another form that an idealistic reading takes is the 'spiritualization' of the Sermon. Ideally, it is something we should all aspire to but it is not meant to be taken seriously. We can find this way of thinking in Martin Luther and in many strains of modern Evangelicalism.[xxxiv] The downside of this interpretation is that like the second view, it dualizes the disjunction between Jesus' teachings and that of the Jewish Scriptures found in the Sermon. The upside of this view, similar to that of the first and second views is that the Sermon is recognized to have an 'other-worldly' character about it, it smells of heaven and God's kingdom, it is different than the way we have typically lived as Christians.

Each of these four views has had its particular influence, depending upon time and place. Is there then a way to take the Sermon seriously without at the same time falling into the traps of legalism, idealism or just spiritualizing away its radical demands? I think there is and I call this the catechetical alternative. By this I mean that the sermon is meant as a form of instruction for candidates who are wondering what Christian living is all about and how it is done.

The Sermon on the Mount as Christian Catechesis

There is a document that helps us to put this view in perspective, a piece of early Christian literature that had some influence on certain parts of the early church called *The Didache.*[xxxv] *The Didache* is the earliest Christian catechism we possess. It was composed (although not necessarily written down) in the first century, perhaps even prior to the Gospels themselves. It was meant to be memorized as it was heard from the mentor who was training the potential convert to the Christian faith. Like so much teaching in the ancient world, it was meant to be heard not read (the literacy rate in the ancient world was quite low and they didn't have the kinds of access to books we have nowadays[xxxvi]). It would have been heard over and over for a period of years and thus would have been implanted deeply in the heart of the convert.[xxxvii]

The Didache and Matthew's Sermon on the Mount share a lot of similarities, so much so that earlier scholars thought that there must be a literary connection between them, some even saying that one document must have borrowed from the other. Current research indicates that indeed there are similarities but that both *The Didache* and Matthew's gospel arose independently of one another.[xxxviii] We may also notice that Luke has a version of the 'catechetical instruction' as well in his Sermon on the Plain (Luke 6:17-49). Together all three witness to the fact that we have a compendium of Jesus' teaching that was found useful to instruct potential converts.

It is suggested that texts like the Sermon on the Mount are for potential converts and not new converts. This is indicated by the fact that much of the material contained in the Sermon on the Mount is found in *The Didache* prior to baptism, the entrance ritual that brought one into the community of faith. Evidently, the practices found in the Sermon were 'tried on', as it were, so that those desiring to be Christians could know just what they were getting into *before* they made their final commitment. Just as a person might try on clothes in a dressing room to see how they fit, so also the catechetical process was a way of helping potential converts 'try on' the Christian life before they made the final decision to live it 'til death. It has to do with "counting the cost" (Luke 9:57-62).

Imagine that! The practices of letting go of anger, turning the other cheek, loving one's enemies, forswearing oaths, living a chaste life, trusting in God for the necessities of life were taught *before* not *after* one committed one's life to Christ. Why was this? I think it is because these values and behaviors were so decidedly different than those commonly found in either Jewish or Gentile cultures. From the outside one could see that the Christians were different, but in order to join them, a trial period of really learning how to live this lifestyle was necessary.

How different this is from today where we encourage people to get "saved" and then, if they are fortunate, we teach them what it means to be a follower of Jesus. For the early church there was not a separation of salvation and discipleship, in fact Christian formation was the prelude to acceptance of salvation, which was baptism into the body of Christ!

As I mentioned before, each person seeking entrance to the Christian community underwent a period of formation. During this time they had a mentor assigned to them, someone to help them as they learned the disciplines of the Christian life, to walk them through difficulties, to pray with them and counsel them. In the Sermon on the Mount Jesus is the model mentor. He is the one who first lives out this life and who invites us to "follow him" as we too journey with him on this new path of becoming a child of God.

What is it then that must be learned if one is to become a Christian?

The Radical Re-Orientating Reign of God

First, one learns that true happiness does not consist of being in the center. The word translated 'blessed' or 'happy' (Matthew 5:3ff) is used of those whose lives are on the margins. There is some talk today about how Jesus wants us all to be healthy, wealthy and living well. This is the so-called prosperity gospel. But there is nothing 'good news' about it. It is as American as apple pie. It simply takes the rights guaranteed in the Declaration of Independence to 'life, liberty and the pursuit of happiness' and says that this is what God wants for us.

But such is not the case. I do not mean that God wants us to be poor, sick and needy. What I mean is that when we live on the edge, when we chose to follow Jesus, our families, our friends and our communities may well marginalize us. It is no small thing to break with relationships that are primarily toxic in character and begin to share in the life of a community where we are loved and cared for. When others around us esteem a go-get-'em, dog-eat-dog' attitude and we find ourselves esteeming others first, we will be seen as foolish. When those around us demand that we hate others who would dare attack and oppress us and we are learning how to turn the other cheek and love our enemies, we will appear to others to be moronic. When our families and friends pile up money in 401K's, IRA's, CD's and investment funds and we begin to give away our resources to feed the poor and support ministries of peace among us, well, we will be criticized. Jesus says as much, "you will be persecuted." When this happens, and we have divested ourselves for the sake of others, when we have sought to be reconciled even with the most obnoxious, spiteful people, when we seek justice and peace in deep and radical manners, indeed, when we grieve over hurting others, Jesus says that this, THIS, is what it is to be blessed by God. This is real happiness.

Can you imagine the early potential convert to Christianity saying to their mentor, "Do you know how hard this is?" The mentor would remind the novitiate that by changing their thinking about life (for that is what 'repentance' means, to change one's thinking'), they will for the first time know what real blessing, authentic happiness is.

Second, the Sermon calls us to a life where we trust God to take care of us. This may seem obvious at first, but the reality is much more difficult than we might imagine. In the fall of 2008 when the global economy collapsed people were glued to their news stations as job losses increased, companies went bankrupt or had to be bailed out, the stock market decreased by 50% and we were told this was the worst economic scenario we had seen since the Great Depression. For many, it felt like the end of the world. Everyone, including Christians began to worry.

Jesus enjoins his disciples "Stop worrying" (Matt 6:25ff). When we worry we feel like the circumstances of our life have gone out of control, we are no longer able to provide for ourselves. We lose our sense of independence and what we had planned, the way we saw the future, now is lost. So we worry and fret and bite our fingernails. Why do we do this? We worry because we think that we alone are responsible for our existence, that in the grand scheme of things there is no one else who will love us.

Yet, Jesus insists, God loves us and will take care of us. The witness to this is the fact that God has provided for the birds of the air. Life on our planet has been sustained for billions of years, not by a distant aloof God, who simply wound up the universe according to immutable laws, and then let it go. Life has been sustained because God is personally involved in all of God's good creation of which we are the most significant part. We are those who have been made in the 'image of God.' Are we not worth more than two sparrows? Surely we are and for Jesus this is the point.

I have several bird feeders around my home. Every day I watch as they come to feast: robins, finches, mockingbirds, starlings, mourning doves, cardinals and yes, lots of little sparrows. Every day I am reminded that God feeds them. When I am tempted to worry about whether or not God will feed me, the birds are my daily reminder that God cares for all life, that I am not alone, that the God of Jesus is not a miser. Yet what about those today in African refugee camps that lack food? What about the homeless in my own community? Does not God care for them as well? Yes he does. Just like I put bird feed in the feeder, so also, as a member of the church I am called to feed the poor and needy.

Life is not about hoarding wealth but about spreading it around. God can act to see to it that the creation is nourished, but he uses us humans to see to it that our fellow humans have their needs met. We live in a world where the poor are daily reminders that we too have an obligation to meet, not only to ourselves but also to one another. In order to do this we, like Jesus, need to eschew three things: comfort, safety and security.

We, like Jesus, will be tested to see whether we trust God for these three things (Matt 4:1-11). Jesus when tempted to secure his own comfort did not turn stones into bread (not for nothing that we refer to 'comfort food'). He knew that he was important to his *Abba*, and so refused to use his power to meet his own needs, to satiate his hunger. When tested to make sure that God would keep him safe from harm, Jesus refused to force God's hand. The temptation to hurl himself off the Temple roof is significant in that the Temple was where God was thought to reside. Jesus is on God's home turf, yet he refuses to prove that God will keep him safe. Finally, Jesus refuses to worship the prince of darkness, of violence, when offered the right to be King of the entire world. Had he done so, Jesus would himself have become the principle of violence-keeping security. He would have grasped his power to rule over all and therefore secured himself at the pinnacle of hierarchy. Thankfully, his way of making peace is not the way of the violent world (John 16:33). Jesus utterly refused to go in this direction instead living out what he will enjoin on his disciples in the Sermon on the Mount. Jesus finds his comfort, safety and security in the giving of himself for others and in the care and vindication of his *Abba* who brings life from death.

Third, the way of the Kingdom of God means that the way we relate to everyone changes. Not just our friends, but also those we despise and those who can't stand us. It is not easy to love the unlovely. When we are attacked, we attack back, when we are threatened, we threaten. Our natural posture is defensiveness. This is true not only on a personal level but also on a political one. Have you ever noticed that when someone attacks you it is always unjust but when you 'attack' another it is always just? It is this problem that the Sermon on the Mount addresses for it lumps all defensiveness under the same rubric. In Matt 5:21ff, Jesus says that to be angry is the same as murder. When you get angry the first thing you do is to have this sort of inane conversation in your head. They said this, I will say that, they will respond thus, I will have that response, etc. Notice how you always win this battle!

Jesus says that the Christian life does not consist of these mental battles. Instead we are to make peace in every way for "Blessed are the peacemakers." More than that, retaliation is not an aspect of Christian existence (5:38ff). When Christians (not people in general) are hassled or persecuted, it is not part of their calling to 'get 'em back.' Christianity is not a gang where if one member is suffering at the hands of rivals, it sends out its members to get the other gang. Instead we are called to 'love our enemies.' How different would the world be today, if so-called Christian America had, instead of announcing war after 9/11, offered forgiveness?

This new way of relating also extends to the way we understand our sexuality. Jesus' admonitions on adultery and divorce are, I suspect, made to men primarily because in his time males were at the top of the gender hierarchy. With the rise of Internet pornography, Jesus' clear call to resist lust has as much to say today as it did then. The problem of pornography is not the sexual acts themselves but what is occurring in the minds of those who watch. Engaging pornography, for men and women, is a vicarious way to have the beautiful lover, to be the object of desire, to be tended and titillated by the 'fantasy lover.' We see ourselves as gods desired and fawned over as the powerful ones who bring or withhold pleasure from our 'lover.' It is clear that sexual fantasizing is a form of idolatry.

Divorce in the Christian community is also forbidden. Why? Jesus wasn't ever married so he cannot be very realistic about this, can he? Divorce among Christian couples is a sign that forgiveness has limits. I will forgive you and stay committed to you only this far. Yet, in the gospels, Jesus teaches us that forgiveness is not for the single event, but is to be expressed "70 times 7." Forgiveness for the errant spouse is a sign of how far God forgives us.[xxxix]

If there is an exception today for divorce I suspect it is not for infidelity, but for abuse. Christian couples are to live in love, not hurting one another, not dominating one another, but in the real egalitarianism given in the Spirit (Gal. 3:27ff). When a "Christian" husband is abusing his spouse (or occasionally a wife is abusing her husband) it is clear the Spirit is not at work in such a person for abuse is violence, and the Spirit of God is not violent. In such a situation my advice would be to flee so that the abused does not give the abuser a place to keep sinning against them (one thinks of those in the early church who sought martyrdom to whom Cyprian offered the same advice).

Fourth, in the Sermon we are shown certain disciplines that will enable further growth when practiced properly. Jesus highlights the problem with spiritual disciplines in that the practice itself becomes an end in itself; it becomes self-serving. We see this all too often when persons who favor a certain practice spend so much energy getting others to practice it as well. What they are really doing is seeking external validation for what they are doing.

Narcissism and Christian Discipleship

Matthew 6:1-18 offers careful correctives in spiritual direction. The dangers of spiritual mimesis (where we imitate another person's religious practice) lurk even in and around our worship. Jesus details three areas that can prove dangerous: giving, praying, and fasting or repenting. In each of these, examples are given of 'bad' *mimesis* (imitation) and 'good' *mimesis.* In no case is Jesus criticizing the faith of Judaism. In each case, the person critiqued expresses their faith in relation to others not to God.

In each case the action that is practiced is done for the purpose of soliciting a response from the collective. If the practice of faith is to elicit a positive response from people and the practice of faith achieves such responses, then as Jesus points out, the goal is reached, "they have their reward." It is not that God will not be gracious to them; it is that they cannot receive what they cannot perceive.

Jesus is critiquing the practice therefore, of religion, not faith. Spirituality expressed in religious terms and forms will always be directed to the other rather than God. Jesus calls these figures 'hypocrites.' We would note that 'hypocrites' is the term applied to actors in the ancient world, particularly where masks were involved. 'Hypocrites' is a term Jesus may have been familiar with from the practice of drama in neighboring Sepphoris and Capernaum.

The truly religious person, the actor, ('hypocrite') is split between the person they know themselves to be and the person they present to others. This metaphoric split is an indication of the rupture of religion and its inability to really make us whole. I find that the distinction Swiss psychologist Carl Jung makes between the persona and the shadow is helpful here. Our persona is the way we wish to be perceived and our shadow is the side unknown to ourselves but often perceived by others. Those aspects we know of our own shadow, we do not wish others to know about, thus we put on 'masks' in public, particularly when it comes to public participation in the divine drama of worship.

Dan O. Via Jr., puts it this way:

> "If the hypocrite is not consciously and cynically pretending, he is still responsible for being unconscious of the dichotomy between self-image

and reality. The hypocrite may not intend to deceive others, but he does lack integrity, correspondence between inner and outer, and is responsible for the deficiency because he has concealed the true nature of the inner person from himself."[xl]

The practice of faith as 'religion before others' serves a two-fold purpose: first it indicates identification with the divine and second, it creates a hierarchical structure where religious practice can be compared and imitated. Soren Kierkegaard named the dangers and the emptiness of this practice in his book, *Either/Or*. It is insidious because it determines itself in relation to the 'other' in the pretense of relation to the 'Other.'

The lie of self to the self stems from the founding lie (5.2, 6.1) that creates the myth of the victim's guilt. Thus, in our own individual religious experience, we become our own prosecutor, judge, jury, victim and executioner (we call this our conscience). Each step in the process is revealed as false, as a lie. Whether repenting, praying or giving, it is our spirituality which expresses our relationship with the *Abba* in our relations with others. Spirituality is not the way we show others our relationship with God.

The desire for recognition is apparent in all three misguided attempts at faith. In the first, the almsgiver desires to seen and known as a benefactor, a good person. In the second, the worshipper seeks to be perceived as faithful to God. In the third, the repentant sinner seeks to be known as a self-flagellant.

In all three cases we can perceive an attempt at differentiation from the masses of humanity. In all three cases, this differentiation sacralizes the practitioner; they desire to be known as 'like God.' The almsgiver desires adoration, the worshipper admiration and the sinner respect. In each case, the religious practitioners have identified themselves with what they believe the divine One desires, namely adoration, admiration and respect. By so differentiating themselves, they 'dedicate themselves to God' and are thus rendered less likely to be picked out in the random lottery of the scapegoat mechanism. That role is left to others allegedly more deserving of that distinction due no doubt to their distance from God, from the sacred.

Jesus assumes we will practice spiritual disciplines ("When you fast, when you pray, when you give alms..."), but it is how we practice them, and the disciple does so in a spirit of authentic yearning to grow in human relationships.

Hypocrisy is a dangerous subject to raise in the church; it is almost always experienced accusatorily, that is, in a satanic fashion. If we use any other model than Jesus to discuss hypocrisy, if we bring up Mr. Jones or Mrs.

Smith or Saint Bill or anybody, we will inevitably doom our people to religious practice. They will have felt the accusation and they will respond out of fear. For Christians, there really is a singular model to follow when it comes to knowing how to live our faith. There is one who has gone the road from baptism with water to baptism with fire and he still brings the message of God's peace, just like he always has.

Finally, we are to be wary of judging others (Matt. 7:1-5). It is not our place to decide whether or not a person is a good, bad or carnal Christian. We do not walk in their shoes. If we did we might see the great strides they have made, even though they may not be on the same part of the journey we are. Jesus, in fact, provides the key to judgment before God and it is not some abstract set of do's and don'ts. When you stand before God, you are measured with the exact same type of measure you use with others. If you measure by the thimble full, don't expect buckets from God.[xli] You get from God what you give to others. This is the way it works in God's kingdom!

God's reign, how shall we describe it? How did Jesus describe it? It seems so upside down from what we know.[xlii] The way God does things seems subversive of the way we humans do things. God is constantly surprising us. In the words of the slogan of the United Church of Christ, "God is still speaking." Yet if we are hearing the Word of God aright, that speaking comes to us as judgment and grace: judgment on our idolatry, grace as the revelation of forgiveness and new beginnings. To Jesus' understanding of his sacred literature we now turn, and why it is we pray "Set apart your name, your character, your revelation, from all the other gods" (= "Hallowed be Thy name"). And so we pray (Matthew 6: 9-13 my translation):

> "*Abba*, reveal Your distinctiveness
> Usher in the reign of Your gracious will
> Feed us today with the Bread of Your glorious Tomorrow
> Come, show forgiveness to us as we forgive others
> Please don't ever put us to the Ultimate Test
> And deliver us from the Accuser
> So say we all."

Chapter 2 How Jesus Read His Bible

2.1 Discovering the Beloved God

We have learned from modern theologians that what one says about Scripture and how one uses it can be two different things and that how one uses Scripture is the real indication of what one believes about it.[xliii] I notice, for example, that many preachers use Scripture as a diving board, they quote it and then jump off into a pool of ideas, leaving the biblical text behind. What they say might be good or true or even relevant but it has little or no connection to the passage under discussion. Other preachers I have heard treat Scripture like they are in a 7th grade science class dissecting a frog. They notice with some repugnance the things they don't like and can be quite critical of the process of having to figure out what lies before them.

Some have a high view of Scripture by which they mean Scripture is the Word of God, inspired and without error, yet the way in which they use it betrays that they really don't take it very seriously. These folks ignore context and a text without a context is a pretext. These folks have what I call the Old McDonald approach to the Bible, here a verse, there a verse, everywhere a verse verse. Contemporary fundamentalist preaching is like this, a string of verses on a chain like pearls that all make whatever point the preacher is seeking to get across.

Protestants frequently argue that because Jesus quoted the Jewish Bible, this means that he accepted its authority as a whole. When they do this they import a modern view of the authority of Scripture back into the past. I noted earlier that there were many and varied views of the authority of the biblical writings and that not all groups in Jesus' time had the same view of biblical authority. It is also true that the way the New Testament writers and Jesus quote and interpret Scripture follows certain patterns in their culture. Groups in Jesus' day had rules or guidelines for interpreting the biblical text. The key question for us, and one that is rarely raised is this: Did Jesus have a way of using his Bible that was different from those around him? I want to suggest that he did.

The key text for us to explore in this section will come from Jesus' inaugural sermon at his hometown synagogue in Nazareth found in the Gospel of Luke (4:16-30). To be fair, many critical scholars see the hand of the Gospel editor all over this text, noting that many phrases are typical of Luke.[xliv] Nevertheless, I suspect that there is an authentic story underlying this text inasmuch as Jesus' first sermon almost gets him killed. As I hope to show, there is also a tremendous congruity with how Jesus interprets the Scripture in this text and his way of understanding both theology and ethics that we saw in chapter 1.

In Luke 4 Jesus returns to his hometown in Nazareth after having been baptized and then tested in the wilderness. He enters the synagogue and is asked to be the Scripture reader.[xlv] In Jesus' day this could have taken two forms, the first is the actual reader (vocalizer) of the Hebrew text that would not have been understood by Galileans.[xlvi] It would be like someone reading from the Greek New Testament in church today. The second role would be that of a translator/interpreter known as a *targumist.* This person would not read from a scroll but recite from memory a 'standard' translation (a *Targum*) in Aramaic that was the common Semitic tongue in Palestine.[xlvii] Luke appears unclear as to which role Jesus took, perhaps conflating both roles into one.

Nevertheless in Luke, Jesus arises takes the scroll and reads from Isaiah:

> "The Spirit of the Lord is on me,
> because he has anointed me
> to preach good news to the poor.
> He has sent me to proclaim freedom for the prisoners
> and recovery of sight for the blind,
> to release the oppressed,
> to proclaim the year of the Lord's favor."

After this he rolls the scroll up, hands it over to the attendant, who puts it away and then Jesus sits down. The sermon was short and sweet. He says, "Today this text has been fulfilled in your hearing." Now what follows is strange for at first it appears that the listeners are quite glad for what Jesus said. But he retorts rather sarcastically and proceeds to cite two examples to justify his sarcasm. It is at this point that the crowd wants to take him out and kill him by throwing him off a cliff.

This really doesn't make much sense. Some interpreters might argue that what got Jesus in trouble was some sort of 'divine' claim, that God had anointed him to be special. But is such the case? In order to see what is happening we shall note three critical but interrelated aspects of the text. First, is the way Jesus cited the text compared to what is actually in Isaiah, second, the translation problem of verse 22 and the third is why Jesus uses these specific examples from Elijah and Elisha.

When teaching this passage I point out that Isaiah 61:1-2 was one of the more popular passages in Judaism. It is cited in the Dead Sea Scrolls and other writings as well as in rabbinic literature. Have you ever seen a football game where, after a touchdown, somebody holds up a sign in the end zone seats that reads "John 3:16?" If they had played football in Jesus' day, that sign would have read "Isaiah 61:1-2." What made it so important was that it was a lectionary passage for the Year of Jubilee. This was a text that expressed the hope of Israel for liberation from the bondage not only of spiritual dis-ease but also political and economic oppression. The vision of Isaiah was one of *shalom*, wholeness in all of life.

The first thing to notice is that Jesus does not cite the entire text but eliminates one very important line, "and the day of the vengeance of our God." The question is why did he do this? Some suggest that now is the time of grace and so Jesus holds off on quoting the text about God's vengeance since that will come later at the end of time. But nowhere else does Jesus seem to quote the biblical text in this fashion, and he never seems to break the work of God into dispensations or periods of time. Something else is going on here.

Second is the problem of translation that arises in Luke 4:22. Most translations indicate that the crowd was pleased with Jesus. These same synagogue hearers then comment, "Isn't this Joseph's son?" The intonation we are supposed to supply would be something like "Oh, what a fine sermon and what a fine preacher Jesus has turned out to be, his father would be so proud!" But is this the case?

The Greek text is quite simple and the King James has adequately translated this "and all bore witness to him." This bearing witness in the KJV is neither positive nor negative. Why then do translators say, "all spoke well of him?" Translators have to make what is known as a syntactical decision, they have to decide whether or not the "bearing witness" is negative or positive. Technically speaking they have to decide if the dative pronoun "to him" is a dative of disadvantage or a dative of advantage; was the crowd bearing witness to his advantage or to his disadvantage? If it is the former case then the intonation we gave to "Isn't this Joseph's son?" above would make sense and Jesus immediately following gets sarcastic for no reason, but if it is the latter then we could just as well translate this text as "and all spoke ill of his sermon", that is, they didn't like what he did, then the intonation of the phrase "Isn't this Joseph's son?" should be rendered something like "who does Jesus think he is coming into our synagogue and saying such things?" With this alternate, preferable translation, of verse 23 Jesus is not being sarcastic but is responding to the negativity of the listeners.[xlviii]

A third point to be made concerns the two examples Jesus cites from two of Israel's greatest prophets, Elijah and Elisha. In both cases Jesus notes that God worked not within the bounds of Israel but outside the chosen people when he sent these prophets to feed and heal. What is the connection between what these prophets did and what Jesus did when he quoted the Isaiah text, and why did the crowd get angry enough with him to want to kill him?

We noted that when Jesus quoted the Isaiah text he did not quote the phrase "and the day of the vengeance of our God." If, in popular opinion, part of the promise of jubilee was that God would deliver Israel from her oppressors, and if that expectation was that God would punish her oppressors, then the phrase "and the day of the vengeance of our God" would be an aspect of the longed for and hoped for deliverance by which Israel's enemies would be cast down. Political deliverance was perceived as an aspect of God working wrath on Israel's enemies. By eliminating this line, Jesus also eliminated the possibility that jubilee included God's wrath upon whoever was oppressing Israel. His words were indeed "gracious words" ("words of grace").

The citation of the two examples of Elijah and Elisha then justify Jesus' exclusion of this vengeance saying for both prophets had worked their healing miracles among foreign outsiders, those whom God was supposed (in popular piety) to hate. In short, Jesus is saying to his synagogue hearers "Jubilee is here, not only for you but also for those you hate; in fact God also goes to your oppressors with this message of jubilee, deliverance and salvation." Now we can begin to understand why they got so mad at him.

But there is a further implication to be drawn from this. By eliminating the phrase regarding God's vengeance, Jesus is removing the notion of retributive violence from the doctrine of God. He is in effect saying that God is not like you think, loving you and angry with those you hate. There is a great bumper sticker making the rounds these days that captures this problem. It says "Isn't it convenient that God hates the same people you do?" Like Israel, we too have a tendency to want to believe that God is on our side and will judge "the other" who is over against us, or different from us. Such was not the case with Jesus. He observed that God makes no distinctions between righteous and wicked, between oppressors and oppressed, they both need deliverance and God's blessing. Did he not say, "God makes rain to fall on good and evil and sun to shine on just and unjust?" (Matt 5:45)

Reading the Bible with Jesus

This is perhaps the most important point I am seeking to make in this book, namely that, like Jesus, it is essential for us to begin to reframe the way we understand the "wrath" or retributive violence of God.[xlix] To suggest that God is nonviolent or better yet, that God is not involved in the cycle of retributive vengeance and punishment will undoubtedly strike many as wrong. Some having read this far are no doubt ready to chuck this book into the fire. If you are feeling this way, then what is the difference between how you feel and how Jesus' hearers felt that day when he preached in his hometown synagogue? Nothing irks some folks more than losing a God who is wrathful, angry, retributive and punishing. This is only because we want so much to believe that God takes sides, and that side is inevitably our side.

So much of Jesus' teaching subverts this way of thinking. One example is the parable of the Pharisee and the tax collector found in Luke 18:9-14 (1.3), where what counts as righteousness is completely and totally turned on its head!

If, in fact, Jesus begins his ministry by asking what God without retribution looks like, and if he acts this way in his ministry, and if he interprets his Bible to say such things, the question arises "Shouldn't we also follow Jesus in interpreting our Bibles in the same way?" That is, is biblical interpretation also a part of discipleship (5.4)? Does following Jesus include more than just living a virtuous life? Might it also have to do with helping folks change the way they envision God? Such was the case for Jesus who called people constantly to "change your thinking." This is what repentance is, changing the way you think about things (Greek *metanoia*). When we change the way we see and understand the character of God, everything else changes and we turn back (Hebrew *shuv*) to the living and true God.

We can see Jesus doing the same thing in Luke 7:18-23 when he responds to the followers of John the Baptist. Herod had imprisoned the Baptist for his preaching against the Herodian family system. John did not want to die without knowing whether Jesus was the one to come. Now what could possibly have created this doubt in John's mind? The answer comes in Jesus' response to John's followers. "Go and tell John what you have seen and heard," Jesus says and then follows a list of miracles. Is Jesus saying, "Tell John you have seen a miracle worker and that God is doing great things through me?" Doesn't John already know these things about Jesus? Surely he does. Healers were rare but they were not uncommon in Jesus' day.[l] What then is Jesus really saying?

Luke 7:22ff is a selection of texts, mostly from Isaiah but also including the miracles of Elijah and Elisha (blind Isaiah 61:1-2, 29:18, 35:5, lame 35:6, deaf 29:18, 35:5, poor 29:19; dead/lepers I Kings 17:17-24 and 2 Kings 5:1-27). The Isaiah texts all include a reference to the vengeance of God *none of which Jesus quotes.* As in Luke 4 what is at stake is the retributive violence of God that was an important aspect of John's proclamation (Luke 3:7-9). John, like the prophets before him, believed that God was going to bring an apocalyptic wrath. Nowhere in Jesus' preaching do we find such and this is what confused John, just as it confused Jesus' synagogue hearers. Jesus implicitly tells John, through his message to John's followers, that the wrath of God is not part of his message, rather healing and good news is. That is, Jesus is inviting John to read Isaiah the way he did![li]

The last thing Jesus tells John the Baptists' disciples is "Blessed is the person who is not scandalized on account of me?" What could have caused this scandal? What had Jesus said and done that would cause people to stumble on his message? The clues are here in both Luke 4 and 7. Jesus did not include as part of his message the idea that God would pour out wrath on Israel's enemies in order to deliver Israel. Violence is not part of the divine economy for Jesus.

Sad to say, most Christians still think more like John the Baptist than Jesus. Christians have lived a long time with a God who is retributive. We say that God is perfect and thus has the right to punish those whom he deems fit. We say that God will bring his righteous wrath upon all those who reject God. We say that God can do what God wants because God is God. All of this logic is foreign to the gospel teaching of Jesus about the character of his heavenly *abba*. Jesus does not begin with an abstract notion of God or Platonic metaphysics, but with the Creator God whom he knows as loving, nurturing and caring for all persons regardless of their moral condition, their politics, their ethnic background or their social or economic status. God cares for everyone equally and alike.

By removing retribution from the work and character of God, Jesus, for the first time in human history, opened up a new way, a path, which he also invites us to travel. Sadly, few have found that this path and church history is replete with hundreds, even thousands of examples of a Janus-faced god, a god who is merciful and wrathful, loving and punishing. Some have said that we need to hold to both of these sides. Jesus didn't and neither should we. It is time for us to follow Jesus in reconsidering what divinity without retribution looks like.

2.2 Davidic Messiah or Son of Man?

We saw that a crucial aspect of the way Jesus read his Bible was to see that even though the Biblical texts asserted that God can be wrathful, Jesus did not do so. We know that Jesus taught love of enemies explicitly (1.4, Matthew 5:43ff, Luke 6:27ff). The question before us in this section is: did Jesus understand his calling and mission to include non-retribution; was it part of his self-understanding?

Before we tackle this it must be admitted that we do not want to make the same mistakes that were made in the 19th century 'liberal lives of Jesus.' We do not want to use the gospels to try and psychoanalyze Jesus. The gospels just do not give us the sort of information to do that, as though we could get inside Jesus' head. But they do give us enough information so that we can plausibly understand how he perceived himself. This is one of the great benefits of the works of (among others) N.T. Wright and Ben Witherington III on Jesus.

When I was a teenager I was 'born again' and began attending a Baptist church. There I was taught that Jesus fulfilled the messianic promises of the Old Testament. I was told that Judaism had a concept of Messiah, that the

Jews of his day rejected him as the Messiah and crucified him. Over the past thirty years I have come to see that neither of these statements is correct.

First, there is no self-evident concept of a Messiah in the Jewish Scriptures. There are anointed individuals, roles played by prophets, priests and kings. The Judaism of Jesus' day had no single concept of Messiah that was believed everywhere by all Jews. There was a plurality of opinion on the topic that we shall return to shortly. The notion that Jesus offered himself as head of the Jewish state is a figment of modern Christian apocalyptic imagination, useful for contemporary Christian Zionists, but not much else.

The fly in the ointment is the second assertion that Jesus fulfilled the messianic prophecies of the Old Testament and could have been accepted as the Messiah but was rejected. Usually this type of thinking says that Jesus was rejected because he was divine, that Judaism could not accept his metaphysical credentials, as it were. Nothing is further from the truth than this.[lii]

There was a plurality of messianic expectations in ancient Judaism. The Jewish Scriptures mention a few eschatological (end-time) figures like the 'son of man' associated with the *Ancient of Days* in Daniel 7:9-14 but for the most part expected that God would be the primary agent of all that occurred in the final deliverance and redemption of Israel. It was in the 100 years before Jesus that we begin to see the concept of a human agent anointed by God in literature like the Psalms of Solomon or I Enoch.[liii]

Even so, messianic beliefs changed over time and from group to group. Rather than speaking of a concept of Messiah, we should speak of Messianic expectations. Sometimes, as with the Qumran community, there would be two Messianic figures, one priestly, and the other kingly. The Samaritans did not have a royal figure like the Judeans, but believed in the coming of a prophet like Moses figure they called 'Taheb.' Others still perceived Messiah within militaristic categories expecting a mighty warrior (Psalms of Solomon 17-18). Others still had some combination of some of these various views.

Trying to Figure Out Jesus

A key text for seeing this occurs in Mark 8:27-30. There, Jesus has left the region of Palestine and moved on with his disciples to the Gentile region which included Caesarea Philippi. He queried his disciples as to who the crowds thought he might be, that is, how the people perceived him. The disciples replied with what we would expect if there were a plurality of messianic expectations for they give a plurality of responses. Some thought Jesus was John the Baptist raised from the dead (Herod may have thought this also), others thought he was Elijah who was promised to come before 'the great and terrible day of the Lord' (Malachi 3:1-5) and still others one of the great prophets of Israel, perhaps Enoch. When Jesus asks them who they think he is Peter's reply is that Jesus is the Messiah. It is at this point that Jesus tells Peter to shut up and be quiet. Why did he do this?[liv]

Scholars for a long time in the twentieth century referred to this as the 'messianic secret.' Jesus supposedly wanted to keep his messianic identity quiet, after all it could get him in trouble with the authorities and he still had work to do. I think that Jesus silenced Peter precisely because Peter misunderstood just what role Jesus was playing in Israel's drama of salvation. This is underscored a few moments later when Peter refuses to acknowledge Jesus' coming suffering and Jesus has to rebuke him. This misunderstanding was not a one time event for Peter, for even at the end, Peter would initiate the first strike in the eschatological 'holy war', cutting off the servant of the high priest's ear when Jesus was being arrested in the garden of Gethsemane (Mark 14:44, John 18:10). It is apparent that whatever else Peter may have thought of Jesus, he believed Jesus to be a figure who would and could use violence to achieve his goals.

A marginal messianic tradition within ancient Judaism was that Messiah would reprise David's role as the great military conqueror. David was Israel's greatest king. He had united the kingdom, started the Temple project in Jerusalem, and expanded Israel's borders. He was the George Washington of Israel's history, a figure which one looked back on with reverence and awe. Every other king in Israel's history would be compared to David, much like we now compare all other American presidents to George Washington or Abraham Lincoln. In short, David was an ideal iconic figure to represent all that one could hope for when one sought national revitalization and liberation (jubilee).

A certain type of Christian fundamentalism, known as Dispensationalism, widely popularized in the *Left Behind* series, affirms just such a portrait of the conquering Messiah. Jesus is supposed to return with a fiery vengeance, slaughtering all God's enemies in a bloodbath of epic Hollywood special effects proportions. This is the portrait of Messiah that John the Baptist, Peter and, I suspect, most of the other disciples expected. It is this portrait of Messiah that Jesus silences, for it does not fit his mission parameters. In short, Peter got it wrong at Caesarea Philippi and Jesus has to correct him. In the same way, it is time for followers of the *Left Behind* series to leave this nonsense behind! The fact of the matter is, as James Charlesworth says,

> "The sayings of Jesus, both those which are authentic and those which were attributed to him, do not contain speculations or prophecies concerning the coming of a Messiah who will conquer the Gentiles, namely the Romans...Jesus' message was certainly apocalyptic and eschatological; but it was not messianic."[lv]

Before we get to the necessary correction Jesus will make regarding how he understands his mission, let us look at another text, Mark 12:35-37. Here, Jesus engages in a riposte, not with his critics, but with a view of the Davidic warrior Messiah. Beginning with what was evidently a commonplace, namely that Messiah would be a son or heir of David, Jesus wants to know how to interpret Psalm 110:1 (see also 4.4). Before quoting the text of the psalm he argues that the Holy Spirit inspired it. Some think that because Jesus says this, that by this he meant the Holy Spirit inspired all Scripture. I think that Jesus says this as a way of preventing the Torah scholars from wiggling their way out of the text; he is using their own view of scripture against them. Psalm 110:1 reads,

> The Lord said to my Lord:
> 'Sit at my right hand
> Until I put your enemies
> Under your feet.'

In the psalm, the first reference to 'Lord' is God; to whom does the second reference to 'Lord' refer? Jesus is arguing that if David wrote the psalm and David referred to the second person as 'Lord' then this person could not be David's son as David would not call his son 'Lord.' This would be against all of the hierarchical aspects of patriarichalism. It just wouldn't work, therefore the second 'Lord', if thought to be Messiah, cannot be David's son. The conclusion to be drawn, for Jesus, is that Messiah is not to be understood in Davidic warrior categories.

Does this mean then that Jesus has no relation to David? The writer of the gospel of Matthew would seem to contradict what is being said here. Matthew structures his opening genealogy on a pattern known as *gematria*, playing on numbers with three generations of fourteen persons each. If you take the numeric value of the three letters in David's name, d+v+d, they total fourteen.

In Matthew's version of the story at Caesarea Philippi (Matthew 16:13-20) unlike Mark and Luke, when asked who the disciples' think he is, Peter replies, "You are the Messiah, the son of the living God." Then follows the blessing to Peter that this was revealed from God and the statement about the keys to the kingdom. I would argue that Matthew has Peter bring together two disparate confessions, one affirming that Jesus is the Messiah of popular expectation; the other that Jesus is the Son of the living God. It is the latter that Jesus lauds in Matthew's gospel, while the former messianic confession is silenced (Matt. 16:20). While understanding the version in Mark and Luke to be more authentic to the Jesus tradition, nevertheless, Matthew's gospel is not asserting that Jesus is to be considered within the popular categories of messiahship; rather, it is the revelation of Jesus sonship which is to be differentiated from that of popular messianic expectation. 'Messiah', as a category, is now to be understood within the discussion of Jesus' relation, not to David, but to his heavenly *abba*.

This brings us back to the question as to how Jesus corrected Peter's misunderstanding of his mission and role. In all three gospels, following Peter's confession, Jesus begins a new series of teaching that has not hitherto occurred in the gospels, the suffering of the son of man. Now the 'son of man' concept is one of the most difficult to get handles on and scholars have wrestled with this aplenty in the twentieth century only to leave us hanging as to where Jesus might have drawn his inspiration from regarding the phrase 'the son of the man.' Many suggest the background of the term is to be found in Daniel 7 and 9, others Psalm 8, others Ezekiel, others see influence from I Enoch, still others argue that it is a round about way, in Aramaic, of saying 'I.'

Son of Man, Last Adam, True Human

It is neither possible nor desirable, in the short run, to have to choose. I think Jesus was far more creative than he is given credit for and would have been aware of all of the nuances that modern scholars are also aware of.[lvi] What holds all of these potential backgrounds together is that the figure 'son of man' is a representative or corporate figure, that is, the 'son of man' stands for the whole of humanity. But more importantly Jesus brings together the figure 'son of man' with another corporate figure, the suffering servant of Isaiah. The suffering servant of Isaiah is both an individual 'person' as well as the corporate people Israel. A corporate figure or personality is one who can represent or stand in the place of the collective people. One sees, for example in the Jewish Bible, a king can represent the people: When the king is good, the people are blessed, when the king is evil, the people are punished. More so if a father commits a crime, the entire family can be punished or wiped out (cf. Joshua 7). The one stands for 'the many.'

Jesus' use of 'the son of man' is significant in that it is his favorite way of referring to himself in the third person. In the Gospels he is the only one to use it, no one else ever calls Jesus 'the son of man.' You may have noticed that I have not capitalized the phrase 'son of man' as you will find it in many translations. This is because I do not think it was used as a title like 'Messiah' or 'High Priest' but, in keeping with the notion of corporate personality mentioned before, functions as a reference to all human beings. But I will qualify that: For Jesus, the awkward phrase 'son of man' (literally 'the son of the man') is a reference both to himself as the 'True Human' and to restored humanity as a whole. Walter Wink's study of this theme in *The Human Being* has been very helpful to me on this topic.[lvii]

In Mark 2:1-12 when a paralytic is brought to Jesus by being lowered through a roof, Jesus confounds his opponents by asking, "Which is easier to say, 'Take up your bed and walk' or 'Your sins are forgiven.'" He then goes on to say "But that you may know that 'the son of the man' has power on earth to forgive sins, I say to you 'take up your bed and walk.'" In this case 'son of man' is most likely a reference to the True Human, the authentic Adam, who, in the image and likeness of God, does God's will, as a human, in forgiving sin. This is precisely the issue at stake for his opponents for whom only God, not any human, could forgive sin. Yet Jesus seems to suggest that as the True Human he can and does forgive sin.

Something similar can be said for the following story in Mark 2:18-27 where Jesus is questioned about his disciple's behavior, breaking the Sabbath law, and he replies, "the Sabbath was made for humanity, not humanity for the Sabbath. So the True Human is Lord even of the Sabbath." That is, what they do is done as truly human, following or imitating him, and thus are not bound to religious taboos.

A final example occurs in Mark's passion narrative (14:61-62) where before the High Priest Jesus gives a noncommittal answer to the question "are you the Messiah?" by answering that it is the True Human who sits at the right hand of God. Such was enough to earn him the charge of blasphemy.

In Mark 8:33 when Jesus corrects Peter, it is not that Jesus rejects the title Messiah; it is that he cannot use it because it had been so over laden with militant and zealous baggage. Later, his followers will refer to him so much as 'the' promised messianic figure and use all manner of titles and roles from the Jewish Scriptures and other writings to describe his person and work that the word Messiah virtually becomes like a modern last name: Jesus Messiah (Christ). Yet during the time of his ministry, Jesus did not refer to himself as Messiah. Instead, he used the ambiguous and many-faceted self-designation 'the son of the man.'

Thus from Mark 8 we must conclude that the True Human is the one who suffers, dies and will be vindicated by God; he is not a conquering, violent Messiah. It is precisely this mention of suffering and dying that sets Peter off to rebuke Jesus. Surely Jesus had it all wrong. Messiahs are powerful figures, warrior-like, always victorious over the enemy for God is with them. How then could Jesus possibly talk about the True Human as one who would suffer and die? Jesus obviously needed to have his theology corrected and Peter was certain he was the one to do it. What Peter, and we ourselves today, barely realize is that what is for us and Peter the solution, was for Jesus the problem, namely, the use of violence to bring about God's will. The one who will follow Jesus does not engage in the use of force such as the Romans use when they crucify rebels and criminals, rather, the follower of Jesus endures the illegitimate use of violence. They are the ones who take up their cross, they do not inflict crosses on others. Their mode of being is not that of coercive power but of trust in the will of God. John Stoner makes this important point,

> "I think that Jesus' intention in using 'the human one' language was not only to clarify who he was, but to identify himself with all who take his way, or all who take his way with himself. So he was describing his movement, his followers, and the destiny of all humanity with that language."

Scholars have made interesting, sometimes tenuous, sometimes well argued connections between Jesus' ethics and his eschatology. Almost always, scholars interpret Jesus ethics in the light of his eschatology. Perhaps it is the other way around. David Flusser quotes the great Swiss Lutheran theologian Leonard Ragaz whose warning was in vain:

> "The notion is quite untenable, that Jesus built a kind of ethic and theology upon his expectation of the imminence of the kingdom of God. This sort of thing may well happen in the study of a theologian or philosopher...the relationship is quite the reverse from what the eschatological systemitizers imagine. It is not the eschatological expectation which determines Jesus' understanding of God and man...but, conversely his understanding of God and man which determines his eschatological expectation....To fail to see this one must have already put on a professor's spectacles."[lviii]

2.3 The Mercy Code

There is a way of living life, a mode of being religious that causes destruction wherever it appears. It is the misinterpretation of the concept of holiness. It was certainly an issue in Jesus' day. The variety of the 'Judaisms' of Jesus' day, the various schools or parties, the rabbinic schools of Hillel and Shammai, the more esoteric groups like the Essenes and those who dwelt in Qumran, mainstream elite like the Sadducees and marginalized Samaritans alike all held to some kind of holiness code, that behavior which made the people right before God.[lix]

Holiness Codes

In Jesus' day (except among Samaritans), the orientation of the concept of holiness was grounded in the Temple at Jerusalem. Arguments over the Temple priesthood fostered such great division that the violence of groups within Judaism matched the bloodshed inside the Temple itself. The Pharisees and Sadducees killed one another by the thousands,[lx] long before the Romans came along. Who had the right to officiate at the altar was a key issue in the centuries before Jesus. Sacral lineage was of paramount importance for the Qumran covenanters as much as it was for the four major families from whom the high priests came. Who presided over sacrifice and how they presided was not a settled issue.

The Temple itself reflected gradations or strata of holiness, from the outer Court of the Gentiles to the Holy of Holies. This meta-map of the Temple was overlaid on Jewish society as well. Just as there were degrees of holy space in the Temple, so also in society various persons had various degrees of holiness; Joachim Jeremias has outlined this in his book *Jerusalem in the Time of Jesus*. It was a hierarchical model, lived out by every group or party except one, that of Jesus.

Jesus refused to recognize the cultural limitations of difference. It made no difference who you were, Jesus treated everyone he met the same, with good intention, with love. Where might this compassion have stemmed from? It is important to know that as Jesus grew up, his *mamzer* or bastard status would have prevented him from participating in the Temple cult.[lxi] Jesus knew what it was like not to be able to share in the privilege of worshipping God as other Jewish males. For those who knew him, Jesus had a questionable paternity that would have had severe social consequences. No one would betroth his or her daughter to him. He would have known what it was like to be excluded from the synagogue or Temple service. He knew what it was like to be a leper or a menstruating woman or someone with a wound that would not heal. It is this experience of marginalization that we must recognize as a crucial aspect of the formation of Jesus' understanding of who God was and how God related to Humanity.

Just as in our own time, so also in Jesus' day, holiness codes kept persons from experiencing the full rich benefit of being in a social community. Likewise virtually every church today has some form of holiness code. These are the rules that we adhere to when we either become baptized or become members. To break these rules is to risk getting kicked out. If you happen to live in a small town or a town dominated by one church, getting the boot may also mean a certain loss of face or shame; it can also mean experiencing ostracism or losing business deals (if you happen to be a merchant).

Holiness codes are the religious equivalent of the secular notion of 'the rule of law.' Humans were religious before they were secular. At Göbekli Tepe, in what is now Turkey, near the Syrian border, archeologists have discovered fantastic remains of what appears to be the earliest archeological evidence of a sacred structure dating from the Paleolithic period (around 9,500 B.C.E.). It has long been assumed that humans would not yet possess the ability to create such structures for another several thousand years. This is an indication that religion predates civilization and in fact, it was the concept of religious 'structure' that would give impetus to that of social organization. All human culture is founded in religion.[lxii] All culture is religious culture, even so-called secular culture, for even when the 'gods' disappear, their social effects remain.

This is why it is not possible for humans to exist apart from laws, prohibitions and commandments. At the foundation of these rules for religious and social order stands something else; victims, both human and animal. Holiness codes, which begin as religious taboos, bring order to a society only because the sacred has been drawn into the center of the community through ritual killing. We shall explore all this in some depth later. I bring it up now because when we come to Jesus and understand how he interacted with the holiness codes of his day, it is essential to keep in mind the relation between 'law' and 'sacrifice.' There is no sacred order apart from death.

We saw that Luke's gospel opens Jesus' ministry with a conflict between Jesus and those who attended the synagogue in Nazareth. Mark's gospel also opens with a series of conflict stories; first it is conflict with the demonic forces, then conflict with religious authority. Mark chapters 2-3 does not give us a portrait of 'gentle Jesus meek and mild, keeper of the status quo,' nor does Jesus appear concerned about religious niceties, nor does he even appear as a concerned citizen who follows the social rules, norms and laws established by his culture. He comes on the scene as a rabble-rousing rebel, a prophet who dares to say and do things that are counter-cultural, against the stream. Time and again, Jesus seems to run afoul of the religious authorities. Imagine today if someone should come to your church, violating your church's most sacred taboos, perhaps criticizing the laxness of your faith, hanging out with questionable folks and generally giving the impression that he or she wasn't all that impressed with your worship. How long would you tolerate such a person? It wasn't just what Jesus claimed about himself that upset the cultural guardians. It was how he acted, how he treated people, and that he frequently treated people and made them well, healing them when his actions contravened the religious tradition!

It was paramount for Jesus' Jewish faith tradition to make clear distinctions between that which was holy and that which was profane or unholy. Have you ever heard of the six degrees of separation? Well, in the Judaism of Jesus' day there were six degrees of holiness, from level 1, least holy to level 6 super-ultra-extra holy. Different things you did, people you had contact with, certain religious activities produced varying degrees of uncleanness. Fortunately there were also various rituals one could engage in to become clean again. In Mark 1:44 Jesus tells a leper he had just healed to go show himself to the local priest and "offer the sacrifices Moses commanded for your cleansing." After Mary gave birth to Jesus according to Luke 2:22, she had a time of purification after which she went to the Temple to offer the appropriate sacrifices. Uncleanness or un-holiness had kept both Mary and the leper from full societal participation. However, by sharing in sacrifice, they were once again deemed fit to live fully in society (at least as fully as former lepers and women were allowed).

Jesus' Contemporaries

To understand this it is essential to realize that the problem of holiness as a socio-theological problem was at stake. It was the way a certain theological method affected social organization and religious hierarchy. "God's in-group is my group." However, there were problems with this kind of thinking and everyone knew it. The Judaism of Jesus' time had three pillars upon which it stood: the Torah, the Temple and the Land. These three pillars were interlocking and all three were holy because God was holy. Handling the Torah caused a certain degree of uncleanness because it was holy, the Temple was a structure with degrees of holiness from the outer courts to the Holy of Holies and the land given to Israel was holy for God gave it and dwelt therein.

During the time of Jesus all Jews agreed that Torah was the supreme revelation and they all agreed that the land belonged to the Jews. There was however a major conflict regarding the Temple. In the several hundred years before Jesus there were huge rifts between those who had legitimate claim to serve as priests in the Temple and those who were perceived as having usurped that authority. If you want to know more about this you can read what happened during and after the Maccabean revolution. As an important and fascinating piece of history, suffice it to say that even Herod the Great's incredible Temple building program, to make it one of the wonders of the ancient world, didn't quiet those who were critical of what went on in the Temple. In order to understand the issues at play for Jesus it is essential to have some idea of the major players of his time.[lxiii]

The Pharisees began as a lay movement of Jews who felt that the priesthood had become so corrupt it was necessary for regular males (remember women were not esteemed very highly) to live the code of conduct for priests in their everyday lives thus becoming 'a holy priesthood.' The lay Pharisees would thus ensure that there was a 'holy remnant' left in the land. The Pharisees believed that there were two Torot, a written Torah and an oral Torah tradition that both ultimately came from Moses. It is absolutely incorrect to think that the Pharisees had no understanding of God's grace or that they taught a 'works-righteousness.' Nothing could be farther from the truth. They were interested in holiness as it related to the fate of the people. Jacob Neusner observes that

> "By keeping the rules of purity the fellow separated from the common man [sic], but by remaining within the towns and cities of the land, he preserved the possibility of teaching others by example.

> The fellows [Pharisees] lived among, but not with, the people of the land."[lxiv]

The Sadducees came primarily from the ruling families of Jerusalem who accepted only the written Torah (and their written interpretation of Torah, the Book of Decrees, that was kept in the Temple) and would not accept any of the oral traditions (the oral torah) of the Pharisees. Because they were wealthy it was in their interest to accommodate the thinking and culture of those who ruled over them. They were religiously conservative but socially liberal. During the time of Jesus they controlled the Temple hierarchy and the High Priesthood.

Shortly before or after the Pharisees emerged on the scene two centuries before Jesus another group of disaffected priests broke away from their group, left the Temple and the city of Jerusalem moving out into the Judean desert and started their own holy community that followed a certain 'Teacher of Righteousness.' We know this community from the ruins of Qumran and the discovery of the Dead Sea Scrolls. Like the Pharisees, those known as Essenes were not a monolithic group; while some lived in the desert, some lived in their own section of Jerusalem (known as the 'Essene Quarter'); others were scattered about villages.[lxv]

Scribes would have been educated Jews who could read and write Hebrew, were able to write legal and business contracts and were most often learned in the intricacies of both oral and written Torahs. A scribe could be attached to any party or no party at all.

Finally there were those who took the issue of holiness to the highest level; they would purge the land of all foreign and alien influence. These Jews were known as 'dagger-men' or *sicarii*, who assassinated both Roman occupiers as well as Jewish colluders. Judas Iscariot and Simon the Zealous (Mark 3:13-19) were most likely from this persuasion. Some thirty years after Jesus' death, persons who thought like this would become known as Zealots, those so zealous for the holiness of the Lord God's Temple and Land, that they would begin the war with Rome that ended in the destruction of Jerusalem.

Each of these groups had certain rules and regulations, they were all interested in holiness or morality, and together they constituted what might be called the 'Moral Majority' of Jesus' Judaism. These were the folks with whom Jesus had most of his problems. Furthermore, almost all of his conflicts centered on the twin poles of holiness and sacrifice.[lxvi]

Jesus was also concerned about the fate of Israel. In one way or another, the Exile of the seventh century B.C.E. had never really ended; the people of Israel had only short periods where they were not dominated by foreign governments. Like many of the prophets before him, Jesus sought to bring about a national restoration in his proclamation of the nearness of the Kingdom of God. This, as we saw when we looked at Luke 4, was the hope of the Jewish people, that God would reign in their Land, that God would once again dwell in the sanctuary of the Temple. Jesus was no different in his aspirations than his contemporaries, but how he went about fulfilling those hopes and dreams would be worlds apart from many of them.

The holiness of Torah, Temple and Land were grounded in God's holiness and it could be said "Be Holy as I (the Lord, your God) am holy" (Lev 11:44). Human holiness was dependent on the holiness of God, not the other way around. Yet, oddly enough we do not find this holiness language in Jesus' teaching. Unlike the constant refrain of holiness in the Dead Sea Scrolls or the later Mishnah, Jesus has another set of lyrics using same melody. Instead of "Be holy as I am holy" Jesus taught "Be merciful as your Father in heaven is merciful." Mercy was for Jesus what holiness was to many of his contemporaries. Notice the same form is used but the substance has changed. Why is this? Because for Jesus, holiness is not a solution but a problem. Holiness caused ostracizing and exclusion; mercy brought reconciliation and re-socialization. Holiness depended on gradation and hierarchy; mercy broke through all barriers. Holiness differentiated persons based upon honor, wealth, family tree, religious affiliation; mercy recognized that God honors all, loves all and blesses all.

Mercy is Better Than Sacrifice

It is striking that in Luke's version of the Sermon on the Mount (Matt 5-7), called the Sermon on the Plain (Luke 6:17-49), the 'perfection' of Matthew ("Be perfect as your heavenly Father is perfect") becomes 'mercy' ("Be merciful as your *Abba* in heaven is merciful").[lxvii] I want to suggest that for Matthew perfection is not about holiness. In the chapter (Matthew 5), which this phrase concludes, there is plenty to do with mercy. Indeed to be merciful is to be perfect; to be perfect is to be merciful. It is not to hastily judge others for you do not know what they have been through. It is to love those who insult you, and pray for those who are spiteful and use you. To be merciful is to be blessed (Matthew 5:7). It is to recognize that 'the one who shows mercy' (Luke 10:37) is the one who loves God and neighbor.

Jesus will have trouble his entire ministry because of the way he shows extraordinary mercies to those who had been deemed outside the grace of God or who were perceived as having been punished by God. Jesus was not like certain television preachers who spend their time hanging out in church with the righteous while condemning sinners to hell; on the contrary, Jesus spent time with these sinners, and ate with them! This caused him serious grief, so much so that he had to spend a fair bit of time defending this practice (see Luke 15:1-2). In short, Jesus would have known the slurs and stares of others because of his assumed *mamzer* status, and this helped prepare him to see just how far God would go to be with those whom society had cast off as worthless wretches.

It was not enough for Jesus to simply try to redefine what it was that constituted social behavior within God's reign. It was also important for him to confront and be confronted by the authorities as we have seen. This kind of confrontation would have been S.O.P. (standard operating procedure), for everything Jesus did seemed topsy-turvy to his religious contemporaries. At the end of ministry (or at the beginning if we follow the chronology of the Fourth Gospel), Jesus would engage in an action that was so shocking and to many so vile that it would seal his fate. He went to the Temple and symbolically tried to shut it down.[lxviii]

Jesus Closes the Temple

We have become accustomed to reading the story of the 'Cleansing of the Temple' as though Jesus came in with his moral Pine-Sol, took his broom and mop and tried to make the place more presentable for guests.[lxix] But Jesus did not 'cleanse' the Temple. No, there was something decidedly wrong with the entire system that could not be fixed.[lxx] Jesus goal was to shut it down. Now, in reality that would have been impossible without starting a major riot and bringing the Roman guard down from the Fortress Antonia to quell the angry mob. This had been done before, many times; Jesus even alludes to one of them (Luke 13:1). What Jesus was engaged in was a prophetic action, an action that was small in scale but had powerful consequences.[lxxi]

Recalling that Jesus quotes Jeremiah 7:11, it is crucial to observe that for both Jesus and Jeremiah the Temple had become the symbol of zealous resistance.[lxxii] We need to remember that any time a foreign occupier destroyed the Temple of the occupied it was considered a victory for the occupier's god.

The question that haunts scholars concerns Jesus' motivation: was he prophesying the destruction of the Temple, engaging in purity issues with regard to sacrifice, fomenting social unrest? These and other motivations have been attributed to Jesus. We may never be certain as to why he did what he did that fateful day but I do believe that his use of the Scripture text (at least his use recorded in the Gospels) relates specifically to the problem of zeal. The Fourth Gospel certainly remembers the story with this in mind (John 2:17) and the text from Jeremiah lends support to this hypothesis.

As we noted earlier it was zeal for holiness that brought about the origins of the various religious groups several hundred years before Jesus. Following in the footsteps of the 'zealous' Maccabees, these various groups sought to keep the Temple and the Land pure, and thus the people pure, so that God would redeem them from their exile and bring them into the great and promised jubilee. The prototype of zeal in the Jewish Scriptures was Phineas (Numbers 25:1-16), who as a result of his zeal in killing an Israelite and his Midianite lover brought a plague to an end. As a result it could be said of him that this act was 'credited to him as righteousness' (Psalm 106:30-31). It is this type of zeal that Jesus forswore and replaced with the mercy code.

Jesus was doing more than just 'cleansing' the Temple of greedy merchants, although that may have been an aspect of his intention. Two other actions are prominent that help us understand that, for Jesus, the entire sacrificial system was problematic. The first action is that according to Mark 11:16 he would not let anyone carry a 'vessel' (*skeuos*) through the Temple courts. The NIV translates this term as 'merchandise' as though he were stopping shoppers in a modern mall, but the term refers to vessels used in the sacrificial process. The second action comes from the Fourth Gospel where Jesus braids a whip and uses it to disperse the sheep and the cattle (John 2:15). By prohibiting sacrificial animals from being purchased and possibly rendering them unclean, and by stopping the use of sacred vessels, Jesus is saying a great big NO! to the system of sacrifice, much like the prophets before him (Ps 40:6, 50:8-15, 51:16f, 69:30, Isa 1:11, Jer. 6:20, Hos. 6:6, Amos 5:21, Mic. 6:6). Nowhere is it suggested that he engaged in violence against human beings, nor is the term for anger (*orge*) used in this story. This is not a story about Jesus getting mad, it is the great prophetic act that the end of all sacrifice had come, that something new, mercy and compassion, replaced sacrifice, which were far more pleasing to God than the blood of bulls and goats.

The interconnecting themes of holiness-zeal-sacrifice-Temple all converge in the narrative of Jesus at the Temple. It is no accident that twice in the Gospel of Matthew Jesus quotes Hosea 6:6 "I desire mercy and not sacrifice." And in Mark (12:32-34) when the teacher of the law comments to Jesus that he agrees regarding the dual nature of the great commandment to love God and neighbor that these "are more important than all burnt offerings and sacrifices", Jesus replies that he "is not far from the kingdom of God." So how far are we from the kin(g)dom of God?

2.4 Kingdom Ethics

Being a Christian is for some little more than having prayed some kind of short 'salvation' prayer. For others living the Christian life consists of a particular set of rules or adherence to a particular political ideology. For even others, being a Christian has to do with the "sweet devotion" of their own inward personal religious experience. Still, for others, the Christian life means being nice to people, tolerant and generally warm and fuzzy around the edges. How far these expressions are from the way of life that Jesus called his followers to live. There is nothing sentimental, narcissistic or moralistic about Jesus' call to follow him in the way of the Kingdom of God. Christians today suffer from one or more of the above when it comes to understanding and living the Christian life.

Kingdom ethics or Kingdom living has 1) one principle, 2) one orientation and 3) one goal.

Principle: Discipleship

If we are going to seriously understand Jesus, it is essential to get these three things right, otherwise what he says about living in relation to others gets ground up into hash. It is easy to dismiss the ethical teaching of Jesus as impractical, which is done by those who relegate his ethics to an interim period of his ministry or to the time in some distant future when God will reign over all the earth. It is also easy to dismiss Jesus' ethics by claiming that they just don't work in the real world, as though Jesus were some sort of philosophical idealist. It is easier still to take the ethics of Jesus and turn them all into command formula to be literally obeyed at all times in all places thus formulating a new law which amounts only to a legalism. Each of these approaches has been tried and found lacking (1.4). I propose a different approach: the recognition that the singular principle, orientation and goal of Jesus' kingdom ethics worked for him and can also work for us who imitate or follow him in this life. This means that 'to know Jesus is to obey him, to obey him is to know him.' This principle, called a 'hermeneutics of obedience' was promoted by the 16th century Anabaptist Hans Denck and suggests that our knowledge of Jesus is not simply intellectual but grounded in the choice to do his will, which is the will of God (John 7:17). Only by so choosing can we both claim to know him and discern how we may live life to its fullest.

One of the primary themes of this book is that the imitation of Christ is not only plausible but also necessary. It is to heed the call to live what Dietrich Bonhoeffer termed 'costly grace.'[lxxiii] Following Jesus does cost a person, and sometimes it can cost them their life. But neither Bonhoeffer nor I want a return to some simplistic legalistic obedience when we speak of the imitation of Christ. One sees this in groups that read Jesus' commands off the page without any interpretation or paying attention to context. Reading texts without interpretation is a form of 'cheap grace.' Reading texts, discerning contexts both ancient and modern, listening attentively to what the Spirit says to the church today, struggling with one another in conversation, debate and dialogue, these are marks of 'costly grace.'[lxxiv]

The imitation of Christ (or the *imitatio Christi*) is an indispensible aspect of the Christian life. Why is this? In 5.1 and 8.2 we will explore some of the new neuro-physiological research that has demonstrated that human beings are hard wired to copy others. For now, I want to assume this research and say that we are all copying someone, all of the time. Jesus calls us to imitate him not each other.

But how shall we imitate Jesus? This is a key question. One might ask how it was that the followers around Jesus got called 'the disciples.' What is a disciple? T.W. Manson compares Luke 14:26 to Matthew's version of the same saying in Matthew 10:37. He noted that while Luke has "cannot be my disciple," Matthew has "is not worthy of me." He observed that the Aramaic Jesus spoke could have been translated one of two ways. If you think Jesus is saying "shau li" you have in Greek "is not worthy of me" but if you translate them as one word "shauliah" you have the word used in Aramaic for "apprentice" like a carpenter, a blacksmith or a weaver's apprentice.

Manson distinguishes Jesus' *shauliah* from the rabbi's *talmidim*. In other words, Jesus had a different type of pedagogy than his contemporaries.

> "It is tempting to see in the choice of the word a definite opposition to the whole scribal system. The talmid of the Rabbinical schools is primarily a student. His chief business was to master the contents of the written Law and the oral Tradition. The finished products of the Rabbinical schools were learned biblical scholars and sound and competent lawyers. The life of a talmid as talmid was made up of study of the sacred writings, attendance on lectures, and discussion of difficult passages or cases. Discipleship as Jesus conceived it was not a theoretical discipline of this sort, but a practical task to which humans were called to give themselves and all their energies. Their work was not study but practice. Fishermen were to become fishers of people; peasants were to be laborers in God's vineyard or God's harvest field. And Jesus was their master not so much as a teacher of right doctrine, but rather as the master-craftsman whom they were to follow and imitate. Discipleship was not matriculation in a Rabbinical College but apprenticeship to the work of the Kingdom."[lxxv]

A disciple is more like an apprentice than a modern student. The Master does not expect the new apprentice to be perfect. A wise Master knows that mistakes will be made. A patient Master will watch progress and affirm it. Following Jesus is just like this.

Following Jesus

A key text for understanding how we come to imitate him is found in Matthew 11:25-30. Jesus says,

> "At that time Jesus said, 'I praise you, Father, Lord of heaven and earth, because you have hidden these things from the wise and

> learned, and revealed them to little children. Yes, Father, for this was your good pleasure.
>
> All things have been committed to me by my Father. No one knows the Son except the Father, and no one knows the Father except the Son and those to whom the Son chooses to reveal him.
>
> Come to me, all you who are weary and burdened, and I will give you rest. Take my yoke upon you and learn from me, for I am gentle and humble in heart, and you will find rest for your souls. For my yoke is easy and my burden is light.'"

Back in 2005 we moved to Lancaster, PA. As I sit here writing this from my home office, I can look out my window and watch the Amish farmer across the way plowing his field with mules. The mules are yoked together with the farmer riding the plow behind them. The yoke functions to keep the mules from going in directions different than the farmer would have them go. I am told that when a young mule is first learning to plow a field, they team him up with a veteran mule that has plowed the field for many years. This way the younger mule learns how to respond to the farmer's guidance because when the older mule turns, the younger mule has to go the same way, the yoke making it impossible for him to go another.

In the same way, we are yoked with Jesus who knows the *Abba's* will. When the Father moves the reins in a certain direction Jesus responds and we respond not by choosing, nor out of our own initiative but simply by submitting to the yoke. The only choice we make is to be yoked with Jesus. After that it is no longer about choice but about something entirely different. It is about 'trust.'

For years I have called this principle 'surrender' but have since decided that while this term in English has some benefits it has too many drawbacks. Some synonyms for surrender are "acquiescence, appeasement, capitulation, cessation, renunciation, submission, white flag, yielding, abandonment, abdication, giving way, relenting, relinquishment, succumbing." You can see that most of these synonyms have to do with loss. In the principle of discipleship to which I draw attention, there is a letting go; a giving up of one's will and choices but it is neither a lost battle nor a loss of identity. To take up the yoke of Jesus is not about trusting that God will guide us but that God did and will guide Jesus. As we follow Jesus God guides us. The imitation of Jesus is not about loss but about gain, gaining our true humanity as we are yoked with the True Human ('the son of man'). This is why I now prefer the term 'trust', which I understand to be a good translation of the Greek term *pistis* that we usually translate as 'faith.'

There are two possible backgrounds for understanding the yoke saying. The first is the yoke of Torah.[lxxvi] Here are several sayings from different periods of time (100 B.C.E. to 300 C.E.) to demonstrate this:

> Ecclesiasticus (Wisdom of ben Sirach, 2nd cent B.C.E.) 51:23-30:
>
> "Come to me you who need instruction, and lodge in my house of learning. Why do you admit to a lack of these things, yet leave your great thirst unslacked? I have made my proclamation: 'Buy for yourselves without money, bend your neck to the yoke, be ready to accept discipline; you need not go far to find it.' See for yourselves how little were my labors compared with the great peace I have found...Do your duty in good time, and in his own good time he will reward you."
>
> Mishnah Aboth 3:5 (Rabbi Nehunya b. Ha-Kanah 70-130 C.E.):
>
> "He that takes upon himself the yoke of the Torah, from him shall be taken away the yoke of worldly government (tyranny) and the yoke of worldly care; but he that throws off the yoke of Torah, upon him shall be laid the yoke of worldly government (tyranny) and the yoke of worldly care."
>
> Talmud Sifra 57b (post 300 C.E.):
>
> "It says in Lev. 11:45, 'For I am the Lord your God who brought you out of the land of Egypt to be your God: you shall therefore be holy for I am holy.' That means, I brought you out of Egypt on the condition that you should receive the yoke of the commandments."

The yoke of Jesus, if it is being compared to Torah, would imply that his yoke is not a legal yoke. It is neither burdensome nor a harsh taskmaster. He would then also be saying that it is his interpretation of Torah lived out that is the interpretation that the Father has given to the Son (Matt 11:25-27). The implication for us is that the Christian life is not experienced as something fearful, for his yoke is easy and light.

However, another possibility exists: that Jesus is referring to the yoke of Rome. Warren Carter argues that the yoke of Matt 11:28-30 is a reference to Roman imperial rule. Part of his argument is that while the word *yoke* occurs 63 times in the LXX (the Septuagint, the Greek translation of the Hebrew Bible which the New Testament writers used), only a few of those times refer to Torah, the majority of the rest refer to imperial power and control.

It's not an either/or when it comes to Jesus' offer. The Mishnah saying above combines the two possibilities of Torah and Empire as backgrounds for the word 'yoke.' Whether religion or Empire (culture) we are under 'the rule of law.' Western jurisprudence grew out of religious taboo. Jesus' yoke takes us out from under the rule of law, religiously conceived, and places us in the rule of love. Our ethics, our social behavior is normed by Jesus, not by an abstract set of morals, values or mores. This means that our choices are developed from a living intimate relationship with Jesus, not from a codebook. Ethics is no longer a question of trying to figure out right and wrong, it is about living in relationship with others in the same manner that Jesus lived in relation to others.

David Flusser has a very important insight at this point. Whatever it is Jesus is doing, he is doing it in a thoroughly radical way. This radicalness of Jesus was his doctrine of God.

> "Jesus' concept of the righteousness of God, therefore, is incommensurable with reason. Man cannot measure it, but he can grasp it. It leads to the Preaching of the kingdom in which the last shall be first and the first last. It also leads from the Sermon on the Mount to Golgotha, where the just man dies a criminal's death. It is at once profoundly moral, and yet beyond good and evil. In this paradoxical scheme, all the 'important' customary virtues, and the well-knit personality, worldly dignity, and the proud insistence upon the formal fulfillment of the law, are fragmentary and empty."[lxxvii]

Orientation: The Reign of God

If the principle of discipleship is surrender as trust what then is our orientation? Which direction are we pointed as we are yoked with Jesus? These questions have to do with our intentionality. Intention is not choice. Choice is the action we take once our intention is fixed. So what is it our intention is fixed upon? It is the same as that of Jesus, the reign of God, God's rule. He said, "Seek primarily God's reign" (Matthew 6:33). When we seek God's reign we bring our intention in line with Jesus who is the revealer of God's reign. You will notice that I have shifted the language from kingdom to reign to emphasize that for Jesus the *basileia Theou* (the reign of God) is not about a place but a manner of existence. To make the 'kingdom' about a place is to valorize real estate as sacred place, something Jesus was loath to do.[lxxviii] In the fourth Gospel he puts it this way to the Samaritan woman: "Kingdom worship is not about real estate but about interior orientation" (John 4:24).

Unlike some of his disciples and many of his contemporaries, Jesus did not put much stock in the physical manifestation of God's kingdom, as it was associated with the land of Israel.[lxxix] His criticism of the Temple is the surest evidence of this and one nowhere finds in Jesus' teaching, as one finds in the eschatology of the Hebrew Prophets, a hope for a restored Temple. For Jesus, God's reign is not tied to the sacred structure of substitutionary sacrifice and zealous nationalism but to the restored human condition:

> Once, having been asked by the Pharisees when the kingdom of God would come, Jesus replied, "The kingdom of God does not come with your careful observation, nor will people say, 'Here it is,' or 'There it is,' because the kingdom of God is within you." (Luke 17:20-21)

Seeking God's reign is our reason for waking up in the morning, living through the day and resting at night. It is the food and drink of our existence as disciples (cf. John 4:34). This is why we pray "*Abba*, manifest your reign, your will be done." God's reign is God's will and God's will is Jesus.

Goal: Service

If our discipleship, our imitation of Jesus involves our trustful surrender to the father's will and if we are oriented to seek or desire nothing other than the father's will, what then is the goal of our discipleship? Why do we follow Jesus? We follow Jesus so that when we die we can get to heaven. Not! As I said at the beginning of this section discipleship is not narcissistic. Frankly, I see way too much self-serving [so-called] discipleship in contemporary Christianity. People claim to follow Jesus for what they can get out of it, whether it is peace of mind, blessing, wealth, health or anything else. These things may well follow ("and all these things will be added unto you" Matt. 6:33) but they are not the goal of our discipleship. The goal, the reason we follow Jesus, is to serve one another as he has served us.

It has long been noted that Mark's Gospel portrays Jesus as a servant-king. The problem with being a servant is that you don't get any of the glamour jobs. Far too many "servant-leaders" are those who are in what I would call glamour positions within the church, they are up front preaching or teaching or leading worship; they might be a high paying bureaucrat in denominational headquarters or an inner city pastor whose 'prosperity gospel' allows them to drive a Benz and live in a twenty room mansion. They can just as easily be the big fish in a small pond: the church elder who gets his way because he is the biggest giver or the secretary who takes great pride in being the doorkeeper everyone must get past. They can be the successful Christian recording artist or the radio talk show host or the author of best-selling books.

The church has its hierarchies and we like to give praise to those visible agents that 'make it happen.' But for every successful 'glamour job' in the church are dozens of unheralded positions where folks share their gifts for little or no thanks. Who really thinks that the person minding the nursery is as important as the seminary trained pastor? Who thinks that the person who takes meals to Mrs. Smith on Thursday is as essential to the body of Christ as the wildly popular Youth Pastor? We expect folks to serve in church under the following rubric: "So when you have done everything you were told to do you should say 'We are unworthy servants, we have only done our duty'" (Luke 17:10).

We miss the goal of discipleship when we are not actively engaging the other person *for their benefit out of gracious compassion and love*. Serving another means getting down in the trenches with them in their disease, their illness, and their troubled circumstances. It means bearing with ignorance, orneriness, anger, depression, self-doubt and other psychological issues. Serving another is not done for praise or money or any other reward, it is done solely for the sake of the other. This is the point of the parable of the sheep and the goats in Matthew 25:31-46. The sheep didn't see Jesus in the poor, the hungry, the lame, the imprisoned, etc, yet they reached out and cared; the goats didn't see Jesus in these folks either and that is why they didn't care.

Again, the goal of discipleship is not about making sure we behave so that God will love us. God loves us deeply and dearly and has demonstrated that in the life, death and resurrection of Jesus. Discipleship is not about participating in an *economy of exchange*, where we give something to God in order to receive something back from God. If we perceive following Jesus as something we do in order to benefit ourselves we will have absolutely missed the point of what it means to follow a servant, whose existence is for the other.

Kingdom ethics is really kin(g)dom ethics[lxxx]; it is really all about maintaining strong and healthy relationships as fellow believers. American Feminist theologians have really helped us male-starched-shirt-kingdom-builders to see this. It is about recognizing that we are all children of God, and treating one another as brothers and sisters. In the words of the Fourth Gospel, service is about laying our life down for each other, esteeming the other, holding the other up. This is what *agape* is, real love, and love is the foundation and end of all God's actions and our response (I Cor. 13:8-13).

Chapter 3 The Mission and Message of Jesus

3.1 The Nonviolent God

Imagine you are back in high school or college and the prettiest or most handsome person, the one who is intelligent and witty, outgoing, the one everyone wishes they could have as their boyfriend or girlfriend comes to you and says, "I want you to know that I really find you attractive, in fact, I love you. I love you so much, so deeply, it astonishes me. I want to be with you forever, you light up my life, you are the reason I exist." Wouldn't that be just amazing? One of the reasons for the popularity of romantic comedies is that the boy/girl is in these circumstances and they end up with the one they so desire. Imagine spending your life with such a person who was absolutely devoted to you, who loved you with an undying love, who cared for you in ways you could not imagine or dream in your wildest dreams.

Now before you could respond with a "Yes" or a "Hallelujah, thank you Jesus!!" suppose they went on to say "But I also want you to know that if you will not love me in return I will make your life a living nightmare, a hell on earth. I will spread rumors and lies about you, I will trash your home. I will make it my life's goal to punish you in every way possible if you won't accept my love for you."

Wouldn't you go to the authorities and at a minimum get a restraining order on such a person? Sure you would. Who wants someone this obsessive to ruin their life? Then why is it that Christians tell essentially the same story with regard to the way God loves the world? We say God loves the world but if God's love is spurned we will be punished with an everlasting punishment. Where can one take out a restraining order on this kind of a God? Job had trouble with this kind of a god and three times in the book of Job he threatens to file a lawsuit against God.

Sadly, most of what Christians think and believe about God is exactly the opposite of what Jesus believed and taught about his *abba*. Have you ever wondered how it is that the Bible says God could command genocide, attempt murder (Exodus 4:24), authorize the killing of innocent children, races and peoples, burn entire cities to the ground like Sodom and act like a terrorist all the while? Yet we accept such a God because whatever the Bible says about God must be true. God has the right to act however God wants because after all, God is God.

Today such a god has been put on trial. People no longer blindly accept that God can do anything God wants to do because God is God. Such an arbitrary deity is now seen as so totally different from Jesus that people who might have an affinity for Jesus can't follow Him thinking he believed in this kind of God. "Jesus Yes! God No!" is something I hear everywhere I go. If we do not accept these behaviors from our fellow human beings why do we accept them from God? If God looks more like Idi Amin or Saddam Hussein than Jesus, something has gone gravely wrong with our understanding and portrayal of the Maker of heaven and earth. Even when God looks more like the most benevolent leader, i.e. Abraham Lincoln, than God looks like Jesus, there is a problem.

The popular understanding of the relationship between Jesus and God looks more like a good cop/bad cop routine than the *abba*-child relationship we find in the Gospels. Muslims and Jews have rightly accused Christianity of tri-theism, a belief in three separate gods. The way we talk about the Father, Son and Holy Spirit and their distinct 'roles', 'attributes' and 'temporal manifestations' lends itself to such critique. When we so differentiate the Father from the Son (and the Spirit), when God can kill and justify all sorts of violence, and yet we also claim that Jesus reveals God, yet Jesus is non-resistant and non-retributive, then we have a problem of epic proportions. Either Jesus does not really show us the character of God or Jesus was deluded to think that he manifested the reign of God in his person and ministry.

We cannot say that Jesus is the full revelation of God and not have to reckon with the fact that Jesus as the revealer of God is quite different than what we find in certain stories about God in the Jewish Scriptures. This is why it was so important for us to see that Jesus read his Bible critically, selectively, just as did many of his contemporaries and in fact, as almost all Christians do today. No one has ever managed to take the entire Bible literally; it must be interpreted. What we have failed to do is to recognize that if Jesus 'imitated the *abba*', the Maker of all that is, then God is like Jesus. I frequently say on my website and in talks I give that what really blew the apostolic church's mind was not whether Jesus was like God, but whether God was like Jesus. The apostolic church started the biggest intellectual shift in human history when they recorded their gospels and letters and throughout had to reckon with the fact that it was Jesus who was recognized as Lord of heaven and earth by virtue of his resurrection and ascension. They began working out the parameters of what a Jesus centered God or theology would look like. We take our cue from them, for their work is not complete and that is why we also, like them, follow Jesus. In fact, we follow them as they follow Jesus.

The Idols We Make

The key question that must be asked today is this: Do Christians derive their understanding of God from the person of Jesus or from the Old

Testament? Rick Warren in *The Purpose Driven Life* says that if you want to know who God is you can go look at all of the various names given to God in the Old Testament, e.g., YHWH, El, Adonai, El-Shaddai, etc.[lxxxi] I want to suggest that if you want to know whom God is you go to one name, the name of Jesus. Why? Because there is a substantive difference between the way 'God' acted in the Old Testament and the way God acted in Jesus. No amount of interpretive gymnastics can hide this; it was a key question wrestled with in the early church. Christians are saying something essential when they assert that God has been revealed in the figure of Jesus. God is known, no longer unknown, no longer hidden, no longer mysterious. God is fully present in Jesus, not partially present, but fully, completely present as Colossians 2:9 asserts, "For in Christ all the fullness of the Deity lives in bodily form." In the fourth century Athanasius, the great proponent of Nicene orthodoxy put it this way: the only difference between the Father and the Son are the terms 'Father' and 'Son.'

A large swath of American Christianity derives its understanding of the character of God by taking all references in the Bible to God and seeking then to delineate certain major characteristics of God. As we saw in 1.1 many popular Christian confessions have a doctrine of God that is like Samsonite luggage: unzip your doctrine of God, put in all of the adjectives and nouns you want, zip it back up and then you have a doctrine of God. This is opposite of the way the early church came to frame its doctrine of God. The early Christians urged people to unzip their theologies, empty out their suitcase and replace it with one article: the person of Jesus Christ. Jesus was (and is) the name by whom God is known.

If in the Hebrew Bible God's holiness, God's otherness, God's inapproachability and majesty are God's primary attributes, in the New Testament it is quite otherwise. In the only instances in the New Testament where axiomatic statements are made about God (God is ________), God is called 'light' and 'love.' These statements about God in I John 1:5 and 4:8 are correlated with the graspability of God in Jesus, the 'word of life' who could be seen, heard and touched.[lxxxii] One can, with Pastor Warren, begin one's understanding of God from references piled up from the Jewish canon or one can look to Jesus; these are mutually exclusive alternatives.

When Christians deal with this problem one of the more popular ways out is to suggest that there is a tension in God. This is just another way of speaking of the Janus-faced God. The frustrating thing about this is when critiquing this position one is frequently charged with 'throwing out the Bible' or some form of 'Marcionism' (4.4). I suggest that both these charges are false, for our task is not to throw anything out of Scripture but to interpret all of Scripture in the light of Jesus, 'to rightly divide the word of truth' (2 Tim. 2:15; see 5.4). Here then is a question often asked. Is it not the case that God appears as a judge in Jesus' teaching? To this we now must turn, for we simply cannot bypass it.

God as Judge

Let me begin with two texts from the Fourth Gospel (John 5:22, 12:47).

> "Moreover, the Father judges no one, but has entrusted all judgment to the Son."
>
> "As for the person who hears my words but does not keep them, I do not judge him. For I did not come to judge the world, but to redeem it."

These texts assert that neither the Father nor the Son judges anyone. What might this mean? Before you start thinking, "Well, there are many other texts about judgment in Scripture," I will concede that point. But we have to begin somewhere and I choose to begin with these texts from the Fourth Gospel. Jesus, as we shall see, certainly talks about judgment, but not in the manner in which Christians for almost two millennia have done. Our views on the final judgment owe more to Jewish apocalyptic imagination, medieval Christian speculation and our own desire to see retributive justice than they do to the way judgment is conceived in the Gospels.

What follows is a sustained commentary on the two verses above. It will not do to simply ask how people in Jesus' time perceived the final judgment as there are mixed indications in the Rabbinic literature, Apocrypha, Pseudepigrapha, Targums and the Dead Sea Scrolls. Claude Montefiore and Hebert Lowe in *A Rabbinic Anthology* offer an important and perceptive comment about the development of final judgment in Judaism that is worth hearing:

> "It will also be seen that if there is a narrowness among the old rabbis, there is also broadness. There are many indications of universalism. The appalling self-delusion which could glibly talk of a God of love and yet believe in an eternal hell was, I think, sooner and more prevailingly lost in Judaism than in Christianity. [Even] the modern Synagogue has moved forward, and has realized that if one single soul were ultimately left out of the bliss of the world to come, the purposes of a God of love would be frustrated forever."[lxxxiii]

We would be wrong to understand ancient Judaism as having a single 'doctrine of hell' nor will we find such in the Bible. What we do find are texts on judgment that, when seen in the light of rejecting the announcement of the nonviolent reign of God, bring us to the possibility of having missed the essential encounter with the Living God.

Yes, Jesus talks about judgment but *how* and *to whom* he talks about it are essential (1.3). I have long been engaged with Christians who will consign to eternal flames those who do not believe what they believe. Their notion of God's mercy is like that of the girl/boyfriend at the beginning of this section. Let us look at several (though not all) judgment texts in the Gospels to see how Jesus uses this theme in his preaching.

First is the parable of the Pharisee and the Tax Collector in Luke 18:9-13. We have already explored this in 1.3. Observe how this parable turns on its head any notion that comparing oneself with another can merit the grace or mercy of God. It is nonsense to think that Jesus' Judaism was a religion of works righteousness as we have for too long heard. This anti-Judaic and wrong-headed understanding has caused many Christians to believe Christianity is a religion of grace compared to Judaism. No, both Judaism and Christianity are religions of grace and both appeal to the mercy and compassion of God, and both have tendencies to fall into the trap of judging others by comparing themselves with others. When we compare ourselves with another, we will always be able to find those who seem to live life in a bent and broken way. There are all around most of us, those whose sins have caught up with them. They are suffering the consequences of many bad choices or rotten circumstances. And it is easy to think that because we made better choices or have better circumstances God must indeed be blessing us. In this parable Jesus turns this logic on its head. It is not the person who thinks God is blessing them because they deserve it, but the one who knows they don't deserve God's blessing who actually receives it. Judgment is pronounced upon the self-righteous.

Our second text comes from Matthew 18:21-35, the parable of the unmerciful servant. In this story a servant owed the king a large sum of money and had no way to pay it back. Begging for mercy, he is set free from the debt. As he walks away he meets a friend who had once borrowed a dollar. He is so ticked off that he throttles his friend who cannot repay; the friend is far poorer than he who racked up several million dollars in debt. The servant who had just been forgiven an enormous debt now sends his friend to prison. Of course when the king gets wind of this he sends the servant to join his friend in jail but with a life sentence! Jesus concludes by saying "Look, this is how it works in God's reign; where you have experienced forgiveness, you are expected to share it." Judgment comes upon the one who having received grace and mercy denies it to others.

Our third text comes from Luke 16:19-31. This is the only text where Jesus uses any kind of description of hell that comes straight out of his culture. Jesus has taken a familiar story and reworked it. Scholars note that this parable has similarities with stories from other cultures (especially Egypt) that speak of a reversal in the after-life. Here the story proceeds to describe what happens when a rich man and a beggar both die. They find that their experience after death is just the opposite of their experience in life. The rich man longs for a drop of water while roasting at 350°. The beggar meanwhile lives the life of luxury he could only have dreamed about when he was on earth. The rich man's sin? Ignoring the plight of his fellow human. Judgment comes to those who live large without considering the needs of those around them.

This same theme is echoed in the final parable of Matthew's gospel, that of the sheep and the goats (Matthew 25:31-46). Judgment does not come to those who won't "accept Christ as Lord and Savior" nor does it come to those who believe the wrong doctrine or attend the wrong church. It comes to those who would love to serve Jesus, but since Jesus is not here think they are not responsible for their fellow humans.

In each of these four instances judgment is not predicated on faith or lack of faith, on right doctrine or belief, the amount of holiness one has achieved or not. Judgment is directly related to the way in which we relate to others in our social world with those whom we think God has rejected because of their sin or circumstances.

This is not all Jesus had to say regarding judgment. He said that those who judge others are in danger of judgment by God. Matthew 7:1-5 is a most important text in this regard (1.4). Here Jesus is saying "Look, if you dispense forgiveness or love or mercy with a thimble don't expect God to use a bucket with you. If you want to know how God will judge you, you are your own measure of judgment. The way you treat others is how God will finally treat you." With the measure you use, God will measure you.

In Luke, Jesus goes even further pointing out that the way you give to others is the way God will give to you (Luke 6:38). Forgive your enemies, show mercy to those you would rather avoid, be gentle and kind to the obstinate and disaffected. Be careful how you measure and be more careful still how you claim God will measure.

You won't hear this kind of stuff from Christian preachers on TV or on the radio as you drive across America. What you will hear instead is how angry God is with sinners. What a substantive difference between how Jesus talked about judgment and how it is presented from tens of thousands of pulpits in this country! The God whom Jesus proclaims is a God who blesses all, forgives all and loves all freely and unconditionally (Matthew 5:45), and who calls us to do the same.

The God in Whom Jesus Believed

In short, what Jesus has done is to say that God is not retributive, God does not engage in a tit-for-tat logic on sin and punishment. God forgives sin, freely, unconditionally, and benevolently. What then does a theology or doctrine of God without retribution look like? First, it is possible to finally speak coherently of Trinity. If the Son is the image of the Father and the Son is non-retributive, so is the Father and the Spirit. There is no division in the Godhead. Doctrines of the Trinity that do not begin with the self-revelation of God in Christ inevitably crash on the shoals of definitions that import characteristics foreign to Jesus and thus to Jesus' *Abba*.

Second, a God seen in the person of Jesus who is non-retributive is totally different from all the other gods of religion who are double-faced at best. If with Jesus we can say, "God is One" then this must mean that God is not internally self-divided between grace and law, wrath and mercy, compassion and punishment, etc. God is not a stew of adjectives raised to the nth power; revelation is not through texts preserved free from error. The revelation of God comes to us as a person, just like us. The texts that bear witness to this person are authentic and rich, but not by necessity perfect, witnesses to that revelation. They are sufficient witnesses and that is all anyone needs in any court of law. This is why the many throughout church history have insisted that it takes both the sacred texts (word) and a personal encounter with the Risen Lord (Spirit) to make sense of God's self-revelation (5.4).

Third, a theology that is non-retributive will issue in an anthropological vision and ethic that is also non-retributive. It is almost impossible for us to imagine this on a grand or global scale, for all we see around us is violence. We laud those who somehow found their way to this new human way of being from St Francis and Gandhi to Dr. Martin Luther King Jr. and Dorothy Day, yet we seem incapable of thinking it a real possibility for ourselves. It is this possibility that Jesus, as God's agent and revealer of the way God governs (or reigns), does bring. It cannot be legislated by Congress, nor can it be required abstractly; the only way to experience this new anthropology is to encounter and be encountered by the Risen Christ, who by the gift of His Spirit makes such a possibility an actuality.

You will not be able to come up with this portrait of God by examining all of the names for God in the Old Testament. You can only come up with this kind of God from a consideration of Jesus' teachings. Yes, they are different and we shall see later why this is so. For now we have to tackle another great misunderstanding that colors our contemporary view of God: If God is a forgiving God, how far does the forgiveness of God extend?

3.2 Forgiveness: The Law of Love

On October 2nd 2006 here in Lancaster County, PA, Charles Roberts went into an Amish schoolhouse in Nickel Mines and took ten girls hostage. He ended up killing five of them and seriously wounding another five before killing himself. This event made headline news around the world. As the days went by and the funerals took place the response of the Amish community also made the news. Rather than speak in terms of retaliation or revenge, the Amish spoke a word of grace and extended their love for the family that Mr. Roberts had left behind, sharing in their grief and setting up a fund for his wife and children with money they received from openhearted donors.

When one elder was asked how they could do such a thing he replied that every day they prayed the Lord's Prayer and in this prayer forgiveness was essential. It would not be the Amish who would continue the spiral of violence by calling either on God or humanity for more blood. As I watched the news unfold on national TV, I was struck by the inability of the television reporters and anchors to grasp the forgiveness as expressed by the Amish. They were befuddled, bemused, frustrated and a few were at times critical that there was no desire for retaliation. But what the world witnessed from the Amish was precisely the heart of the Love of God for the world.

Retaliation and Violence

I compare this to the reports I frequently see on CNN where loved ones of murder victims cry out for retaliation, justice or vengeance. I note that these loved ones often hope that the murderer will "burn in hell" or "get what they deserve." This language echoes what our societies are built upon: retributive vengeance. We live in a world where we think that justice is a tit-for-tat mechanism, where everyone wants his or her "pound of flesh," where the justice of "an eye for an eye" prevails. But as Gandhi has admonished us "an eye for an eye makes the whole world blind."

Violence in all its forms is the single reality that most scares us. Violence can take many forms but they all have the same goal: the destruction of the other. There is verbal violence such as insults or gossip, put downs and nasty rhetoric; there is emotional violence such as obsession, coercion and hatred; and there is physical violence from the beating of a child and domestic abuse to rape, murder, torture and war. Many books try to define violence arguing that some of these actions are not violent. However, they fail to see that all violence leaves deep and lasting scars on human relationships. Moreover violence inevitably calls forth more violence; it is a spiral or a cycle with no end.

Violence is like a virus that spreads almost imperceptibly. Take anger for instance. Dad has had a hard day at work and the boss yelled at him, calling him incompetent. Fuming on the drive home Dad wonders how he can get back at his boss. Upon arriving home, his wife has dinner prepared but his latent hostility comes creeping out when he criticizes her cooking. Mom gets mad but doesn't say anything, later she will yell at the kids because they are watching TV and haven't finished their homework. Sonny walks out of the room and gives Brutus, the family dog, a kick to get out of his way. Brutus, who has no one to kick, slinks away. In this scenario anger is like the game of hot potato; no one wants it so it is non-consciously passed along finally given to one who cannot do anything but endure it.

Lethal violence spreads like this as well. Gang warfare in the inner city is rife with the contagion of violence. It is played out on a global scale between nations. As I write this North Korea has threatened "a thousand-fold" retaliation against the United States should they perceive we are at war with them. A thousand fold! Imagine that. Here, even the rhetoric of violence has spiraled out of control. The war on terror has been declared to not have a foreseeable end because whatever the terrorists do to us, we will do to them and when we do to them they turn around and do to us. Back in the spiral of violence again...and again...and again. It just never stops.

The violence of our time is not unusual. Although the twentieth century was the most violent on record for the number of people killed, violence has been with us from the beginning. Remember Cain and Abel? The problem of violence that has plagued human culture since its origin also had a powerful structuring role in Jesus' world. Other empires had long dominated Israel with their tyrants and taxes. In the Jewish historian Josephus, we read page after page after page of violent acts committed upon and by the Jewish people. There seems to be no end to killing and like Ehud in Judges 3:15-23 or Phineas in Numbers 25:6-9, a lot of killing was done in the name of God, the Most High. Christians eventually adopted this posture (4.2) that killing in the name of God can be sanctioned.

There is a deep irony to the problem of violence: my violence is good, your violence is bad. I always have reasons for my violence; you only have excuses for yours. Have you ever noticed when someone wrongs you, how much time you spend justifying your response in that conversation in your head? We will have more to say on the problem of violence in chapter 5; for now let us say retributive violence is the disease of the human condition. Justified vengeance is what is killing us. It is important to recognize that the problem of social retribution is real and after all the time we have been on this planet as a species we do not know how to deal with it.

If retribution or getting even is one way to deal with the problem of violence, there is another, as shown by Jesus, the way of forgiveness.

Forgiveness is the only way that forever cuts short and ends the cycle of retributive violence. It is the way of Jesus' life and death.

At this juncture I want to say that where the term 'nonviolent' has been used with reference to God, the better term would be 'forgiving.' 'Nonviolent', however, calls attention to the fact that the opposite of nonviolence is violence. This negative term gets under people's skin because the word 'God' is associated with references to stories in the Jewish Bible where God acts in a violent manner. To speak of God as nonviolent brings these Jewish texts under critical scrutiny. 'Forgiveness' is the positive way of speaking of nonviolence; from this point on I will use them interchangeably.

The Many Dimensions of Forgiveness

Forgiveness is *The Heart of the Matter* as Don Henley put it. Forgiveness *is* the heart of the matter and the song expresses this in a poignant and beautiful way. Scholars have sought a key to understanding Jesus for centuries. In the twentieth century it was the phrase 'the reign of God' that most seemed to think was the center of Jesus' message. This phrase may very well capture Jesus' central concern but at the heart of his kin(g)dom message is the problem of human violence and the solution of divine forgiveness. One way to observe the centrality of the theme of forgiveness is to note all of the various genres or types of story and teaching where it can be found.

Forgiveness is a theme in miracle stories. In Mark's gospel (2:1-12), the story of the paralytic, Jesus works with the common Jewish understanding that sin and disease have a common root (cf. John 9:2). Modern medical research has shown that there is an intimate connection between the state of our psychology and our body. What affects our minds, our self-esteem, has its effects in our physical self. Jesus does not dispute the connection but uses it to demonstrate that, as a human being (the True Human), God has given him power to do what belonged only to God, the authority to pronounce forgiveness, done apart from any structure of sacred authority.

Forgiveness is a theme used to great effect in Jesus' parables as we have already seen in the parable of the unmerciful servant. It is the key implicit theme of the parable of the Waiting father (Luke 15:11-32) as it is also in the parable of the good Samaritan (Luke 10:25-37).

Forgiveness can be found in the conflict story of Luke 7:36-50 where Jesus attends a banquet at the home of one Simon, a Pharisee. Here, Jesus is anointed by a woman whose reputation as a woman of ill repute has preceded her. Jesus, after a brief riposte with Simon, announces to the woman that her sins are forgiven. At this point the crowd begins to murmur amongst themselves, "Who is this who even forgives sins?"

One can also find general teaching on forgiveness, e.g., in Matthew 6:14-15 or Matthew 18. Here we note that receiving forgiveness from God is tied directly to forgiving others. In the New Testament Christians are enjoined to be "imitators of God" (Ephesians 5:1). In the Gospels the language of imitation (*mimesis*) is not used but another term is: *to follow*. The verb *akolouthein* is a technical term for discipleship: following Jesus is to act like Jesus acted.[lxxxiv] Interestingly, the only place where we ask God to imitate us is when it comes to forgiveness. In the Lord's Prayer we pray "Forgive us our sin, as we forgive others who sin against us." The little word 'as' is the key word. In the same fashion we forgive, or with the same measure we forgive, we are asking God to forgive us.

Forgiveness is a central theme in the Jubilee Year. We saw in Luke 4 Jesus quoted the jubilary text from Isaiah 61 (2.1). The phrase "to release the oppressed" uses the word for forgiveness. It is important to note that forgiveness is more than spiritual; it is also economic. Judaism used the words sin and debt interchangeably. To sin was to incur debt. This is why in the two versions of the Lord's Prayer Matthew has 'debt' and Luke has 'sin.' Yet, to be in economic debt was seen as oppressive as to be in moral debt. In Jesus honor/shame culture, there was plenty of economic exploitation and the vast majority of the non-aristocracy was indebted to the rich. Jubilee was a longed for time when not only would moral debt be forgiven but there would also come release from economic deprivation due to economic debt.[lxxxv]

Forgiveness is the theme that suffuses the Last Meal of Jesus with his disciples. When Jesus takes the cup and says (Matthew 26:27-28) "This is my blood of the covenant, which is poured out for many for the forgiveness of sins" we are to think of the echo of the promise of a new covenant found in Jeremiah 31:31-34 where the Lord declares that "the time is coming when I will make a new covenant...for I will forgive their wickedness and remember their sins no more."

Last, forgiveness is expressed by the dying Jesus in Luke's Gospel: "Father, forgive them, they do not know what they do" (Luke 23:34). Admittedly, this is a textual variant, a saying not attested in certain Greek manuscripts. Whether or not it is authentic (and I suspect it is) it certainly expresses what we have seen of Jesus' teaching and is congruent with the way he understood the importance of human relationships.

One cannot escape that for Jesus forgiveness of the other, restoring relationship with the other, was of paramount importance. In fact it was so important that it took precedence over worship. In Matthew 5:21-24, Jesus is in effect saying "If you decide one fine Sunday to get up and go to church and on your way begin thinking about the person who has wronged you, don't bother going to church. First, go to the person who has hurt you and make peace. When you have done that, then come before God in worship." Imagine if everyone who had something against someone else decided to follow this rule. Churches would be empty on many a Sunday morning! The world would certainly be a different place the rest of the week.

It is the theme of forgiveness which will differentiate Jesus from John the Baptist, for while it is true John's baptism was a baptism of repentance for the forgiveness of sin and the washing away of uncleanness. John's message contained nothing regarding forgiveness for the enemy other. Jesus' message on the other hand, resounded with this theme of enemy forgiveness and enemy love. As we saw in Luke 7, it is this forgiving aspect of Jesus' ministry that so disturbed John who was looking for God to judge and overthrow the Romans (and possibly Herod and a 'corrupt priesthood.'), while Jesus counseled a new way.

Forgiveness: Limitless and Free

In order to really see this new way it is important that we understand some elusive theological terms. If I ask you to define 'love' or 'grace', you will undoubtedly be able to give me an answer. There is no doubt that both 'love' and 'grace' are relational terms, that is, they imply some kind of intercourse between persons. When we speak of God's love or God's grace it is important that we do not take it out of the realm of the personal and turn it into a thing. Grace, for example can mean unmerited favor, but that leads us to other questions: What does unmerited mean? Does this mean that God can be or is unfavorable at times? You have to load up these terms with meaning from prior questions. Terms like grace and love are then self-referential within the system of language they are used in. Pelagians and Augustinians, Calvinists and Arminians must define terms like grace and love from positions already taken with reference to such terms.

We are better off asking about *agape* by looking to I Corinthians 13. In addition to many other aspects of what an *agapaic* lifestyle looks like, here it can be said of *agape* that it keeps no record of wrongs. This does not mean that wrongdoing isn't going on all the time; otherwise there would be no need to talk about records. It is characteristic of *agape* to forgive. Paul uses the same logic when speaking of the cross in 2 Corinthians 5:18-19, "God was in Christ reconciling the world to himself, not counting sins against sinners." What did Jesus say about forgiveness? Is it congruent with all this?

The answer is a resounding Yes! Forgiveness is absolutely about not counting sins. Remember Luke 23:34, "Father, forgive them, they don't know what they are doing?" His prayer is to ask God not to reckon our sins against us; this is what he prayed for that day as he hung dying. The reason that we can say things like "Christ bore my sins" is not because of some heavenly transaction. It is because we recognize had we been there we would have been Pilate, or Caiaphas or any one of the Sanhedrin, or the disciples or the mob. There is no place we can hide, from the greatest to the smallest. Everyone is named in the passion narrative, and Jesus forgives everyone. That was the Father's will, that kind of forgiveness.

Forgiveness is like the Energizer Bunny: it goes on and on and on and on… Remember when Peter asks Jesus "How many times should I forgive my brother, seven times?" Jesus replies "No, seventy times seven." "No Peter, it's not about counting, it's about living a life of forgiveness." Then, according to Matthew's narrative, Jesus continues with *the parable of the unmerciful servant*! The climax though, is that Jesus goes on to interpret the parable for them with reference to God who, he says, will treat us in the same way we treat each other from our heart. You don't get the God you believe in, you get the God you live. It is because we keep count, it is because we humans are bent on 'reckoning' and 'justice' that we limit the power of total forgiveness. We want *that* from God, but it seems so hard to 'imitate God' whom Jesus is imitating when it comes to forgiveness.

Why is this? Why is forgiveness so hard? Why do we seek so many ways to qualify it? Why do we feel the need to hang onto our anger? Why do we always seek to justify our anger, resentment or bitterness? Even though we may know that God's forgiveness is 'free and unmerited', why do so many spend so much time trying to earn it?

Where does the notion that it might be earned or merited come from? Is forgiveness extended to a person the moment they say a prayer at the back of a tract? Or when they choose baptism? Or when they became holy enough? Or when they join the community of faith? Or when their parents had them baptized? When is the moment of forgiveness? None of these? The moment of forgiveness took place long ago, historically on Good Friday, theologically, 'from the foundation of the world.' We have always stood in a forgiven relationship to God; that is God's posture with us. This is why he is like such an overjoyed *abba* when his prodigal children come home. Restored relationships counts far more than reckoning sin, thus, forgiveness.

How Did We End Up With An Angry God?

So, I have now described how I understand the word 'forgiveness' in the life and teaching of Jesus. How did we get to the place that we seem to confuse forgiveness with something merited? The answer is both old and new; it goes back to our earliest human ancestors and is found in all kinds of new age or monotheistic or pagan or any other tradition that could qualify as a religion. It is known as '*the sacrificial principle.*' Just like we have our biology and aspects of our development coded within our genes, so we also have coded into our brain certain social responses we humans have developed over time. One of these is our relation to divinity. Augustine has said "Our hearts are restless until they find rest in You, O God." It may well be that there is some sort of god-shaped vacuum in human experience, but it is not provable. What is demonstrable is the anthropological fact that we humans, unlike our primate ancestors, are a religious species. Archeological evidence of the earliest human remains indicates a fascination or tremendous fear of death...and what lies beyond.

As humans have evolved, views of god have changed. It has taken over ten thousand years but our views of divinity have made significant shifts. Neolithic humans would have lived in great fear of transcendence that they experienced as the raw force of nature and death. A significant indication of a shift in 'Divinity' was when god concepts were harnessed by the earliest civilizations (Empire), complete with priesthoods and Temples for all manner of sacrifice. Now 'the God' or gods, in addition to being feared, could also be worshipped and adored, for the God/gods could bless the people it represented. If the people were doing well, it meant that Divinity or the gods favored them. In this process god became double-faced or Janus-faced; god as master and lord of both good and evil. But notice this: the concept of god does not go from good to bad, but from terrifying to also good, thus 'two-faced.' This Janus-faced god, the god who is both to be feared and to be praised and loved is the newer development in the history of humankind's religious maturation. The two-sided god is the god of civilized religion (or in modern terms the god of Empire). Where some might see blessing in this, there is also bane. The god who loves and hates, forgives and damns, blesses and curses is the god we humans have made a thousand-fold repetition of, each calling itself 'the true religion.' All can see human history is replete with the human sacrifices we have made to this kind of divinity in order to secure our lives here on earth.

The *sacrificial principle* is expressed by the act of giving and receiving and captured in the Latin (Roman) phrase "*do ut des*" which roughly translated is "I give in order to receive." Why do I make an offering to the gods? Because I seek something that is not in my power, I make a gift before I make a request. In an honor/shame society, like so many Middle Eastern cultures, it would not be honorable for the receiver of a gift not to reciprocate. In religious practice the same was true. Religion is doing something in order to get something from God. Religion is about sacrifice. It has been well said that in the ancient world the real question wouldn't be "Which god do you believe in?" but "To which god do you sacrifice?"

When we think of Christian forgiveness in the way religions think of it, it will always carry the qualifications of giving and receiving. That is why almost every theology needs a moment when forgiveness is 'actualized' in the individual person. There is an incomplete transaction until someone makes a conscious choice. That is the person's payment. The reaction to this is to decry the concept of 'free-will.' This is a correct reaction that unfortunately devolves into a very abstract doctrine of double predestination or fate when God comes to decide who is forgiven, who made the requisite choice or payment. In the next section we will see how this all gets deformed in popular versions of the doctrine of the atonement (what Jesus' death means).

When there is an exchange between givers/receivers we are dealing with what is called an *economy of exchange*. We all live in the midst of an *economy of exchange* but never really think about it. We all trade (give) our time (a job) in order to receive money that is then given in exchange for goods and services. That is why we can be so attached to our possessions; they represent the value of our time. Our very existence is oriented to an economy of exchange as is our religion. In a future chapter (5.2) I shall talk about culture and religion having the same common root, but for now it is only important that we begin to see the big difference between the way forgiveness is perceived within an *economy of exchange* and the way that Jesus talked about and lived out God's jubilary, boundary-crossing, endless forgiveness.[lxxxvi]

The opposite of forgiveness is retribution, which is the negative side of an *economy of exchange*; here, the balances must be even, order restored. To be unforgiving is to seek retribution. In earlier times retribution was like the Wild, Wild West. It was dispensed without mercy by any who were wronged. Eye for an eye, tooth for a tooth. You killed someone from my family, tribe, nation or gang, and I will kill one of yours. The cycle could and frequently did go on for generations, even centuries.

This is what makes Jesus' ministry (and priesthood) of forgiveness so important. We who killed him do not need ever fear his retaliation. He has sought and received our forgiveness from God and has himself given it to us when he appeared to us after his resurrection and said "*Shalom*."[lxxxvii]

Forgiveness abolishes *the sacrificial principle*. It is simply, freely and profusely given us by God; God only relates to us as forgiven. This is why Jesus can say (in Luke 4) to the Nazarene synagogue hearers, "God goes to your enemy with jubilee blessing." The *abba* of Jesus is not Janus-faced. God forgives and we too can forgive. This is why he can say that the reign of God consists in forgiveness between humans. Gospel forgiveness breaks down any notion that it can be earned or merited. It comes completely as a gift; it is still there even if the gift is not taken. It is a gift 'given before' thus for-given. It is a total posture or orientation, not a response. The gift of forgiveness is not withdrawn and then replaced with anger or wrath. When we confess that Jesus is Lord, we are confessing that the Maker of heaven and earth looks upon all of us with mercy and calls us to live as children of God's image.

3.3 The Nonviolent Atonement

I saw this on a church sign while driving this past week:

"Either Jesus Pays...
...Or You Do"

There is a lot of theology packed into those few words. Let's unpack some assumptions. First, payment is required. Second, Jesus has to pay or we have to pay, a clear indication we are in an *economy of exchange* and operating with *a sacrificial principle.* This indicates we are dealing with a transaction. Third, Jesus or we have to pay someone. Fourth there is an implicit assumption that someone is owed. Fifth, Jesus can do something for us we could have done, as either one of us can somehow pay; he can function as a substitute.

All of this and probably more are implied in those few words.

When I became a 'new' Christian thirty-four years ago, I learned, or heard or understood for the first time, what the death of Jesus meant. It meant all of what is written above. Jesus came to die for my sins, to pay the price, to save me from hell. "I came to seek and save the lost", "I have not come to call righteous but sinners", "I have come that they might have life abundantly" and "I have come not to destroy the law but to fulfill it." These sayings all somehow related back to atonement; "Jesus paid it all/all to Him I owe/Sin had left its crimson stain/He washed it white as snow."

All of these "I came" sayings do in fact come round to atonement and God's purposes. But it makes a huge difference when one relates the "I came" to the God we have been describing or the Janus-faced God, the one who is both wrathful and forgiving. Which God sends Jesus? When you place Jesus in relation to these two very different structural descriptions of God, two very different atonement theories emerge: a sacrificial/religious and a non-sacrificial/non-religious one. A sacrificial or religious reading of why Jesus came must explain itself not only to forgiveness but also to retribution. And this can only be done *using the language and logic of an economy of exchange.*

The Problem of an Angry God and Jesus' Death

This kind of logic entered the way Christians thought about the death of Jesus in the late 11th century with the Archbishop of Canterbury, Anselm, and the publication of his book *Why God Became Human.* That's a good question, which Anselm tried to answer by interpreting Christ's death as liberation from sin and a restoring of the order of God's universe. The death of Jesus was a logical necessity, given the human condition and God's sense of justice.

Anselm finished editing this essay while sitting with the Pope on the battlefields of the Crusade.[lxxxviii] The Christian/Muslim conflict was in full swing. Life was tenuous. It is no wonder that Anselm wanted order and hoped that Jesus' death somehow brought that order. Anselm said that Jesus was a substitute for us. He then leapt to the conclusion that Jesus' death was necessary because we could not balance the scales of God's justice. Is this conclusion correct? The witness of the New Testament is not of a God who is some humongous Judge Judy waiting to get us all. The Judge of the New Testament is, if anything, a gracious and merciful Judge who becomes judged by humanity, by you and me (1.3). God is 'The Judge Judged in our Place' as Karl Barth puts it.

Jesus came to change everything in Anselm's understanding of ushering in God's reign. But Anselm assimilated Jesus' death to that of the pagan *sacrificial principle* and made God the object of Jesus' atonement. Jesus did something for God and in exchange earned our salvation. What was that something? Satisfaction? Payment?

From Anselm until the present, much discussion of Jesus' death has been conducted with reference to the Janus-faced God. This is precisely where medieval atonement theory breaks with the New Testament, for the apostolic church did not relate Jesus' death to a wrathful deity. They say the opposite: the initiative for our reconciliation comes from God (e.g., Romans 5:6-11, 2 Corinthians 5:16-21).

It wasn't Anselm that took the cruel step of seeing the cross as punishment. The most influential Reformer, John Calvin made explicit that Jesus' death is related to the 'dark side of God.' In his *Institutes* he said:

> "In short the only reason given in Scripture that the Son of God willed to take our flesh, and accepted this commandment from the Father, is that he would be a sacrifice to appease the Father on our behalf. 'Thus it is written, that the Christ should suffer...and that repentance be preached in his name.' (Lk. 24:46-47) 'For this reason the Father loves me, because I lay down my life for my sheep...this commandment He

> gave me.' (Jn. 10:17, 15:18) 'As Moses lifted up the serpent in the wilderness, so must the Son of Man be lifted up.' (Jn. 3:14) Another passage, 'Father, save me from this hour...but for this purpose I have come to this hour. Father, glorify your son.' (Jn. 12:17-28 conflated with verse 23)."[lxxxix]

The entire purpose of Jesus' death is attached solely to the 'dark side of deity.' The problem? Jesus' atoning work on the Cross is no longer seen as an act of grace by a generous and merciful God; it is morphed into the most violent image, that of child sacrifice. Yes, in this image, God sacrifices God's Son, like Abraham would have sacrificed Isaac. But unlike Abraham, God went through with it. Jesus' satisfactory death becomes fully penal (Jesus is punished on our behalf) for the wrathful side of God must be placated.

A recent group Bible study by a major Evangelical publisher makes exactly this the content of the gospel message. They begin with the story of Adam, Eve and the Serpent. When the human couple disobeyed God "to meet the demands of his own perfect judgment, God judged them for their sin and...all of creation entered into a fallen state." "When Adam and Eve rebel against God, his perfect justice demands that he punish them for their sin." What then is our hope? Jesus is the one who "fulfilled Scripture and accomplished our salvation by paying the penalty of death for our sins."[xc]

With this final shift, authentic Christian thinking about Jesus' death went straight out the window.[xci] This logic is foreign to the apostolic writers; it contradicts their emphases and language. It is this *sacrificial logic* that has been under attack in the debates around atonement for the past thirty years. The proponents of this logic are never completely wrong for they do manage to capture Jesus' death as a benefit, a positive thing. It is the way they capture it that is the problem. They understand Jesus' death *in the framework of an economy of exchange and the sacrificial principle.*

How Did Jesus Explain His Own Death?

So the question is: did Jesus understand his death as an appeasement of his *Abba's* wrath? We have already dealt with Psalm 22 (1.3). There is no wrath of God implied in that text or Jesus' use of it. So how did Jesus understand his death?

A good place to begin is Mark 10:45:

> "For the Son of man did not come to be served, but to serve and give his life a ransom for many."

It's the little word 'ransom' (*lutron*) that causes such problems. Ransom suggests payment. It implies an *economy of exchange.* But what is exchanged with whom? Who is the object of the ransom here? Is it the devil? Is it God? How is it paid? What is the nature of the debt? There are no clear answers if we understand this saying a) apart from its context and b) interpreted through the lens of *the sacrificial principle.* The context is about the problem of hierarchy and authority. First, James and John come seeking the best seats in the house. They want Jesus' right and left hand side in his kingdom; they were after all, '*sons of rage*' (not 'sons of thunder' a common mistranslation[xcii]; see Mark 3:17) who would see the world changed through divine violence and themselves as agents of God's wrath (Luke 9:51-56). Jesus tries to get them to see who he is and what he is about. It takes the disciples' hearing this and getting pretty indignant about the Zebedee's request before Jesus can show them clearly. He does this by comparing his mission to pagan authority; he then says that following him means abandoning pagan thinking. To become the opposite of pagan leaders they must assume the role of lowliest servant? What could this mean? Scot McKnight has some wonderful, illuminating comments:

> "The use of the term 'for' (*anti*) indicates either exclusive substitutionary death (his death instead of theirs, Lev 27:11) or benefit for the many (his death brings freedom for the many; cf. Matt 17:27)...What is unobserved by the substitution theory advocates is that the ransom cannot be a substitute as we might find in theologically sophisticated language; where death is for death and penal judgment for penal judgment. Here we have a mixing of descriptions: a ransom for slaves. Jesus, in Mark's language doesn't become a slave for other slaves. He is a ransom for those enslaved. The difference ought to be given special attention...The ransom does not thereby become a substitute so much as a liberating price. The notion is one of being a Savior, not substitution. The best translation would be that Jesus is a 'ransom for the benefit of the many.'"[xciii]

McKnight is saying that this text can be and has been read with a sacrificial meaning imported into it since it is not there to begin with; it has to come from somewhere other than the language itself. There is nothing to suggest that either God or the devil is the recipient of this ransom payment. Mark 10:45 then, can be lifted out of a sacrificial interpretation and given a new look. This new look focuses on Jesus' humanity as given for us and to us, a gift from God, a service of God. It suggests that the language of slavery is an apt a description of our human condition and that Jesus does what he does for everyone.

Theologically speaking this is what Willard Swartley calls "redemptive solidarity."[xciv] The movement in atonement is from top down, the Word becomes flesh. Incarnation is already atonement. For the Word to assume flesh also indicates a prior decision by God to do so, thus assuring us that reconciliation with us is God's highest priority. God intends to overcome our estrangement and restore our true humanity. Incarnation and atonement are the single act of the God who Serves.

That Jesus understands leadership and authority in a way completely at odds with the pagan understanding is clear. Mark 10:45 brings together the problem of kingship/leadership and atonement. This is not the first time these two themes came together for Jesus. After the miracle of the feeding of the 5,000, Jesus takes his innermost circle of disciples to Caesarea Philippi and speaks about his death. What happened at that feeding to cause Jesus to realize his death was a virtual certainty? The answer can be found in the Fourth Gospel where Jesus withdrew into the hills, by himself, because the crowds, and possibly the disciples, intended to make him king by force (John 6:15). Viva la revolution!

If this is what the crowds wanted then Jesus knew then his message had failed. The crowds did not seem to understand it was not about violence or revolution, justified or any other kind. It was all about forgiveness, about so caring for one another that we might well be perceived as slaves. This is what his *abba's* reign was about. Jesus would make peace but it would not be with any means using coercion, force or threats. That was the way of the world; the way of the *Pax Romana* (the peace enforced by Rome).[xcv]

Second, this saying is not about an *economy of exchange*. Nowhere in the Gospels does Jesus say God is angry or wrathful with sinners, nor does he ever say or imply that God's wrath must be appeased before God can accept sinners back into the fold. None of the logic of *the sacrificial principle* can be found in anything Jesus says regarding his death. If Jesus death was not a sacrificial act, relating to the logic of giving and receiving then what was it?

First, it was a political act. It was Pilate, as representative of Caesar, who gave the order of execution. It was pagan Empire that actually carried out the crucifixion. Although it is true that Jesus was 'handed over' to the Jewish leadership by one of his disciples, and it is also true that Jesus was 'handed over' to Pilate by these same religious authorities, it was the pagan sacrificial system of Empire that killed Jesus. The Nicene Creed captures this when it says Jesus was 'crucified under Pontius Pilate.' The Creed does not say Jesus was crucified 'by the Jews.' To be sure, they played a role but it was we Gentiles who did the heinous act. The politics of the event can be seen in the *titulus* at the top of Jesus' cross which Pilate commissioned in three different languages: 'The King of the Jews' (Mark 15:26). As we have seen, it is kingship that is the problem that leads to Jesus' death. Jesus' death was seen as an act of the state against someone who would subvert the state.

Second, the Passion Narrative has a certain structure that is familiar to readers of ancient stories, the structure of all against one (5.2, 6.3). As we noted earlier, virtually everyone with the exception of a few women, participated in the execution of Jesus. No one is left out. To put it bluntly, Jesus was lynched by an angry mob. Like the victim of Psalm 22 or the servant of Isaiah 53, he was alone; no one came to his aid, no one stood up for him, no one cried out that what was being perpetrated was an injustice. Sometimes Christians look at the cross of Jesus and see a singular unique event. The fact that Jesus so clearly ties his death into the deaths of other victims (like Psalm 22 and Isaiah 53) ought to indicate that he does not see his death in these terms. In fact he sees a clear connection between his death and all of the unjust deaths of his sacred history. In Matthew 23:29-36 Jesus addresses his contemporaries with a warning: they will experience the cataclysm of social disintegration because they persist in using violence against individuals to solve their social crises.

> "I am sending you prophets and wise men and teachers. Some you will kill and crucify; others you will flog in your synagogues and pursue from town to town. And so upon you will come all the righteous blood that has been shed on earth, from the blood of the righteous Abel to the blood of Zechariah son of Berekiah, whom you murdered between the Temple and the altar."

Jesus points out that the history of the Jewish people is a history bounded by murder: the very first murder of the Jewish 'canon' was that of Abel (Genesis 4:8) and the last murder, that of Zechariah (2 Chronicles 24:20-21). His death will be like that of every prophet sent by God to Israel. The difference between Jesus' death and that of the prophets, from Abel to Zechariah, was that their deaths took place in or by sacred altars; it was in the context of sacrifice, near a bloody altar that they die. Jesus does not die in the Temple or near an altar. His death is completely secularized; he dies on a hill "outside the city gate" (Hebrews 13:12). This becomes an important clue that Jesus' death was to be interpreted as other than the usual sacrificial practice of making an offering to appease the deity.

So, Jesus' death is not to be interpreted in the logic of *the sacrificial principle* but as the subversion and end of it. Jesus' death is God's way of coming into the machinery of sacrifice and tossing in a wrench to stop it from working ever again. The *sacrificial principle* is the dark side of religion of which Jesus' death is the light.

Mark Heim in his book *Saved from Sacrifice* sums it up best:

> "The truth is that God and Jesus together submit themselves to human violence. Both suffer its results. Both reveal and overcome it. God does not require the death of the Son anymore than Jesus requires the

helpless bereavement of the Father. Jesus' suffering is not required as an offering to satisfy God anymore than one member of a team undertaking a very dangerous rescue mission 'requires' another dearly loved member to be in a place of peril or pain. They are constantly and consistently on the same side. By virtue of their love and communion with each other, each suffers what the other suffers. They are not playing out a war in the heart of God."[xcvi]

3.4 Eye Opening Parables

If you have made it this far in this book you will have experienced three major challenges: first, is your understanding of the Bible, second your view of the atonement and third, is the way you understand God's final judgment (known as eschatology). You may feel as though I am asking you to throw out the Bible, toss your salvation and forget worrying about your future. Actually I suppose the last is not such a bad idea. I also affirm that Scripture is essential to the life of the Church and the Christian, all of it, not just some parts of it, and that Jesus' life and death are that reality apart from which we can neither know God nor be saved.

You will recall that in the Introduction we saw that there is as much deconstructive work to be done as reconstructive. It is the deconstructive work that is painful because we have learned to emotionally invest, not in Jesus, but in our theology. A good test to determine whether Jesus or our theology takes precedence is to discern the degree to which we are willing to unlearn something and learn something new about Him. Jesus doesn't change, "He is the same yesterday, today and forever" (Hebrews 13:8). But we do change and our understanding of Jesus changes. If we are careful listeners to His Spirit we will find that an aspect of what God does in our lives is to change the way we think.

We have seen that the use of violence or retribution did not form any part of the way in which Jesus perceived God's working in the world. But how do we communicate that God is not like people have been taught? If people think that God is retributive and that justice consists of retribution, payback or a balancing of the scales, how do you let them know this is not God? Can you just come out and say, "Oh by the way, you have got God all wrong. Our sacred texts do indeed speak of God being violent, retributive, angry and vindictive, but really, they don't mean what you think."

There will be many readers of this book who will balk at this very point. Just as Christians today think they are clear with regard to the character of God, so Jesus' contemporaries' thought they also knew God. I understand my contemporaries' reaction; it is the same reaction Jesus received in his hometown synagogue. When teaching this I have sometimes received this reaction from laypersons, church officials, pastors and even theologians.

People just do not want to let go of a wrathful God, a God who punishes evildoers. They fear that if they do they will lose all moral footing, that life will descend into anarchy and that there will be no justice in the world. And they are right! All of this could happen. But the 'all of this' is the problem not the solution because the 'all of this' is grounded in a mechanism of scapegoating violence. Their theology is grounded in fear but 'perfect love casts out all fear' (I John 4:18). What is needed is a way to communicate this.

Some Eskimo tribes have twenty or thirty words for snow; each different type of snow is a different word. But how would you talk about snow to an aboriginal native that lives in the hot desert climate of Arizona? In the same way when entire peoples are embedded in a system of sacrificial logic, how do you talk about grace and forgiveness? If the only thing people have ever known is a Janus-faced God how do you let them know that "God is light and in God there is no darkness at all" (I John 1:5) or that God does "not change like shifting shadows" (James 1:17)? If justifying anger is what people know how do you tell them "human anger does not bring about the righteous life that God requires" (James 1:20)? Bono sums it up when he says, "Explaining belief has always been difficult. How do you explain a love and logic at the heart of the universe when the world is so out of whack?"

What is needed is a method of speaking about God that both relates to what hearers know and yet carves out a new path in their knowing so that not only what they know but also *how they know something* changes. This is exactly what a parable does and Jesus was the master parable teller. We've explored some of the parables of judgment in section 1.3. A parable is not an illustration; it does not simply paint a moral in story form. It is a form of communicating that places the unknown next to the supposedly known and says 'Look here, this is what you think you know, this other, well, this is what is real. They may look similar but if you probe more deeply you will find a greater discontinuity. Then the choice is yours, change your way of thinking or stay stuck in your old mindset and suffer their consequences."[xcvii]

In this sense a parable is a puzzle, a kind of theological Sudoku. Parables require work, hard intellectual work in order to grasp their 'meaning.' A parable creates a new possibility just by its being told. It is a door opener, a light on new paths. Jesus' most prominent way of speaking was through parables. A simple yet adequate description of what constitutes a parable, specifically Jesus' parables, comes from British scholar T.W. Manson.

> "The true parable is not an illustration to help one through a theological discussion; it is rather a mode of religious experience. It belongs to the same order of things as altar and sacrifice, prayer,

> the prophetic vision and the like. It is a datum of theology, not a by-product. It is a way in which religious faith is attained and, so far as it can be, transmitted from one person to another. It is not a crutch for limping intellects, but a spur to religious insight; its object is not to provide simple theological instruction, but to produce living religious faith."[xcviii]

The Complex Simplicity of Parables

Now the major burden of Jesus' parables concerns the 'kin(g)dom of God' the way God reigns or rules. This being the case, then what Jesus is doing in his parables is helping us to change the way we think about God and the way God is God, the way God rules. We saw in the last section that we bear faithful witness to God, by not acting as autocratic tyrants but as lowly servants. A God who serves? What kind of a God is it that serves? Gods are by definition majestic, holy, powerful, mighty and exalted. We only exist to serve God. What does this mean that God is our servant? What could this mean? What is it exactly that the parables open us for us? What is it that needs changing?

We can find some help here in the way certain scholars group the parables. I have chosen three scholars who have different ways of describing the grouping of Jesus' parables but all point to something essential about their orientation. T.W. Manson says Jesus' parables fall roughly into two categories 1) God's governance and 2) Ethical behavior. Michael Goulder suggests that Jesus' parables are to be classified into 1) The Indicative and 2) The Imperative. Finally Old Testament scholar Claus Westermann says Jesus' parables are about 1) Proclamation and 2) A Call for Action. What each of these writers recognize is that Jesus' parables fall into one of two categories 1) theology and 2) ethics or 1) The Way Things Are and 2) The Way we Can Conform to the Way Things Are.

Jesus' parables fall into exactly the same two categories as his understanding of what constitutes the greatest commandment, what it means to love God and love our neighbor. The parables then are an invitation to participate in this new way of being and living and loving in the world which reflects the authentic character of who God is, not as abstract, but specifically who God is in Jesus, the True Human.

From this observation on the parables and the greatest commandment I want to draw a conclusion: Life is all about interpretation, about the way we interpret our sacred texts, our experience and the world around us. There is no life without interpretation. As we saw in 1.2, the context for the greatest commandment in all three Synoptic Gospels had to do with interpretation; likewise the parables have to do with the way we interpret God and ourselves in relation to each other. It is not a question of whether or not we interpret. We do. We are not automatons who simply live a program; we humans seek meaning and significance in all of life, from the smallest thing to the biggest event. Jesus' intention is to draw us out of the box of our pagan sacrificial logic, out of our idolatry, and into the wonderful mystery of his compassionate *Abba*.

Jesus cannot do that straight out. He tried in Nazareth (2.1) and found that if he told it like it is, he could get killed. He needed another means by which to communicate this message indirectly in order that his hearers would be challenged to come alongside his new logic, to think through to the conclusions that he also drew. Some may have been able to do this, although the Gospels don't give us much indication of Jesus' success as a teller of parables. We are never told that the crowds went wild when they understood what he was saying; and it is apparent that the disciples didn't get much of what was going on. So it should not surprise us when we do not quickly grasp the parables. The real question is: Have they grasped us? Have they hooked us so that no matter how much we struggle we are caught on their line, finding ourselves being reeled closer and closer to....truth?

Jesus' parables no longer challenge Christians; we have domesticated them beyond recognition. We have turned them into morality plays or innocuous assertions. What we have rarely done is to allow the parables to totally change the way we think. We come to them asking them to fit into our theology, rather than come to them seeking ways to allow our theology to change and fit them. We do not hear them as they are intended to be heard. No surprise here for parables are for "the one who has ears to hear" (Mark 4:9). Parables are not guarantees of our 'getting it'; parables are linguistic risks of communication. Jesus demonstrated this risk in a parable he told about parables, the Parable of the Sower.

In this parable the sower sows seed on a landscape that includes the good soil, the shallow ground, areas full of weeds and a path that cut through the field. Then the field was ploughed. This is the opposite of Western farming practice that first clears the field, then plows furrows, then plants the seed. Jesus' parable works on what everyone knows to be true: Farmers first sow seed then they plow. In Jesus' parable there is no mention of the sower plowing, only sowing. Once the seed has been sown, what is important is the soil into which it falls. If no other action is taken, only sowing, then it all depends on the soil. Such seems to be Jesus' interpretation of this parable about parables in Mark 4:13-20.[xcix]

The parable of the sower is about how proclamation occurs in God's reign. It is gently sown; it is not forcefully plowed under. Given the types and conditions of the soils, we might be surprised that the yield is only 25% or less of the actual seed sown. Most of the seed goes to waste. Most people cannot hear what Jesus has to say about God and God's reign. But for those with ears to hear, the growth is extraordinary, as much as a hundred fold. Some people really get it! What is the mystery of the kingdom that some folks get? It is *Shalom*, God's holistic peace, the way God reigns.

When Jesus says what he thinks, it gets him into trouble. Parables help the listener by bringing the listener into the thinking process that facilitates change. Parables are thus a gracious form of communication that requires work on our part as humans in order to make the transition from our faulty ways of thinking into the new thinking of the Kin(g)dom of God. After almost two thousand years of church history and millions of books of theology written, and billions of Christians and hundreds of thousands of churches and sects, the question remains: Have we heard Jesus and is it Jesus we are following or do we need to be parabled?

Important Considerations When Interpreting the Parables

When you interpret the parables it is important to note to whom Jesus is speaking, for different groups needed different challenges to their thinking. In this vein we may note that the groups break down into three categories: the disciples, the crowds and Jesus' interlocutors (those who seek to trap Jesus with their questions).

Here is a partial list of audiences and parables according to Manson:[c]

- the crowds
    - the sower Mark 4, children in the marketplace Luke 7:31f, light under a bushel, Luke 11:33, mustard seed and leaven, unfruitful fig tree Luke 13:6
- the disciples
    - stones for bread Luke 11:11, Lord returning from feast, robbed house Luke 12:35-40, talents Luke 16:13, city on a hill Matt. 5:14, several parables of eschatology Matt. 13:24-52, the unjust steward 18:23-35
- the interlocutors
    - parables of Mark 2-3 (children of the bridal party, new patch, new wine, divided kingdom, strong man), vineyard Mark 12:1-11, two sons Matt. 21:28ff, marriage feast Matt. 22:1-14, two debtors Luke 7:40f, Good Samaritan Luke 10:30f, the 3 'lost' parables of Luke 15, Dives and Lazarus Luke 16:19ff, Pharisee & publican Luke 18:9-14

Gospel scholars note that sometimes the church supplies the audiences as they passed on the parables. Therefore, when interpreting them it is helpful to at least ask why they chose this or that audience to apply them. Sometimes Jesus' parables are strung together to create a 'teaching discourse.' Either way there is a teaching method in the parables that still challenges us as much today as it did then.

In Matthew's Gospel, a chapter on parables (13) introduces the double theme of parable listening: what happens to those who hear the truth of the parables and what happens when the parables remain...riddles. Some scholars see Matthew 13 as a filling out (technically known as a midrash) of Mark 4 (on the assumption that Matthew used or edited Mark's Gospel). This is possible, although an airtight case cannot be made for it. I will assume this possibility in the following discussion.

Our theme of parable hearing is buttressed by several observations on the context of Matthew 13. First, it is the center of five discourses. Second, it is bounded by stories, like bookends, of those who cannot hear Jesus. Third, it has an expanded quotation of the problem of listening/understanding from Isaiah. Fourth, it contains both parables of growth and parables of judgment.

First, Matthew chapter 13 is the central discourse of five major discourses. Prior to this comes Matthew 5-7, the Sermon on the Mount and Matthew 10, the Missionary Discourse. After this is Matthew 18, the Church Discourse and Matthew 24-25, the Discourse of Finality. In this structure the center text is the key text for understanding what went on before and why it changes afterword. Even Dispensationalism (the view that God acts different ways at different periods of time) observes the key place Matthew 13 plays in Jesus' supposed offer of the kingdom to Israel.

Second, right before the parables comes the short narrative on who constitutes Jesus' authentic family (Matthew 12:46-50). Jesus observes it is not his biological family whom he calls relatives but anyone who hears and does the will of God. The section on parables is followed by Matthew's version of Luke 4 and the response of Jesus' hometown synagogue hearers. Matthew records that they tried to connect him, not to God, but to his biological family (which Jesus had already disconnected) and then they were 'scandalized' at his words. We recall in Luke 4, they were scandalized precisely by the 'words of grace' and enemy forgiveness he spoke when citing Jewish Scripture, then tried to kill him.

Third, Matthew expands Mark's quotation from Isaiah. Compare Mark 4:12 with Matthew 13:13-15. This expansion clarifies a potential translation problem in Mark. Some read Mark 4:12 as though Jesus were saying he speaks in parables to intentionally cause people problems in hearing them.[ci] Most translations of Mark 4:12 make it sound as though Jesus speaks in parables "in order that" those who see might become non-seeing. But the word "in order that" (*hina*) has been shown in itself to be a mistranslation of Jesus' mother tongue Aramaic. Jesus probably used a word that functioned as a set of quotation marks to introduce the citation from Isaiah. The quotation from Isaiah is a justification for why parables are necessary. Jesus must speak in parables because although his hearers think they hear, they really don't and do not know it. They are in denial. Parables, then, cause them to think outside the box in which they are accustomed to thinking. Matthew's expansion of Mark's quotation of Isaiah 6:9-11 makes this clear. The point of the parables is if they would just realize their incomprehension and the way they cling to their false view of God with such stubbornness, God would heal them. God's orientation is not one of judgment but one of healing. So also the parables are not intended to cause intellectual or spiritual blindness and deafness but healing. The result all depends upon the soil into which the seed falls.

Fourth, Matthew makes clear just what happens when people both hear and do not hear what is occurring when Jesus speaks in parables. Whereas Mark only has parables of growth, Matthew includes parables of judgment. Why is this? Because there is a consequence when we chose not to listen to Jesus, when we refuse to conform our theology to his understanding of God. That consequence is more than just blindness. It is the reality that our lives will become further entangled in the spiral of violence and the violent retribution we give and justify by calling upon a retributive God. Again, parables offer us a way out or they take us deeper into our own twisted logic.

The parable of the Weeds and the parable of the Net have more often than not been used to explain why some people go to heaven and others go to hell. Jesus' explanation has nothing to do with the separation of good and bad people; his parables already themselves by the very hearing of them occasion a person's destiny. How we respond to his parables is how we shall end up. If we respond positively, changing our thinking and our ways from one of retribution to forgiveness, we shall then be gathered as children of the kingdom. If we refuse we shall only be able to live within the idolatrous sacrificial framework of religion with its sometimes merciful, sometimes angry and wrathful deity. The wicked in the parables are not general sinners, or those that don't attend church or even the unsaved; the wicked are those who will not hear what Jesus teaches about God and God's reign of mercy and forgiveness, adjusting their theology and ethics accordingly. We too, like Jesus' hearers, are being parabled today. We can either walk away uncomprehending or we can let them infect us and change the way we think and live.

As we conclude these first three chapters on Jesus we have seen a completely new way of thinking emerging that cannot simply be labeled 'conservative' or 'liberal' or 'pietistic' or anything else. We acknowledge a debt to all facets of the Christian tradition. When Jesus' life and teaching are taken with utmost seriousness and explored in the light of his culture and time, his mission and message become powerfully brighter and thus transformative, particularly in the way he wove all of his message together. Sadly, this light would begin to dim within decades of Jesus' resurrection, taking on new forms, some for good, some for ill. How did this happen? What mistakes were made in the early church that we no longer need keep on repeating today?

Chapter 4 Constantinian Christianity

4.1 Peacemaking in the Early Church

Have you ever been asked if you speak another language? When asked this I reply, "Yes, in addition to English I am fluent in Lutheran, Methodist, Roman Catholic, Pentecostal, Reformed, Evangelical, Pietist, and many dialects of Baptist." Christian denominations really do speak in different tongues. It would appear as if there was incredible diversity in Christianity. But they can each be traced back to a common ancestor. Just like we can trace the romance languages (Spanish, French, Portuguese, Catalan, Italian and Rumanian, etc) back to Latin, so also even though they sound different and have different vocabularies, there is a common thread in all of the churches today. That thread is ancient and runs deep in the DNA of Christianity, but it is a mutation, a shift away from the purity of the gospel. How did this change take place? This is what we shall explore.

This chapter will take a slightly different rhetorical tone. It will be a little more technical (but not too much). It is important to pay attention to details, but it is also crucial to have a grasp of the big picture. We will attempt to keep an eye on both when it comes to the church of the second through the fourth centuries. Many are the reasons Christians turn to the early church to find inspiration and guidance. Some turn for theological guidance but, as we shall see, shortly after the apostolic period significant changes occurred in the way theology was done. It is possible to do early church theology without doing apostolic theology. They are done from totally different sets of presuppositions and backgrounds.

The Playlist

For readers unfamiliar with the players in the drama of early church history, it will be important to get to know the significant figures and some important documents circulating at that time. Using the following list of characters you can also get a big picture view of where they fall in the church history timeline as I have attempted to put them in chronological order. You may, as have others when first encountering the history of our theological beliefs, be surprised to learn how many of our dearly held beliefs which we perceived to have come directly from Jesus or the apostles actually arose much later in the scheme of things within the community of faith. Here is the cast that you can refer to as you read this chapter:

The Playlist

Cast	Date Range C.E.	Description
Philo	c. 20 B.C.E. –50 C.E.	Jewish interpreter of scripture, merged Greek philosophy w/ Torah
Didache	c. 50-80? (100-125?)	1st Jewish-Christian catechism, taught prior to Baptism
Clement of Rome	c. 100	Bishop of Rome, author of a letter to Church at Corinth
Marcion	c. 110-150	Arch heretic, claimed to follow Paul but threw out Hebrew scriptures
Papias	c. 130	Bishop in Asia Minor, collected information related to the Gospels
Epistle of Barnabas	c. 110	Supercessionist, allegorical document from Alexandria
Justin Martyr	c. 140-160	1st Christian apologist, converted from Greek philosophy
Irenaeus	c. 160-185	Bishop of Lyons, major writer on heretics
Clement of Alexandria	c. 180-200	Like Philo and Origen, would merge Greek philosophy & Christian ideas
Origen	c. 200	Brilliant thinker, catechist and prolific writer in Christian theology
Tertullian	c. 200	Converted Latin lawyer, joined "Early Pentecostals"
Cyprian	c. 250	Bishop of Carthage, wrote on Baptism and Church leadership
Lactantius	c. 300-318	Wrote "Divine Institutes," the first Latin systematic theology

Eusebius	c. 300-335	Bishop of Caesarea, friend of Constantine, Church historian
Constantine	c. 306-337	First "Christian Emperor," convener of the Nicene Council
Nicene Council	c. 325	Gathering of Eastern Bishops which dealt with the divinity of Jesus
Donatus	c. 350	Bishop of Carthage who defrocked traitorous priests, "post persecution"
Augustine	c. 384-430	Theologian who laid foundation for all Western Christian thought

We note at the outset that as the early church developed they claimed to follow apostolic tradition. They showed great care in seeking to make sure that their leaders were followers of the followers of the apostles; that the literature they read in worship was congruent with the apostolic oral teaching that had been passed on; and that continuity was maintained with the church of the previous century in every way possible. In fact, so strong was this oral tradition that a significant early theologian, Papias, preferred it to written (gospel) texts!

What American Christianity misses today that was part of early Christian experience was to be a persecuted minority. Empire was a totality of existence and dominated every aspect of a person's life. But one could not confess both Jesus and Caesar to be Lord; it had to be one or the other. So when Christians confessed, "Jesus is Lord" they were automatically suspected of treason and harassed, exiled or killed. The sacred texts that authorized such a confession were also seized and burned.

It is a fact that nowhere in the New Testament does any author explicitly authorize violence against Empire. It is also a fact, Romans 13 notwithstanding, that nowhere in the apostolic literature does anyone encourage complicity with Empire. The road between revolution and complicity is narrow. Yet we see time and again that Christian defense of faithfulness to Jesus was radical, contrary to the norms and values of Empire and, indeed, quite subversive of it. A conclusion we can draw from all this is that the literature produced by the apostolic church and collected in the New Testament was done under the all seeing eye of Empire[cii]; an Empire which persecuted and prosecuted to the full extent of the law any and all who had any other Lord but Caesar.

It is quite different for us today in so-called Christian America, for the lines between Caesar and Jesus have become blurred to such an extent that it is hard to know where the one ends and the other begins. American civil religion is more predominant in many churches than is the exclusive worship of Jesus. Flags and crosses both adorn sanctuaries; hymns to God and patriotic songs both fill the hearts and minds of the faithful; success is the same whether it is Christian mission or the exportation of American values. Little wonder it is so difficult for many Christians to wrap their minds around the concept, so crucial to early Christianity, that allegiance to Jesus was exclusive and total.

In light of the way I interpret Scripture I am sometimes asked if I believe there are absolutes in the universe. My answer is affirmative; the one crucial absolute for the Christian is complete and total dedication and surrender to Jesus as Lord. This mystifies those who cannot comprehend just how much this simple affirmation changes everything. Not just some things, but everything, our relation to each other, to money, power, fame, community, our inner psychology, our ethnic commitments and more, including how we see God. It was this way for the earliest followers of Jesus who were baptized into a communion that completely subverted the normal social values of Empire. For in baptism, all racial, economic and gender distinctions had been abolished (Gal 3:28ff) and baptism brought all Christians into a single-family system where hierarchy had been deconstructed.

Sadly, many in the early church did not perceive the radical character of Paul's understanding of baptism and would soon develop sacred structures of apostolic succession, would undervalue the role of women in leadership and eventually would capitulate to serving both God and wealth. This deviance from the egalitarian posture of Jesus and Paul took centuries to fully blossom. When it did, as we shall see, it is no mistake to talk about the fall of the church, a fall from being the new community of the Spirit to a community that looked just like any other group in Empire.

Again, this took centuries, not happening overnight. But it did happen and we have to live with the decisions made then, particularly the way those decisions have affected us in the two millennia since. One of those decisions had to do with God and war. The early church fathers accepted the Jewish canon as their Bible. The God of those texts both engaged and authorized warfare against Israel's enemies. Many of the second century writers took these texts at face value arguing that God had acted this way in the past but had brought a change in Jesus. Since Jesus, God has called believers to explicitly reject violence and retaliation. Others, uncomfortable with this warrior God would spiritualize these stories and make them about spiritual warfare between the Christian and the devil. Very few of these writers would go as far as saying that the God of the Old Testament was against violence and war.

The early church was only marginally pacifist in its theological orientation though. The injunctions toward nonviolence in early Christian catechesis, found e.g., in Matthew and the Didache, taught the Christian convert a new way of relating in the world, a way that forbade reciprocal vengeance. This is reflected in virtually all of the Christian writers of the second and third centuries. It is common to describe the early church as pacifist. Yet that is not quite accurate. While they renounced violence as a tactic for returning evil for evil, still they did not think this through as Jesus had done. Their pacifism was grounded in a dispensational shift; God acted that way once, now God acts this way.

Concomitant to this was the recognition by these same writers that the church was going to be around for a while; Jesus had not returned as quickly as some thought he might. Because of this an uneasy alliance between church and Empire had to be forged and the later second century writers who did this were called Apologists, as their writings reflect a defense of the Christian faith in the midst of Empire. They will frequently talk about how Christians are good citizens, the contributions Christians make to their communities, and how the lives Christians live are filled with virtue. They will argue that the Christian faith is compatible with the prevailing philosophical ideologies, often taking over from these philosophies definitions of God and God's relation to the world, importing them and adjusting them to Christian thinking.

All of this was done to keep the Empire from persecuting the little flock, persecution that they perceived as unjust and unnecessary. What they did not do was to resist Empire. From their perspective, the calling to be a peacemaker meant to be quiet, live out of the spotlight and not call attention to one's self. Now it must be noted that the early Christians did not live in the kind of democracy we have today in the United States. The Roman Empire was a totalitarian regime; it dominated the whole existence of the person and the community. Caesar was Lord. Total allegiance to Empire was a *sine qua non* (indispensible), much like many Christians experienced in the 19th and 20th centuries under fascism or communism, and even today experience in many places around the globe. To be a Christian meant that the possibility of persecution by the authorities was always around the corner. But, resisting Empire then meant certain death even as it does today under totalitarian regimes.

It is little wonder these early Christian thinkers would seek to find ways of making peace with Empire. However, this attempt at conciliation had one fundamental drawback. It caused these writers to miss the fact that Jesus did not teach quietism nor doormat pacifism but nonviolent resistance. One of the (many) important merits of the work of New Testament scholar Walter Wink is his clear demonstration that Jesus' injunction in Matthew 5:38-48 does not counsel letting others abuse you.[ciii] The Greek verb used (*antistenai*) does not mean be a doormat, it means that when you are abused (persecuted), you 'speak truth to power' by engaging in actions which, while nonviolent, are also resistant. Turning the other cheek does not mean letting someone strike you over and over. It is a way of calling attention to the abuse in a nonviolent fashion such that the abuser will recognize the futility of their actions.

Early Christian Involvement in Violence

It is no surprise when it comes to the issue of early Christian involvement in military service, writers from just-war traditions can find evidence that such was possible in the early church. What they fail to recognize is that at this stage of the church's development, the examples they adduce are rare and marginal. One simply never finds evidence that Christians justified military service as a possibility; killing was against the instruction they had been taught as members. There is no record of which I am aware where a convert to Christianity in these first three centuries asks if killing can be justified. It was not done, at all, period. It may well be true that there were converts to Christianity who served as bureaucrats in various capacities in the military, but these would have been few and far between.

Some scholars note that early Christian objection to military service was not due to the possibility of violence but rather to the problem the Christian would have encountered with sacrifice and idolatry. This is not completely true. A major writer from the late second and early third century, Tertullian, of Carthage in North Africa, offers both the problems of violence and idolatry as reasons why Christians could not serve as soldiers. The focus is more often the issue of idolatry, leading some writers to say that contemporary objections to Christian participation in military service using conscientious objection to killing as a reason don't cut the mustard. No one in the early church really groused about the problem of killing, why should it be an issue today? The early church really didn't maximize the issue of violence. Therefore they really weren't all that into pacifism were they?

These kinds of questions are red herrings for they fail to take into consideration the emphasis on nonviolence found in the teaching of the church. This would be akin to saying that just because abortion isn't mentioned in the New Testament, and only rarely in the early church, we can use the early church as an example of a community that must have thought it morally feasible to practice abortion. Hardly. The early church was totally pro-life, including stringent prohibitions against killing of any kind, even for so-called Christian soldiers. It is disingenuous to try and use an argument from (virtual) silence to justify contemporary practices.

One clear sign of the early church's acceptance of a nonviolent posture can be seen, among other places, in the attitudes of the church fathers toward military service and military involvement in violence. Hans von Campenhausen summarizes the position of the early church when he points out that "not a single one of the Fathers doubted that, in the world as it is, war is inevitable, and consequently, they saw no reason to condemn the military profession in particular. It is of the very essence of the world to be obliged to shed blood, whether in war or in legal process. They themselves, however, would have nothing to do with war service."[civ]

In other words, the church fathers recognized that human culture was violent. Following the example of Jesus and the apostles they refused to participate in the military or in violence. Adolf von Harnack is his *Militia Chrìsti* suggested that prior to 170 C.E. there was no discussion about military service simply because it was not yet a live issue. But does this mean that had it erupted prior to 170 it would not have been answered in the negative? The "pacifism" expressed in the Gospel accounts, as well as the pacifism found, for example, in Clement of Rome, would seem to indicate that a definite Christian attitude prohibiting violent retaliation was established. At any rate, from 170 C.E. the majority opinion of the church fathers is that military service is a banned profession simply because it could demand bloodshed, and Jesus' teachings prohibit bloodshed and violence. To be sure, as Harnack points out, there is some evidence to the contrary, but it seems the majority opinion is that military service and war are prohibited to the Christian. As Lisa Cahill has submitted in summing up the early fathers, "violence is not part of the new dispensation."[cv]

Tertullian, Cyprian, Clement of Alexandria, Origen, and Lactantius, major figures all, have the common opinion that violent retaliation was foreign to the spirit of the gospel. As the Apostle Peter suggested in his first epistle:

> To this you were called, because Christ suffered for you, leaving you an example, that you should follow in his steps. "He committed no sin, and no deceit was found in his mouth" (Isaiah 53:9). When they hurled insults at him, he did not retaliate; when he suffered, he made no threats. Instead he entrusted himself to him who judges justly (1 Peter 2:21-23).

The early church fathers struggled on many fronts with many issues, as the Jewish gospel of Jesus made its way into the highways and byways of the Greco-Roman world. It is not our place to criticize them for failure to see things as we do today. We not only have the advantage of hindsight but also almost 2,000 years of history and theology under our belt. It will always be profitable to turn to these great figures to see the ways in which they engaged their cultures, but we need not repeat their mistakes, false turns or dead ends. We do justice to their memory to think along with them and beyond them. By so doing we can continue the hard work they began relating the good news of the gospel to all of our various contexts, in whatever country we find ourselves and therefore amidst whatever empire rules over us.

4.2 The Influence of Constantine and Augustine

Church history is full of change. One can hardly study a time or place where significant change is not occurring. But not all change is the same; some changes have consequences that are far more profound than others. Who would have thought that when a monk posted a dispute about indulgences it would lead to the kind of theological Reformation that occurred in the 16th century? Who would have concluded that a pastor writing a commentary on Romans in his parish study at the end of World War I would change the way we now do theology? Yet Martin Luther and Karl Barth both changed the theological landscape of the church. In the same way, who would have thought that an emperor's vision of a cross in the sky would permanently alter the way the church conducted itself amid Empire or that a little girl singing would bring about the conversion of one of the most, if not the most, significant Christian thinkers ever? Yet such happened in the early fourth and fifth centuries to Constantine and Augustine respectively.

Christians, ever since the time of Constantine and Augustine have seen the changes brought by these two men as laudable. Constantine ended persecution, Augustine provided the framework within which we have done theology ever since. Now there is much to say when persecution ceases and theology matters. Constantine and Augustine are not the bogeymen of the early church but their actions and writings have hampered the church's ability to see issues relating to violence and war ever since.

Constantine would be the first "Christian" (he wasn't officially converted until his death bed baptism) to use the cross, an instrument of imperial torture as the official emblem by which he would wage war. His vision in 313 C.E. at the Milvian bridge of a cross in the sky and the words "by this sign, conquer" were emblazoned on the shields of his military before that great and consequential battle which resulted in his becoming sole emperor. Bishop Hosius of Cordoba gave the church's official interpretation of Constantine's vision and ever since that fateful day, church and Empire have been strange bedfellows. Five centuries later Charles the Great, a.k.a., Charlemagne, would unite church and state even more closely into the Holy Roman Empire and four centuries later this state religion would initiate the Inquisition.[cvi]

The new church-Empire relationship brought about in the hundred years from 313-413 C.E. has been the single determining reality for how

Christians pursue the task of theology. We can talk about this now for two reasons: first, we live in the age of post-Christendom. This is the first time since Constantine when we can no longer talk about the Christian West; the West has become secularized.[cvii] Second, there are those who have looked at church history, seeing not only the benefits of the Constantinian era, but also its debits and refer to this era as the "fall of the church" comparable to the fall of Adam and Eve in Eden. In the hundred years following the ascension of Constantine more Christian died at the hands of Christians than had died the previous 250 years at the hands of Empire.

What happened during this century that produced such tectonic shifts in Christian theology? Simply put, the church capitulated to Empire. It caved in. It had had enough of persecution, of being on the outside. It was tired. So when Constantine had his vision it was only natural that the bishops rejoiced. They would cease being martyred!

With the church as an accepted cultural institution, even the spirituality of martyrdom undergoes the subtle transformation from the bloody "red" martyrdom to the ascetic ideal expressed in the "white" martyrdom. The "white martyrdom" transfers the outer hostility of persecution inwardly, thus providing a foundation for the hatred of "bodily passions," passions which if excited would lead to mimetic conflict. The age of martyrs gave way to the rise of ascetic monasticism.

Constantine's ecclesial chronicler, Eusebius of Caesarea, is primarily responsible for our interpretation of Constantine. Eusebius is one of the first figures in the early church to seek to discern the patterns of ecclesial history and the divine involvement in that history. What is striking is that in the earliest editions of his *Church History,* Eusebius was a pacifist! It was not until after the Constantinian peace that Eusebius appeared to sanction violence as a Christian possibility. He even leaves out of his church history Constantine's murder of Crispus, his own son and potential heir to the throne. Apparently Eusebius, the primary model of historians in the early church, came to accept the violence of the state as the price paid for peace from persecution.[cviii]

As historian Robert Grant observed, it was also the fate of the Jews that played a prominent *raison d'être* for Eusebius' chronicles. Judaism and Christianity now became the two dominant religious traditions caught in conflict. The Cain and Abel character of Jewish-Christian relations' ends with Jews becoming official scapegoats and Christian anti-Semitism becoming an institutional reality. The church that began as a persecuted community now becomes the persecutor, thus sealing its fate with those who had in times past killed the prophets.

The Most Influential Christian Ever

Approximately 100 years after Constantine, violence and persecution sanctioned by the church came to the fore in the life and thought of Augustine. The Donatist problem was the occasion for Augustine to set forth his views on violence. In the words of Peter Brown, "Augustine, in replying to his critics, wrote the only full justification in the history of the early church, of the right of the state to suppress non-Catholics."[cix]

The Donatist controversy began as a result of persecution. At stake was whether or not priests who had lapsed, i.e., those who had become *traditores* by sacrificing or handing over Scriptures to the local magistrates, could remain priests within the church. Donatus argued that anyone who denied the faith was out. It was as simple as that. This attitude of extrusion toward the lapsed betrays Donatus' involvement in a rivalry with the lapsed, understandable enough in view of the pain which persecution had brought to the martyrs. Augustine demonstrates that he was "hooked" into this rivalry from the other side, the side of the lapsed. His response to the crisis was to turn the Donatist Christians into victims, scapegoats, to resolve the conflict and bring peace to North Africa.

The alternative available to Augustine and to Donatus alike is illustrated in the writings of Cyprian who stood with Augustine against Donatus and his harshness, calling for forgiveness and reconciliation on the grounds that all are sinners in need of grace. It would have been prophetic thus to instruct the Donatists, but unfortunately violent to victimize them.

In his profound and often moving biography of Augustine, Peter Brown has analyzed this painfully difficult period in the life of the Bishop of Hippo. Brown notes several crucial aspects of Augustine's thought that bear upon the sacrificial reading he will give the Christian tradition. First, the doctrine of double predestination (where God determines who will end up in heaven and hell) had grown more deeply rooted in Augustine. There can be little doubt that Augustine is the first major systematic writer on the subject. It is clear that Augustine did not have in mind the dual predestination that many of his medieval followers would have. Nevertheless, Augustine suggests that prior to creation God had determined to damn most of humanity, and to admit only a few to heaven.

While it is true that in Augustine, election is gracious and life giving, it is also true that he refuses to delve into why God does not choose all. I would contend that, for Augustine, the doctrine of predestination provided a theological justification for victimizing, since God himself arbitrarily chose victims in eternity past. Therefore, since all would be foreseen as sinners, all were justly damned and punished. Any gracious election of a few only underscores the depths of God's mercy.[cx]

Second, Augustine's attitude, according to Brown, can be summarized in the word *disciplina* (discipline). Augustine argues that in the Old Testament, disasters were divine punishments. Augustine seems to see retributive justice clearly in his notion of discipline, because he sees the punishment of the Donatists as "another controlled catastrophe imposed by God, mediated, on this occasion, by the laws of the Christian Emperors." Brown also points out that Augustine had accepted the "severities and violent deeds" of God in the Old Testament and that they no longer shocked him.

Why did Augustine so easily engage violence as a solution? The downfall of Rome, the collapse of Roman culture, the invasion of the barbarians, as well as the license and promiscuity so prevalent for Augustine, all probably contributed to such a crisis for Augustine. As a bishop, Augustine could have sought to encourage his followers by the example of Christ, as the early fathers had done. However, Augustine had long since accepted the Constantinian synthesis and would admit that humanity required more than spiritual pressure to keep from violating cultural and Christian prohibitions.[cxi]

We may with Peter Brown call Augustine the "first theorist of the Inquisition."[cxii] We are suggesting that Augustine baptized the victimage mechanism with Christian theology. Little wonder that Augustine himself felt a *tremendum,* a sense of awe and foreboding. Augustine sacralized (made sacred) the martyrs who had been persecuted in the early church as well as others who had been victimized, thus continuing to pave the way for "the cult of the saints." Augustine merged all holy dead, since all had been scapegoated. Thus, from the perspective of sacred violence, all scapegoats share in the sacralization process.

It is ironic and significant that when Augustine engaged in a defense of persecution, the awe he felt in the face of the persecuted is the same as that which is felt in the face of the scapegoat who ends the misfortune of the community and brings a saving cohesion (5.2). Augustine had set in motion a mechanism cycling both forward and backward in time, a sacral screen for violence, plundering both the persecuted and the persecutor in the church of the treasure of the Gospel of peace. Unknowingly he merges the Donatists he persecutes with the holy martyrs, even Jesus himself, in the indiscriminate blur of sacralized violence. *Tremendum* indeed!

The persecuted Donatists became the first official victims of Augustinian "Christian" culture, a culture reflected in his influential *City of God.* It is in truth an anti-Christian culture, east of Eden in violence. It is a culture for which Augustine justified the victimage mechanism from biblical texts using the sacrificial hermeneutic exposed and opposed by the prophets and by Jesus in the Gospels. Essentially, Augustine accepted that Empire was here to remain and the church had better find the appropriate ways to work together with it.

Why Does It Seem That Everybody Is Talking About Empire?

Empire is a big topic these days. Books now abound and will continue to be published for the foreseeable future that feature the word Empire in their title. Why is this so? Writers on Empire are beginning to see clear connections between the current American Empire and the Roman Empire and we could also add the Constantinian Empire. These authors argue that the early Christians did their theology amid a totalitarian state, a state that demanded complete and total authority, a state in which Caesar was Lord. Our current political reality is such that no matter where you travel on the planet, the ultimate authority is the government wherever you are. Even so-called democracies, which are supposedly of the people, by the people and for the people have been reduced to national security states. Citizen rights have been reduced or stripped in the interests of securing borders, economies and ideologies.

We are truly living in an age of Empire. Western history is the history of Empire. There has been the Holy Roman Empire, the Spanish, French and English all laid claim to Empire and now we live in the time of American Empire. It was the same for the bishops and laity after the year 313. In order to be able to secure the church as an institution, they had to recognize the state as an institution also ordained and favored by God. Thus, when the demands of the state contravened the ethics of Christian catechesis, when the demand for violence required the renunciation of nonviolence, the bishops had no where to go but to affirm that there were two distinct but complimentary realities, the church and the state. This capitulation following Constantine's conversion would lead the bishops to begin to formulate Christian theology in different categories than they had hitherto utilized. Bridges were built everywhere with reigning philosophies and political ideologies so that the new church-Empire relationship would be vigorously mutual.

Certain characteristics of theology that has capitulated to Empire can be seen down through the ages. These are present in varying degrees but they are all a sure sign that theology has left behind the message of Jesus and the apostolic church, surrendering to the reigning powers and principalities. Others may also be identified. These are:

- Triumphalism/Supercessionism
- Docetism
- Marginalization of the Poor

- Justification of Violence/War
- Defense of Institutions

First is the problem of triumphalism. A theology is triumphalist when it grounds itself in power. Its vision of God is a God of power and might, who crushes the enemies of the church, who gives power to Empire in order to facilitate the proclamation of the gospel. We can see this most clearly from about the year 800, with the rise of Charlemagne and the Holy Roman Empire. The church believed that God had aligned church and Empire as two distinct but parallel agents of power in the world. This view has continued down to our own time.

Triumphalism manifests itself theologically as supercessionism, the view that Christianity replaces Judaism as the true religion, that the church replaces the Jewish people as the true people of God. This replacement theory has its roots early in the second century when Christians wrangled with Jews over the interpretation of the Jewish canon. As the church began to recognize its own canon, it was a short leap to say that the Jewish canon was 'old' while the Christian canon was 'new.' As this move occurred, a concomitant line of reasoning was also taking place in early Christianity that would have horrid consequences in our own time: the rise of Christian anti-Semitism. Once Judaism is labeled as 'old' and the new time of the church is identified with the kingdom of God, there develops the view that the Jews were Christ-killers. Anti-Semitism of the ancient world was brought into the very heart of Christianity leading to almost two millennia of persecution of the Jews by Christians, climaxing in the Nazi Holocaust of the mid twentieth century. A triumphalist Christianity loses its heart and soul when it abandons Judaism and the Jewish Jesus.[cxiii]

Triumphalism in Christian theology today has other forms that are more pious but are nevertheless also more deceptive. One form was experienced by millions in the 18th and 19th centuries when in the name of God, the British Empire colonized large parts of the world, bringing the cultural religion of the time with them as they converted the masses of 'ignorant savages' of the Americas, Africa and Asia. This way of thinking can be clearly seen in the doctrine of 'Manifest Destiny.' We are not at the end of this way of thinking yet, for the United States has also walked this path in the 19th and 20th centuries, sending out missionaries and militaries to pacify entire populations, rendering whole peoples subservient in order to sustain the American way of life.

A second mark of church-Empire complicity manifests itself today in docetism, the view that Jesus only appeared to be human. When Christians deny the full and robust humanity of Jesus as the locus of God's revelation it is but a short step to believing our earthly life doesn't matter much and that it is all about getting to heaven. The way we treat one another, the way we treat the created world is no longer under the mandate of service and stewardship but becomes determined by the principle of domination in a misreading of Genesis 1:26ff. We surrender the humanity of Jesus, and thus all of created reality to Empire and allow it to determine how we are to live in this lifetime.

A third mark of the church-Empire tango occurs when the church concedes to Empire the right to marginalize the poor in order to sustain the lifestyle of a few. In the Middle Ages, the poor were the majority whose very existence was to serve the landed aristocracy. In our own time, the poor are those whose countries our multi-national corporations rape and pillage in the name of freedom and democracy in order to sustain our American way of life. A recent United Nations survey indicated that 1 in 6 people (roughly 1 billion) suffer from hunger. It is not that there is not enough food to go around; it is that we who live in the midst of Empire revel in our meals full of meat, fancy sauces and desserts.

The poor are necessary to Empire for it is on their backs that we are able to drive our cars, take our vacations and say grace before our meals. Yet, Empire driven theology thanks God for its blessings and assumes that the more you have, the more God has blessed you.[cxiv] This type of thinking lies behind certain political theories regarding the poor; they are lazy, they should work, if God were with them they wouldn't be poor etc. We then go on and praise God while others suffer around us. Later on I will show that religious culture needs scapegoats. For now I only want to suggest that when we marginalize the poor we have left Jesus behind and succumbed to the civil religion of Empire.

A fourth sign that Christian theology has been seduced by the power of Empire is when it justifies violence and war. Saying this is certain to rub many people the wrong way, but as suggested earlier, the apostolic church and the early church did not take this route. Instead they forsook all manner of retaliation. When the church accepted the Constantinian synthesis of church-Empire, from that point on it had to also accept that if the Emperor (or President) decided to go to war then a way could, and should, be found to justify the Emperor's plans, for after all the Emperor obviously had the best interests of the church in his heart.

Sadly, even the so-called Historic Peace Churches (Mennonites, Brethren and Amish) capitulated to this logic when they rejected the use of the sword but allowed its use by the State to protect its interests and punish evildoers. They easily slid into a two-kingdom theory, where the church sought to save souls but the Empire determined how life was to be lived. This way of thinking has had disastrous consequences for both the church and the world. It led to a Christian quietism, an unwillingness to engage the world, and a passive-aggressive separatism, none of which has to do with following Jesus.

The last signal that Christian theology has bought into the religious culture of Empire can be seen when energy is spent defending institutions, in whatever form they may be found. The failure to recognize the deconstructive character of Jesus' teaching regarding religion, family and Empire (see 5.2 on the pillars of culture) has led many theologians to assume that institutions, once begun, must remain forever. When this occurs, people become secondary to the permanence of the institution and are sacrificed for the institution.

In the early church one form this took was the office of bishop and the concept of apostolic succession. Not that bishops are by any means a bad thing, but when the office becomes more important than those being served, the office has become institutionalized, in short, it becomes a principality and power. Or take the modern charismatic revival, where the gift of 'speaking in tongues' once meant a manifestation of the Spirit. Now in certain traditions it has become an indispensible proof of being 'born again.' Worship styles may also become institutionalized and any deviation from what 'we have always done' is seen as giving up on the church's heritage.

One can also see the defense of civil institutions, such as the modern nation state or economic theories being touted by many across the Christian spectrum. We shall see later that the problem with institutions is they are grounded in violence and need to be nurtured from time to time with scapegoats in order to insure their survival. These five marks of theologies grounded in the Constantinian era are what we should be on the lookout for when we seek to identify where the church has 'fallen.' They are the surest indicators of a faulty and dangerous way of thinking.

4.3 Scripture and the Early Church

Most Christians have been told that the early church collected the Bible. Books that were recognized as authoritative were in, while questionable books were out. Some Christians believe God superintended the process of canonization and that the current (by which they mean 'Protestant') canon of 66 books are those God wanted the church to have. It follows for them, that these are the books authored by God's self; God simply canonized his own writings through the church. Whether this may be true or not, it is not as though we have a divine telegram telling us it was so.

The Church undertook the canonization process during a time of persecution. This canonization process recognized books that had also been written under social duress. For the early church, these books validated a story that they already knew, the story of the mission and message of Jesus, his trial and execution...and on the third day, his resurrection. This story was their hope as they too experienced the kind of reaction Jesus got when he preached the life of God's reign.

Jesus predicted persecution for his followers (e.g., Matthew 5:11). Preaching this good news was not going to be an easy sell. By the end of the third century things had ebbed and flowed regionally regarding persecution in the Christian empire. But at the end of the third century, Diocletian unleashed a program of persecution to eradicate Christianity. A key element in these persecutions was the confiscation of the church's books. The question was, "which books are worth saving, worth dying for?" or "In which books do we hear most clearly the story of Jesus?"

The early church lived in two worlds at once, that of discipleship and that of evangelism. Scholars have long noted the catechetical process people underwent to become a Christian. Aaron Milevec points to *The Didache*, an oral tradition he argues is as early as 50 C.E. is actually a catechesis to be heard and memorized. When a person became a Christian ties with all one's past were severed, family, community, nation. All ties. A new allegiance was called for, an exclusive allegiance to Jesus and his way.

When it came to learning the Jewish Scriptures it is my opinion that the church until the early second century (for the most part), interpreted the Scriptures in the light of Jesus rather than Jesus in the light of the Scriptures. Jesus' life, death and resurrection brought about a pivotal change in how one understood the Jewish Scriptures. The apostle Paul, the authors of the Fourth Gospel and of the Epistle to the Hebrews all reflect this orientation.

This suggests the apostolic church had a Jesus centered Scripture not a Scripture centered Jesus. This distinction might seem like splitting hairs but there is a substantial difference between these two perspectives. Contemporary conservative American Christians have a tendency to go to the Jewish Bible and find Jesus under every rock, in every verse, particularly where a triumphalist or sacrificial reading can be inferred. The two may sound the same but they are very different. The early church read the Bible while on the margins sociologically; Christians read the Bible today as those on top who have triumphed!

As we saw, a triumphalist reading of Scripture occurs when we read about God's power, might or authority and then apply it to our life situation and ourselves. What we do not realize when we do this is that we are already persons of power in the world and we have used our power to dominate other peoples. When we read the Bible from this perspective we give ourselves authorization to continue putting our foot on the throat of another "in the name of God." This kind of reading also includes reading passages of comfort or consolation for ourselves when in fact they are really directed to those we oppress.

A term we shall use to describe this way of interpreting the Bible is *a sacrificial reading*. A *sacrificial reading* is when we go to Scripture in our guilt and shame and seek solace for the forgiveness of our sins in the mechanism of retributive violence. Now, most Christians have thrown out the ritual aspects of sacrifice in the Jewish Bible as having been superseded by Christ; nevertheless, they will also interpret the death of Jesus as the supreme sacrifice analogically, by turning to the Old Testament sacrificial system and believing that God required the sacrifice of His Son in order to achieve human redemption. This is something we have looked at, and critiqued from the perspective of Jesus; later we shall turn to Paul. For now it is sufficient to point out that neither of these were perspectives of the earliest church when they interpreted Christ's death for us.

The Bible(s) of the Early Church

Some historical context about the actual Scriptures is necessary if we are to understand the early church's theology. When we talk about the early church's use of the Bible it is crucial to remember that it was not the Hebrew Old Testament they used, but the Greek translation, the Septuagint (abbreviated as LXX), which was translated about 200 years before Jesus. It is, in many respects, substantially different from the Hebrew text.[cxv]

Every translation is an interpretation and this can readily be seen in the LXX. Here is one example, although there are hundreds of places where this could be shown in more dramatic fashion. Psalm 8:5 (RSV) reads: "Yet thou hast made him little less than God, and dost crown him with glory and honor." The word for God used here is 'Elohim', the same word for God found in Genesis 1 and throughout the Jewish Scriptures. It is the plural from the noun 'El' which means divinity. The Psalmist, by this translation, is saying that humans are created on a plane just slightly lower than God's self. Now by the time of the LXX translators, references to God suggesting human characteristics ('the arm of the Lord,' 'the eye of the Lord' etc.) were being edited out of translations both Aramaic and Greek. So the LXX translators translated the term 'Elohim' with reference to divine beings that were with God, '*angeloi*' or angels, which is how the KJV also translates it.

This might not seem important but the question remains, are humans below God on the scale of worth and value or are they also below the angels in the hierarchy of created beings? One of the crucial arguments of the Letter to the Hebrews is that Jesus was fully human and not some semi-divine angelic being. The text the author uses to justify his assertion is the LXX translation of Psalm 8 (see Hebrews 2:6). Had the author of Hebrews used the Hebrew text of the Jewish Bible he could not have used Psalm 8. It was the interpretive shift from God to angels when translating 'Elohim' that allowed the writer to conclude Jesus was just like us humans, a little lower than the angels.

Why is this important? Because virtually every single New Testament writer and every single church theologian (with four significant exceptions, Hegesippus, Origen, Epiphanius and Jerome) used the Greek, not the Hebrew Bible, with all of its significant differences in theology. Modern translations are made using the Hebrew text and modern theories of inspiration argue that it is the Hebrew text that is inspired. No one in the early church would have come to this conclusion. The LXX was the dominant Scriptural basis for interpreting Jesus in the early church. Even today, the Eastern church (the Greek and Russian Orthodox) believes that the LXX is the inspired version of the Old Testament.

There is something else to consider as well. The LXX contains some literature not found in the Hebrew canon, the so-called Apocrypha. Protestants, with a few exceptions, do not accept the Apocrypha as canonical, although interestingly enough the first editions of the King James Bible included these writings. These writings contain much valuable information particularly with regard to the problem of the encroachment of Greek culture and thought within Judaism.

These two indisputable historical facts ought to give us pause when we begin our theology by asserting a theory of the inspiration of Scripture that is more modern than ancient. The dominant contemporary view of the Bible is that it is all of one piece, "God's Word" and that the early church canonized the writings that are inspired. This is not the case and the earliest Christians knew this.

The Greatest Heretic Asked the Most Important Question

However, a more significant piece of data to consider is the problem that arose in the second century about the use of the Jewish Scriptures for Christian theology and life. Sometime in the early decades of the second century a wealthy ship owner from the area around the Black Sea made his way, first to Ephesus and then on to Rome. Marcion (80-150? C.E.) was a gifted teacher who asked the key theological question that has plagued Christianity ever since: "What does the violent God of the Jewish Scriptures have to do with the gracious, compassionate God taught by Jesus and Paul?"

This really is a conundrum if we will admit it, for it appears that God changes from the Old to the New Testaments. There have been a number of ways to solve this apparent problem but until recently none have proved satisfactory. Marcion's solution was to throw out the Jewish Scriptures and collect New Testament documents that had been purged of this Jewish influence (Luke and some of Paul's letters).[cxvi] Influenced by the polytheism of his time and emerging Gnosticism, Marcion taught that there were two gods, the Creator God of the Jews and the higher God, who was Spirit, this latter God revealed in Jesus. By rejecting the 'violent God' of the Jewish Bible, Marcion also rejected the world made by the Creator, the world of flesh, blood, sweat and semen. His churches practiced rejection of sexual relations (even in marriage) and other ascetic practices.

The church leaders who opposed Marcion contended otherwise when they said it was one and the same God; that the God who created was the God who redeemed. This was the orthodox solution, which would soon run into a host of major problems and one in particular: how to reconcile the character of God as found in the Jewish Scriptures with the character of God found in the person of Jesus. Many and varied are the ways by which the early Christian Fathers tried to bring the two 'Testaments' into relation. For Justin Martyr, they stand in a schema of promise and fulfillment, where the emphasis is on the fulfillment of ancient prophecy. For Clement of Alexandria they are pedagogically related, God could not reveal God's self all at once and so accommodated revelation to our limited but growing understanding. For Irenaeus and Cyprian they are related as differing historical dispensations; God acts certain ways at certain periods of time. Augustine's theory, which included aspects of all of the above, goes under many names but is dualistically inspired by his neo-Platonic philosophical background: the Testaments can be related as letter-Spirit or even law-gospel, but his dictum that 'the new in the old is concealed, the old in the new is revealed' has been the maxim determinant in western Christian understanding of the testamental relationship for sixteen hundred years.

The majority solution, while rejecting the two gods theory of Marcion, tended to unify all biblical statements about God in just as much of a dualistic paradigm as Marcion's. By the time we get to Augustine (400 C.E.), the most influential figure in Christian history after the Apostle Paul, God's character has two sides, light and dark, loving and wrathful, merciful and punishing. This two-faced view of God (the Janus-Face) has dominated Christian theology ever since.

As we saw in a previous chapter, the early church was by and large committed to the way of peace and nonviolence. As they struggled with how to relate the apostolic writings to the Jewish canon they would gradually begin to accept that God, like all the other gods, was retributive. As we saw in the last chapter, it is short step from a doctrine of a punishing God to a view that Christian ethics can also be penal in its outworking.

It would be easy to criticize the early church fathers for their inability to see that something startlingly new had occurred in Jesus. The fact is they were working out their theology from a perspective dominated by the categories of Greek philosophy. The first important apologist of the second century, Justin Martyr, was a student of many Greek philosophical schools before he became a Christian. Clement of Alexandria and Origen were deeply influenced by Plato. Augustine would drink deeply from the well of Neo-Platonic thought. The problem with this is that God was already a 'known' quantity; what God could or could not do, what God was like had already been discussed and decided apart from God's revelation to the Jewish people throughout their history and ultimately in Jesus Christ.

These early theologians were trying to put a square peg in a round hole by bringing together the dynamic revelatory God of Judaism with the static unchangeable thought patterns of Greek philosophy. One can see this over and over again. The God of Exodus 3:14 ("I will be who I will be") who will not be named, labeled or boxed became the god who is unchangeable, without feeling, apart from space, time and history. This is a god who cannot suffer and who is not affected by the human situation. This god is remote and far removed from the vicissitudes of human existence.

Therefore the early church fathers rejected the dualism of Marcion only to succumb to philosophical dualism. This affected the way they interpreted their Scriptures, both the Jewish canon and the emerging New Testament. They began to develop a doctrine of God that was both parts oil and water, Jewish and Greek, biblical and pagan. To put it quite bluntly, the definition of God that comes out of Greek philosophy cannot contain the biblical revelation of the dynamic character of the Trinitarian God known as Father, Son and Holy Spirit.

4.4 Interpreting the Bible

Our journey through the early church has led us to see some of the incredible distortions of the gospel already being formulated in the early second century just a scant hundred years after Jesus' death and resurrection. Those who want to naively 'return to the pristine early church' do not realize how changed it had become from the church of the apostolic era. In fact, it can be argued that some of these changes were already underway in some of the later New Testament literature, such as the letters to Timothy & Titus.

Juxtaposing two critical thinkers from the mid-second century, Marcion and Justin Martyr, highlights this problem of biblical interpretation. We have already had occasion to discuss these two thinkers, now we shall look at a specific example of biblical interpretation. How did these two thinkers handle the problem of the violence of God in the Jewish Bible? The way they handled this issue has been the starting point for almost all subsequent discussion. If they handled it poorly, it is incumbent upon us to re-open the question so we today can answer it in a more consistent and coherent fashion. Some of what follows may seem technical to some, but hang in there for the explanation.

An explicit dualism remained in Marcion's thought. The rigorist response of Judaism following the collapse of the Temple, an anti-Greek literal rendering of Torah and anti-Jewish sentiment all contributed to Marcion's rejection of the Hebrew Bible. The conflict between Synagogue and Church in Pontus only reinforced Marcion's dualism and his rejection of the Creator God and thus the covenant God of Judaism. When the early church leaders went about establishing the relation between the Testaments I think they were on the "right track" but they got on the "wrong train."[cxvii]

We can compare Justin Martyr's theory of the relationship of the Testaments with that of Marcion. Several reasons for this comparison propose themselves. First, Justin's influence on early Christian theology, particularly on Irenaeus, is well known. Second, it is with Justin that the church achieves the first working hypothesis of the relationship between the Testaments. Third, Justin claims to have written a treatise that responds to Marcion. Justin's appropriation of the Hebrew Scriptures would set the tone for the next 1900 years. It is therefore all the more important to note Justin's Platonic background. Both the heretic Justin is fighting and Justin himself are seeking to work out their interpretation of the Hebrew Bible in the context of Platonic dualism. Justin does this when he engages prophecy-fulfillment and allegory, both rabbinic models of exegesis. This is the apparent consonance with New Testament exegetical traditions. But the appropriation of rabbinic hermeneutics mingled with Platonic presuppositions is something else. The methods of rabbinic exegesis are congruent with those of the New Testament authors, but those of Platonic origin are not. Kenneth Woolcombe contends, "in the sub-apostolic age the historical typology of the Bible was at once obscured and overlaid by the symbolic typology of Hellenistic Platonism."[cxviii]

Justin' use of Platonic ideology in exegesis can be seen in the number of times he uses the word '*symbolon*' to refer to a Jewish *pesher* type reading where biblical prophecy is equivalent to current history. Only, in this case, Justin's appropriation of the Hebrew Bible is still sufficiently christologically centered so that if it is said in the Hebrew Bible it can be fitted to the history of Jesus. This method is taken to extremes in the *Epistle to Barnabas*, reminiscent of Philo and foreshadowing Origen.

Justin missed significant distinctions between the Hebrew prophecies and the history of Jesus. Rene Girard says this occurs in "the habit of tracing structural analogies between the Passion and the sacrifices instituted by other religions. The sacrificial reading is capable only of seeing such analogies of this kind."[cxix] Justin missed the strategic difference between the gospels and pagan mythology claiming that while both had the same symbolic structure, only the gospel was historical. To be sure Justin does not have as developed a sacrificial understanding of the death of Christ as does say, Melito of Sardis. Nevertheless, his habit 'of tracing structural analogies" laid the groundwork for a sacrificial theology to take hold.

Justin found a theological connection between the Testaments in the typology of the scapegoat Jesus but the fusion of type and prototype obscured any significant differences between them. Thus begins the "Christian" myth. Justin's Platonic typological exegesis opened the door to read the Gospels through a sacrificial lens, the very interpretation they demystify. While Justin fought to keep out Marcionite dualism from coming in the front door, Plato slipped in the back.

As an example we can cite Justin's use of Psalm 110. In early Christianity it is the most frequently quoted text from the Hebrew Bible, particularly verses 1 and 4.

> The Lord said to my Lord:
> "Sit at my right hand
> Until I make your enemies
> A footstool for your feet."
>
> The Lord has sworn
> And will not change His mind:
> "You are a priest forever,
> In the order of Melchizedeck."

In the New Testament there are over twenty-five citations of these verses. Psalm 110 probably originated prior to the exile, but was used by the post Maccabean family (the Hasmoneans) to justify their royal and priestly prerogatives. In addition to the priestly Melchizedeck, they also claimed the violent Phineas as a model (see Num. 25: 6-18, I Macc. 2:26ff). The violence of Psalm 110, verses 2-3 and 5-6, admirably suited a militant interpretation of the Psalm (2.2).

However, in the New Testament, only verses 1 and 4 are quoted. David Hay suggests that this can be traced back to Jesus himself offering an anti-Hasmonean interpretation of the text.[cxx] The Hasmoneans were the succeeding generations of the Maccabee family in both the high priesthood and the kingship of Israel. For Jesus, a violent interpretation of the Psalm would be a misinterpretation of his mission.

I would say that verses 2-3 and 5-6 are omitted in the New Testament discussion of Jesus' messiahship because they participate in the *sacrificial reading*, a way of thinking I believe Jesus intentionally sought to expose.

The first Christian to quote Psalm 110 in its entirety is Justin Martyr who incorporates both sacrificial and non-sacrificial elements in his exegesis. Justin's influence on Irenaeus whose theory of the canon was to have a profound effect cannot be underestimated. Augustine's dictum that 'the old in the new is revealed and the new in the old is concealed' is little more than a paraphrase of Justin. Such a position continues to be propagated to the present.

Examples of Non-Sacrificial Early Christian Writers

This does not mean that Justin Martyr has a full blown sacrificial theology; that cannot be demonstrated. But it can be shown that Justin's exegetical presuppositions allowed sacrificial thinking to begin to penetrate the developing early Christian theological tradition. Though to be fair, there are elements of a non-sacrificial reading in Justin's *Dialogue with Trypho*.

Justin says, following the Hebrew prophets, that the rituals and prohibitions of the Torah were given because of the tendency of the people to sin. Justin also quotes extensively several anti-sacrificial texts from the prophets, including Amos 5-6 and Jeremiah 7:22ff. Even the Temple is not "commanded by God but used by concession that you [Jews] in giving yourself to him might not worship idols." Irenaeus, apparently taking up a common tradition will pick up this same anti-sacrificial motif. Sacrifice in the early church would become rapidly spiritualized in a positive direction where the appropriate sacrifices were those of praise and thanksgiving.[cxxi] But the damage had been done with Justin's equation of the *Logos* of Greek philosophy with that of Christianity.

Some circles were apparently more aware of their non-sacrificial interpretation. Epiphanius records a saying of Jesus in the *Hebrew Gospel* that read, "I have come to abolish sacrifices and if you do not cease from sacrificing, the wrath of God will come upon you." This is an instance of what is called an *agrapha*, a saying of Jesus found outside of the gospels.[cxxii] Acts 20:35 has a saying of Jesus not recorded in the Gospels, "It is more blessed to give than to receive." If we acknowledge that the saying above found in the *Hebrew Gospel* could have come from Jesus then we have a further proof that Jesus was decidedly anti-sacrificial.

In an early Christian document titled *Timothy and Aquila*, Deuteronomy is rejected as non-inspired because it was "not dictated by God, but 'deuteronomized' by Moses; this is the reason why he did not put it in the *aron*, that is, in the Ark of the Covenant." We also see this in the Pseudo Clementine *Recognitions*; God was in the process of weaning the Jewish people from sacrifice. Sacrifice was allowed for a season until the prophet like Moses should come to take away all sacrifice. In addition, the Pseudo

Clementine *Homilies* assert that the Hebrew Scriptures say both true and false things about God!

Finally, I must mention the *Epistle to Diognetus*. Of all early Christian literature outside the New Testament it is the most consistently non-sacrificial. It can be said here that 'violence is not an attribute of God.' In this little essay, the Jews are reproved for thinking God needs sacrifice (3:3-4); God has called Christians to the post/role of scapegoat (6:9-10); the proof of the Christian message is found in the Christian ability to endure being scapegoated (7:7-9); God is, was, and always will be long suffering and free from wrath (8:7-8); there is an awareness of desire (*epithumia*, 9:11); Christ in becoming the scapegoat par excellence who restores humanity to God, becoming a ransom on our behalf (*lutron hyper humon*, 9:2-6). Finally, imitation of God is possible (10:4) by which a human may become like God. This imitation consists in caring for those weaker than oneself (10:6-7) and rejecting imitated desire (10:5).

Doomed to Repeat the Interpretive Mistakes of the Early Church?

As interesting as these few cases may be, an anti-sacrificial interpretation really had no chance to take hold in the early church as soon as Plato was introduced into the discussion. His notion of reality as a duality between real and the 'created' was the framework that Christianity (real) understood itself in relation to Judaism (created). The anti-sacrificial prophetic tradition, and consequently Jesus were muted when Plato was inserted into the discussion.

Observe three critical areas where the early fathers missed important aspects of the non-sacrificial hermeneutic witnessed to in the Hebrew Bible and exploited in the New Testament. First, most of the early Christian leadership failed to understand the critique of propitiatory sacrifices in the Hebrew prophets. That is, they missed the insight that there was a development away from all sacrifice, and that God neither wanted nor desired sacrifices (Psalm 40; Jer. 7; Amos 5; Psalm 51, etc). Had they perceived this they would not have lain the framework for the later church to speak of God in almost schizophrenic terms. In what appears to become a tortured discussion in later Christian theology, the work of the Son somehow appeases the wrath and hatred of the father who loves (sic) humanity. God's anger and mercy battle like mythological Titans. And this battle is still reflected in contemporary doctrines of the atonement.

Second, many early Christian interpreters missed the significance of the founding murder in Genesis 4. Only in *I Clement* and a century later in Irenaeus are Cain and Abel even mentioned. The crucial role of imitation in Genesis that issues in violence and sacrifice and the unmasking of the victim in Genesis 4 is muted when Augustine interprets Genesis 3 through his neo-

Platonist glasses and blames humanity's fall on sexual desire. The other significant person to pick up on this some 1500 years later also, namely Sigmund Freud, like Augustine, missed the founding murder. Sexual desire, like before, became the culprit.

Finally, I would contend that early Christian thinkers tended to miss the selective use of the Hebrew Scriptures in the New Testament; a hermeneutic approach I believe can be traced back to Jesus' exegesis of the Hebrew Bible. There is no wholesale appropriation of the Hebrew Scriptures in the New Testament. In short, the church's indulgence in dualistic categories set up conflict in all of its subsequent theological discussion.

The disastrous dualism that plagued early Christian controversies continues to do so to the present day. Colin Gunton claims that what the doctrine of impassability (that God the Father cannot suffer) was to the church fathers, post-Kantian dualism is to modern theology (the split between what you know and what is really there). God is 'beyond' and there is no bridge between there and here; hence, there can be no suffering God. Indeed the patripassionist debate of the second and third centuries (could God suffer, did the Father also suffer or just the Son?) is, according to Jaroslav Pelikan, the same issue that faced Marcion and the Gnostics, viz., "the crucifixion and death of the one who was called God." It is no mistake that the very crisis of bringing together the two Testaments, and the two different understandings of God, was also the time when the church turned to the Platonic notion of the unchanging God. Either God changes or God doesn't change. Or we have got God wrong. And this last is tough to admit. So tough in fact as to be unthinkable for those who were transforming Christianity from a persecuted movement into an institution of power.

The point of exploring this issue is to note that the troublesome problem of the violence of God in the Hebrew Bible played a key role in how the early church understood God. While it is true that the ethics they taught were nonviolent (as we saw in *The Didache* and the Gospel of Matthew), they could not see what Jesus also taught was the theology of a nonviolent God. Their Platonism blinded them.

We are at the end of the first half of this study. The call to discipleship, to follow Jesus in every aspect of our life, theology and spirituality has been front and center. We have seen how the apostolic church took its cue from Jesus and worked out its ways of presenting his story. He was their Alpha and Omega and the Way between their starting and ending points. We also took a small detour into the church of the second through fourth centuries to show how quickly and easily the message of Jesus got mixed up with pagan religious concepts. Our goal is to get back to Jesus, the Jesus of the Gospels, the Jesus borne witness to by the apostolic church, the rabbi from

Nazareth, the True Human, the incarnate logic (*logos*) of God. Just as we have needed to deconstruct our Doctrine of God in light of the cross of Jesus, so also now it becomes important to deconstruct our understanding of what it means to be human.

When we say that we believe that Jesus is truly human, or Jesus assumed our humanity or Jesus knows what it is like to be human, the question is begged, 'What do we understand by the term 'human?' In the next chapter we will look at a more fruitful way of understanding what being human is all about. Then it will become clear why it is so essential for us to follow Jesus, the True Human, and how and why following him changes the way we think.[cxxiii]

Chapter 5 Understanding Human Culture

5.1 What Does It Mean To Be Human?

Terms like culture and humanity are easily thrown about on the assumption we all mean something we have agreed upon when we use them. If I ask you what it means to be human, what constitutes humanness, you might say rationality or language or the ability to invent or free will, self-determination or any of a host of other terms.

The study of what it means to be human has branched out into all kinds of disciplines, some physical, like biology or neurophysiology; others are interpretive like psychology, cultural anthropology, theology, political science and philosophy. Many are the ways we could describe what it means to be human. We most likely have as many disagreements about what it means to be human as we have disagreements about what it means for God to be God. This is our dilemma. We have not settled, as a species, on the way we understand ourselves.

In this chapter I will introduce a new way of understanding what it means to be human. It has been emerging for the last fifty years and is the only way of thinking I know of that makes sense of scientific data from both the human and physical sciences. We ought not bypass science in our description of humanity, even if we take our definition of what it means to be truly human from Jesus. This new approach is a great benefit to the modern church because it understands humanity holistically. More so, to our benefit, it takes conversation with both science and the Bible seriously.

The battle between science and the Bible, in quarters both left and right, is a straw man. Both sides come to the Bible with the presupposition that the Bible is rightly interpreted literally. So, for some two hundred years the battle has raged with apologists on the right trying to prove the veracity of the Scriptures and those on the left showing the utter absurdity of believing in such an archaic text. Neither side is right. Both sides miss the true purpose and message of the text.

Three important writers have influenced me in this regard: Alister McGrath, Thomas Torrance and John Polkinghorne. From them I have learned that science and theology can be partners and that each can illumine the other. These writers do this on the level of physics, theology and epistemology (how we know what we know); I will do this by bringing anthropology into dialogue with the Bible.

In 1996, a group of researchers in Parma, Italy, made a discovery that would change the way we understood the brain and behavior. They discovered 'mirror neurons.' These are cells in the brain that we once thought had to do only with action. Cells 'fired' and we moved our arm to wave goodbye. What the scientists discovered was that these same neurons fired for perception as well as action. They deduced from this that there are cells in our brain that function like little imitation or copy devices. When we see someone waving goodbye these same cells 'fire' as if it was our own arm waving. Monkey see, monkey do is now monkey see, monkey thinks he do. The same is true for humans: we see, we do. We learn by imitation, more so, imitation is learning. We don't first learn to imitate, and then start copying others (as we were taught by the great developmental psychologist Jean Piaget); instead, we are hard-wired to imitate *and do so from birth.*

You may have seen the poster or heard that 'children learn what they live.' The thing we now know is that this is true until the day we die. We are all copying each other (and others in our culture) all the time. There is not a time when we cease copying, when we are somehow free from imitation. When we say we are 'made in the image of God' we are saying we are copies; we are meant to copy or imitate God. But we have not done that; we have learned to copy one another in our brokenness and that is our downfall. The Scripture does not say that sin entered the world through Eve but through the male, Adam (Genesis 3:6-7). Why is this, didn't she also disobey? How is it that sin is not reckoned to her? Because it was Adam who initiated the copying, Adam imitated Eve's desire, rather than God's desire.

In our culture we can see the effects of this imitation everywhere. Take fashion for example. What is a fashion or a fad? It occurs when masses all appropriate the new in-thing. They copy the initiators. Or take Madison Avenue. Advertisers use celebrities to endorse products. Why? Because if we buy the product the celebrity endorses we are validated by that person, we can be like them in some way. Why do business people always dress for success? In order to imitate the successful. Have you noticed that when a hit movie comes out there are a slew of others like it that follow in its wake? Even this book has recommendations on its back cover on the assumption that if popular, credible people like it you will want to read it too.

As much as our views of God need changing, so also the way we view ourselves needs to change. Ray Anderson affirms this in his book *On Being Human*:

> "The implicit anthropological assumptions we bring to contemporary issues - whether sociological, psychological or ethical - affect theological conclusions we draw in the areas of soteriology and

> ecclesiology, not to mention the doctrines of justification and sanctification" [cxxiv]

Can we really change the way we think about God if we don't change the way we think about ourselves and what it means to be human? Can we hope to change the way we think about ourselves if we do not change the way we think about God? One of the debits of western Christian thinking about God stems from Augustine and his reflections on the doctrine of the Trinity. Unlike the East that begins with the three divine ('aspects, modes, persons'), Augustine began, in typically Platonic fashion with the unity or Oneness of God. This way of thinking has profound ramifications for how Augustine understood the human being.

> "A monotheistic theology, in which God is understood as a communion of autonomous but totally interdependent persons in relationship, will yield a very different picture of the humanity which is made to reflect and mirror the life of such a God in its own."[cxxv]

Tom Smail goes on to point out that Augustine found an analogue to the Trinity in the interior life of the human thus replacing relationality with rationality as the *imago Dei*.[cxxvi]

The way I will speak about being human has two parts: what it means to be human phenomenologically (what we can discern from our senses) and what we can discern from what the New Testament has to say about the True Human. The first step will be in relation to the cross of Jesus, where this type of 'mimetic' humanity is exposed, judged and forgiven. The second step will be discussed in the light of the resurrection of Jesus, who comes to us in order to restore to us our full humanity. They both involve imitation.

Escalating Violence & The Mob Mentality

In the chapter on the atonement (3.3) we saw that everyone is implicated in the death of Jesus. The mob that gathers includes leadership, the disciples of Jesus and the crowds. Mobs are difficult to understand; for in an instant the complexion of a mob can change. This is what makes mob violence such a frightening thing. At any point a small act of aggression can blaze through a group of people and morph into a full-scale brawl. What can account for this phenomenon?

It has to do with the process of escalation. Studies done at the University of Texas provide interesting data in this regard. Researchers took students and using a device that measured pressure, put x pounds of pressure on a students hand. This student was in turn to apply the exact amount of pressure to a fellow student, who in turn was to apply that same amount back and so on. What the research uncovered was that although the perception of the students was that they were applying the same amount of pressure as was applied to them, in fact, they were ratcheting up the pressure they applied to each other incrementally. Their actions did not match their perceptions. When they thought they were responding tit-for-tat, they were actually upping the ante.

The escalation of aggression or violence in a group of people is in proportion to their justification of equitable retaliation; giving to the other exactly what they gave. If one slaps, then a slap back is due; if one punches, then a punch is due. The aggressor thinks they are giving exactly what was given but the person who is being hit knows there has been an escalation, however slight, and so another greater blow must be given in order to level the playing field. As both aggressors believe that the other is escalating events but they themselves are just returning tit-for-tat, there will always be justification for the response but the blame will be transferred to the other who is perceived as escalating the conflict.

What is happening is that persons are imitating one another in violence. Unlike animals who have a dominance/submission hierarchy and who stop fighting as soon as one animal submits or walks away, we humans will keep on fighting, justifying or rationalizing our responses all the while, even to the point of killing the other.

This is what makes the specter of mob violence so frightening. As soon as an act of violence occurs, and the retaliatory response is escalated beyond control, the mob becomes energized by a new energy, the energy of passing on the violence to another. Someone bumped me, I bump back, someone else struck me, and so I strike back. Soon an entire group can be caught up in the escalation. We become more and more like each other in violence. One can see this, e.g., in inner-city gang conflict but also at European soccer matches. Of course we have seen plenty of this kind of thinking between nation-states in the twentieth century, it is the logic of the arms race, and the erroneous notion of nuclear deterrence commonly called Mutually Assured Destruction.

Religious & Cultural 'Solutions' that Moderate Violence

Controlling the mob or the group becomes the primary social concern; this is the role that religion played in our earliest human ancestors. It is ancient but it is also modern. It is the mob out of control, the populace smitten by the contagion of anarchy that is the #1 threat to any contemporary government. This is why in the age of the 'national security state' mass gatherings or demonstrations are so closely monitored by the government. As the old camp song says 'it only takes a spark to get a fire going.'

In the passion narrative of Jesus we see the effect of the contagion of violence upon the mob. First there is the defense of the disciples when Jesus is arrested (Mark 14:47). Second comes the false evidence (rumors and gossip) that race through the crowd like wind through trees (Mark 14:55). Third is the presence of 'transcendent violation' in this case the charge of blasphemy (Mark 14:63-64). Fourth comes the fear of identification with Jesus. This fear is grounded in the dawning awareness that Jesus may well be the victim of mob violence (Mark 14:66-72). The gospel narrative lays out in clear fashion the problem and dynamics of the escalation of violence in groups. All that is left is to find a solution. That solution is also given in the passion story:

> "It is better that one man should die than the whole nation perish." (John 11:49-50)

The solution to the problem is to find a scapegoat upon whom the hostility of the community can be transferred or in other words, one who can bear the sins of the conflicted group. This too is found in the passion narrative. It is the crucial moment in the story and it is the result of an imitation run amok.

At the cross, therefore, we can speak of a group imitation or social formation only in the sense that the mob has imitated and escalated its own internal conflict all out of proportion to its ability to deal with the crisis of its own making. We might call this the problem of original sin. The resolution to this imitated hostility and violence is only quelled by the even greater sin of taking a life. Great violence is necessary to alleviate the internal destructive violence of the group. If a suitable scapegoat is not found, the group/mob will implode.

We are by nature creatures of imitation and when we are in groups we tend to do as the group. When in Rome, as the saying goes, we tend to do as the Romans. It is essential to grasp this crucial element of mob imitation. Before the cross we are little more than copies of one another. This may well be what the church has meant by original sin, that is, we are all caught up in this matrix of sin; we learn it from each other. None of us grows up in a family without it, we are socialized into it from an early age, we learn it in our schools and in our modern consumer society, and it crushes us under its overwhelming call. However it is not very original, for all sin is but a copy, a mime. That is why Karl Barth says that sin has no reality of its own. Contrary to some recent arguments, we do not possess a 'violent gene' nor are we disposed to violence. It is not a thing that is passed on genetically; it has no being or substance. It is learned (imitated) behavior. We, as a species, are sinful and extremely rare is the one who has escaped its clutches.

As copying creatures we all seek to be different from each other. We desire the desires of others though, and so we are undifferentiated. It is this intolerable situation we have remedied with the religious/cultural experience termed 'sacrifice.' Guy Vanheeswijck summarizes it nicely when he says, "

> "This situation of chaos, in which people in order to be different from each other shed all differences, is both the origin of civilization and the continuing threat of the end. This process of violent undifferentiation is hanging over men's heads as the sword of Damocles...Hence, 'culture' is always – in any form whatsoever – the endeavor of human beings to avoid backsliding into this original violence."[cxxvii]

Jesus' Solution to Eradicate Imitated Violence

If this is so, then how are we to find our way out of this mess? The answer the New Testament gives is that we are redeemed through both the death and resurrection of Jesus. In his death we express our sinfulness when we kill him, and in his death Jesus sought forgiveness for this sin against him. In his resurrection, we encounter the victim who is not retributive but comes to us, one who brings the reconciling word '*Shalom*', and by this word indicates that we are forgiven. But it is more than that, for in his encounter with us as the Vindicated Victim, Jesus also offers us new life. Paul in Romans 5:10 puts it this way, "for if when we considered God to be our enemy, we were reconciled through the death of his son, how much more, having been reconciled shall we be saved through his life." Jesus death restores our relationship to God, we are forgiven persecutors (sinners); his resurrection is the foundation of a totally new existence; peace, *shalom*, forgiveness.

It is our encounter with the Vindicated Victim who forgives us and restores our relation to God that is the basis for the new imitation. We are still creatures of imitation even after we have been forgiven and reconciled so it stands to reason that we will also continue to imitate, but in the encounter with the Risen Lord, we are given choice for the first time. We can either continue to imitate each other and end up again and again before the cross with our victims, or we can now choose to imitate Jesus. It is not the historical Jesus we imitate, it is the living Lord.

This has great significance because we do not imitate a model that is 2,000 years old, but one who is present with us. One of the problems with the older medieval notions of the imitation of Christ was that it took the gospel record and sought to live in the present as Jesus had lived in the past. This is an aspect of what we shall call good or positive imitation, but it has for its example a textual model. Because we have encountered a living Lord, our model is not simply the 'dead record' but a real live virtual encounter with this same Jesus who lived and ministered so long ago. The disciples of the gospel records do not have an advantage over us because they were there; they knew Jesus. We too, know Him as they knew him, as the Risen Lord. The Danish philosopher Soren Kierkegaard wisely remarked, "We are all disciples at second hand." The first generation disciples do not have an advantage over us.

Our contemporary imitation of Christ is grounded in the two-fold aspect of our encounter with him in our present and the disciples' encounter with him in our past (their present). This is an example of why it is important to hold both word and Spirit together, to recognize that while the gospel records are essential to following Christ, they are also incomplete apart from his presence. As I have said twice now "to know Jesus is to follow him, to follow him is to know him." Groups of faith, taking the time to work through the gospel texts, in the light of the present Christ (the *Christus praesens*), will indeed be able to discern the best ways to follow him in their unique and distinct communities.

In the imitation of the Risen Jesus we become like him, just as when we imitate each other we become like each other. The difference is that when we become like each other, we experience the need for differentiation, the need to be different *precisely because in our imitation of one another we have become more and more like each other*. This need eventuates in the non-conscious expulsion of our hostility onto a scapegoat. In our imitation of Christ, the Vindicated Victim, our need for differentiation is transformed, for while we will never be Jesus, the movement is from differentiation to undifferentiation, that is, our goal is not to be different from Jesus but to be like him (see I John 3:2).

It is this likeness to Christ or conformity to Christ that lay at the heart of all early Christian catechesis as we saw when we explored *The Didache* (1.4). There is plenty of talk these days about Christian spirituality, the Christian faith, the Christian life but really very little talk about Christian formation. One theologian who explored this concept carefully was Dietrich Bonhoeffer. Bonhoeffer, who lived through the terrible atrocities of Hitler's Germany, probed this issue of conformation to Christ from his earliest writings to his last letters. His famous book, published in 1937 at the height of Nazi power, *Discipleship*, is a specific exploration of both the Sermon on the Mount and Paul's theology (unheard of among Lutherans at that time). That there is congruence between the theological model of Paul and the Life of Jesus has not been so clear to many throughout modern times. But for Bonhoeffer, as for all who take up this theme of Christian formation, there is always a two-fold emphasis: the gospel record and an encounter with the Risen Christ. This is why teachers in the church have always insisted that young Christians spend most of their time studying the life of Jesus.

The model of humanness I am proposing is neither brand new nor without foundation but it is very different from what most moderns have come to understand as what constitutes being human. We have a long tradition of seeing ourselves as autonomous individuals, each responsible for ourselves, each making choices that define who we are. We have failed to recognize that this way of 'being human' is a false construct. The reality is that we are all in this thing of humanness together; there is no such thing as 'free will' if we are always copying each other non-consciously. The emphasis that Augustine and Martin Luther laid upon 'the bondage of the will' has a real ring of truth to it for it recognizes that we are unable to get ourselves out of the mess we have been entangled in, the mess of sin, the mess of mimetic contagion that spirals into retributive violence.

So many contemporary philosophical, political and social problems could be solved if it were recognized that we are not really autonomous but interconnected as a species. We need a new word that describes this phenomenon. Perhaps, following a suggestion by Rene Girard, we might say we are '*interdividual*.' This is why at the beginning I stressed the importance of the discovery of the 'mirror neurons' in the human brain. It is also why I began this book with a discussion of the Christian life and not a doctrine of sin, for we would not know our sin unless we had been confronted with it and forgiven. I presuppose that everyone can and may have an authentic encounter with the Risen Jesus, not as a religious experience (although to many it has felt that way), but as recognition that Jesus brings something to the table that no one else has. This is my understanding of Gandhi's encounter with Jesus and why, for me, Gandhi is a more radical follower of Jesus than many Christians.

What does it mean to be human? It means that we are a corporate entity, that our lives are not discreet packages boxed separately. It means that we see ourselves as joined in every way, in sin, as well as in redemption.

5.2 Mimetic Realism: The Nutshell Version

One of the distinct advantages of living at the beginning of the twenty-first century is that we are able to think new thoughts in new ways while, at the same time, rethink older thoughts in new ways and see the value and importance of those who traveled before us. Too frequently we hastily dismiss out of hand those thinkers of previous generations who are (so we think) passé, old fashioned or out of touch with the contemporary world. We dismiss too easily those who also struggled to understand the human condition. We have the benefit of hindsight and so can be courteous to those in our past even where we move beyond them.

One of the most important thinkers of our generation is still quite unknown. He has been called 'the Einstein of the human sciences' because his work is changing the way we understand what it means to be human in the same way that Einstein's theory of relativity helped change the way we understand physics. Rene Girard, now retired from Stanford University, is the person I would like to introduce to you in this section. His work has for a long time gone by the name 'mimetic theory' which may sound strange, but is really easily grasped, you were given all the major parts in the last section.

Following Robert Hamerton-Kelly, I propose we change the term mimetic theory to mimetic realism. The word 'theory' has for many the sense of the unreal or the abstract. This new way of understanding humanity is neither. I have held off naming it until now because it is important to understand that mimetic realism is not something imported into the biblical text, but is exported from it. Mimetic realism is one of the few modern anthropologies that takes the witness of the entire Bible seriously.

As mentioned in the last section the dominant way of understanding humanness is that of the 'autonomous individual.' I challenged that with an understanding of our corporate character pointing out that neuroscience has shown that our brains are hard wired so that we are always imitating one another. As Aristotle the Greek philosopher long ago said, "Humans are the most imitative of all creatures (*Poetics* 4:2)." When we talk about imitation it is not as if this idea just burst on the scene, but the scientific evidence for it has now made it an accepted reality, hence we speak of mimetic (or imitative) realism. We are not autonomous; autonomy is not real. Instead we are connected in deep and powerful ways with everyone, those we love and those we despise.

Rene Girard

The journey of Rene Girard in his uncovering of mimetic realism is both fascinating and complex. What follows is the nutshell version, if you wish to follow this up there are any number of excellent introductions to the development of his thought. In the late 1950's as a young professor of French, Girard assigned to his students texts to read from some of the great French masters. He noticed that the interaction of the characters in these novels could not be explained by current literary theories. Something else was going on there. Expanding his reading to other great Western novelists, Girard began to see a pattern. In 1959 he produced his first book on what he saw occurring between the characters of these writers (Proust, Stendhal, Dostoyevsky, Cervantes and Shakespeare) *Deceit, Desire and the Novel.* He observed that characters were influenced in their actions in the way they copied other characters. This can be seen especially in the so-called 'love triangle.' A man has grown desperately bored with his wife. One day a friend comes to visit and shows a keen interest in the wife. This sparks a new found interest in the husband for his wife. But it took a third party to create that interest. Why?

Girard argues that humans use each other as models. This should not strike us as odd, for we often speak of having certain role models in our life that we emulate. But the key insight that he discovered was that it is not simply human action but human perception that we imitate (8.2). He perceived that we humans copy each other's desires. I want something only because I first observe someone else want it. Desire does not arise spontaneously from within autonomously; it arises from without, in another whom I then imitate. It is precisely this insight gained from a study of literature that has been vindicated this past decade in the study of the brain.

If I not only copy your actions but also your desires, do I do this consciously? No, says Girard, the copying of another's desire occurs below the level of consciousness, it is simply the brain doing what the brain does. We do this kind of nonconscious living all the time. Have you ever gone out to your car and left your home only to arrive at your destination not really remembering the ride at all? Perhaps you were thinking about the morning meeting you were going to have or listening intently to the news or caught up in a conversation. Because you have been driving for so long, you were able to 'multi-task' and focus on something other than your driving. One might say you got where you were 'nonconsciously.' In the same way when we imitate each other's desires, it is done below the level of our awareness; we do not know that we are doing it. We think that when we want something, it is because the desire arose within us all on its own. In fact it arose because we saw it expressed in another. Girard calls this 'mediated desire.'

OK, so we imitate each other not only in our actions but also in our desires. So what is the big deal? Have you ever spent any time babysitting children? What happens when you put more than one child in a roomful of toys? Do they share everything equitably or at some point does an argument erupt about a particular toy? I'll bet this has happened to you and you wondered, "Why can't we all just get along? There are plenty of toys in this room, why are you fighting over one toy?" Seems silly doesn't it? Here is what happened according to mimetic realism.

All of the toys had equal value before the kids entered the room. But when *child A* became focused on a particular toy, that toy now had a special 'value' attached to it, it became an object of fascination. *Child B* watches *child A* and nonconsciously imitates *child A's* desire for that specific toy. It may well be that *child B* first laid eyes on the toy but because it had no 'value' left it alone until *child A* began playing with it. *Child B*, not knowing of course, that this desire is imitated, thinks she has a right to that toy because she first spied it before *child A* began playing with it. Both children then engage in an argument over who gets the toy because both want it!

The big deal is this: mediated desire inevitably leads to rivalry. Let's go back to our love triangle. A husband, bored with his wife does not take an interest in her until someone else does. He emulates (imitates) that interest. The wife however, pays attention to the male friend who is paying attention to her thus causing jealousy in the husband. The husband thinks that she should be paying attention to him; he has a prior claim on her, since he is her husband. So, a rivalry ensues between the friend and the husband over the wife's attention. Same scenario as two children in a room full of toys with far more potentially disastrous consequences.

We can recognize this kind of structure to human life because we all experience it all of the time. Two co-workers are up for a job promotion but there is only one slot to be filled; two drivers on the road, both in a hurry; two high school friends both like the same guy; two shoppers going for that last pair of sale shoes, and the list could go on and on. When two persons both seek to grasp the same object of desire, a rivalry inevitably ensues. Rivalry is the consequence of nonconscious imitation. In the last section I mentioned studies done on the escalation of rivalry. In the phase of rivalry we imitate each other *in violence now* as we both seek to appropriate the desired object whether it is in words or actions. Thus far, both of Girard's insights about mimesis (imitation) and its escalation into rivalry have been validated by scientific studies.

After a period of seven years research Girard produced the book that gained him global attention, *Violence and the Sacred*. This book explored the phenomenon of sacrifice. Girard began digging into the origins of culture and religion in a time when everyone else thought this area had been thoroughly plowed. Girard argued that when humans were emerging as a species, over a period of tens or hundreds of thousands of years, they had to deal with the problem of intra-communal rivalry and violence and the response of retribution. Unlike the animal kingdom with its built in braking mechanism of dominance/submission, humans escalated violence all out of proportion to the issue at hand. Some way had to be found to deal with this or there would never be community formation, sharing of tasks and the survival of the species. Our earliest ancestors found a way to head off the problem of intra-species violence in the shocking act of transferring their collective hostility onto a random victim, a scapegoat. At some point in our history humans realized that this was a mechanism that worked if repeated and so began the process of our becoming civilized. Over time, as we developed, we used this scapegoating violence to temporarily stop our own internal communal violence.

For Girard, the act of repetitive ritual sacrifice, our using violence to stop the threat of greater violence, is the place to begin our reflection of what it means to be human. This is the great gain in understanding made by mimetic realism. The turn to collective scapegoating is what helped enlarge our brains that allowed us then to create language, generate religion and foster the development of what we call civilization. In 1978 Girard published his greatest work, *Things Hidden from the Foundation of the World,* where he systematically explored this theme of cultural development in the light of sacrifice. What makes this book so significant was that Girard brought the Bible into conversation with anthropological science.

It would be difficult to try and explain all of the nuances Girard unpacks with regard to the way the Bible and cultural anthropology interface. This is perhaps the most fruitful aspect of Girard's work for contemporary Christianity, for he is able to show that not only do Scripture and the science of anthropology not contradict one another, but that when the Bible is read from the perspective of the problem of sacrifice, it clarifies essential elements when discussing religion.[cxxviii] More so, Girard brings to absolute clarity the real distinction between the Old and New Testaments and why they must be kept together. Not separated, but distinct, telling one story, both sides, from Genesis to Revelation.

Girard further developed his reading of the Bible with a book on *Job: The Victim of His People* and *The Scapegoat* in the late 1980's and a decade later at the turn of the millennium in *I See Satan Fall as Lightning*. Girard has always had an interest in the genius of Shakespeare and in 1994 published *The Theater of Envy*. His latest work is on the impending human created apocalypse that he sees foreshadowed in the work on the German military strategist Clausewitz.[cxxix] All of us who have had the privilege of knowing Girard attest to his gentle but uncompromising manner, his meekness laden with conviction. In 2007 Rene Girard was inducted into the French Academy, a group of 40 French intellectuals who take over seats among "the Immortals" in a tradition going back hundreds of years. The greatest French scholars have been the one's to people this body. It was a great honor to see just how valuable Girard's work has become to so many working in all manner of scholarly endeavor both within and without the church.

The Pillars of Culture

Soon, we will look at Girard's understanding of the two Testaments, but we first need to have a big picture. Following this all too quick survey of Girard, I now lay out a model of what constitutes mimetic realism or a way of looking at ourselves as human beings, and hopefully recall having already encountered this when we looked at Jesus' life and teaching.

Mimetic realism is about the way we human beings encounter one another. It begins in the deep structure of nonconscious human desire that has predictable effects across the entire species. It is a three-step process from human encounter to human sacrificial violence:

1. Imitated Desire
2. Escalation of Rivalries
3. Collective Transfer of Hostility onto a 'Scapegoat'

Now as has been mentioned, the first two phases have clinical work to support them as working premises. The Bible also has these phenomena as part of its anthropological perspective. Here then is a place where science and the Bible can have an authentic dialogue, right at the heart of the matter: what does it mean to be human? It is far more than shifting chemical equations and electrical discharge. In the light of mimetic realism we see how we humans have been caught in the spell of 'original sin', how we are 'in bondage' to a certain way of thinking and behaving, and how Jesus liberates us from that life and shows us an entirely new way of relating to both our fellow human and God. This new way of relating is grounded in solidarity with our fellow crucifiers and our reconciliation with the Crucified. It is God's work in Christ that effects our new relationship to God and others.

The passion of Jesus tells the story of humanity as both persecutor and persecuted. The story of divinity is told from the perspective of the persecuted. Authentic theology can only arise from this perspective. When we tell the story of God from the perspective of the persecutor as well as the persecuted we end up with the Janus-faced god we talked about in the first four chapters. What mimetic realism uncovers is that it is only as the persecuted that God's story is told. God is truly known only in the lowliness and abasement of the cross, the place where humanity turned on God and murdered God. While we may have sung, "We Are the Champions", God sang a dirge of forgiveness.

There is one final piece of the puzzle, the pillars of culture. What has formed us as groups and kept us surviving under imitated rivalrous desire? Girard speaks of the three pillars of culture, the three elements every human culture needs and has used: these are prohibition, ritual and myth. These pillars are generated by the mechanism of the scapegoating process. How does this happen?

How many of you have that one family member who comes to family gatherings and makes a fool out of himself or herself? They can be argumentative or drink too much. Isn't the gathering always better when they are not present? Have you ever noticed that at some point during the day talk turns to this one and everyone is glad and agrees it is better off without him or her? When you were in high school, were you part of a group whose identity was grounded in "we are not like them!" "We are different, we are better." Group identity is forged in relation to the victim; *we* are not *that*.[cxxx]

When a mob is in a mimetic frenzy, when objects of desire lead to jealousy, envy and hatred, these negative feelings will bear fruit: that fruit is the common act of violence against the one. The group must displace this negativity because if they don't they will start tearing one another apart and the group will not hold together. It is impossible to create the first historical scenario of this, and most likely thousands of scenarios like it were repeated. At some point what is being described as the "original" scenario of scapegoating became the fixed point of the group. This fixed point would have occurred when someone remembered that the last time a crisis like the "original" one occurred, the all against one mechanism stopped the intra-group violence. It is when this mechanism is intentionally triggered, as in regularly reenacted sacrifices, that we have the first fruits of human culture and religion being born. It is at this point that we humans 'become aware' and take steps to bring these crises under control, so we can maintain our group cohesion.

However, the crisis and its resolution are too much for the community to take on a regular basis. So we humans learn to put taboos on those very things that cause the most conflict, food and women. Our earliest human taboos relate to sex and hunger, two natural instincts now being controlled by prohibition. We develop the institution of law to govern our existence; we come under 'the rule of law.' These laws help ameliorate somewhat the potential for mimetic crises, but they don't stop it completely, crises still occur because desires are still imitated. From time to time the group must be refreshed by blood, by the sacrifice of a victim. The repetition of this sacrificial process will have a certain formal structure or a ritual aspect to it. Certain things must be done certain ways in order for the sacrifice to be effective. From the structure of ritual we humans will develop the ultimate structure, the institution (and god help us, bureaucracy). This is *how* the New Testament *means* when it refers to The Powers (7.3).[cxxxi]

Finally after the group has completed its sacrificial process, the experience of catharsis and the new found "aahhhhhh" or peace takes hold. The story of the sacrifice is told in such a way that the victim deserved what they got and the community was blessed by doing what they did. We tell the story of our lynching from the perspective of the persecutor, the assigner of guilt and we justify what we have done. This is what mimetic realism means by the term 'myth.' It is a false story, not because it accepts a three-tiered universe (Bultmann), but because it hides the unjust treatment of the victim.

The three pillars of culture are prohibition, ritual and myth. From these we derive the way we structure our human relationships, or what we call our 'civics.' But the victim actually produces more. This is where it gets really interesting. The victim produces human language. How is this so? Like modern primates we humans may have learned to identify objects with specific 'grunts' or 'sounds.' But when humans engaged the sacrificial mechanism we were brought for the first time into the presence of symbol, that which is both like and unlike, that which can have more than one 'meaning.' This occurs when we first believe the victim guilty of some crime and worthy of death and after the sacrificial catharsis, believe the victim to bring benefits that we lacked, such as peace, unity, stability or cohesion. The victim is the first 'thing' we would have attached two totally different meanings to. So, our ability to communicate, which is symbolic in character (compared to primates which is literal, word = thing), stems from our primordial violence. Our very words betray us. We will learn more about this in 5.4.

There you have mimetic realism in a nutshell. Plenty of evidence has been gathered and many books written on all the parts of the mimetic mechanism. For now you can see how it helps us to become aware of the source of human violence and our human solution of generating victims to alleviate that potentially destructive violence. You can also see why the story of the Passion of Jesus is so important, for in the Cross, as Mark Heim puts it, Jesus didn't get into God's justice machine, God in Christ entered ours.

5.3 Culture, Violence and Religion

It is time to put together many of the insights we have been setting forth.

First, we talked about how the Christian life and Christian theology must begin with Jesus. The greatest commandment, for Jesus, was a way to interpret the Old Testament that was lived out by Jesus. Jesus spoke of God, the *abba*, as one rich in mercy and not prone to retribution. We looked more closely at the Sermon on the Mount as a model of Christian existence.

Second, was a look at how Jesus read his Scriptures to discern more clearly how love interprets the Bible. We saw that Jesus rejected the notion that either he or God were retributive in character and asserted that authentic existence consisted of mercy, forgiveness and compassion. Jesus had a clear critique of the relation of violence (sacrifice) to religion (Temple). We analyzed discipleship in terms of its major principle (trust), its orientation (intentionality) and its goal (service).

Third, we explored Jesus' understanding of God as non-retributive while looking at major parables of judgment. We saw that forgiveness was a major theme in Jesus' teaching and life and that his death was not to be conceived in terms of religion, the *sacrificial principle*, but in new terms, in terms of freely given gracious forgiveness.

Fourth, we turned to the early church, the church that put together the New Testament as we know it, to see where and how they dealt with the question of the relation of Jesus to God and learned that when the Jewish gospel went out onto foreign soil, it changed, not always for the better. I also suggested that there was a clear emphasis on forgiveness and non-retaliation in discipleship (catechesis) in the early church.

In this chapter we have explored the work of Rene Girard and mimetic realism, particularly as this impacts our reading of the Bible. The model of humanness (anthropology) proposed by Girard makes the most sense of the vast majority of data out there, including biblical data. By learning to separate God from violence, we begin to see the clear difference between the way we humans tell the story of our encounter with divinity and the way that God tells the story.

You see, the Bible is not pointing to something different from what other cultures said in their myths and histories; but it is *saying it differently*. It introduces what theologian James Alison calls "the intelligence of the victim." This is a key insight into why we must begin our theological reflection with Jesus on the cross. Only then can we see the power of the revelatory character of forgiveness in the framework of a scapegoating mechanism designed to use violence for maximum benefit. The story the Bible tells is how God in Jesus entered the cultural religion of sacred violence, suffered its most horrible side effects and revealed that the mechanism is ungodly and doomed. In the cross, scapegoating violence is shown to be the emperor with no clothes; at the cross God pulled back the curtain to show that the wizard was impotent. Jesus was raised from the dead in order to prove his innocence against all notions of justice; for we humans had thought it just that he should die. His resurrection is the raising of the Son of Man, true and authentic Humanity, who comes in peace and offers new life, who is the Model of the true image of God, who calls us all to discipleship so that we may be like him.

Why don't we seem to get this? Robert Hamerton-Kelly puts it in the form of a joke,

> "Holmes and Watson are camping, and they wake up in the middle of the night. As they lie there looking up at the profusion of stars, Holmes asks Watson what he deduces from this magnificent display. Wishing to be thorough Watson says, 'Meteorologically speaking I deduce it will be a fine day tomorrow; astronomically that it is mid-summer; philosophically that there is order in the

> universe; and theologically that God is in His heaven and all is right with the world.' 'Watson, you're a fool,' snaps Holmes. 'Why,' asks the crestfallen Watson? 'What do you deduce Holmes?' 'That someone has stolen our tent!' Mimetic theory is like that tent; its evidences are everywhere but many miss its presence, many like Watson are too thorough to pay attention to the simple things in front of them because they believe that the true account must be deep and complicated, and cannot be banal like the mob and the French Triangle."[cxxxii]

What I am suggesting in this book is not that complicated and neither is mimetic realism! If the Gospel of Jesus actually liberates us from imitated desire, rivalry and violence it would need to be simple and address root, stalk and flower. It is and it does.

What is it then that we are liberated from? The violence of human culture. Why only violence? Because violence is the seed which contains the fruits of culture and religion. How is this so? The rest of this chapter will seek to answer that question. It is an exercise in cultural analysis and it comes from two directions: anthropological science and the Bible. What we have to do is to understand the role of the Victim in relation to culture and religion. It is the victim that is the soil within which the seed sprouts.

It is impossible to read the Bible and not be aware of the cry of the victims. From just after "in the beginning" to "the cry of the widow and the orphan" and the "righteous afflicted" the Bible is replete with cries of the outcast, the unjustly persecuted, the marginalized, the crucified. It is far too easy for Christians to identity with victims, for whenever anyone criticizes us we whine and claim we "are being persecuted for righteousness sake. They don't like me because I am a Christian." Everybody is a victim nowadays. We are a people obsessed by victimage and possessed by victims. In fact, I tried to think of another way to write this book and avoid talk about victims. I couldn't. The principle 'take the log out of your own eye first' applies here.

The Violent Seduction of American Christianity

We North Americans have for over 200 years been involved in the dark side, exterminating Native Americans, enslaving African-Americans, exploiting women and children and every new wave of immigrants, as well as participating in the creation and extermination of poor peoples all over the planet to fuel our mimetic desire for consumption. We are the persecutors; we are the Empire. It is from this perspective we have learned to tell the gospel story. We live by a theory of Christian myth, seeing ourselves as righteous and the other as evil, corrupt or damned. From

Manifest Destiny to The Patriot's Bible we see the worst of this false "Christianity."

North American Christianity is caught up in Christian myth.[cxxxiii] Myth is the importation and validation of violence as divine retribution or punishment. This is precisely what Jesus came to show was false in his tradition. To make god after our likeness is idolatry, making god in our own sacrificial image.[cxxxiv] Anytime someone justifies their hatred or anger, resentment or bitterness, anytime anyone blames the other or accuses the other of breaking social laws and then makes God out to agree, entirely misses what is going on in the Bible. They miss what is called gospel, good news, news that brings gladness and joy. It is to have a theology (a doctrine of God) without a christology (a doctrine of Jesus).

How did we get to such a place? There are many contributing tributaries but a significant one can be found in the Swiss Reformation theologian John Calvin. Many others had and have taught this but he is clear about it. Calvin said that all humans could know God just by looking at the creation. In very Platonic fashion, Calvin argued that there is " 'a sense of divinity' or a 'seed of religion' implanted within every human being by God."[cxxxv] Alister McGrath observes three consequences that Calvin notes of this natural theology: "the universality of religion (which if uninformed by the revelation of Jesus degenerates into idolatry), a troubled conscience, and a servile fear of God."

Calvin's alternation between 'sense of divinity' and 'seed of religion' suggests that God and religion are one. What he does not perceive is that they are only so as a result of the generative mimetic scapegoating mechanism. The god whom Calvin would have us believe in is the violent Janus-faced god of human religion. This is why Calvin's three consequences are so telling with regard to his anthropology (humans live in mortal terror of the All-Seeing, All-Knowing Judge of the Universe), a view that has infected North American Christianity. The god of religion and the God and Father of Jesus are totally different. The first will always be sacrificial; the latter will always be gracious, freely forgiving and always merciful, full of love (1.3, 7.2).

It is imperative that we do not come to the Bible seeking justification for our sacrificial practices, for when we do, we dishonor God's work in Christ and God's work in us by the Spirit. These are the very things God came to destroy and replace with his only begotten son. It is so very important to begin Christian theology by looking at the life, person, work, mission and message of Jesus. If we fail here, we might as well quit trying to be the church, the body of Christ.

We also need to see the generative scapegoating mechanism for what it is: the satanic impulse of deception and murder (John 8:44). We must not first think of ourselves as persecuted but as persecutors. We do this first by recognizing our role in the death of Christ; we do it second by looking at all of the subtle and not so subtle ways we are enmeshed in mimetic desire and scapegoating. Our own victims stare us in the face; all of those unkind words that cannot be taken back, all of those friendships broken off because of a rivalry; all of our failed relationships and marriages, our estranged children, our abandoned elderly, our ignored poor. They are all around us and in every memory. When we do these two things, as we shall see with the apostle Paul (7.1), we are not converted from one religion to another but from religion in general to an entirely different mode of existence. We have no right to embrace victim status if we don't first see ourselves as victimizers.

What reveals this to us? The cross of Christ. We name ourselves as sinners before the cross of Jesus, as those who unjustly accuse, prosecute, persecute and execute. Yes, it was our sin that killed Jesus. Not as some transaction where God takes our sin and somehow transfers it onto Jesus; but as the actual rejection of his life and message. In the light of his forgiveness, his promise of no retaliation, his '*Shalom*' we repent of our psychological projection of guilt and shame, turn to Jesus for new life and a new way of life. We can only do this when we come as 'the violent ones' who would take Jesus kingship by force (Luke 16:16), when we admit we prefer a violent God. As our very humanity is destructured and restructured by the cross, we experience significant destabilization, enough to bring about a radical transformation. Our satanic expression of violence at scapegoats, narrated as the history of God in Christ on the cross, is brought down by the winds of the Spirit to be shown as the old dead tree it really is. That old devil has been thrown down. Hallelujah! Girard says that on the cross, God in Jesus was:

> "...Depriving the victim mechanism of the darkness that must conceal it so it can continue to control human culture, the Cross shakes up the world. Its light deprives Satan of his principle power, the power to expel Satan. Once the Cross completely illuminates this dark sun, Satan is no longer able to limit his capacity for destruction. Satan will destroy his [own] kingdom and he will destroy himself."
>
> "In the triumph of a victorious general the humiliating display of those conquered is only a consequence of the victory achieved, whereas in the case of the Cross this display is the victory itself; it is the unveiling of the violent origin of culture. The powers are not put on display because they are defeated, but they are defeated because they are put on display."[cxxxvi]

This is more than revelation; the cross of Jesus is an act of transformation, a real defeat, and an ultimate triumph. The passion of Jesus is the most destabilizing force in the world when read from the perspective of the persecuted.

But when read from the perspective of the persecutor the cross becomes justification for retribution in theology, rendered authoritative by the *sacrificial principle* in an *economy of exchange*. When this happens the passion of Jesus itself is gagged and bound and cast out by Christianity. But that doesn't mean it is not influential. One of the ways that I have seen this expressed comes from Tony Bartlett. Tony enjoys good movies and is a fascinating critic (watch a movie with him sometime!).[cxxxvii] He notes that there is a direct connection between the gospel and violence in Hollywood filmmaking. He says that whenever there is a scene of great violence, death, blood and guts, one almost always finds an allusion to the death of Jesus, whether it is the girl with a crucifix around her neck, a church scene, a pieta, a bell tolling, or someone saying "Jesus Christ." A great example is the baptismal scene at the end of the first Godfather movie, where interspersed with the ritual of death and new life are scenes of retributive violent executions as the new Godfather Michael, evens the score and then some. I see this now a lot in teen 'slasher' films as well. Our filmmakers recognize the religious dimension of violence and the sacred character of retribution. Do we?

The gospel and human myth do not mix, anymore than does the way God's reign mix with the way Caesar, Ba'al, the White House or Beijing reigns. They are two completely different realities, as different as forgiveness and retribution. They may have the same structure but their content is totally different. It is because the perspective is different. The gospel can only be proclaimed as the perspective of the persecuted, the scapegoat, the crucified. We recall what happened to the gospel from the second century apologists on through Constantine and Augustine when the voices of the persecutor and the persecuted became indistinct, when followers of Jesus morphed into The Persecuting Persecuted.

It is my sincere hope that you can see the value of utilizing mimetic realism as a tool to rethink what it means to be human. By so doing, we can understand ourselves as mimetic creatures that couldn't control violence except with violence. This allows us to see clearly how the death and resurrection of Jesus changed everything!

5.4 Two Ways to Read the Bible

In the last three sections we have looked at ourselves from a new perspective. What are the implications of this way of seeing, this theory? Our word 'theory' unfortunately connotes for many the abstract or the unproven. 'Theory' comes from a Greek root and is easily translated "to see"; theory is the way we see, it is our perspective. There is no such thing as pure raw 'seeing.' All seeing, all knowing, all theory has a perspective. We all have grids. Many think they have 'the right grid, God's grid.' They don't. Their theory, their way of seeing and understanding God, does not begin with deconstruction by the cross of Christ; it begins with the presuppositions of *the sacrificial principle* (3.2 & 3.3).

In order to show these two ways, theories or perspectives in the light of mimetic realism, we will use a section of an essay I wrote on reimaging biblical authority. I will then comment on what is written in order to clarify some of the denser statements.

> Girard says that the Hebrew Scriptures began a hermeneutic enterprise that is only clearly brought to light in the gospel texts. This enterprise is the demystification of the mechanism from which religion and culture stem: the unanimous violence against the scapegoat. This unanimous victimage occurs when a mimetic crisis reaches feverish proportions and demands an outlet so that internal mimetic aggression will not lead to an all-encompassing destruction.
>
> The demystification process, i.e., the process of exposing the true character of violence, begins by pointing out the origin of myth in the false attribution of guilt to the scapegoat. The failure to discern the mimetic process eventuates in the expulsion of the victim, as seen in non-biblical mythology. This expulsion or sacrifice in turn generates the rituals and prohibitions of both religion and culture while the justification for this generation is enshrined in its mythology.

Girard is saying that the Bible contains within itself the very method it wants to be interpreted by; that method is to see that the Bible contains both perspectives, that of the persecuted and that of the persecutor. The Hebrew Bible is the earliest literature we possess where the voice of the victim is heard, where the loser gets to tell the story. All previous literature and cultures only tell the story from the perspective of the winner.

The project of the Jewish-Christian tradition is to expose the roots of violence in our everyday lives and show us a way to live in peace. We continue in our religious and cultural violence and justification of violence because we fail to discern that the very thing we justify is our own 'righteous' scapegoating. In the generative process of human enculturation, as we saw in the last section, violence produced those very aspects of culture we rely upon to survive. It is these very things that the gospel has demystified, exposed as lies, and trumped in their ability to keep us spell-bound to its power.

> The Judeo-Christian tradition exposes the victimage mechanism offering a distinctive treatment of myth.[cxxxviii] It is precisely the intervention of God in the 'founding murder' of Abel that differentiates the Jewish myth from other ancient myths. The innocent Abel may indeed be the ground of Cain's city, but it is a city doomed to disintegrate because it is grounded in a mechanism that will ultimately fail. This is clearly seen in the glorying of Lamech regarding the escalation of human violence and vengeance. (Gen. 4:23-24)

This false perspective is called 'myth.' It is the perspective of the hunter, the angry mob, the warrior, the executioner, the hater of enemies. Myths are early human stories about origination. The Bible has originary stories too. It has a story about murder at the very beginning. The Cain and Abel story has parallels in other cultures; it is referred to as *the founding murder myth*. We should not be surprised. When humans talk about their origins, where we came from and how we got here, we find stories of a murder in the beginning. Why? Because cultures need victims. The difference between the way other cultures talk about the *founding murder* and the way the Bible speaks about it is in the perspective (6.1). Outside the Bible the story is told from the winner's side. This other had to die in order to save the community (from collapse due to mimetic desire out of control). Our civilization, so they say, is founded upon the winner of the battle, not the loser. Not so the Bible.

In the Genesis story we encounter a different voice, the voice of the God who takes the side of the victim unjustly violated (6.1). Of course we recognize this voice in the Prophets and their concern about widows and orphans, but have we read the Cain & Abel story from this perspective? When we do, we also see that 'Cain went out and built a city', but it was already exposed as faulty. There has always been something wrong with the way we humans have civilized ourselves.

As in the story of Lamech (Gen. 4:23-24), the problem of violence tends to escalate out of control. Right from the beginning of the Bible, the connection between violence, sacrifice and civilization is being made.

> The earliest stories of the Jewish people are stories that share violence, death, and victimization of the poor, the needy and the outcast. They differ from mythology in that God does not take the side of the aggressor but the victim. This new viewpoint ties revelation to the victim. Whose perspective do we hear when we engage Scripture? The perspective of the persecutor and the

perspective of the victim are intertwined throughout the Bible. In the light of the passion of Jesus, we can see the structural similarities between these two perspectives. Thus, unlike Marcion, we need not jettison the Hebrew Bible *in toto* for it is initiating a necessary step, albeit a penultimate step, in assisting us to discern revelation from religion. Girard suggests:

> "In the Hebrew Bible, there is clearly a dynamic that moves in the direction of the rehabilitation of the victims, but it is not a cut and dried thing. Rather it is a process under way, a text in travail; it is not a chronologically progressive process, but a struggle that advances and retreats. I see the Gospels as the climactic achievement of that trend, and therefore as the essential text in the cultural upheaval of the modern world."[cxxxix]

The key thing is to connect revelation with the voice of the victim. This is why the cross of Christ is so important as our starting point. Because this one theme carries through both the Jewish and Christian Testaments, they belong together. The New Testament interprets the Old Testament only in the light of the cross, only in the light of the voice of the scapegoat.

> To listen to the Bible from the perspective of the scapegoat is the internal biblical logic, the Bible's own internal hermeneutic. This perception of what Bonhoeffer would call 'the view from below' is the signal merit of the biblical text and is what grounds its authority. Girard concludes,
>
> > "The Judeo-Christian scriptures should be regarded as the first complete revelation of the structuring power of victimage in pagan religions, and the question of their anthropological value can and should be examined as a purely scientific question, in the light of whether or not myths become intelligible when interpreted as more or less distant traces of misunderstood episodes of victimage. I believe that they do."[cxl]

Girard is arguing that, in the light of the way the Bible tells its story, the question is: does the Bible have something significant to say about what it means to be human? The answer is, 'yes it does.' To be sure, it also has plenty to say about God, that is really the point of the Bible, but first we must see clearly that we have been reading the Bible in the light of the very principle it is criticizing (known as idolatry or sin). By seeing that the Bible has something to say about the connection between violence, sacrifice and culture, we are in a position to read the Bible differently than we have done previously.

> For Girard, the unity of the two Testaments stems not from a theological datum such as God or covenant, but from an anthropological datum, unanimous victimage. The propensity of humanity to turn to violence presents a theory of humanity. As Andrew McKenna wryly put it, "In the beginning was the weapon." Girard has been influenced in this regard by the anthropological thinking of Simone Weil. In a personal conversation Girard affirmatively quoted her saying that "in the gospel there is a theory of humanity." The Passion of Jesus is *the* key to interpreting the entirety of the biblical tradition inasmuch as "at the anthropological level, therefore, the Passion is typical rather than unique; it illustrates the major events of Gospel anthropology, namely, the victimary mechanism that appeases human communities and reestablishes, at least provisionally, their tranquility."[cxli]

I said earlier that we must begin our theology with Jesus and not an abstract definition of God. Because the heart of Jesus' story is the violence he endured as he was tried, tortured and executed, we must begin with that reality, and we have at every turn. Mimetic realism takes it cue from the Bible when it demonstrates that, at its very core, both Testaments are first of all helping us understand our violent selves, and then, in the light of the True Human, being transformed into authentic humanity.

> This anthropology is the framework within which revelation takes place. Revelation is then not to be conceived as a transcendent communication, a divine telegram but as a clear exposure of what we humans do when we sacrifice others and sacralize our victims. As a people, the Israelites were called out of paganism with its orientation to human sacrifice. Their texts reflect both their bondage to the mythic structuring of their religion as well as the work of God in delivering them from the bondage of reciprocal vengeance. This theme of mimetic violence "is found only partially in the Old Testament accounts. The mimetic crisis and collective violence are there, but the third phase of the mimetic cycle is absent: the sacred revelation, the resurrection of the victim."[cxlii]

When God Speaks

Now comes the key: *recognizing that there are two trajectories in the Hebrew Scriptures and that the Gospel specifically and intentionally follows one and not the other*. Rather than simply tie revelation to language or words as has been done since the early third century (in most Christian circles), we will tie it to the mechanism that generates language in the first place, namely, sacrificial violence. The Bible can then authentically reflect on the process by which God was revealing God's self throughout the history of the Jewish people as it's sacred texts contain both strands: dark and light, death and life, power and powerlessness, myth and gospel. Here is an example.

Dale Allison Jr. observes that Luke 9:51-55 is a text about the universal rejection of violent vengeance and stands in direct contradiction to the violence of Elijah in 2 Kings 1:9-12. He marshals evidence that the problem of the 'violent' God texts of the Jewish Scriptures already produced a problem for Judaism. The rabbis before and after Jesus' time had to wrestle with the internal contradictions about God found in their Scriptures. So did the early Christians.

> "In some Christian circles, the implied critique of 2 Kings 1:9-12 in Luke 9:51-56 made it, at least by Marcion's time, part of a case for distinguishing between the God of the Jews and the God of the Christians. But the problem of conflicting theologies was not born with Christianity. That predicament was already internal to Judaism. The indiscriminately compassionate God of Ezekiel 33 and Wisdom 11 is not easily thought of as heeding a pitiless prayer for fire, and some Jews saw this plainly enough. If, after Marcion, the issue for Christians became which God to acknowledge, this was only a later variant of the earlier question, 'Which texts should we sanction."[cxliii]

Thus, the two strands of the compassion and the vengeance of God are precisely that which are brought to the fore in Jesus' teaching and as we have shown, form a hermeneutical principle by which Jesus says we may know the truth about God from falsehood attributed to God by biblical writers. However there is more. The Bible contains more than just these two strands, it also contains a third strand: the new transformative power of resurrection.

> The resurrection is thus the keystone for both biblical revelation and biblical hermeneutics. Because this is so, the relationship between the Gospels and the Jewish Scriptures becomes clear in that both have the same project, "the reduction of all human religion and culture to its generative mechanism."[cxliv] The biblical texts are the "first in human history to allow those who would simply become silent victims in the world of myth to voice their complaint as hysterical crowds besiege them."[cxlv] It is this voice, the rehabilitation of victims that leads Girard to articulate a principle of major importance when discussing revelation: "The reversal of the relation of innocence and guilt between victims and executioners is the keystone of biblical inspiration" and "the refusal to deify victims is inseparable from another aspect of the biblical

> revelation, the most important of all: the deity is no longer victimized. For the first time in human history the divine and collective violence are separated from one another."[cxlvi]

If the cross really shows us humans for what we are, then the resurrection offers the possibility of new life. The Bible, from the get-go, criticizes the way we humans have been 'doing humanness.' It does not simply stop at criticizing but also offers all of us a real way out, the transformation of humanity into the true 'image of God', first Torah, then Torah lived, Jesus Christ. Most important though is Girard's last statement that "the divine and collective violence are separated from one another." I'm not a believer in progressive revelation; I am however a believer in progressive understanding. That revelation? God has revealed God's self to be forgiving (non-retributive). In other words, the texts in the Jewish canon that reflect a 'violent' God stem from the projection of humanity, the texts that reflect a redeeming, compassionate and suffering God reflect revelation.

> "The Gospel revelation is the definitive formulation of a truth already partially disclosed in the Old Testament. But in order to come to completion, it requires the good news that God himself accepts the role of the victim of the crowd so that he can save us all. This God who becomes a victim is not another mythic god but the one God, infinitely good, of the Old Testament."[cxlvii]

The above quote from Girard spells out that to read the Bible this way is not the same as throwing out the Jewish Scriptures as did Marcion (4.3 & 4.4). God, maker of heaven and earth, God of Abraham, Isaac and Jacob, and Moses and the prophets, is the God of the Jewish Jesus and of Christians. One God, two literary trajectories, one book. Indeed, this God is the only true God. In fact, as we shall see (7.2), it was the very way Paul read his Scriptures.

> To break free from the Platonic influence in biblical interpretation it is necessary to reexamine the matrix within which Christian theology developed, and as we are suggesting, by particularly examining the underlying presuppositions concerning the relationship of the Testaments. A more holistic and consistent approach is needed in our investigations if we are to find the distinctive element of the anthropology, and the theology, of the Bible.

In Chapter 4 I specifically pointed out how the influence of Greek philosophy betrayed the gospel in early Christian theology. The theology of the second century church does not flow seamlessly from the apostolic period. Virtually the entirety of Christendom will relate the two

Testaments with presuppositions about God generated from a perspective that is alien to the Bible.

> Summarizing Girard, the Bible is in the process of showing that violence is a human characteristic not a divine one. In the words of the second century *Epistle to Diognetus*, "violence is not an attribute of God." And this is really the same problem that faced Marcion, what do the violent texts about God in the Jewish Bible and the gracious God of Jesus have in common? And so we have come full circle back where we started. A strategy is thus unveiled that allows us to recognize that the Scriptures, as collections of sacred literature in synagogue and church, are in the process of disentangling God's revelation from human projections.

There you have it. For many this will be a difficult jump. It is so ingrained that one does not question God's Word. But the prophets critiqued their own biblical tradition. Jesus followed suit, so who are we not to follow them? When we don't, when we stand blindly under the arch of 'biblical authority' and a theory of inspiration, we make the Bible say something it is not saying, and is in fact, asserting the exact opposite. Only a new image of biblical authority can take us out of this sacrificial reading of the Bible. This will happen when the text is brought into proper relation to both Jesus and the Spirit, and consequently formulated under the control of a *theology of the cross.* Let me be clear on this: the New Testament does not show an interest in the Old Testament itself *as a salvific book*; rather the apostolic churches interpreted the Old Testament in the light of the events surrounding the life, death and resurrection of Jesus Christ. He and he alone could make sense of the Jewish Scriptures.

Interpreting the Bible As Discipleship

James Alison, who proceeds to develop this encounter of Christ and Scripture as the matrix for biblical hermeneutics, affirms the assertion that it is only an encounter with the Living Christ that can authorize Scripture (that is, render it authoritative). This step is essential for the Bible must be interpreted, the question is: who authorizes the interpretation if not the author? If we claim to know this author as the Risen Lord, it means our interpretation(s) of the Scripture must comport with the revelation that has been given in his life, death, resurrection and ascension.[cxlviii]

For the inerrantist, error in Scripture would mean that Scripture couldn't be trusted. James Alison asserts, on the contrary that,

> "It is one of the advantages of the anthropology that I have been trying to set out that, by insisting on human alterity rather than some supposed imbued transcendental relation to God as

> constitutive of what it means to be human, it permits us to consider divine revelation as a process of human discovery. That is to say, it is not frightened of the utterly contingent, human, historical process by which cultures arose and declined, events occurred, peoples were formed, previous events were reinterpreted, the texts themselves edited and reedited. It is not as though divine revelation needs somehow to be protected from all such happenings, in order really to be divine revelation."[cxlix]

Rather than perceiving revelation as a divine communication or telegram, we ought to be able to recognize that revelation occurs constantly in the anthropological process of discovery. Alison asserts that "this means that the slow development of the understanding of who human beings are and the slow development of the understanding of who God is are a simultaneous process, and impossible the one without the other."[cl] Is this substantially different from John Calvin's opening assertion at the beginning of his influential *Institutes* that, "Nearly all wisdom we possess, that is to say, true and sound wisdom, consists of two parts: the knowledge of God and of ourselves. But while joined by many bonds, which one precedes and brings forth the other is not easy to discern."[cli]

Thus, the act of interpreting Scripture is constantly reframing not only how we see ourselves but also how we perceive God. This new viewpoint would not be possible apart from the resurrection of Jesus from the dead for it is in the resurrection that we are given the perspective of "the intelligence of the victim', that other-worldly logic given to the disciples on the road to Emmaus (1.1). Because we have "a foundational scene of origin in reverse, in which the victim is uncovered and given back in order to permit a new sort of foundation that does not depend on a cover up", then "the resurrection is the possibility of a completely new and previously unimaginable human story, a re-reading of all human stories from a radical perspective that had previously been hidden."[clii]

Alison is moving toward what has been a commonplace in Anabaptist hermeneutics since the sixteenth century, viz., "no one may truly know Christ, except he follow him in life."[cliii] It is the revelation of the resurrected victim that creates the possibility, hitherto an impossibility, for reading texts outside the box of our anthropological mythmaking and justification of reciprocal vengeance. Christopher Marshall also points to this way of understanding our changed relationship to God:

> "God's perceived involvement in the infliction of violence is over. God no longer fights fire with fire. God has changed – or, perhaps more accurately, the human experience of God's association with violence has changed. God no longer permits his identity to be defined by violence; God actively repudiates the violent behavior

> which has hitherto clouded his character so that the duplicity of violence itself may be exposed and defeated."[cliv]

Alison's observations about the intelligence of the victim have profound implications for interpreting Scripture. I will list the five essential aspects of the hermeneutics of this reading of Scripture as a result of an encounter with the Risen Jesus:

1) "The Risen Lord permitted a completely new rereading not only of his own life and death, but of the way that life and death reinterpreted the Scriptures."[clv]
2) "The difficulty of Jesus' teaching had something to do not in the first place with its own content, but with the constitution of the consciousness of those he was teaching. It was as if they had a veil over their eyes until after the Resurrection."[clvi]
3) "After the resurrection, then, Jesus' moral teaching and his teaching concerning discipleship were able to be understood not as extra features of his life, unrelated to his passion, but structured by exactly the same intelligence of the victim that led to his passion."[clvii]
4) "The first of the two key shifts permitted by the intelligence of the victim was a new perception on humans as formed in violence, and with victimization as the constitutional base of human awareness" and
5) "The second is the shift in perception that this affords with relation to who God is...so it becomes possible to understand God as entirely without violence."[clviii]

Alison's correlation of hermeneutics with the resurrection and discipleship are the three legs of the stool of a new paradigm of biblical authority. This anthropological reading of the text is a formative new paradigm for framing the specifics of how the Bible is to be read, understood and lived within the Christian communion.[clix] It is a liberating paradigm for it moves beyond the contentious debates regarding the relation of truth to language and brings to the fore the key problem that has bogged down the church since Marcion on the relation of violence to divinity. The lens of the Cross and Resurrection of Jesus reveals our total sin and God's total grace. It is a paradigm that calls for more than just intellectual assent; indeed it requires the risk of obedience to Jesus so that, just as he is the Light of the World, so we too, in listening to him and following him, may be light to our world.

Rather than start the book with this chapter and then explore the gospel story, I wrote it the other way around. I hope I have been able to show that this way of reading Scripture comes from Scripture itself. Some in the scientific community, who use mimetic realism in their discipline, don't particularly like all of the 'Bible talk" Girard engages in. But for us in the church there ought to be no qualms when it comes to talking about the Bible. The fact is that the insights of the Bible make an essential contribution to mimetic realism, as a way of understanding what it means to be human. This chapter concludes with some thoughts I wrote for an essay celebrating Rene Girard's life and work.

> We may also find ourselves naming the mimetic processes, just like the ancient prophets. It must be said that evil does not take kindly to being exposed any more in our time than it did in Jesus' day. There is a certain risk in distinguishing myth from gospel. Cultural mythology does not take kindly to its unmasking. Whether that myth is expressed religiously, politically or academically does not matter, the voice of myth has many mouthpieces. And yet, like the prophets, we are not frightened by 'the center that will not hold.' We know that this center must fail, because it dehumanizes. By sharing in the sufferings of others and living and teaching forgiveness we contribute to the deconstruction of victimage thinking and culture. Evil has lost its power in the event of the cross. In the death of Jesus Exile has forever become Exodus.
>
> I still consider theology the most joyful of disciplines and I am glad to be able to share in exploring how mimetic theory illumines biblical texts. How has the work of Rene Girard changed my thinking? It has focused me and at the same time has allowed me to see a bigger picture, more than I could have ever dreamed or imagined. The simplicity of mimetic theory brings focus, its applicability vision. I can no longer do theology *etsi Girard non daretur (as though Girard did not exist)*. Rene does not have all of the answers, he is not always right. But he is the best guide for where humanity needs to go in its thinking and Christians in their theology as we begin this ominous twenty first century.[clx]

Chapter 6 Interpreting the Old Testament

6.1 Genesis 1-11

The opening chapters of Genesis are a gold mine of testimony to the anthropology we have been considering. Genesis is a record of dysfunctional family systems and rival brothers Cain-Abel, Isaac-Ishmael, Jacob-Esau and Joseph-his brothers. But Genesis is divided into two clear but interlocking parts: the founding stories of chapters 1-11, and the historical drama of the family of Abram. The model of humanness explored in Genesis 1-11 can be traced throughout the stories of sibling rivalry eventuating in the story of the mob of brothers against the lone Joseph. The entire human story, and its resolution, can be found in the book of Genesis. Genesis contains the entire gospel story from the fall, sacrifice and civilization, to redemption and Joseph's forgiveness of his brothers and consequent reconciliation with them.

This text could be explored far more deeply than we can do in a few pages. Rather than burden you, we will take a bird's eye view of Genesis 1-11, highlighting those themes we have already touched upon in our work so far. In so doing, we will see that Genesis 1-11, yes, the 'mythology' of the Bible, has far more to say about humans than we may dare wish, yet strikes us as true and redemptive. In order to facilitate this reading we are going to focus almost exclusively around the question of violence and nonviolence, since this is what is given to us in the cross of Christ (our violence and his forgiveness). My goal then is to seek ways to use these texts as we continue to reconstruct the way we see ourselves in the light of the Bible.

Genesis is a book of doubles. Just as there are stories of twins and siblings, so also there are stories told twice. The Noah story, e.g., is a mixture of two ways of telling the story of the flood. Likewise there are two creation narratives. The first narrative is Genesis 1:1-2:3, the second in 2:3-24. There are several important observations one could make about the first creation narrative. I will limit myself to authorial context, the perspective of the story, what it means to be human, and what the responsible task of humanity is to be.

The narrative of Genesis 1 is assigned by many to the priestly class exiled in Babylon. The Exile was the formative event that defined Judaism. Restoration hope was preached by many of the prophets including the followers of Isaiah, the priest Ezekiel, the prophets Daniel and Joel. Out of this land where they sat by the rivers and wept (Psalm 137), where the Babylonians held captive the wealthy families, the elite religious and political establishment, they forged a new hope. This hope was that God would redeem them, but not like the gods of those around them. They yearned for something new.

The priestly writer of the first creation narrative brings to the table this hope, for no matter how the world looks to us humans God says, "The creation is very, very good." Do not despair, he is saying, The Maker of all that is will bring to beautiful and harmonious completion all that is. How does he do this? By telling an 'originary myth', a story about how things came to be, the same kind of story told by all other cultures and civilizations. Our author is saying that God's people tell God's story differently than the gentiles tell their stories. Their creation myths involve gods murdered and body parts strewn to make the physical universe. Their creation myths have violence, and concealed scapegoats. The priestly creation story has none of this; God simply calls the world into existence by the power of his word. Creation is not an act that occurs as violence or retribution, but as grace, ordered and beautiful.

This was a courageous act. It is akin to Isaiah 40 in its boldness. Before the exile Israel had lived among its neighbors as *henotheists* (those who believe in multiple gods). While they believed the gods of the other peoples around them were real, their God, the God of Moses, was the supreme God. During the exile Israel would live among the gentiles in a new way, that of being dominated by a foreign power. This is when Israel made the shift to monotheism, the belief that there was only One God, that all other gods were idols of human crafting. When the priestly writer narrates his nonviolent account of creation, it is in the context of an empire built on blood and conquest. The priestly writer breaks the connection between creation and divine violence. He was not the only person of his time to do so (see 6.3).

If creation is a benevolent act, what might it mean to be made in the 'image of God?' For a long time Protestants have been told it is our ability to reason that is the analogue between God and us. If we lived in the world of The Borg, maybe (not Marcus, but the Star Trek variety). It is our ability to reason, to communicate, to invent, which is singled out. But the Genesis creation narrative is not speaking about modern autonomous humans. It is pointing out that the 'image and likeness of God' has to do with relationality; the male and female are created together and together spoken to by God. We were created in relationship not as 'individual entities' that may or may not interact. We are our relationships. Girard would say we are '*interdividual*' rather than individual. Bonhoeffer saw this back in 1933 (*Creation and Fall*) when he said that to be made in the image of God is to be created in relationship. He could refer to the church as 'Christ existing as community." The priestly narrative gives us a glimpse of what real covenanted community without violence looks like.

The first creation account sees humans as stewards of the earth, not as dominators. Humans were not meant to rape the earth but to care for her. The humans were to tend the garden, not chop down all its trees to build a house. This fruitful relationship with God, each other and the earth is the vision of the priestly writer, longing for the day when Israel's God will be the God of all the nations and peace will reign on earth as in heaven.

Why Are There Two Creation Stories?

There are real and substantive differences between the first and second creation narratives.[clxi] The image of God has changed; God, the abundant provider of Genesis 1 becomes God the Withholder in Genesis 2. The egalitarianism of the creation of the male and female of Genesis 1 is replaced with the hierarchy of male dominance. Third, the prohibition gives away a clue that already, even chronologically before the story of human descent into sin, the victimage process has begun. Fourth is the ritual saying on marriage in 2:23, and it's institution in a legal ruling (2:24). These last two signs alert us as to why the view of God has changed, for this view of God (Genesis 2) presupposes sacrifice. Genesis 3 then explains the presence of the prohibition and the ritual in chapter 2, which may be consequent to it in the text, but is presupposed by it.[clxii]

The writer of the second creation story is a bit of a mystery. He is referred to as the Yahwist because he prefers the unpronounceable name of God, YHWH. Scholars debate about whether this account was conceived at the beginning or end of the monarchy (from the 10th-6th centuries B.C.E.). For our purposes this does not matter much. What does count is that the second creation story goes from 2:4-4:26. While there is apparently no rift in the universe in the first creation story, the second one explains just how the world has come apart.

The stories of Cain and Abel and Lamech cannot be separated from that of Adam and Eve. This suggests that what is considered the 'fall' encompasses more than just a 'free independent moral decision'; it points to the relationship between all of those aspects of mimetic realism we have been discussing: imitation, transfer of blame/hostility, sacrifice, rivalry, murder, the founding of civilization and the problem of the exponential escalation of violence. All of these themes are mentioned, tied together or developed in Genesis 2-4

Jesus tied Genesis 4 to Genesis 3 when he observed that the function of the satan is to lie and to murder (John 8:44). The very two essential items for an effective scapegoating are a ritual death and a lie that mythologizes the way the story is told about the event. The second creation narrative is meant to be read as other great stories of civilization were meant to be read, as founding narratives, only this time *the way the story gets told is going to be different.*

Torah has both creation stories, not just one. Why did the compilers of Torah include two creation stories that were so different (even to their use of the name for God)? The second story is not simply rehashing the first in more detail. The second creation story does not have a seventh day. This Sabbath rest is essential to the first creation story where, when God has finished the job all up, it was all "very, very good." The second creation story begins on the sixth day of the first creation story; it is all about the human. The promise and process of redemption begun in 3:15 is not completed until the Day of YHWH. Human history is what day six is about. Day six runs from Genesis 2:4 to Revelation 21:1. The Yahwist connects humanity to the problem of evil and the bondage of pagan civilization with that of sacrifice and murder. It should come as no surprise that we are dealing with the elements of mimetic realism.

Genesis 3 and 4 recount the beginnings of the descent of humanity into a world dominated by sin, violence and idolatry. Rather than trace the fall of Adam to the breaking of a covenant (which is not mentioned in the text) or to pride (which is not mentioned in the text), or to sex, which occurs after the problem in the garden, we can see the 'fall' as the human descent into violence, sacrifice and culture.

Notice that there is no mention of the devil or the satan in this story. The Genesis story may later be interpreted in the light of oriental dualism, as one finds in the prologue to Job, e.g., but originally it was not cast in those terms. There are two players who lived in the garden, the human and the serpent. Both were *arum*. In 2:25 it says that "the man and his wife were both *arum* and they felt no shame." In the very next sentence (3:1) it says, "Now the serpent was more *arum* than any of the wild animals the Lord God had made." What might this *arum* mean? How are both the human and the serpent alike? We might say that the couple were both 'nude' and the serpent was more 'shrewd' if we wanted to make a play on words to capture this *arum*.[clxiii]

Wherein lies the deception of the serpent? In suggesting that God's withholding had gone all the way, they could not eat of any tree (3:1). The woman clarifies that the serpent has misrepresented God but then she also does what the serpent did: she buys into the image of a God who withholds: not only are they forbidden to eat the fruit, now they are forbidden to touch it. By adding the prohibition, the woman and the serpent become one. They both share in common the presupposition that God is in rivalry with humankind.

In 3:6 after the woman eats it does not say that she felt guilty or had any qualms. The serpent's promise was not fulfilled that when she ate "her eyes would be opened, and she would be like God" (3:4-5). The woman ate of the fruit and had not changed at all. So she gives some to her man. Her change does not occur until after the male imitates her and eats the fruit. It is only then that they together become aware that they are *arum* (3:7).

What then might the serpent represent? The serpent perfectly represents the mechanism of object-mediated desire. One can see the very psychology of human desire being played out in these few short verses. Remember monkey see, monkey think he do? Here it is, at the beginning of the whole story. It is all about imitated desire and its consequences. Not to mince words, but the devil is an anthropological category not a theological one. The devil is about us humans, our violence, our projection, our victimizing, our idolatry. It is not about some supra temporal being, that God created (8.3). No, we humans created the satan, the moment the male imitated in paradise. The satan dwells within us, creates our communities, rules our ideologies. It is the most terrifying 'thing' that exists because of its ability to keep us enthralled as a species for so long. The satanic has a highly developed sense of deception and a powerful voice that creates great fear. The satanic requires sacrifice. Human sacrifice.

That is who we are. In the Fourth Gospel, this is exactly the connection Jesus makes between Genesis 3 and Genesis 4 when he refers to the satan as a deceiver and a murderer. To be born human is to be born into sacrificial culture. This is what is learned, this is what is imitated. We, mired in the imitation of our violent culture, express, corporately and individually, the satan. Jesus confronted this possibility within himself in the temptation narrative (1.4). Unlike the couple, Jesus thwarts the deceiver's argument and so cannot be ruled by it.

There is also grace. It is experienced as banishment. God casts the couple out of Eden, not because they were bad or naughty or proud, but because, if they stayed, they might remain perpetually in their wretched mimesis (3:22). Banishment was a redemptive move on God's part. It was not punishment.

If in chapter 3 we see mediated desire being played out, in chapter 4 we find its consequences. It is here that we are introduced to the themes of sacrifice, rivalry, murder and cover-up. Just as in Genesis 2-3 we saw that the appearance of the prohibition is an indicator that the victimage mechanism is presupposed, the same phenomenon of retrojected history can be seen in Genesis 4; for there is already sacrifice, even though no one has "invented" sacrifice (and won't until chapter 9). None of this is in the first creation narrative!

In the way Girard understands the anthropology of the Bible, Cain and Abel play a significant role in the human story. Girard compares the founding murder myth to that of other ancient cultures and finds that they are telling the same story from different perspectives. Other cultures have myths that describe the origin of their civilization or their race. In these stories the victim is always guilty, they get what they deserve. The brother or sibling who dies got what was coming to him. Not so in the Genesis story, where for the first time the victim has a voice, it cries out from the ground for vengeance. Not only does God hear it but Cain is afraid others will hear it too and avenge the murder of Abel.

God does two very important things in this story. First he acknowledges that Abel's voice has been heard, he has been unjustly murdered. Second, though, is that God marks Cain. Now some interpret the phrase "if anyone kills Cain, he will suffer seven times over" as referring to God bringing the vengeance. Such is not the case. God is marking Cain as a way to stop the process begun in sacrificial crisis. It is less a threat and more of a prophetic warning "Look, if you keep on killing, it will escalate out of control." Eventually it will.

Now Abel's voice is the same voice that was silenced in other versions of founding murder myths, it is the voice of the victim. But Abel's is the voice of the retributive victim, the one who wants justice done, an eye for an eye. God does not honor Abel's cry, even if Abel's sacrifice was preferred. God intervenes only to stop violence from escalating. If in the Bible the voice of the victim is heard, and that voice is retributive, this does not mean the voice of the victim doesn't also undergo another shift, for it does. Genesis may begin with Abel but it ends with Joseph, who could have been retributive but was reconciliatory. To put it in terms of *a theology of the cross*, "Jesus' blood speaks a better word than that of Abel" (Heb 12:24) because it cries out for mercy, not vengeance.

Finally, we note that after Cain traveled east, he "built a city." Why a city? Why not a hut or a yurt or that he decorated a cave? Why a city? This is the real clue we are dealing with the effects of the founding murder as it relates to the beginnings of human civilization, human culture. Cain's city may have been made of brick, but its mortar was human blood.

What happens next is utterly amazing. Within a few short generations, retributive violence has spiraled to its utter limit. Lamech will take seventy- fold vengeance if anyone seeks retribution against him for killing a young boy who only wounded him (4:23-24). This kind of escalation of retributive violence at the origin of our species was the biggest threat to our survival. A short time later, the story unfolds that "The earth was corrupt and full of violence" (6:11). The corruption of our species is not that we have become morally degenerate; this is but a side effect. Our real corruption is the problem of violence that spirals out of control (6:13). Noah's time was very dangerous; it was a violent time. People were killing people right and left. It was like Mad Max meets the Terminator without the technology.

Humanity failed to heed the mark of Cain, and retributive vengeance (justice) had become socially unmanageable. If left to their own devices humans would appear to be on a course of mutually assured destruction. The human project would fail. God did not allow that. If the only alternative was to help speed up the process of the inevitable and start over, then the flood can also, like the expulsion from Eden, be seen as a redemptive act, not a penal one.

Mutually Assured Destruction?

You will notice that I skipped from Lamech to Noah and completely avoided the difficult verses 6:1-4 on the Nephilim. It is the Priestly writer that has an interest in the Nephilim as part of his narrative, but treating the Nephilim passage would be lengthy so I will forego it even though that is where the writer takes the creation story. The genealogy of chapter 5 and the first four verses of chapter 6 are how the writer of the first creation story continues from 2:3 where he left off. Notice the repetition of themes in 5:1-2 (from the sixth day in 1:24-31) that echo 1:26-28. The priestly writer also goes into further detail when telling the story of Noah than does the Yahwist.[clxiv] The Yahwist and the Priestly writer give two different reasons for why the flood was necessary.

The Yahwist comes first; God sees that the evil *yetzer* had taken over humans. The rabbis taught that humans were created with two *yetzerim*, one for good, and the other for evil (8.3). A *yetzer* is the way your heart inclines, leans toward, and tends to a direction. In Genesis 6:5 is a very pregnant statement about the human condition: "Every inclination of the thoughts of their hearts was only evil all the time." Every inclination, not just some of them. Only evil, not a mixture of evil and good. All the time, not just occasionally. The explanation is psychological; it concerns the "thoughts of the heart" or as we may call it, mediated desire.

The Priestly writer explains the occasion for the Flood by saying that "the earth was corrupt in God's sight and full of violence" (6:11). To be corrupt and full of violence is one and the same thing; this is what scholars call parallelism in Hebrew writing. The Priestly writer, working within the sacrificial system, understands all too well the problem of violence outside the boundaries of the ritual apparatus (this is one thing that makes the book of Leviticus so profound). But are the Yahwist and the Priestly writer contradicting one another? Not if these stories are read in the light of mimetic realism. The Yahwist takes the problem to the source, the evils of imitated desire. The Priestly writer speaks of the conclusion of the problem of mediated desire, namely rivalries spun out of control and retributive vengeance. Both writers together then point to the broken or fallen character of the human, so much so that for the Yahwist, "the LORD was grieved he had created humans" (6:6).

From Eve and Adam through Cain and Lamech to the generation of Noah, the story of the human condition in it's fallen state is described with all of its crucial pieces, mediated desire, rivalry, scapegoating, the problems of prohibitions, sacrifice and retributive vengeance. This is one of those things that make Genesis 1-11 so strategic in interpreting what is happening in the Bible. When one spends time trying to defend its historical veracity or disapproving it by mocking its naiveté, all of the rich anthropological data it contains can be missed.

It is important that the story be told two ways for this indicates that there is more than one way to tell a story. Torah is not a monolithic voice, it never has been. If it were one voice, the rabbis would never have had to be as skilled as they were (and are today) to interpret it. Torah has two voices, that of the human persecutor and that of the human victim and it is the latter to whom God turns and whom God favors.

The story is not at an end though. If we had time we would look at Noah's sacrifice and an introduction to the Janus-faced God (8:20-21), who because of sacrifice, changes his mind. I note again that when a Janus-faced God is found in the text, it is already an indication we are in the world of myth (an account given by the victor to justify their sacred violence). Even if the story is struggling to break out of it, the starting point is the religious myth of human projection. The double telling of the human story, our side and God's side are both essential elements of the biblical text.

The opening mythology of the biblical text ends dramatically. The humans are going to declare themselves divinity by building "a tower that reaches to the heavens" (11:4). If there is a god that god will fall. They do this for two reasons, 1) "to make a name for ourselves" and 2) so they "will not be scattered over the face of the earth." The first reason is the desire to be the model, the one whom all will imitate. To make a name for oneself is to be publically acknowledged in what one does. The second reason is to alleviate the possibility that some kind of internal implosion would blast them around the planet. This is the indication that rivalries have escalated out of control, that the community is in a crisis and it needs help now.

The Tower, it is the Tower that will save them. By means of the Tower they will have an effective antidote to their rivalrous crises. The Tower was meant to be a permanent fixture; instead of stones and mortar, it went high-tech with bricks and tar. It would secure the community's future and guarantee its prosperity. What was this Tower? It is commonly referred to as a ziggurat, a pyramidal building with a flat top. What do you suppose was at the top of this building? An altar, blood, a priest, humans to be sacrificed, knives, bowls, fire; in short, everything that any good Neolithic cleric would need. If you need a visual on this check out Mel Gibson's movie *Apocalypto*. The thing at the top of this Tower that will save humanity is the enactment of the originary murder, the ritual repetition of which is the mechanism that generates the structure and power of human culture. This is why it has to go, from God's perspective it must be destroyed.

God saves humanity from becoming forever beholden to the allure of power and violence. As with all of the other stories in the Genesis mythology, the Tower story is ultimately redemptive. It is not for nothing that some scholars see a direct allusion to the Babel story on the Day of Pentecost (Acts 2:1-13). The language of humanity, which had been put asunder, is now restored by the speech of the Spirit of God as witness is given to the work of Jesus.

This has been a very brief foray into these eleven chapters. Genesis will continue to develop all of these themes in the stories of the patriarchs, Abraham, Isaac and Jacob. This way of reading the Genesis text is, I think, far more illuminating and potentially transformative than either an apologetic or a dismissive approach. We will now see how some of these Genesis story lines play out in some other Jewish Scriptural writings.

6.2 Psalms and Job

In a humorous look at the question of David's authorship of many of the psalms, Bono says:

> "David was a star, the Elvis of the Bible…it is not clear to me how many, if any, of these psalms David or his son Solomon really wrote. Some scholars suggest the royals never dampened their nibs and that there was a host of Holy Ghost writers. Who cares? I didn't buy Leiber and Stoller…they were just songwriters…I bought Elvis."[clxv]

David is a strange figure within the pages of the Jewish Bible. He has many sides. Some scholars observe that there are really a number of ways David's story was told and they all made it into the biblical canon! No wonder David appears to be all over the map emotionally, morally and geographically from Samuel – Chronicles.[clxvi] Nevertheless there is something about the underdog winning that we connect with in David's story. From Shepherd to King, David's story as told in the Bible is like a Disney tale directed by Quentin Tarantino. The highs and lows make for constant suspense, yet his ultimate triumph over Saul, the king nobody wanted, not even God (I Samuel 8:1-9), and David's expansion of the kingdom and the Temple project were destined to make him great in the folklore of Judaism. David: Shepherd, Rock Star, Warrior, King.

The Psalms, perhaps some of them by David, were the songs of the Jewish people, primarily sung by the priests and Levites in the Temple. However, the people sang some, like Psalms 113-118 at feast times. Songs have a way of saying things that words alone cannot say. The combination of music and words into a song is something we all understand, from those who love Mozart to Deadheads.

Reading the Book of Psalms is not like walking into a small town hardware store; it is more akin to going to a Super Wal-Mart! Not only are there oodles and oodles of psalms but they also seem to naturally fall into certain groups. Walter Bruggemann (*Message of the Psalms*) says that the psalms can pretty much fit into three categories:

- Orientation
- Disorientation
- New orientation

Some psalms help orient the people of God to God's promises. Some question God's existence or love. Finally some reorient to a new perspective. But it is all three together that constitute the songbook. The Psalter gives us a method: orientation, disorientation and reorientation. Its very structure says that reading the Bible will change your theology. If it doesn't you are not reading it the way it gives itself to be read. This three-fold model is identical to that proposed by philosopher Paul Ricoeur who said we first accept blindly what we are told (orientation), then we begin to question what we have been told (disorientation) and finally we arrive at an informed belief (reorientation). Ricoeur called these phases' first naiveté, critical distance and second naiveté. These are the intellectual steps we take as we are moving from religion to revelation, from childish steps to adult wisdom.

This use of the Psalms can be seen in the songs of U2. Their hit song '40' based on Psalm 40 became their signature show ender.

> "I waited patiently for the Lord
> He turned to me and heard my cry
> He lifted me out of the slimy pit
> Out of the mud and mire."

Like the Psalmist, Bono's lyrics frequently question the way we look at the world. His words and metaphors are deeply informed by Scripture, but they are not religious. They reflect the way of seeing that we have been describing, the perspective of the outcast, the marginalized, and the poor, the scapegoats of our world. It is no surprise to find that the Psalms have been influential for Bono, as they have been for songwriters and poets down through the ages, and for Jesus too.

Richard Hays has shown that the early church read many of the Psalms as though Jesus was the speaker. He says,

> "How widespread was the hermeneutical convention of hearing Christ's voice in the Psalms: John, the Synoptics and Hebrews all bear witness, independently of Paul and of one another, to this interpretive tradition."[clxvii]

In psalm after psalm one hears a new voice, the voice of the downtrodden, the depressed, the suicidal, the bitter, the angry and the lonely.[clxviii] We hear the voice of those who have lost some hope, those who have lost all hope and others who can't imagine what hope is. Donald Juel says,

> "Nor is it surprising that Jesus' followers turned to the Psalter to understand his crucifixion. The suffering of the righteous was a matter of considerable interest to the religious community out of whose experience and for whom the Psalms were composed."[clxix]

The agony of so many psalms grabs us viscerally and can bring us to tears. Our tears may be insincere, however, if we walk away from our reading and then do to someone that which happened to the psalmist. Our tears are salvific when we see ourselves as the persecutor and so seek ways to make amends and mending in our relationships. Late Antique theologian (c. 579-649) John Climacus said, "Tears are a second baptism."

Some psalms are notoriously difficult to read today because our notion of vengeance and its relationship to justice has changed dramatically. We no longer hope that a blessing is given to those who seize our enemy's infant babies and, holding them by their little legs, smash their heads against boulders (Psalm 137:9). Nevertheless there is an invective in some psalms; the desire for retribution is intense. A kinsman redeemer is sought (a *go'el*): one who will even the score for the victim's clan, a champion of justice. These psalms are known as Imprecatory Psalms: the word imprecatory refers to being cursed by God. The psalmist is so angry that he invokes the Almighty to rain down vengeance with a passion.

Interpreting the Imprecatory Psalms

The Imprecatory psalms are 7, 35, 55, 58, 59, 69, 79, 109, 137 and 139. We will take a look at these psalms. Some interpreters come to these psalms and mistakenly see a one for one correspondence between the viewpoint of the writer and theological data. John Piper is a clear exponent of this view:

> There is a kind of hate for the sinner (viewed as morally corrupt and hostile to God) that may coexist with pity and even a desire for their salvation. You may hate spinach without opposing its good use. The imprecatory Psalms were not avoided by Jesus. At least one of the most severe of them (Psalm 69) seems to have been a favorite from which Jesus, in his human nature, drew guidance and encouragement and self-understanding. (John 15:25=Psalm 69:4, "They hated me without cause." John 2:17=Psalm 69:9, "Zeal for your house has eaten me up." Matthew 27:24=Psalm 69:21, "They gave me gall for my food.") This is a Psalm which prays, "Pour out your indignation on them, and let your burning anger overtake them" (69:24).[clxx]

Piper concludes that because Jesus referred to the Imprecatory psalms he thereby accepted the implicit theology of the psalms. In earlier chapters we saw that such is not the case when Jesus read his Bible. Strangely Piper says these psalms provided comfort to Jesus' 'human nature.' Does this mean that Piper recognizes what we have been saying all along, viz., that God is non-retributive? That the 'divine side' of Jesus would have nothing to do with imprecation? This may not be what Piper is consciously saying but it is suggestive. So let's look at some of the Imprecatory psalms. It will be very helpful to have a Bible open at this point so you can read the entire psalm. We begin with the observation that in each of these psalms something has happened to de-center or destabilize the speaker; they are in a state of disorientation.

Psalm 7 is a psalm of the righteous suffering person. Nowhere is God asked to slay anyone. What is more is that the apparent militant justice of verses 12-13 is never dispensed, from on high at least. Divine justice allows evil consequences to come back upon the head of the evildoer (Psalm 35:7-8). Nothing very imprecatory here.

Psalm 35 is a prayer for vindication. While it is allegedly a Psalm of David, notice who is talking: "the poor and the needy from those who rob them" (35:10). The psalmist is in the position of the scapegoat at a trial in a kangaroo court where there are "ruthless witnesses" "slanderers" and "mockers." He is being unjustly condemned. He does not want to be the victim that keeps violence at bay, he doesn't deserve to be and asks God to vindicate him but nowhere does the writer ask for hellfire and brimstone.

How do you feel when a good friend turns against you? This was what distressed the author of Psalm 55. What is the problem as the author sees it? "I see violence and strife in the city" (55:9). There it is again, the problem is violence. There is also the threat of violence and the deception of violence (55:11). Our singer believes that God afflicts the wicked (55:19) but does not say how except to note, "God will bring down the wicked into the pit of corruption."

The writer of Psalm 58 felt the same way. It begins, lo and behold, with, you guessed it, the problem of violence

> Do you rulers indeed speak justly?
> Do you judge uprightly among men?
> No, in your heat you devise injustice
> And your hands mete out violence on the earth.

This writer's anger is boiling over against his enemies, it borders on the venomous. He asks God to break their teeth right in their mouths (58:6, God as Jack Dempsey on steroids), indeed "the righteous will be glad when they are avenged, when they bathe their feet in the blood of the wicked" (58:10). This is a person who is having more than a bad hair day. What they are facing is systemic injustice from the elite who are at war with one another. While I can certainly empathize with this writer's sentiment, I also know that, unlike myths where the victim has no voice, our author does have a voice. His victim state is one caught up in retribution, like that of Abel. We should expect these kinds of psalms, for they are true to how people can feel about their experiences. But there is no reason to presume that the view of God assumed by the psalmist was correct.

"Don't kill them, torture them." This is what the writer of Psalm 59 wants (59:11). He wants them to be eventually annihilated: "Consume them in wrath, consume them till they are no more" (59:13). Notice that like many of the imprecatory psalms this is the story of an individual being pursued by "enemies" plural, by a group or a mob. It is totally understandable why they feel the way they do.

Psalm 69 is, as we have seen, a key psalm for those who assert that the view of God presumed by the psalmists is theologically correct. Piper says that "The apostle Paul quoted the very imprecatory words of Psalm 69:22-23 in Romans 11:9-10 as having Old Testament authority. This means Paul regarded the very words of imprecation as inspired and not sinful, personal words of vengeance." I could not disagree more. This again, is a single victim at the mercy of the many: "Those who hate me without a reason outnumber the hairs on my head." The entire community is dead set against this one. The scapegoating mechanism is about to claim another victim, another human sacrifice. The lies and innuendos have made him a person without favor; his own family has turned against him, he is reduced to a Job-like state. This writer too seeks the ultimate retribution that the group be annihilated "May they be blotted out of the book of life and not be listed with the righteous." The writer is asking God not to do what God did with Cain, but to let the mechanism of scapegoating violence crash in upon itself (69:22-23) as an expression of God's wrath (69:24). The emotion is again understandable but God is Janus-faced for this speaker.

Some psalmists can get really nasty, especially when it comes to matters of national security. In Psalm 79, Israel has been plundered by the Babylonians and reflects the distress at this great event. It is the nations that are allied against Israel that are the problem; they are invaders and have pillaged the Federal Reserve and Ft. Knox, have defiled the National Cathedral, and leave death in their wake. The singer thinks that God is angry at Israel and can only interpret the Babylonian conquest in this way. In the next chapter we will see how certain followers of the prophet Isaiah began to think in a different frame about God and Israel's Exile. The writer of Psalm 79, however, is still stuck in *the sacrificial principle* and longs for a national tit-for-tat. When the writer asks God to "pay back into the laps of our neighbors seven times" he is imploring God, not to stop violence, but to be a murderer like Cain, and Lamech!

Well, it had to happen, someone finally has had enough and wants the mob to stand accused! Bring in the Satan, the heavenly prosecuting attorney, the Attorney General himself (106:6). The Satan, the accuser of the peoples, the Grand Inquisitor is called to the stage to fulfill his role not as the mob accusing the single victim, but as the single victim accusing the mob. This is where Satan tries to cast out Satan. Everyone stands accused. This makes for an intolerable situation. In the words of the pop song, "Everybody wants to rule the world." The victim still adopts the posture of retributive justice and would continue the cycle of violence. This is not the way Jesus responded.

There are three types of victims. There is the victim of myth, the one who believes they are guilty as charged. There is the innocent victim like Abel who seeks retribution but whose voice is heard. Then there is the victim like Joseph who seeks to be reconciled to his "enemy brothers." Jesus is not like Abel but like Joseph. The writer to the Hebrews first pointed this out for us when saying, "Jesus' blood speaks a better word than that of Abel" (Hebrews 12:24).

In Psalm 139 the psalmist writes about their personal experience of God as just and kind and how "precious to me are your thoughts O God" (139:17). Yet the problem for the author is how to get rid of violence and the only way out for him is to ask God to do the dirty work and get rid of "evildoers, bloodthirsty men" (139:19). This does not conform to anything we know about Jesus and his view of God's relation to the problem of human violence. The Psalmist and Jesus are as different as Abel and Joseph.

There is nothing about the Imprecatory psalms' desire for vengeance that we could find in Jesus, but the problem of victimizing is pronounced in both. Again, we are not rejecting parts of the Bible; we are simply insisting that they be interpreted within the framework given by Jesus and the apostolic church. The corollary between Jesus and the psalms is not to be found in their theologies, but in the description they give of the victim scapegoating mechanism. The anthropological insight of the victim is why Jesus turned to the Psalter.

The Book of Job

This brings us to the Book of Job. Job is an extended psalm of lament. What Job allows us to see more clearly than the various psalms is the way that an original text about victimizing becomes mythologized. Scholars have long recognized that the opening chapters (1-2) are quite different in vocabulary, style and theology than the dialogues of chapters 3-37. In the Prologue to Job (1-2), it is the heavenly Attorney General (the satan) out for a little stroll who initiates all of Job's woes. In the Dialogues (3-37) there is no mention at all of the kinds of things that occur in the Prologue, in fact just the opposite. In the Dialogues Job has gone from being a hero figure to being a down and out victim of his community.

Rene Girard in his book *Job: The Victim of His People* has made the case that the Dialogues present us with the 'truth' that is papered over in the dualism of the Prologue. The victimization of Job by his community is turned into a heavenly prosecution. This reflects the tendency to mythologize the process of victimage by turning it into divine will.

> "Strangely enough, over the centuries commentators have not paid the slightest attention to that cause [the human victimization that Job laments in the Dialogues]...they seem not to notice it. Ancients and moderns alike, atheists, Protestants, Catholics or Jews – none of them question the object of Job's complaints. The matter seems to have been settled for them in the Prologue. Everyone clings religiously to the ulcers, the lost cattle, etc. And yet exegetes have been warning their readers for some time about this prologue."[clxxi]

The book of Job has for too long taken as its solution the very problem of the text: the mythologizing of an originary lament by the victim.[clxxii] The voice of the victim is now taken up into the sphere of divine arbitrariness. This kind of God can only respond with a macho attitude (chapters 38-41). Little wonder that the response of God to Job has brought little satisfaction to readers.

The Job of the Dialogues is no different than so many of the psalmists who have become victims of an unjust accusation. But as Girard points out what makes the book of Job so valuable is that the other side, the side of the persecuting community is now also heard. We have Job's friends seeking to help him accept his guilt, as any good victim should so that the sacrificial process can move forward. This, Job consistently refuses to do and rightly so. His friends (who actually play the role of prosecutors) can now be seen for what they really are: counselors of the scapegoating mechanism trying to get Job to go along with his victimage. Little wonder that Job calls for help from heaven. He calls on God against God. Three times he threatens a lawsuit against God. Finally he seeks a heavenly advocate. If at first he can say, "my own lament is my advocate with God" (Jerusalem Bible), yet he knows that he has another advocate (Job 19:25-27):

> [25] I know that my Redeemer lives, and that in the end he will stand upon the earth. [26] And after my skin has been destroyed, yet in my flesh I will see God; [27] I myself will see him with my own eyes—I, and not another. How my heart yearns within me!

What Job hopes for is a heavenly Defense Attorney that as we shall later see (8.3) is promised by Jesus. So even in the Jewish Scriptures there is already a keen awareness that somehow God must be better than God seems to be. The voice of the victim continues to come to expression through the Jewish sacred writings. After the exile, a new component will be introduced, something so new, so radical, that it will change our understanding of victims entirely. It was this new radical thing that Jesus seized upon as his own understanding of his mission. To this we now turn.

6.3 Isaiah 53
(Tony Bartlett)

(Note from Michael: We are almost at the pinnacle of the mountain. Tony will be our Sherpa to the top. The air is rarified up here. Tony is opening up a radical reading of Isaiah 53. His case is made broadly and deeply. This is the top; enjoy the view. After this it's all downhill!)

The passage Isaiah 52:13-53:12, renews themes seen before in Isaiah 40-52, that of Zion, the holy city, and then the Servant. On both counts the writing reaches new heights of expression, but it is of course with the second that the pivotal interest lies. We will return to each separate theme when we examine the text in detail, but a prologue to "the fourth song of the Servant," establishing some of its fundamental meaning and relevance, seems immediately called for. A passage that has had such a profound effect on the whole Christian movement and whose critical meaning is endlessly discussed cannot be treated as if the interpretation were somehow neutral. *Entering the world of the text is at once to enter a world that we have constructed around it but which it has also served to construct, and in ways that may well exceed or subvert the way of thinking we are used to.* We must, therefore, first clearly and honestly recognize a dynamic relationship between our world of understanding and the fourth song of the Servant. What follows are sketches in that direction, without pretending to be exhaustive or definitive.

According to Paul Hanson the Servant songs are a redefinition of power.[clxxiii] Right there something enormous is suggested. We could argue that so much that has gone before in the Bible is about redefinition of power. But the great national epic contained in the Torah, Joshua and Judges can be interpreted as the violent revolution of an underclass (Norman Gottwald). Going on from there, the story of the monarchy in Samuel through Kings can be read as a religious nationalism, with insistence on obedience and fidelity to a single God. For sure, the prophets pleaded for social justice and cried out passionately against oppression and violence. And on the way they came to a notion of relationship between God and God's people that went deeper than any formal legal or national-religious understanding. But at what point did the tradition achieve the constitutive break with the universal form of human culture toward which it was always yearning? To have a single God, over against the gods of the nations, and to hold that this God was committed to justice, are not in themselves claims of a truly radical break with the given human culture. The general monotheism of western nations and their many revolutions for the sake of liberty and justice do not significantly mark us off from the empires of Assyria, Greece or Rome, or, for that matter, from that of Solomon. Any schoolboy could tell us that.

I take Hanson's words, therefore, with a sense of something truly new. Only here, with the Servant, do we have the valuation of something truly other in a story of humankind formed simultaneously by epic brutality and its epic forgetting (or mythologizing of history). The nation of Israel had been decimated by a ruthless conqueror, its leading elements, political, military and technical, cut off at the legs and carried to a far land where the assumption was "assimilate or die." Israel, however, did neither: through the remarkable activity of its prophets, Jeremiah and Ezekiel, and probably the teaching of its priests and scribes, it survived as a kind of fantasy of itself. It remembered what it had been and that memory became what it was and what it would yet be. But this did not alter the abject change of fortune it had experienced. It had lost its existence as a state. It had lost its sacred place that guaranteed it before God. In face of the rise to power of the Persian Cyrus and of his enlightened administration in letting captives return to their homelands, the prophet of 2nd Isaiah urged the people to leave Babylon, to "depart, go out from there!" But evidently the agency which brought about this possibility was not their own, and when some of them responded it was entirely without any security derived from traditional forces or institutions. They had to rely on the security offered by the Persian empire, and through and in that means alone, the power of their God. They had been reduced to wretched national weakness. They had become in the prophet's hard-truth words "you worm Jacob, you insect Israel!" (41:14)

If the identity of statehood and temple were removed and yet God still related to them, and did so with an intensity and tenderness not seen before, it meant they were—anthropologically speaking—denuded before him. Yet at the same time there was something about this actual situation God valued. It was a horribly unwelcome human situation, but one rich in astonishing theological possibility. The prophet began to understand that this very weakness was important, willed by God, and productive itself of God's purpose. This is the developing thesis of the Servant songs, running in order from "not grow(ing) faint or be(ing) crushed," through "spend(ing) my strength for nothing and vanity," and "giv(ing) my back to those who struck me," to the full-blown alienation and destruction of the fourth song.

Here now we pivot on the edge of an almost intolerable human breakthrough. Who, in what century, in what land, in what culture, could possibly value a human identity in abjection? Thus with this prophecy there at once begins a struggle of interpretation, and one evident even in the text itself. What do the very words mean? And what in fact is the agency of God in the suffering of the Servant? It is well known that the Aramaic translation of Isaiah (*Isaiah Targum*)[clxxiv] completely re-writes the suffering of the Servant, overturning the text so that the suffering now applies to the nations not to the Servant. The later Christian interpretation of the text has restored the honor of the Christian God (and so, of course, of Christian men and women) by reading the suffering as precisely that—willed by God to restore his honor and justice in a punitive crushing of the Servant. So the mechanisms of power and violence remain intact, and indeed are horribly reinforced, hence the emergence of culturally specific "Christian violence." But these brutal renderings cannot be the meaning of the prophet, if only because our contemporary thought-world allows us to see this brutality for what it is, allowing other possible readings to surface, running counter to it. It is possible to understand that the text itself has disclosed the brutality before we ever see it clearly for what it is.

Could the author really propose a single individual afflicted by God to compensate for his punitive wrath against the many? Morna Hooker sees the exclusive mechanism of such an idea as anomalous, "without parallel in Old Testament thought."[clxxv] Certainly, it's hard to deny that the language of Isaiah 52-53 is sacrificial, seeming to imply a single victim. But then if the prophet intends sacrificial metaphors does he use them in a truly sacrificial sense, i.e. with a compensatory mechanism? This is highly improbable. We know a prophet could well be asked to take on a life-style of suffering and even of punishment. Ezekiel was told "lie on your left side, and place the punishment of the house of Israel upon it; you shall bear their punishment for the number of days, three hundred ninety days..." But this is an enacted meaning and not the famous "vicarious suffering" attributed to the Servant, a suffering in place of the suffering of others. Ezekiel, and others like him, while undoubtedly suffering, does so within a structure of declarative meaning. They are not suffering *instead of* the people, they are suffering *in order to manifest to* the people what is about to happen to them, and why.

Generally, this declarative, teaching purpose should be the presumed interpretative frame of the Isaiah text, rather than one of compensation or transaction. This becomes even more compelling when we think of the Servant in the collective sense. If we take the Servant in the collective sense as Israel then that pulls the meaning in a direction of visual demonstration of a truth rather than substitution. It is much more intelligible that 'the one who silences kings' does so because of a transformed human meaning, rather than some kind of transaction made with God. Destroying a nation in order to appease a god would not startle nations or shut the mouth of kings, unless indeed there was some inspired knowledge of the innocence of that nation before God and their inflicted punishment being a substitute for everyone else's. All of which sounds incredible, but is really only a projection backward on Israel of medieval Christian doctrine about Christ. Much more humanly likely is a first-hand response to the endless nonviolence of the "Servant" turning the heart of an observer to peace and forgiveness. And then the writer universalizes this direct experience, as a destiny for all in response to Israel's suffering. Even if we see the prophet talking first and foremost about Israel in some visionary scene of suffering before the nations, it would amount to the same thing. The prophetic mind is still extrapolating from a deep sense of the transformative teaching power of a totally nonviolent response accompanied by an infinite trust in God.

The strong possibility of the pedagogical (*teaching*) function of the Servant is given textual backing if we turn to one of the verses of the fourth song (the only time I'll do this in this introductory sketch). It seems the most explicitly "penal" verse of the whole poem: "Upon him was the punishment that made us whole, and by his bruises we are healed" (53:5b). The word for punishment in the LXX text is *paideia* and the whole phrase in the first part is *paideia eirenes emin ep' auton*. The word *paideia* can be translated as "teaching, education, discipline, correction." (The Hebrew behind it, *musar*, has the same semantic range: out of its seven occurrences in Jeremiah the NRSV translates it three times as correction, and, one time each, as discipline, punishment, instruction, lesson.) The whole phrase may be rendered then as "the teaching for our peace is on him and by his bruising we are brought to health." The word *paideia* is also used by the LXX in the third song, in the dynamic sense of the Servant as the one who may be both the object and subject of the teaching: literally "the Lord gives me a tongue of instruction" (*glossan paideias*, 50:4a). Thus we have in the NRSV: "The Lord God has given me the tongue of a teacher." There can be little doubt that the Septuagint translators understood the Servant's role as divinely instructional toward others, in and through his intense learning.

The Birth of A New Paradigm

Where then does this lead? Or, rather, where has the text already led us by its own power? For even as I make this argument—about the pedagogy of the Servant—there can be no doubt that the fourth song again and again insists on the Servant's suffering for or on behalf of others. So, even as I dismiss a transactional interpretation there still remains a strong other-directed sense, and this in turn is so powerful that it becomes somehow objective, something in its own right. This is why the sacrificial language is employed, or is understood as employed. It would seem to be the only cultural resource able to speak about what is occurring. Something new has emerged and it is framed according to the language of sacrifice even as it is pedagogical and disclosive, rather than sacral and compensatory. The prophetic community gathered round the theme of the Servant understood the amazing figure entering the role of the sacrificial lamb but without pursuing it to its final sacred closure. Rather it is displayed for all to see in its terrible and subversive pathos. Here is the animal scapegoat, the lamb for the slaughter, and yet it is a human being and one who is suffering terribly. So even if there is no transaction, no penal exchange, there is someone doing something absolute for others. And that absolute act, while opening up brutal human reality to view, is itself something, something in itself. In the past that was called sacrifice; but now we don't have a word for this new thing, unless it is an impossible love, so impossible it has to be named with the name of God itself.

Understanding the text in this way we are assisting in a tectonic upheaval. We're moving from a standard system to something else than cannot truly be called a system. The standard system works by excluding one—so the system in fact is the system-minus-one. But the one has to be added to again and again, so the system actually ends with a vast pile of extruded items, a trash heap of history bigger than history itself. The choice then is between the standard system accompanied by a colossal human trash heap and something wholly new emerging in the fourth song of the Servant. The Servant takes on the role of the excluded one and pursues its track, to the outside, to the "ex" beyond the closure. The opening to the outside and the movement there produces what might be called (with some hesitation) a "new ontology" (a new way of being). For the track opened by the Servant toward the outside produces an empathy with that track, and this is the Servant's pedagogy. His endless non-retaliation or nonviolence teaches and invites imitation and this imitation then creates an entirely "other" sense of being. The Servant's patient pedagogy is rooted in fact in an original ontology beyond being, beyond "things" constituted as they are in the fatal exchanges of desire and killing. By creating and tracing the path of absolute giving-self-away he leads us into a pre-primordial world of utter love. And thus we are made "right" or "righteous."

You could even imagine that this "other" sense is packed away in traditional sacrifice itself, but under the fatal misrepresentation of violence, a counterfeit-because-forced version of the movement to the outside. Because we cast the other out, for that reason we think the world exists, and in a sense we are right because the movement to the outside does create the world. But really we produce a shallow world, a foreshortened, brittle and dangerous world. Instead of the depth of love we have created an arena where our violence is "satisfied" but only for a time. Sacrifice is a terrible palimpsest (an older manuscript that is written over with new text), achieved by a few savage brushstrokes, overlaying the original self-giving of God. It both replays that self-giving and closes it off and denies it by filling that space with the victim. This is why the world continues to turn on the basis of sacrifice, and all its blind philosophy and violent metaphysic appear plausibly true. There *is* something to it. But it is still only a grotesque distortion of the original movement of love. It takes the Servant in his fearful abjection to break through to the original "non-being" of self-giving. Thus he demonstrates the falsehood of sacrifice, because he not only retraces the violence in his body, but also re-traces it, or traces it for the first time, as endless love. It is only because of the appearance of truth that something else can be shown as false. Only theology is able to give full and free expression to that. To put it another way, mimetic anthropology has to be recognized for what it is, the offshoot of theology, not the other way round. For theology, therefore, to truly fulfill its destiny in our contemporary situation, must begin with the astonishing challenge to being and its violent system that the Servant of the Lord has taught.

Commentary on Isaiah 52:13-53:12

52:1-2. These verses continue the Zion oracle that began at 51:17, which is one of several appearing from 49 onwards (49:14-26, 50:1-3, 51:1-8, 51:9-11, 51:17-52:2, 52:7-12, 54:1-17). Up to chapter 49 the most prominent addressee was Jacob or Israel; after that point it becomes Zion. I have not highlighted these oracles perhaps as much as I should. As we can see, there is an impressive parade, and they fill almost all the space around the second, third and fourth servant songs. They act as an unmistakable counterpoint, and the question arises of how does this female role fit with the Servant, if at all?

The oracles are part of what is known as "Zion theology." What this means in short is a powerful theological accent on the city of Jerusalem as the place of God's blessing and promise. In 1st Isaiah it is in connection to the figure of the Davidic king or messiah, but in 2nd Isaiah the Davidic figure drops out and the city of Zion stands forward as the sole protagonist, without the need for a monarchy. Right from the beginning she is addressed for her own sake, "Speak tenderly to Jerusalem" (40:1). Very likely the origins of Zion theology is in standard civic prophecy, claiming divine protection for any city which achieved regional dominance. However, in the case of Jerusalem this has to be read in the context of Yahwism, from the initial conquest of the city by the Yahwist king, David, and the progressive integration of the covenant and law into the city's imagination and identity. Thus at Isaiah 2:2-3 we read that all the nations shall come to Jerusalem to learn there the Lord's ways, "for out of Zion shall go forth instruction and the word of the Lord from Jerusalem." When the city's destruction and exile occurred this religious identity received a severe blow, which in any other case would have been fatal. But that is precisely where the prophet of 2nd Isaiah stepped in, telling Jerusalem that her suffering had reached its term, and that, instead of suffering, Jerusalem was to now be the "herald of glad tidings" (40:9).

The Zion oracles then continue in this spirit, constantly reassuring the city of divine comfort, relationship and destiny. She is addressed as mother (50:1, 51:18) and also as bride (49:18, 52:1, 54:5-6). The Lord declares, "I have inscribed you on the palms of my hands; your walls are continually before me" (49:16), and he assures her that even if she has lost so many of her children, many, many more will return to her (49:20-22). Probably these oracles were produced independently in the immediate years before and just after the return from Babylon in 537 B.C.E. Their clear and urgent purpose was to encourage people in face of a devastated city, without walls, temple, palace or populace, to see these things and yet still imagine a triumphant purpose. Their poetry soars in almost inverse proportion to the depressing reality. There is a continual affirmation of God's positive intention right there in midst of destruction and failure.

The suffering of the city obviously puts it in a parallel situation to the Servant, but unlike Israel the city is never addressed as Servant. At the same time, some of the things said to her are also said to the Servant: "Kings...with their faces to the ground shall bow down to you" (49:23b; cf. 49:7c); "You offered your back like the ground, like the street for them to walk on' (51:23c; cf. 50:6a). And, perhaps most important, in respect of both, "The Lord has bared his holy arm before the eyes of all the nations; and all the ends of the earth shall see the salvation of our God" (52:10; cf. 49:6c, 53:1). There is clearly a degree of crossover between Zion and the Servant. But Zion also has a history and character that is independent from that of the Servant. She was punished for her sins (40:2c) whereas the Servant is never seen as guilty. And her offering of her back can be read as unwilling and resentful. Moreover, because she is never named Servant (as Israel is) there is no textual ambivalence between them. Thus, despite a sympathy of features, the two represent different identities, with a dramatic tension between them. They are both the work of YHWH and for the sake of the nations, but Zion is generally the object of a passionate future hope, while the Servant is passionately active in the present.

The oracles were very probably not composed as a counterpoint to the Servant songs, but the final collation of the two themes produces a rich emotional field for the reader. There is the continual sense of loving relationship toward Jerusalem in its crisis, and in the meantime a mysterious redemptive figure emerging from exactly the setting of its crisis. Thus Zion is the scene of the Servant, and the Servant is the strange shadow companion of Zion. In other studies I have described him as a "new physics," or, as above, a "new ontology," and if this is the case then Zion is the human setting where this newness will be lived. The last oracle in chapter 54 approaches a sense of human transformation, and the writings of the third division of Isaiah, from 56 onwards continue to develop this vision. Then finally in the Christian testament, in the book of Revelation, very many of the Isaianic images are picked up and asserted of "the new Jerusalem coming down out of heaven from God...as a bride adorned for her husband," a place where God will dwell with humankind. Thus the pathway of transformation is completed. But it is begun here, in the mysterious and beautiful twinning of themes. The marriage between a God of infinite self giving and a humanity which has finally surrendered to a love beyond being will be nothing less than the collapse of heaven into earth.

1-2 The actual verses, call on Jerusalem to awaken, from a kind of coma or depression. Her catatonic state has been caused both by being taken captive and by the presence of "unclean" aliens within her. But now there will be a return of purity, for the impure shall enter her no more. What is purity? At this point it is a distinction from the nations, from the conquerors who bring a sense of physical contamination. But the Servant will break through this: he more than anyone is marked with impurity—he is covered with iniquity and is given a grave with the wicked—and yet he transcends its grasp. Underlying the phenomenon of uncleanness that afflicts Zion is the violence of the nations that removes the sense of her God from Jerusalem. Circumcision is simply the externalizing of the harsh distinction that keeps the nations at bay. But of course it is itself achieved by a form of violence. Thus the Servant is the most radical possible reply to the purity demand, because he overcomes the uncleanness of violence from within, replacing it with a completely fresh principle of existence.

3-6 A different type of oracle addressed not to Zion but to the people. It asserts that the exile was unjustified—"my people are taken away without cause" (5). It is a statement that parallels the Servant song at 53:8—"by a perversion of justice he was taken away." The claim is a contrast with 42:24-5 and 43:26-8 etc. which says the exile was just punishment for the people's sins, and suggests a different voice here, one less influenced by the Deuteronomic mindset. Is it possible that the proximity of the Servant who "makes many righteous" has allowed this other viewpoint access to the text? Are we are already under the influence of this new way of reckoning and un-reckoning human guilt? On the other hand, the contextual insistence on external purity, at verse 1 and again at 11, suggests that this is not yet the nonviolent solution of the Servant. We could well be witnessing a priestly-style assertion of the people's purity, perhaps under the effect of a more sacrificial reading of the Servant.

7-10 Part of another Zion oracle, these words are some of the most famous in the Old Testament, providing a key locus for the term "gospel" or "good news," mined almost certainly by Jesus, as well as by Paul (Romans 10:15). The good news is about the return of the Lord to Zion that is proof that "God reigns," and thus an announcement of "the kingdom of God." It forms a doublet with the similar passage at the outset of the book at 40:9-11. There the messenger or herald is Zion herself, but here it seems to be one who returns to Zion. The displacement of "beauty" from the face or mouth of the messenger to his "feet" poetically catches the immense joy of this double return, of God and his people. Jesus rehearses the same joy, in a similar but expanded frame, in the "gospels." The poet expresses an uncontainable exuberance that commands the very ruins—symbols of death and horror—to break into singing. It is this enormously felt reversal that constitutes then the "bared arm" of the Lord, a figure that normally refers to a warrior's might in battle. But in this case it speaks to the effect of human experience astonishingly transformed and overturned in its very root. The doublet with chapter 40, the beginning of the prophecy, already tells us that we are reaching a climax in the overall composition, and then the trope (*figure of speech in which meaning is altered from the usual or expected*) of the Lord's arm before the eyes of the nations (10) is almost immediately repeated in relation to the Servant, at 52:13a and 53:1b. The oracle then stands at the threshold of the fourth song and announces it internally and with striking emphasis. It is also, therefore, the place where the themes of Zion and the Servant are most fully sutured. In effect the joy of the return to Zion is used to preface the shocking appearance of the Servant. The sequence also suggests then that both are different phases of the same reign of God, hinting as well that the Servant is the means of the glorious return at a deeper mysterious level.

11-12 A reiteration of the theme of purity but in the context of the departure from Babylon—the returnees are to "touch no unclean thing" as they go, purifying themselves as they carry the sacred vessels that had been removed by Nebuchadnezzar from the temple. It is noteworthy the temple is not itself mentioned. All the emphasis is on those who return; they will not depart in haste as in the Exodus from Egypt but with a much greater security in this new exodus. These verses seem to be a clumsy addition to the theme of joyful return to Zion, backtracking in imagination to Babylon. Is their effect to draw a clear line under the oracle, marking a difference—

despite the earlier suture—with the truly startling figure of the Servant? Or is a further connection to the Servant in fact intended, a hint that the work of the temple is now fulfilled and made redundant by the "sacrificial" role he will undertake?

13-15 And so at last we arrive at the fourth song. The Lord is speaking and declares the exaltation and triumph of the Servant, anticipating the end of the poem when the Servant receives "a portion with the great." But it is fascinating that the exaltation seems to derive directly from his abasement, so that the latter is somehow productive of the former. "*Just as* there are many who were astonished at him [because he did not look like a human]...*so* he shall startle many nations; kings shall shut their mouths because of him" (14). At the least there is no clear move from abasement to exaltation as visibly different conditions.

What then is the marring of appearance, so that the person no longer has the form of a human? The picture is a contradiction of Genesis where man and woman are made in the image of God; it is both a human and theological reversal, an absolute dehumanization. If we take the scene before the nations and kings in the collective sense, of another nation, Israel, which stands before them, then perhaps the form that is lost is statehood, including a ruling monarch, an intact temple and a graceful city. The word translated "marred" means ruined, wasted, trashed, smashed, which could certainly apply to a city. But reading it purely that way loses much of the shock of the disfigurement of human form and in fact reduces the impact of the metaphor applied to Israel. Its vigor as metaphor seems to demand that we "see" an actual human deprived of human form. So what then is the marring of a human? Illness, poverty, brutalization, humiliation? We cannot say, but in any case the Servant is described outside the society of men. And it is seemingly in exactly that condition he will shut the mouths of the powerful. From the perspective I have developed, the logic that makes this work is that of the Servant who *as* excluded being, is the one returned to view. It is his loss of appearance, his going beyond the human, which places him outside the system. But it is precisely as the one driven out that he now returns to view. So a total novelty is disclosed to the nations and kings. What else could possibly provide the shock to silence kings but this revelatory non-humanity? The hidden victim upon whom the whole edifice and power of nations and kings depend is now plainly on view. No wonder they are struck dumb!

This reading would in turn make sense of "That which had not been told them they shall see, and that which they had not heard they shall contemplate." It is structurally the thing that has no name, does not even belong to language; this is the thing that they will look upon, that they will contemplate in the sense of a spiritual awareness. What a profound, earth-shaking contemplation!

The Servant of Isaiah

53:1-3 Beginning at this point is what is known as the "We" material, running to 11b. It features a first person plural speaker, in contrast to the Lord as before and after. The difference has led some to conclude that the unit is detachable and probably earlier than the framing verses built round it. In contrast others read the material of chapter 53 dramatically and seamlessly, so that it is the kings introduced at 52:15 who are then the first person speakers. But in this case the introduction is very poor: you have to go from the Lord's address to that of the kings without any signal of change, in addition to the fact that the kings have only just "shut their mouths." It seems better to see the thing critically, envisioning an original unit that is then framed by an address from the Lord, and the change to plural speakers is open in reference rather than dramatically closed. In other words, "we" can mean anyone, including of course the kings and the nations. This, I would submit, is the poetic feeling of the text, with its blunt and striking announcement seeming to speak for everyone: "Who has believed what we have heard?"

If this is the case it then becomes possible to speculate about the existential "we" behind the unit. Were they members of the Isaianic community who had witnessed at first hand the maltreatment of an individual? The shift to an individual "servant" that this brings goes along with the autobiographical second and third songs, demanding a single person, as well as the pronounced prophetic and teaching role of this figure. It would be much easier to go from a single individual like this to a representative metaphor, rather than the other way. (The figure of "Son of Man" in Daniel 7 is clearly already a representative metaphor, and nowhere before or after does he then speak in the first person, i.e. become existentially single.) We can then add, as already mentioned, the impact of the intensity of suffering. It is very hard, hearing these words, not to think of a single persecuted man.

We have the description of one who is young and grows up in arid ground, without human consolation or refreshment. We then hear "he had no form or majesty that we should look at him, nothing in his appearance that we should desire him." The reference to form and appearance invokes 52:14 and could well be one of the bases on which the frame is elaborated. But here the poverty in appearance is not the passive result of "marring;" it appears personal and proper. This individual was possibly crippled, or at the least unimpressive, unattractive, deprived. The note "majesty" suggests a king, the kind of bearing that a king should have, and this hint turns our thoughts to the actual exiled king of Jerusalem, Jehoiachin. He was the son of Jehoiachim whose rebellion brought down the wrath of Nebuchadnezzar on the city. When his father died Jehoiachin was only eighteen years old. He lasted just three months on the throne and then surrendered the city and was carried off in the first deportation to Babylon (597 BCE). The Book of Kings never explains why his leadership crumbled so rapidly, especially given the resistance of the nobles subsequently under Zedekiah, something vividly portrayed in the book of Jeremiah. Jeremiah in fact has very dismissive words for the young king.

> "Is this man Coniah [another name for Jehoiachin] a despised broken pot,
> a vessel no one wants?
> Why are he and his offspring hurled out
> and cast away in a land they do not know?
> O land, land, land,
> Hear the word of the Lord!
> Thus says the Lord:
> Record this man as childless,
> a man who shall not succeed in his days;
> For none of his offspring shall succeed
> in sitting on the throne of David,
> and ruling again in Judah." (Jeremiah 22:28-30)

The "broken pot" recalls Jeremiah's prophetic action, smashing an earthenware pot at the entrance to the valley of Hinnom, in symbolism of the disaster coming on the city (19:1-15). Thus Jeremiah's assessment, just like the Deuteronomist's (2 Kings 24:19), holds Jehoiachin accountable for the sins of the city and the Davidic dynasty that ruled it. The word "despised" in the first line is *nivzeh*, (niph'al masculine participle of *bazah*), the same Hebrew word used twice in Isaiah 53:3: "He was despised and rejected by others...he was despised, and we held him of no account." It's also noteworthy that in the final reversal of the Servant's condition "he shall see his offspring" (53:10c), something that may also be seen as referencing Jeremiah's prophecy.

The exiled king's situation could hardly be more worthy of contempt. Whatever the reason, he gave up without a fight. And before and aside from whether he was prepared to fight, he was judged and rejected by the greatest prophet of the time and then by the scribes who wrote the history. As an imprisoned trophy of war his situation was one of constant humiliation before the mighty of Babylon, and with the words of Jeremiah ringing in their ears his fellow exiles could easily have held a parallel, if not greater disdain. He was "one from whom others hide their faces." And yet Jehoiachin survived and, according to 2 Kings 25:27-9, after 37 years he was released from prison and given an honored seat at the king's table, "above the other seats of the kings."

His story is manifestly one of humiliation and reversal. I recount it not because I wish to make a case for his being "the servant of the fourth song," but because it shows how reasonable it can be to believe in an actual historical individual behind the text and how that individual can give life to the anthropology emerging in the text. It is entirely possible that Jehoiachin bore his fate with dignity and patience and it was for that reason that he finally rose to be an ornament at the king's table. At the same time, before the eyes of his fellow exiles—busying themselves building houses, planting gardens and eating their produce (Jeremiah 29:5)—his constant and isolated presence of suffering may eventually have given rise to an opposite emotion from rejection. It is an entirely new existential situation where one king does not succeed another but the defeated one stays alive in captivity as an object lesson in disgrace; and if we add to that the prophetic and scribal denunciation of this individual the result could be nothing but collective revulsion. But then in an amazing response, he sustains his condition with silence and integrity, and it is precisely this that could give rise to something unprecedented.

A transformation of emotion must be conceivable, wherein the object of contempt by virtue of his own lack of resentment, hatred or despair, pulls people round to himself. Contempt is a mimetic transfer, discharging a steady collective violence on another; but then if that mimesis meets a free space filled with peace, trust and non-retaliation then inevitably—by almost a law of mechanics—that transfer will begin to mutate into those very opposite emotions. All that is necessary then to complete the trajectory is that a prophetic mind understood—in a flash of revelation—that it was precisely this individual who filled the role of the temple victim, of the lamb for the slaughter, but without the temple. Here was the afflicted one who was not afflicted for his own sins but those of others, yet by means other than temple ritual. And then all the language of striking, wounding, crushing and, in and with that, of exchange, all of that falls into place as an amazing and amazed litany on the part of the prophet. The prophet appears to use the language of sacrifice because that is what he is indeed seeing on the surface, even as he senses, at a deeper level, something very different happening. He cannot help but recount the process, blow by blow—because that is what actually happened— even as he registers a seismic shift from sacrifice to mimetic human peace and true repentance.

4-7 Surely he has borne our infirmities
And carried our diseases;
Yet we accounted him stricken,
struck down by God, and afflicted.
But he was wounded for our transgressions,
crushed for our iniquities;
upon him was the punishment [education] that made us whole,
and by his bruises we are healed.

All we like sheep had gone astray;
We have all turned to our own way,
and the Lord has laid on him
the iniquity of us all.
He was oppressed and he was afflicted,
yet he did not open his mouth;
Like a lamb that is led to the slaughter,
and like a sheep that before its shearers is silent,
so he did not open his mouth.

The experience recounted is very dense. It cannot be read simplistically as the Christian tradition has done, if only because the tradition is not itself simple: to arrive at it took a number of convolutions of thought that were not (and are not) consistent with the bible in general and the gospel in particular. For God to carry out punitive intent and damage against an innocent individual because of the sins of others is deeply antithetical to biblical grace. At the same time, such is the volatility of mimetic transfer in a world of violence it is easy to imagine that along with an original mimesis of peace a sense of the scapegoat can quickly be imported to Isaiah 53. Thus the text seems fatally easy to misread—as the simple substitution of "punishment" for "teaching" or "education" shows. In many ways the prophecy has to be read with the purity of the Servant in order to understand the Servant.

8-9 What can help steady our reading is to bear constantly in mind that it is not the death of the Servant but his prolonged suffering that carries the weight of the text. It is the Servant's suffering nonviolence that provides the mimetic pathway of transformation, and his death is simply its final, abyssal moment. Unlike in sacrifice (or successful scapegoating) where everything pivots on the death and the violence leading up to it is forgotten, here everything turns on the suffering, and death is simply its ultimate moment. Pursuing our exemplary interpretation of Jehoiachin can again reinforce this. We have already seen how his apparent guilt at the root of his abyssal suffering, little by little is replaced by a sense of innocence, and with this of course there would be a feeling of a perversion of justice. Then finally he did die in Babylon. He was "cut off from the land of the living," and "they made his grave with the wicked and his tomb with the rich," a fate likely for a captive but honored king. And certainly Jehoiachin had "done no violence and there was no deceit in his mouth:" He surrendered his city and throne to Nebuchadnezzar after only three months where there was not time for maneuvering or duplicity.

10-12 Having the concrete figure of Jehoiachin in mind has helped us imagine the event of mimetic transformation, and avoid abstract atonement metaphysics. He has provided a springboard to the concrete anthropology whereby nonviolent suffering is somehow a lesson of healing that can be learned. However, as I have also pointed out, it has needed the prophet to see and record all this, and probably more than one prophet. I think the "original" 2nd Isaiah was the author of the autobiographical second and third songs of the Servant, and then a disciple wrote the fourth song reflecting on the violent fate of this figure. Something like this is still possible, even if I have now made a hypothetical case for Jehoiachin being the "servant" of the fourth song. Jehoiachin-as-servant still leaves the self-reporting figure of the second and third songs, and for the reasons I gave earlier—that this figure would have had to be central to the prophetic community, indeed the "original" prophet—I believe that he does act as the core interpreting agent of the Servant songs. It was from deep inside his own personal inspiration and experience of suffering that he was able to articulate this new thing and for the first time. It was through him that the Deuteronomic judgment on the king and on Israel began to be reversed from the inside, from the very abyss in which it had thrust them; "Speak tenderly to Jerusalem...that she has served her term, that her penalty is paid..." Perhaps then this original voice penned the "We" section, and then a disciple's hand added the frame. Or, possibly another disciple under the influence of the original prophet wrote it. These details do not really matter; what is important is the prophetic insight that recognized the transformation taking place.

The prophet sees that everything that had happened to the Servant had been the will of the Lord: "... it was the will of the Lord to crush him with pain" (10a). Read instrumentally, with a violent mimesis, this sounds like the Lord was cruel and sadistic. But, on the contrary, we may now understand the will of the Lord was the whole process of mimetic transformation, including all its pain, and with an amazing newness as its outcome. Looked at from this end point we can more easily accept it was the Lord's will; but the prophet starts with the brutal reality of crushing because that is exactly the phenomenon before his eyes, in all its astonishing immediacy and fullness. The prophet's angle of reading which sees pain and transformation holistically as the Lord's will is extremely important, because it means ultimately that the Lord is "crushed" by his own will. For in this case the Lord is identified with what he wills. Because the Servant's crushing is not instrumental—a means to an end—but is itself the scene of transformation (a *paideia*), then when the Lord *wills* this thing he wills his own absolute loss of violence. The vintner who crushes the grape wills the amazing novelty of wine and will surely claim identity with the vintage. Even more so does the Lord when he produces the wine of a new creation. Up to now the Lord's will is identified with the generative principle of culture, which is violence. But now he wills this new generative humanity into history and so is immediately identified with its nonviolent principle. But he wills this "new thing" because it is his very self from eternity.

Logically then, on the basis of the witnessed phenomenon, the prophet makes the key ontological claim of the poem. "When you make his life an offering for sin, he shall see his offspring, and shall prolong his days" (10b&c). The word translated "sin offering," *asham*, is made to sound like a temple sacrifice and it has carried that resonance throughout the Christian era. However it is regarded as "enigmatic" by the commentators and is basically a variant for the much more common and technically appropriate term *hattath*. This is the word used for sin-offering throughout the whole of Leviticus. *Asham* is used in Leviticus for another kind of offering, sometime called a "guilt offering," but it seems to belong to late sections and the original sense of the word seems to have been broader, a "guilt-payment" or "restitution" Thus it seems plain that the prophet deliberately avoided the more regular cultic word and used something vaguer which both echoed the cult and yet was wider than it. I would suggest that the phrase is much better translated as "when you make his life a setting-right." The fact that it has been confidently translated as "sin-offering" masks its anthropological openness.

However, it still seems that some kind of compensation or exchange is being named. And because of that it appears as an ontological claim, a setting right in the overall order of things. But at a deeper level we understand this is a barely-understood change to the order itself—everything in the past was set right by temple sacrifice, and thus preserved the principle of violence itself; but now the Servant has side-stepped that principle into something new, a "new ontology." The phrase could rightly be paraphrased as: "When you make his life a new setting up of everything." This new setting up/setting right exceeds every compensation and exchange absolutely even while the language seems almost inevitably to fall back into the old way of thinking—until finally we grasp the fact that something *really* new has happened! Naturally, then, because everything is new the Servant shall "see his offspring," he shall see the birth of the new in people and the birth of new people. In the same spirit the Servant himself shall "prolong his days..." It is precisely because a new order is at work the Servant shall continue in life. If it were the old order then the Servant would be dead and the temple would prolong its days.

11-12 How this happens is then made plain in the final frame section, a reflection which strikingly endorses everything I have been arguing. In the Qumran manuscripts and Masoretic texts the word "light" in verse 11 is missing, and if we add to this a very possible alternative parsing of the latter half of 11b plus 11c the result is: "Out of his anguish he shall see and shall find satisfaction. Through his knowledge the righteous one, my servant, shall make many righteous, and he shall carry their iniquities." As Paul Hanson points out the verbs "bear" and "carry" refer back to chapter 46:1-4 where YHWH is contrasted with the gods of Babylon who have to be carried by their devotees. Instead the God of Israel carries his people, and now the Lord provides another means of bearing, in this case of the people's sins (cf. 6b: "the Lord laid on him the iniquity of us all.") But again it is the actual means of this carrying and bearing that are at issue. According to the Lord, now speaking, in his anguish the Servant shall see and be satisfied. In effect he shall *see* the profound meaning of what is happening to him and come thereby to a new theological-anthropological truth. This interpretation is proven by the immediate mention of the Servant's "knowledge," and simultaneously we see this transformative knowledge as something he communicates to others. By his knowledge he makes others righteous; i.e. the meaning the Servant sees becomes also his teaching, his revolutionary *paideia.* Thus it is by means of a profound re-education that the Servant relieves the burden of the people's sins. Indeed what better way of relieving sin than bringing someone to an entirely new existential condition where sin's violent power and power of violence are undone? The simple displacement of "through his knowledge" to "satisfaction" neutralizes the message of human transformation through anthropological awareness and returns us to a standard sacrificial sense. But connecting this knowledge with the making righteous fits conclusively with the theme of *paideia* and the mimetic peace underpinning the whole song.

Because of this the Servant is given "a portion with the great" and "divide(s) the spoil with the strong." We could perhaps be back here at Jehoiachim kings' table in Babylon, but the deeper and wider prophetic meaning now achieved expands the reference enormously. I am reminded of Jesus' binding of the strong man, by which he liberates others from the control of the strong, of the violent. The Servant shall set many free from the world system of generative violence. And the reason for this is given one more time, and in perhaps the most resonant anthropological phrase of the whole song: "Because he poured himself out to death and was numbered among the transgressors." The Hebrew can be rendered as: "He laid bare/he poured out his soul to death" and it captures in one line the abyssal surrender of the Servant's life as the means by which he overcomes the violent. The Hebrew soul is the self-identical life of the person in its fragile and mortal reality; and it is also the natural appetite and desire that goes with such life. It is the experience we all have of wrapping this tenuous existence around with all the protections we can assemble, including the objects of mimetic desire. Pouring all this out willingly to death while being counted as one of the wicked is the antithesis of this "natural" life. It is not stated here in any passive sense of a sacrificial object, but in an absolute personal sense. It is not the object *asham* that works, but the subject's pouring out! Then, in the final couplet of the song, the Servant's bearing the sin of many and making intercession for evildoers are placed in parallel to this personal movement. It is no longer a matter of the Lord laying a burden on the Servant, but of the human movement by the Servant. Here is a picture of an unconditional entering of an individual to a space furthest from God, and endlessly so (a "pouring out"). It is because the Servant does this without reciprocal violence—i.e. without despair or the promise of retaliation—that he makes this non-place of nonbeing the absolute opening to the new, the beyond-being of love for all those who find themselves separated from both being and love.

And so we reach the end of the Servant songs. We have discovered that the figure of the Servant has multiple references, and that the prophetic voices and hands that shaped the figure are also certainly plural. The Servant may be conceived as Israel, as the collective reality of the people, because the prophet saw them as such. At the same time a cast of significant individuals, Cyrus, Jehoiachin, the original prophet, and others perhaps we do not know of, emerge as essential protagonists in delineating the revolutionary humanity of the Servant. This is no abstract corporate figure. It is a human being who has drunk the dregs of existence, has plumbed its depths, and in that condition has discovered something wonderfully, eternally new. A collective could never have done this. Could a collective write Mozart? But, even as this individual discovers the music at the bottom of our existence, he begins to play it for all to hear. And then of course it can become a collective reality, because everyone can and does resonate to its unheard-of harmonics. So the circle is completed. Israel is the Servant, and will yet be the Servant. And all the nations can learn from servant Israel, and can themselves also become the Servant. Why not, if his meaning is not a grim transaction, benefiting only those in the account of the "saved," but a transformative education, a *paideia*, open to all?

In the history of the tradition sacrificial transaction took over as the meaning of the Servant because what the Servant does is in the area previously occupied by sacrifice. It has been extremely difficult for violent humanity to take off its old lens of sacrifice and see the new thing beneath it. Forgiveness pre-empts sacrifice, but from the point of view of the violent forgiveness can only be understood in terms of sacrifice. It is a massive testimony to the power of Isaiah's Servant, and of Jesus, its first historical interpreter, that slowly forgiveness has shone through the misrecognition and misconstruction of violent anthropology.

6.4 Wisdom, Torah, Word

From Genesis to Malachi (in the Christian structure of the Jewish Bible) retributive violence is the one theme that dominates our horizon. It is executed by victors, desired by victims, initiated by 'God' and lamented by God. We saw in Genesis 1-11 that all of the themes of mimetic realism were already present in the way the writers of Torah told their stories. The Psalms provided another opportunity to see the difference between retributive victims and victims who sought vindication. Tony Bartlett's study of the fourth servant song of Isaiah clearly demonstrated the new revelation regarding divinity and nonviolence that was bursting forth in Israel's consciousness as the Exile was coming to a close.

There is a further development of this theme of the victim in literature produced after the Exile commonly referred to as wisdom literature. Technically we have already looked at some of this in 6.2 on the Psalms and Job. Before and during the time of Exile, suffering was couched in terms of the corporate, the people, the nation. After the exile the corporate victim, perhaps under the influence of such texts as Isaiah 53 and Ezekiel, becomes individualized and is known as the *suffering righteous person*. The all against one of the servant songs is expressly given utterance in Wisdom, particularly in a book known as the Wisdom of Solomon (found in the Old Testament Apocrypha).

As we saw, Job is a good example in wisdom literature of an innocent person who suffers unjustly. So also is the figure in Wisdom 2-3 (from the Revised Standard Version). Let's look at this text more closely. The writer is reflecting on his/her persecutors.

> ***2:1*** For they reasoned unsoundly, saying to themselves, "Short and sorrowful is our life, and there is no remedy when a man comes to his end, and no one has been known to return from Hades.
> ***2*** Because we were born by mere chance, and hereafter we shall be as though we had never been; because the breath in our nostrils is smoke, and reason is a spark kindled by the beating of our hearts.
> ***3*** When it is extinguished, the body will turn to ashes, and the spirit will dissolve like empty air. ***4*** Our name will be forgotten in time and no one will remember our works; our life will pass away like the traces of a cloud, and be scattered like mist that is chased by the rays of the sun and overcome by its heat. ***5*** For our allotted time is the passing of a shadow, and there is no return from our death, because it is sealed up and no one turns back. ***6*** "Come, therefore, let us enjoy the good things that exist, and make use of the creation to the full as in youth. ***7*** Let us take our fill of costly wine and perfumes, and let no flower of spring pass by us. ***8*** Let us crown ourselves with rosebuds before they wither. ***9*** Let none of us fail to share in our revelry, everywhere let us leave signs of enjoyment, because this is our portion, and this our lot.

These folks are nihilists. There is no Judge, there is no judgment. There is only this life, nothing else. So what do they do? They fulfill their desires (vs 6) to the fullest, they are the ultimate consumers. Eat, drink and be merry, for tomorrow we die! But what are these 'signs of enjoyment?' Are they dirty dishes, empty wine bottles or trashed hotel rooms? No.

> ***2:10*** Let us oppress the righteous poor man; let us not spare the widow nor regard the gray hairs of the aged. ***11*** But let our might be our law of right, for what is weak proves itself to be useless. ***12*** "Let us lie in wait for the righteous man, because he is inconvenient to us and opposes our actions; he reproaches us for sins against the law, and accuses us of sins against our training. ***13*** He professes to have knowledge of God, and calls himself a child of the Lord. ***14*** He became to us a reproof of our thoughts; ***15*** the very sight of him is a burden to us, because his manner of life is unlike that of others, and his ways are strange. ***16*** We are considered by him as something base, and he avoids our ways as unclean; he calls the last end of the righteous happy, and boasts that God is his father. ***17*** Let us see if his words are true, and let us test what will happen at the end of his life; ***18*** for if the righteous man is God's son, he will help him, and will deliver him from the hand of his adversaries. ***19*** Let us test him with insult and torture, that we may find out how gentle he is, and make trial of his forbearance. ***20*** Let us condemn him to a shameful death, for, according to what he says, he will be protected."

The signs of enjoyment are all those made miserable and execrable by these nihilists. It is the oppression of the righteous poor person, the one who has no defense; it is to require of widows payments that cannot be made, and utter ruination of the elderly. How do they rule? By might makes right (vs 11). They have the stones and the guns, the crosses and electric chairs. Their goal: to weed out the weakest among them, a social euthanasia. But why this poor defenseless person? Because they are defenseless, an inconvenience and a testimony to the evil of their own sacrificial power.

The righteous poor woman, by her very existence sears the conscience; her ways are different and she avoids the example of the oppressor. Note that vs 16-17 sound like the story of Jesus; the act of lynching has been hatched. As I mentioned before the structure of myth and gospel are the same, they have the same elements. It is no surprise to us then that Jesus is pre-figured in the Jewish Scriptures, it is where this pre-figuration is clearest that we should take our starting point which is to be the cross. We are looking for the pre-figured Crucified as we read the Jewish Bible.

> ***2:21*** Thus they reasoned, but they were led astray, for their wickedness blinded them, ***22*** and they did not know the secret purposes of God, nor hope for the wages of holiness, nor discern the prize for blameless souls; ***23*** for God created man for incorruption, and made him in the image of his own eternity, ***24*** but through the devil's envy death entered the world, and those who belong to his party experience it. ***3:1*** But the souls of the righteous are in the hand of God, and no torment will ever touch

> them. ***2*** In the eyes of the foolish they seemed to have died, and their departure was thought to be an affliction, ***3*** and their going from us to be their destruction; but they are at peace. ***4*** For though in the sight of men they were punished, their hope is full of immortality.

The victim now speaks. The logic of the persecutors is to mock the victim with the ultimate slander: If the victim succumbs, then it is obvious God was not on their side and probably doesn't exist. The victim says differently. Both sides get to tell their story, one of them is myth, the other is the underbelly of myth. The victim trusts that God is on their side, that God has greater purposes for suffering than they might be aware of, and that God is to be trusted. The mob lynched its victim and justified its violence with lies, believing that God too judged the victim and accepted their death; but the victim knew that there was something on the other side of this life.

For a moment I want to recall that Israel was the nation chosen by God to come out of paganism and become a different people. It would only be natural for this people to tell their stories from the dual perspective of the cultures they came from and their experiences with this God. That is, their literature reflects both God's saving activity and the religious view (*the pagan sacrificial principle*) that God's saving activity includes violence against Israel's enemies. In chapter 12 the writer of the Wisdom of Solomon connects Israel's taking of the Holy Land to an ethnic cleansing. The primary issue is sacrificial human violence that fouls the land.

> ***12:3*** Those who dwelt of old in thy holy land ***4*** thou didst hate for their detestable practices, their works of sorcery and unholy rites, ***5*** their merciless slaughter of children, and their sacrificial feasting on human flesh and blood. These initiates from the midst of a heathen cult, ***6*** these parents who murder helpless lives, thou didst will to destroy by the hands of our fathers, ***7*** that the land most precious of all to thee might receive a worthy colony of the servants of God.

The current mob that afflicts the righteous poor of chapters 2-3 is now exposed as pagan in its orientation, for they participate in the slaughter of the innocent. Sacrifice is a highly ritualized event in the hands of the heathen. Our author understands that the social ostracizing he is going through is the same as human sacrifice. When mimetic realism therefore connects social scapegoating with the practice of human sacrifice it is not the first to do so, already Jewish wisdom literature had begun making the connections.

Jesus: The Wisdom of God

There is another even more interesting aspect of Wisdom literature we can profitably explore. I have already mentioned how Jesus can be seen as 'pre-figured' in certain texts of the Jewish Bible, all related to the victim of the cross. Wisdom too, like Jesus, comes to dwell among her own (Proverbs 8-9 and John 1:14). What is Wisdom? She is God's agent in creation (Proverbs 8:22-31 and John 1:1-5). As time went on in the centuries before Jesus, Wisdom could also be known as the Torah and even begins to get assimilated to the Greek philosophical notion of *The Logos* (8.1). Wisdom is the Word of God: the word of God comes in textual form as Torah, therefore Wisdom = Torah.

In the New Testament a major theme is the comparison of Jesus to the figure of Wisdom. Paul does it in I Corinthians and Colossians, the author of Hebrews, the writers of the Fourth Gospel, of Luke and of Matthew also do so in their use of the Jesus material. Ben Witherington III has written a detailed tome titled *Jesus the Sage* that traces Wisdom as thoroughly as one could wish.[clxxvi] Witherington shows that the comparison of Jesus and Wisdom goes back to Jesus himself, particularly Jesus' parables. If so one would suppose that the theme of the righteous poor sufferer would be found in the parables...and it is! We see exactly this in the widow in Luke 18:1-8 or the beggar Lazarus in Luke 16:19-26.

Wisdom in the Jewish Scriptures is Torah lived purely, without blemish. In regard to God, Wisdom is described in personal or intimate terms in Proverbs 8:22-31. The Wisdom of Solomon makes connections in this way and also adds another.

> ***10:1*** Wisdom protected the first-formed father of the world, when he alone had been created; she delivered him from his transgression, ***2*** and gave him strength to rule all things. ***3*** But when an unrighteous man departed from her in his anger, he perished because in rage he slew his brother. ***4*** When the earth was flooded because of him, wisdom again saved it, steering the righteous man by a paltry piece of wood. ***5*** Wisdom also, when the nations in wicked agreement had been confounded, recognized the righteous man and preserved him blameless before God, and kept him strong in the face of his compassion for his child. ***6*** Wisdom rescued a righteous man when the ungodly were perishing; he escaped the fire that descended on the Five Cities.

Wisdom in found all through the stories of Genesis, according to this text. It is Wisdom who appears in the garden and delivers Adam (but how?) and it is the story of Cain and Abel that are the 'fall.' It was Cain's legacy of escalating violence that created the generation of the flood; it was Wisdom that steered the ark. Furthermore it was Wisdom who was present in the three messengers that saved Lot from destruction at Sodom. The writer goes on to suggest that every time there was an act of deliverance, that deliverance came through Wisdom. Wisdom then is a salvific figure. Little wonder that Jesus would see himself in Wisdom terms.

The New Testament writers surely do. Take the description of Wisdom in Wisdom of Solomon 7:25-26

> ***7:22*** for wisdom, the fashioner of all things, taught me. For in her there is a spirit that is intelligent, holy, unique, manifold, subtle, mobile, clear, unpolluted, distinct, invulnerable, loving the good, keen, irresistible, ***23*** beneficent, humane, steadfast, sure, free from anxiety, all-powerful, overseeing all, and penetrating through all spirits that are intelligent and pure and most subtle. ***24*** For wisdom is more mobile than any motion; because of her pureness she pervades and penetrates all things. ***25*** For she is a breath of the power of God, and a pure emanation of the glory of the Almighty; therefore nothing defiled gains entrance into her. ***26*** For she is a reflection of eternal light, a spotless mirror of the working of God, and an image of his goodness. ***27*** Though she is but one, she can do all things, and while remaining in herself, she renews all things; in every generation she passes into holy souls and makes them friends of God, and prophets; ***28*** for God loves nothing so much as the man who lives with wisdom.

You will notice in this description of Wisdom that there is nothing to indicate any wrath or anger or hostility or arbitrariness; the description is entirely positive, as it is in Proverbs 8. Now compare the language of verse 26 with Hebrews 1:2-3:

> "The Son...through whom God made the universe.
> He is the radiance of God's glory
> And the exact representation of his being
> Sustaining all things by his powerful word."

Or the Christ-hymn of Colossians 1:15-20. Jesus is:

> "The Image of the Invisible God
> By him all things were created
> He is before all things
> And by him all things exist.
> He is the head of the body
> He is the beginning
> And the firstborn from the dead

For God was pleased to dwell fully in Jesus
And through Jesus to reconcile everything."

Jesus as Wisdom personified is another way, like the son of the man, where Jesus used figures from his Scriptures, in this case, the figure of the wise person who suffers unjustly. We saw that the teaching on the 'son of man' was tied to the cross and of course the servant of Isaiah 53 is a sufferer. Each of these figures, son of man, the righteous sufferer, the suffering servant all have to do with the problem of violence.

Jesus, the Wisdom of God (I Cor. 1:24) is also God's lived Torah.[clxxvii] In 8.1 we will look in detail at how the writer of the Fourth Gospel uses this Wisdom/Torah/Logos connection to argue that it is Jesus, not a text, that is Torah enfleshed, a here's-how-you-do-it model. For now it is important to be able to reaffirm a thesis we have been advancing since the beginning of this book, namely that for the apostolic church, Jesus, not the written text (or the oral torah) was the Word, the express revelation of the fullness of divinity. God was revealed as a human life.

These are just a few of the figural uses of Wisdom by the writers of the New Testament. Did they come up with this on their own? Ben Witherington III thinks that Jesus intentionally used wisdom thinking in his teaching. His extensive research suggests that Jesus was intentionally reframing the wisdom tradition in his use of short sayings, parables, and metaphors. But what is really suggestive for our argument that Jesus had a 'critical' approach to his sacred texts is that,

> "One may also be surprised to discover how many of the major themes of proverbial Wisdom are totally or almost totally *absent* from the Jesus tradition. For example there are no proverbs urging the seeking of Wisdom, or suggesting that acquiring it is difficult. Nor does Jesus urge that the fear of God is the beginning of Wisdom. There are, furthermore, no proverbs or sayings urging hard work or character building exercises *per se*. Jesus offers nothing like the conventional androcentric and patriarchal Wisdom about women found in Proverbs."[clxxviii]

First, Witherington notes that many central themes of wisdom are absent from the teaching of Jesus. How could this be unless Jesus was reading this literature through a lens that required him to look critically? If these central themes were 'God's eternal truth' surely they would have found a way into his teaching, at least on the margins, but they don't. A dominant theme of Wisdom is that if you work hard, you will be blessed, but Jesus seems to subvert this with his "Blessed are you Poor." This would be an example of the way Jesus critiqued the Wisdom tradition.

Second, there are no proverbs inculcating the seeking of Wisdom, for Wisdom is not absent but present in Jesus. Nor are there any proverbs encouraging the follower of Jesus to fear God. This is crucial, for if fear is the beginning of Wisdom, then Jesus is not the Wisdom of God. He says, "Do not be afraid" (Luke 12:32). We fear a god who punishes, we trust a God who loves and forgives, heals and vindicates. If we mix them we believe only partly in God for we affirm that God is two-faced, Janus-like.

Third, Witherington contends that there are no 'How To" character building types of sayings. What a contrast to the modern bookstore, both secular and sacred with their shelves loaded with *"How To"* _____ (you fill in the blank). Imagine Jesus today looking over the titles in a Christian bookstore. "You want to live a successful Christian life? Hmm, start by selling all you have, give the proceeds to the needy and join me in almost certain death." Or "How to Get God's Blessing? Yes, that is important. Well, in order to do that you have to learn what it is to be dispossessed, sad and depressed all the time, very gentle, never hurting a fly, always wanting the right thing for everybody. You would also let every insult go, making peace wherever you went. Yep, I'd call that blessed."

Finally, Jesus breaks through the very clear male domination logic of the Jewish Scriptures. In order to do this he would have had to be able to recognize, as he read these texts, like Isaiah 61, the Psalms and Wisdom, when and how God was speaking. Just because the text says 'God' doesn't mean it is Jesus' *Abba*. This is a *sine qua non* (indispensible) part of the logic of Jesus' use of the Old Testament. It has taken almost 2,000 years since Jesus for this aspect of his message to get home to the world, and it still hasn't arrived in a lot of places.

Jesus is the human personification of God's Wisdom, God's Instruction, God's message (Wisdom, Torah, Word). The apostolic church certainly thought it so as we saw in the Christ hymns in the New Testament (1.1). When we read the Jewish Scriptures the way Jesus read them we will find the God he proclaimed and the reign of that God. As long as any of us, pastors or congregations, continue to ignore Jesus as our starting point and begin with a theory of inspiration, we will be relating back to Torah and Wisdom as though Jesus had not interpreted both. It is time for Christianity to let go of all that hinders it and start over by acknowledging just Jesus, the beginning, the middle and the end. God will provide the rest.

Chapter 7 Paul

7.1 Paul The Converted Persecutor

There are always three things I look for when reading scholars who write on the apostle Paul. What letters do they consider authentic? How do they use Acts in framing Paul? What is their relation to the Augustinian reading of Paul?

I accept the standard undisputed letters: Romans, I & II Corinthians, Galatians, Philippians, I Thessalonians and Philemon. Included in my Pauline canon are Colossians, and at its margins II Thessalonians. I read Ephesians as an 'orthodox' editing of a document highly dependent on Colossians; it is a beautiful summation of the Pauline emphasis on the universal grace of God.

I am comfortable with Luke's method of history writing in Acts, it is already familiar from his gospel. To be sure, there is an agenda in Acts, like any excellent history, it is more than a collection of 'facts'; good history is told as a tale. Where there are differences in chronology or theology between Luke and Paul, I side with Paul's letters.

In 1963 New Testament scholar Krister Stendahl published his very influential essay on "*The Apostle Paul and the Introspective Conscience of the West.*"[clxxix] This essay showed that when interpreters read Paul, their emphases are not Paul's emphases. I have since been interested in both the old and 'New Perspective on Paul.' This new perspective has helped revitalize Paul by placing him back into his Jewish context, a context he never left! But even the New Perspective can still occasionally labor under the presuppositions of an Augustinian interpretation of Paul.

Franz Overbeck once said that only one person came close to understanding Paul in the history of the church and that person was Marcion, yet even he misunderstood him! The author of II Peter in the early second century writes, "Paul's letters are difficult to understand (2 Peter 3:15-16)." Yet, oddly enough, it has been the re-discovery of Paul's letters by Augustine, Luther and then Barth that produced the big intellectual shifts in Christian theology. Difficult or not, they are worthwhile to know. First we need to understand what is commonly called the 'conversion of Paul.'

Acts records Paul's conversion three times (Acts 9, 22 and 29), but Paul recounts it only once in Galatians 1:15-17. Paul says that his encounter with Jesus was an apocalypse (this is the verb used): 'God revealed (*apocalypsed*) His son in me." The deep structure of Saul changed and became Paul. His entire way of thinking was shattered and rebuilt on a new foundation, Jesus Christ (I Cor. 3:11). The way he had perceived and directed his life to this point was entirely transformed.[clxxx]

Acts records that Paul was blinded by a dazzling light (9:3). Paul converts to Jesus and is saved and promised heaven when he dies. But is that what happened? Not hardly, not by a long shot. Paul is not asked if he has heard of the four spiritual laws. He is not asked to be born again. He is not asked if he would like to become a Christian convert. He is asked about his violence. "Saul, Saul, why do you persecute me?" (Acts 9:4) This was the big question for Paul. Why indeed did he persecute Jesus by persecuting his followers? What was it about Jesus that deserved persecution?

Paul speaks to this in one of his very few autobiographical statements in Philippians (3:4-6).

> 3:4 If anyone else thinks he has reasons to put confidence in the flesh, I have more: 5circumcised on the eighth day, of the people of Israel, of the tribe of Benjamin, a Hebrew of Hebrews; in regard to the law, a Pharisee; 6as for zeal, persecuting the church; as for legalistic righteousness, faultless.

Paul's pedigree is excellent. He lists three ethnic categories and three categories regarding his religious orientation. Paul says his orientation to the Torah was as a Pharisee. He doesn't tell us which school he was disposed to although Acts records that he studied under the Hillelite Gamaliel. Hillel and Shammai were the two great rabbis in the decades before Jesus and helped to shape the way Pharisees interpreted Torah. I think the statement in Philippians, "as for zeal", possibly suggests that Paul moved away from his more liberal Hillelite training (if one follows Acts in this regard) and joined the camp of Shammai, the more conservative group of the Pharisees. It was the Shammaite Pharisees that would line up with the zealous rebels during the war of 66-70 C.E.[clxxxi] Paul gives a concrete measure of his zeal; he was a persecutor. Like Phineas, Elijah and the Maccabees, Paul's zeal knew no limit, even death was compelled, and so Paul persecuted the church. Acts records he gave consent to Stephen's 'lynching.'

The Problem of Justifying Violence

Zeal for Torah was a problem not a blessing. In the phrase 'zeal for the law' Martin Hengel says that,

> "Here we have the zeal for the law of which Phineas (Numbers 25) and Elijah (I Kings 18) were the model, and which in particular had been part of the ideal of radical groups since the time of the

> Maccabees. Such a 'zealot' was unconditionally prepared to use force in order to turn God's wrath away from Israel, giving his own life to protect sanctuary and law against the serious lawbreaker...This was an attitude which was very popular in contemporary Judaism and, as Luke rightly indicates with the addition 'as all of you are today' (Acts 23.2), also provoked the mob organized against Paul."[clxxxii]

The logic that Paul used when persecuting Christians is now the logic used against him. Yet before his 'conversion or call' Paul could follow this logic and still, from his perspective, be a model of perfection when it came to fulfilling the requirements of the two Torot (oral and written Torahs). The question Paul would have to ask himself in the coming days was, "if I thought I was doing everything right, but now know I was doing something really wrong, including how I read my Bible, then everything I thought about God now has to be changed in light of the fact that God has exalted Jesus of Nazareth to the right hand of Majesty."

If we are going to call this a conversion narrative it is not Paul's conversion from Judaism to Christianity, he does not change religions. It is his conversion from persecutor to persecuted, from villain to martyr, from blameless Pharisee to least among the apostles and chief of sinners. It is not a change in his faith tradition. Paul was a Jew, just like Jesus, they never ceased being Jews and from the beginning to the end of their life would express their faith in a Jewish manner.

Krister Stendahl raises the question: Was the Damascus Road experience a conversion or a call? If it is not a change of religions but a call, to what is Paul called? In Romans and I Corinthians (Rom. 1:1, I Cor. 1:1) Paul asserts he is "called to be an apostle" and in 2 Corinthians and Colossians (2 Cor. 1:1, Col. 1:1) he says he is "an apostle of Jesus Christ by the will of God" while in Galatians (Gal 1:1) he says he "was sent not from men nor by any man but by Jesus Christ and God the Father." Paul's language echoes that of the calling of the Jewish prophets, notably Isaiah and Jeremiah (Isa. 6:1, Jer. 1:1-4). Paul therefore, was not converted from Judaism; he was changed within it.

We have already noted that it was a zealous interpretation of Torah from which Paul was converted. What exactly was the problem with Torah? Was it not "holy, righteous and good" (Romans 7:12)? Yes it was but it had one fatal flaw: it "was powerless in that it was weakened by sinful flesh" (Rom 8:3). How was it weakened? It has nothing to do with the capacity to keep the commandments, for Paul himself was "blameless" in this regard and I would imagine so were many others. Nor did it have to do with some kind of works-righteousness, as though Judaism was not a religion of grace. The Torah was weakened in the way we humans interpreted it in a zealous fashion. For Paul, to interpret Jesus "according to the flesh" was the acknowledgement that

> "he once knew Christ 'in a fleshly way.' He had possessed an inferior type of knowledge about Jesus. All this can mean in the light of what he says about the persecution of the church (Phil. 3:6) is that he once shared the estimation of Jesus common among his contemporaries, namely that he was an heretical teacher and a turbulent agitator whose activities had with justice brought him to a scaffold. This, Paul now recognizes, was a false judgment which he had abandoned."[clxxxiii]

When Torah was interpreted from the perspective of the persecutor, Torah authorized social retribution in the name of God. This is what Paul saw. But Torah had another reading, another perspective on how it can and may be interpreted in the light of the life and death of Jesus of Nazareth. It can be interpreted in terms of love (1.2, 2.1, 3.2). This is Paul's argument in Galatians 3:15-22. He uses the term 'law' (*nomos*) to refer to the covenant at Sinai and the giving of, at a minimum, the Ten Commandments. He contrasts this with 'promise' (*epangellia*). Because of the 'violence justifying' texts in Torah, when seen as God's Word, the 'law' could only be a death dealing instrument (Gal. 3:21, Rom. 7:10), and that in more than just a spiritual sense, but in the real sense of community sanctioned death.[clxxxiv]

Paul and the Two Trajectories of His Bible

The problem lies not with Torah, but with human interpretation of Torah. This human interpretation is already contained within Torah *along with divine revelation*. J Louis Martyn asserts that part of what Paul is doing in Galatians is developing this insight. He queries "is there some sense in which Paul speaks in Galatians 5:3 and 5:14 of genuinely different aspects or voices of the Law?"[clxxxv] Martyn observes:

> "Whereas Paul in 5:3 refers to the voice of the Sinaitic Law that curses and enslaves (Gal. 3:10, 13, 19, 4:3-5, 21a, 24-25), he speaks in 5:14 of the voice of the original, pre-Sinaitic Law that articulates God's own mind (3:8, 4:21b)."
>
> "Paul draws a sharp contrast between two voices, the blessing/promise voice of God and the cursing/enslaving voice of the Law."
>
> "[in] writing Galatians 3 and 4, Paul has in mind a Law with two quite distinct voices, one false and cursing, and one – representing God – true and promising."

> "In Galatians the Law's relationship to Christ is a subject best approached by noting first, that the Law has done something to Christ, and second, that Christ has also done something to the Law…Christ has defeated the cursing voice of the Law…[and] Christ has brought to completion the imperative of the Law's original voice…the Law is permanently secondary to Christ."[clxxxvi]

There would be then two ways to read the Bible according to Paul. I have sought to establish throughout this book that there are two perspectives in the Bible, the voice of the victim and the voice of the victimizer. Martyn, among others, makes this assertion regarding how to read the Bible a biblical datum, when he argues that Paul himself makes this distinction. Douglas Campbell has followed this up in his recent groundbreaking book on Paul.[clxxxvii]

Campbell absolutely demolishes the conventional reading of Paul that sees justification by faith/grace as the center of his thought.[clxxxviii] In a thorough re-reading of Romans 1-4, Campbell details in meticulous fashion that Paul is engaging a specific false teacher and that in Romans 1-4 Paul lays out both his *and the teacher's* theology. When read as a 'debate' between Paul and the false teacher, Romans 1-4 in fact underscores the gospel preached by Paul in Galatia by showing that, for the teacher (and other false teachers), Christ has not come to end the Law, but to validate it for Gentiles.[clxxxix] Paul never claims an eternal validity for the whole Torah. Like Martyn, Campbell claims that Paul has a different view of God than that of 'the [false] Teacher.'

> "The Teacher has not taken Christ's disclosure of God's benevolence with full seriousness; that disclosure has been subordinated and assimilated to some prior conception of God that is retributive…hence, fundamentally different conceptions of God are at stake at Rome."
>
> "His [Paul's] gospel is rooted in a *dikaiosune theou* (often translated as 'righteousness of God'). The Teacher's gospel is rooted, however, in an *orge theou* (often translated as 'wrath of God') – an anger that responds to all actions retributively, and to sinful actions punitively. *These two basal conceptions of God could not, in this sense, be more different.*"
>
> "In short, for Paul, God, as revealed by Christ, is benevolent."[cxc]

The argument that the Bible has two distinct voices has support then from both Jesus (2.1) and Paul. So does the argument that at stake in the gospel is the way we understand the Janus-faced god in relation to God in Christ (1.3, 3.2). The separation of the voices (or discerning the spirits) is necessary in order for us to hear what is really good about the gospel (5.4). There is an important text in 2 Corinthians 3:13-18 where Paul explores two possible ways to read Torah, veiled and unveiled.

> 13We are not like Moses, who would put a veil over his face to keep the Israelites from gazing at it while the radiance was fading away. 14But their minds were made dull, for to this day the same veil remains when the old covenant is read. It has not been removed, because only in Christ is it taken away. 15Even to this day when Moses is read, a veil covers their hearts. 16But whenever anyone turns to the Lord, the veil is taken away. 17Now the Lord is the Spirit, and where the Spirit of the Lord is, there is freedom. 18And we, who with unveiled faces all reflect the Lord's glory, are being transformed into his likeness with ever-increasing glory, which comes from the Lord, who is the Spirit.

To read Torah veiled is to read it knowing that that which was glorious about it was fading. What does it mean when glory fades? Notice Paul does not say the text loses its glory, but the interpreter of the text; it is Moses who wears a veil. The Israelites had identified Moses and the text, if Moses' glory faded, then it might also be possible to say that the glory of the text was also fading. Moses avoided this by wearing a veil. Denying the fading glory of the interpreter is tantamount to becoming "dull", "stubborn" or "without feeling" (*poreo*). Dullness of heart or the inability to interpret the text rightly stems from the refusal to see that the text is not divine. It is not the letter (*gramma*) of the text that is revelation (2 Cor. 3:6-8) but the interpretation of the text in the light of the Spirit, who is Jesus.

Paul pursues this line of reasoning saying that both the ancient Israelites and his contemporaries read Torah 'veiled.' They read it from the perspective of divinely sanctioned death, through the lens of zeal, that which authorized killing in the divine name. The only way to read the text aright would be in an encounter with the Risen Jesus, the Lord who is the Spirit. It is only Jesus who can help us see that there is another way to read the Bible, in an unveiled manner, transparent, open and free. Such was the case for the apostle Paul for it was his encounter with the Risen Christ that transformed him from a zealous persecutor to a defender of Christians and the gospel message.[cxci]

The Challenge of Paul When Reading the Bible

We know that Paul's message was not easily heard nor widely accepted. Not only were there "false teachers" in Galatia and "false apostles" in Corinth; Paul also had a rocky relationship with the Jerusalem church headed up by James and Peter. He shares his side of the story in Galatians 2:1-14. Peter, James and John are "reputed pillars" of this community, but whatever anyone else thinks of them is not important to Paul (Gal. 2:6). Peter caused a stir at Antioch by first eating or breaking bread with Gentile Christians then, after the appearance of men under James' authority, would no longer eat with them.

At stake for the Jerusalem community was the role of the Torah; should Gentiles be required to become Jews in order to become Christians? If so, then they would be kosher and any Christian Jew could eat with his fellow converted Gentile become Jew *and not have to be concerned about pollution from idolatry*. For Paul it had to do with the way Torah was interpreted. The way it was being read along exclusionary lines by the Jerusalem church leadership (no Gentiles allowed) was for Paul, the same kind of reading that got Jesus crucified in the first place. Jesus' persecutors and evidently the Jerusalem Christian leadership both read Torah from the perspective of exclusion, which is the same thing as reading the Bible in the light of a 'holiness code' (3.2). What Paul is saying is that the way he read the Bible that authorized his persecution of Christians was the same way Peter was currently reading the Bible. The exclusionary principle may have shades of grey (from shunning to execution) but it is all the same. To read the Bible from this perspective leads not to reconciliation and life, but to estrangement and death.

My friend Jonathan Sauder puts it (almost tongue in cheek) this way:

> "If we believe that Jesus is really the Wisdom and Logic of God then we are faced with the same issue that divided Peter and Paul in Galatians 2:11-19: Is Jesus allowed to reformat our basic understanding of God's cosmic Order? Peter's answer was 'No.' Jesus gives us what could be called a 'dispensation', an exception, valid in certain times and places, to kosher food laws. But at the end of the day we must concede to the guardians of the canonical tradition (the visitors from Jerusalem) that kosher is written into the fabric of the universe and is not to be discounted.
>
> Paul's answer was 'Yes.' He did not accuse Peter of merely being insensitive to his new Gentile brethren. Paul thought that the very gospel, the very claim that Jesus is God's way of being righteous, was what was at stake here. Either Peter had to stop thinking of the nature of God in terms of cultural taboos or he had to acknowledge that Jesus gives him permission to violate God's Order, thus making Jesus, in Paul's words, a 'minister of sin' (Gal. 2:17) – a facilitator of deviance from the taboo based order of God's created cosmos.
>
> Peter the Dispensationalist partially desacralized kosher taboos and social segregation but in the eyes of Paul this incomplete deconstruction meant building again the ways of thinking about

> God's holiness that had driven men of religious conscience to kill Jesus as an enemy of God's Order."

Peter's way of reading Torah is similar to the 'opponent's' attacks on Paul. In Acts 21:27-28 on his final trip to Jerusalem (in the summer of 57), Paul is accused of teaching "all people everywhere against our people, our law and this place (the Temple)." Others perceive Paul as having a "Torah-less" gospel.[cxcii] They would be right that Paul is reading his Bible differently than he had done before; they would have been wrong in thinking Paul rejected his Bible. Paul was not a Marcionite. The difference between the way pre-converted Saul read his Bible and the way post-conversion Paul read it after that event is that afterword he read the Bible understanding the problem of sacred violence (the belief that violence can be God's will).

What then, was Paul's understanding of Torah? This is perhaps one of the most complicated issues in Pauline studies for the past fifty years, even perhaps, the last 2,000 years! We have seen that Marcion made this the preeminent issue in the second century and that in response to Marcion the church began to read the Old Testament differently than Paul. Modern studies on Paul and the Torah illuminate this quandary by seeking to show how Paul argued in a Jewish manner or how he used the Scriptures or that he accepted that Torah was still valid for Jews but not for Gentiles. They are all correct, but only a few writers observe that it is the problem of zealous violent interpretation of Torah that is at the heart of Paul's argument with both his fellow Jews and Jewish-Christians (and in the case of Galatians, converts to Judaism).

James Dunn captures all of these issues in a short summary when he observes that

> "Paul's negative thrust against the law is against the law taken over too completely by Israel, the law misunderstood by a misplaced emphasis on boundary-marking ritual [kosher, Sabbath, circumcision], the law become a tool of sin in its too close identification with matters of the flesh, the law side-tracked into a focus for nationalistic zeal."[cxciii]

The issue of boundary marking is the problem of differentiation we observed in community formation around a scapegoat; the law exacerbates sin in that prohibitions cannot stop the hemorrhaging of mimetic conflict, and in fact increases it; and, the law can be interpreted in a zealous fashion, justifying all manner of retribution and scapegoating. This is what Paul was arguing against.

Robert Hamerton-Kelly says it very well when he writes,

> "For Paul, the reading of the Torah by his Jewish contemporaries on the other hand brings death because like a veil of ignorance it comes between the readers and Christ. The letters of the text function to obscure rather than to reveal the true goal and purpose of the Law, which is to point to faith in Christ by revealing the sin of Adam and the victimage on which the world is based. If the Mosaic Jews were to read Moses in the light of the crucifixion, they would see the revelation of the distortion of the primal prohibitions by the faithlessness of Adam, and understand how it is that the Law brings death – that is, they would read it as Paul read it. By the same token if Christians were to read the Torah in the Jewish way, they would lose sight of the One whom the law cursed and crucified. The Law kills because the Mosaic interpretation covers up the surrogate victim mechanism and spins the sacred web of self-delusion through observance of holy rules and rituals."[cxciv]

The problem for Paul as Hamerton-Kelly and Dunn see it is an interpretive one. This is why we have spent so much time in this book arguing that the problem is not the Bible itself, but the way the Bible has been and is currently interpreted within the grid of sacred violence. Theologians and clergy abound, complete with PhD's, books, articles, dictionaries and the latest Bible software who, in spite of what Scripture says about itself, interpret Scripture against itself. It is no different today than it was in Isaiah's day or that of Jesus and Paul. The gospel message has always had an uphill journey as it challenges the false structuring of religion, no matter what form it takes.

What Paul is arguing against when it comes to the Law is that there are times when what one perceives as doing the right thing is wrong; just because the Bible 'authorizes' violence does not mean that it is God's will. This is the shift in perspective that changed Paul's life upside down. For Paul, the only thing that mattered was "faith expressed as love" (Gal. 5:6). Christ had brought an end to zealous Torah interpretation (Rom. 10:5) by becoming the object of the people's wrath (Gal. 3:13-14), the victim unjustly prosecuted by the requirements of Torah. If love is the lens by which to interpret Torah, as both Jesus and Paul do, then it must be said that the grace-filled compassionate interpretation of Torah found in many synagogues across North America is more 'Christian' than the wrath filled, hellfire and brimstone preaching of many churches. The issue for Paul, as it was for Jesus (1.2), was not that of Judaism vs. another religion, but how we read our Scriptures in the light of the Compassionate Maker of heaven and earth. It is not our relationship to the Bible that counts but our relation to Jesus, God's interpreter.

7.2 Paul's Hopeful Vision

"Have you been saved?" "Are you born again? "Will you go to heaven when you die?" Over these past thirty years I have been asked these questions a few times as have many readers. This is laudable because behind these questions lies the belief that Jesus can be known *just like we know other human beings.* The real question is: Which Jesus are we following?

Paul experienced in his churches, especially Galatia, Corinth and probably Colossae, that there were false ways of rendering Jesus' story. He will tell the Galatians that if anyone, even the highest angel, should preach a different gospel than the one he preached, well, let's just say that things could go very bad for them (Gal 1:8). In 2 Corinthians, in what is known as the 'tearful letter' (2 Cor. 2:4 = 2 Cor. 10-13), Paul goes on the offensive against 'super-apostles.' There were different ways of telling the story of Jesus (2 Cor. 11:4); some had evidently put the *em-PHA-sis on the wrong sy-LA-ble.* Paul knows himself to be an authentic witness to the Risen Jesus and the message of salvation in Christ. But what exactly is this salvation? Is it forensic justification by faith? Is it acceptance of right doctrine? Is it baptism in the right church? Is it religious feeling? Who is included in this salvation? Some? Many? All? A few? How is this salvation effected? Where and when does it take place? Is salvation the act of redeeming personal autonomous subjects or is it corporate redemption of all the peoples of this world?

The first thing we note from Paul is that salvation is always at God's initiative. It is the opposite of religion, which always begins with human initiative. It is God who "set forth Jesus as a propitiation for sin" (Rom. 3:25) and it is God who "demonstrates his love for us in this: while we were yet sinners, Christ died for us" (Rom. 5:8). 2 Corinthians 5:17-18 says, "If anyone is in Christ, the new creation has arrived. All this is from God." Salvation is not something we dream up, nor is it just icing on the cake of human culture. It is an entirely new thing and it comes from God.

The second thing we notice is that salvation occurs in the person of Jesus. Jesus is the center of Pauline theology and thus of Paul's understanding of God's work in Christ. How Paul understood this work will be the burden of the next section. There are numerous texts in Paul's letters to support this thesis, and I doubt there would be any serious disagreement about this. That Jesus was central to Paul's theology can also be demonstrated by how his successors did their theology. An example of how one of Paul's followers did theology can be found in Ephesians 1:3-14.

> 3Praise be to the God and Father of our Lord Jesus Christ, who has blessed us in the heavenly realms with every spiritual blessing in

> Christ. 4For he chose us in him before the creation of the world to
> be holy and blameless in his sight. In love 5he predestined us to be
> adopted as his sons through Jesus Christ, in accordance with his
> pleasure and will— 6to the praise of his glorious grace, which he
> has freely given us in the One he loves. 7In him we have redemption
> through his blood, the forgiveness of sins, in accordance with the
> riches of God's grace 8that he lavished on us with all wisdom and
> understanding. 9And he made known to us the mystery of his will
> according to his good pleasure, which he purposed in Christ, 10to be
> put into effect when the times will have reached their fulfillment—
> to bring all things in heaven and on earth together under one head,
> even Christ.
>
> 11In him we were also chosen, having been predestined according
> to the plan of him who works out everything in conformity with the
> purpose of his will, 12in order that we, who were the first to hope in
> Christ, might be for the praise of his glory. 13And you also were
> included in Christ when you heard the word of truth, the gospel of
> your salvation. Having believed, you were marked in him with a
> seal, the promised Holy Spirit, 14who is a deposit guaranteeing our
> inheritance until the redemption of those who are God's
> possession—to the praise of his glory.

Here we have what appears to be a song (see 1.1) of three verses with a chorus, 'to the praise of his glorious grace,' as it were. Each verse tells the same story from a different aspect, first the Father, then the Son, then the Holy Spirit. It is one God named as Father, Son and Spirit, not three gods, but one singular God named three different ways as Creator, Reconciler and Redeemer.

Over eleven times in these verses one can find the words "in Christ", "in Him", "through Jesus Christ," and so forth. This christological emphasis on the work of God is not without significance for far too many Christians today have a view of God that doesn't look like Jesus very much. The God of Christendom is frequently Janus-faced and all too often distant, aloof, almighty and out of reach (1.3). The God and Father of Jesus chose to share our existence, not remain in distant mysterious transcendence. The *Abba* chose us in Jesus before the world began, to be *for us* in Jesus, forgiving us our sins and redeeming our relationship with God's self. And so in being *for us* from time immemorial, God also chooses to be *with us* in our present, as the one who comes *to us* from the good future. God *with us* and *in us* and *for us*, the Holy Spirit, the Spirit of the Risen Jesus. All that can be comprehended of our salvation can be found in this longest single sentence in the New Testament (202 words).

The salvation that occurred in Jesus affected the entire cosmos (Col 1:15-20). If the consequence of sin that affected the entire human story was the result of the disobedience of one man in a garden, the deconstruction of that consequence was the result of one person's obedience *in another garden* (Rom. 5:15-16). Jesus' obedience brought life to all (Rom. 5:18). Just as Adam's story is the story of Everyone, so also the story of Jesus is the story of All. This is why when the early church talked about salvation they referred to Jesus as Lord of all, not just a few, not just some, but all.

Compare this to the "I, me, my" ways we speak of salvation in contemporary Christianity. Persons are encouraged to tell a personal salvation story when they attend church. No longer does the salvation wrought by God in Jesus have corporate dimensions, no longer is it the salvation of the world. The way we tell the story of salvation is frankly narcissistic.

If the work that God has done in Jesus is for the whole world this means that when we speak of salvation we do it in such a way as to include the whole world. So why don't we? There are three reasons I think that we don't. The first comes from the early church and its rejection of Judaism. By arguing that the Old Testament belonged properly to the church, and not Judaism, Christianity has lost contact with its 'parent.' The gospel is seen less as the dynamic activity of God with the world and more in terms of a metaphysics, which we explored in chapter 4.

The second reason, which we mentioned in 4.2, was Augustine's theory of predestination or election. When we divide the world into two camps, good and bad, saved and unsaved, we import Platonic dualism into salvation. It is true that Augustine's doctrine of election was meant to protect the grace of God against those who would assert that salvation was from human initiative, but his 'a few go to heaven and the majority go to hell when we all deserve hell' does not capture the incredible manifestation of God's grace in the New Testament.[cxcv] It is true that some marginal New Testament documents appear to share Augustine's sentiment, but we should expect these misinterpretations of the gospel message. The apostolic church was not error free. While the New Testament contains gospel there are also indications in this literature of a slide into myth (e.g., the denigration of women in the Pastorals or Jude's apocalyptic dualism).

The third reason we don't speak of salvation for the world and tend to speak of salvation in terms of ourselves stems from the development of the concept of the autonomous human being beginning in the Renaissance in 14th century Italy and flowering in the 18th century Enlightenment. I have already critiqued that trend (5.1 & 5.2). North American Christianity buys into all three of these mistakes in far too many churches.

And Deliverance for All

For Paul (as well as for Jesus), salvation had an explicit sociological dimension: Christ's death was to be the means by which both Jews and Gentiles were reconciled (Eph. 2:10-22, Rom. 9-11). In the Introduction I mentioned the growing interest in both ancient Judaism and Christianity in the twentieth century and that we have clearer handles on the relationship between the two. We also better understand the nature of the hope of post-Exilic Judaism. That hope was not that Jews would dominate Gentiles nor that God would wipe out the Heathen Evil Empires but that the entire world would acknowledge that the God of Israel, the Maker of heaven and earth is the true God. Isaiah gives expression to this:

> 60:**1** "Arise, shine, for your light has come, and the glory of the Lord rises upon you. **2** See, darkness covers the earth and thick darkness is over the peoples, but the Lord rises upon you and his glory appears over you. **3** Nations will come to your light, and kings to the brightness of your dawn. **4** Lift up your eyes and look about you: All assemble and come to you; your sons come from afar, and your daughters are carried on the hip."

Zechariah (14:16) also, even if his prophecy is bounded by the mythological notion of punishment asserts that,

> "Then the survivors from all the nations that have attacked Jerusalem will go up year after year to worship the King, the Lord Almighty, and to celebrate the feast of tabernacles."

The hope of Israel after the exile was for God and God alone to reign over all the nations. For Paul this took the form of Jesus, the King who reconciles all his subjects, for it was both Jew and Gentile who conspired and executed him. How did this work out for the Apostle Paul in concrete terms? We recall that Paul had trouble with those Jewish Christians who followed their compatriots in reading Torah through the lens of a holiness code requiring Gentiles to become Jews before they could become Christians. Yet this did not stop Paul from reaching out to them by going to his congregations and seeking donations to help the poor in the Jerusalem church (Rom. 15:26, 2 Cor. 8-9). This symbolic gesture was an expression of the Jewish prophetic hope that Jews and Gentiles would be one family, all recognized as children of God.

The gospel, for Paul, has profound sociological consequences; it is not just a ticket to get into heaven when one dies. The gospel transforms relationships: where once Jews and Gentiles had been mortal enemies, now they are seen as siblings. Dietrich Ritschl expresses this notion that Christianity and Judaism belong together poignantly:

> "It is important to be exposed fully to the shame of the scorn, trivialization and usurping of God which has continually become a historical reality as a result of Jewish and Christian theologies, as a result of persecution of Jews by Christians, and as a result of Jewish isolation and Christian claims to a monopoly. It is the only honest evaluation we can make of our common Jewish and Christian history. If in the last resort, it is God who is the accuser, the rejection and mockery of Jewish life in accordance with Torah and the Christian conviction of faith and theology in our time is sufficient occasion no longer to do theology after Auschwitz to the exclusion of this fundamental wound. If the very question of a loving God in the face of a single fellow human being who suffers the hatred of humanity is sufficient occasion to enquire into the first and most central statements about God's relationship to humanity, how much more is the total failure of the relationship of faith and love between individuals who speak of a God who loves, is ready to suffer yet at the same time is righteous: Jews and Christians, Israel and the Church."[cxcvi]

If Paul were here today I suspect he would make a similar case. How can this type of reconciliation occur? The Roman Catholic Church made a step forward in this direction during Vatican II. In a prayer attributed to Pope John XXIII this can be seen:

> "We recognize today that many centuries of blindness have veiled our eyes so that we no longer see the beauty of your elect people and no longer recognize on its countenance the features of our first born brother. And we understand that we have a mark of Cain on our forehead. Over the centuries our brother Abel has lain in blood that we have shed – and he has wept tears that we have caused because we forgot your love.
>
> Forgive us the curse which we wrongly attached to the name of Jews. Forgive us for nailing you to the cross a second time in your flesh. We did not know what we were doing."[cxcvii]

Christian anti-Semitism ought to be an oxymoron, an impossibility, but is sadly all too real throughout the history of Christianity. If, for Paul, salvation was global and included the Gentiles in the hope of Israel, it stands to reasons that we modern Christians may acknowledge not just our debt to Judaism but also our gratitude. Many aspects of Torah interpretation in parts of contemporary Judaism are remarkably closer to Jesus and Paul than that which is preached from many 'Christian' pulpits.

There is, however, a need to address one fundamental distortion of this reconciliation: that of Christian Dispensationalism with Jewish Zionism. Western guilt following the Holocaust combined with British mismanagement to create a 'homeland' for the Jews, the state of Israel. In order to do so, those who had peopled the land for almost 2,000 years were 'forced into exile.' The decision to make a Jewish State lies behind much of the current 'war on terror.' If it was not a good decision to force tens of thousands into forced exile so others could come home from their exile, it is certainly also not a good decision to justify the retaliation we have seen from Hamas, al-Qaeda and Hezbollah. Both the Christian Left and the Christian Right have bought into taking sides in this conflict.

I am not saying that the Jewish people do not need a homeland, for they have endured wandering for more than 1,800 years. Nor is it anti-Semitic to raise questions about the role Zionism plays in modern Judaism; there have been many internal Jewish critiques of such a position. I am saying that the problem that both Jesus and Paul confronted, namely zealous nationalism, is the primary issue that also faces us today whether it is Arab, American, Jewish or European. It was the phenomenon of nationalism that killed Jesus.

N.T. Wright comments that for Paul the plight of Israel was mirrored in his pre-conversion assessment of the way to handle the followers of Jesus: they deserved to be killed for they had critiqued Torah, Temple and Land.

> "Near the heart of the critique we find the accusation that Israel is sinful, but the critique cannot be reduced to terms of 'human sin, with Israel as a special example.' Near the heart of the critique we find the analysis of Israel as double-minded, but the critique cannot be reduced to terms of existentialist muddle with Jews happening to play the leading role in the Sartrean drama. At the very heart of the critique we find the rebellion of Israel against the covenant purposes of God, *seen* as the acting out by Israel of the primeval sin of Adam, coming to full flowering in 'national righteousness', the meta-sin against which the gospel of the cross struck with its scandalous force, and resulting in Israel's rejection of that gospel."[cxcviii]

North American Christians should not feel smug that 'they have accepted' Christ' while Jews continue to disavow him, for if someone today were to suggest that American Christians were not meant to have a homeland they would literally be up in arms (after all we have the second amendment to defend). The confluence of church and state, going back to Constantine has made zealous nationalism just as much of a problem for contemporary American Christianity as it was and is for Judaism.

Salvation, for Paul as for Jesus, had to do with the healing of all relationships, but especially the relationship between the people of God, the Jews and those 'not called God's people', the Gentiles. Ralph Martin summarizes Paul's doctrine of salvation by observing that Paul

> "Announced the arrival of a new age and cast his lot with the new beginning that had been made in world history. On the basis of a global reconciliation that embraces the cosmic powers, the forces of sin and death, and humankind as a sinful race in Christ's victory over evil, he moved to proclaim deliverance from all human ills that afflicted both his society and his readers."[cxcix]

If Paul were around today I suspect he might ask all those committed to peace to gather together, Muslim, Christian and Jewish, to seek ways to each call their own faith traditions to once again recognize that the Maker of all things is a God of Peace. "Salvation is for the Jew first, but also for the Gentile" (Rom 1:16). We must each in our own way challenge the notion of zealous nationalism and a zealous reading of our sacred texts. If we do so we bring light into the darkness of human conflict; if we won't we can only expect things to end up in human catastrophe.

7.3 The Significance of the Death and Resurrection of Jesus

We have already begun to explore the role that the death and resurrection of Jesus play in the apostle Paul's theology. In this section we want to look more closely at how Paul describes the effects of God's work in Jesus. What was God accomplishing by becoming a human being?

In the last section I pointed out that for Paul, salvation had primarily a corporate thrust while critiquing our modern solipsistic (ego-centered) appropriation of God's work for us. This is not to deny that salvation is personal; the fact is that we each experience and appropriate God's redemptive work according to our own personal story.

For the apostle the work of Jesus on our behalf affects four significant areas of our lives: the personal, the theological, the social and the ethical. It is personal because in our baptism we make a pledge (I Peter 3:21) to live with clear consciences and seek to be transformed in the renewing of the ways we think (Rom. 12:1-2); it is theological for the work of Jesus transforms not only our thinking about ourselves but also the ways in which we have thought about God. It is social because in Jesus' death we see that forgiveness is offered to all (I Cor. 15:22) and thus achieves reconciliation between enemies (Eph. 2:14-21) and it is ethical, for by dying and rising with Jesus in baptism we learn how to think in new ways that affect the ways we relate to each other (Col 3:1-4). In short, the work of Christ, his person, his message, his life, death, resurrection and ascension are all done for us in order to recreate us and restore the image of God within each of us and all of us.

In this section we want to explore how the death and resurrection of Jesus changed the way we live together before God. In 3.3 we looked at how Jesus understood the consequence of his mission and what rejection of his message would mean. We found that, in the Gospels, there is nothing to suggest that on the cross Jesus was appeasing an angry God.[cc]

Where shall we begin? Let's look at a well-known passage, Romans 3:23-26:

> "23for all have sinned and fall short of the glory of God, 24and are justified freely by his grace through the redemption that came by Christ Jesus. 25God presented him as a sacrifice of atonement, through faith in his blood. He did this to demonstrate his justice, because in his forbearance he had left the sins committed beforehand unpunished— 26he did it to demonstrate his justice at the present time, so as to be just and the one who justifies those who have faith in Jesus."

There are several key questions we must resolve in order to interpret this text. The first concerns the translation of *hilasterion*, which the NIV translates as "a sacrifice of atonement." The KJV translates this term as "propitiation" while the RSV uses "expiation." To propitiate a god is to make a sacrifice to appease wrath, anger or a curse. We are already familiar with this as *the sacrificial principle*. On the other hand, to expiate sin is to remove it, it looks to the object causing sin rather than God as the object to be appeased. There has been quite a bit of ink spilled over which translation best captures *hilasterion*. Those who reject an angry divinity prefer *expiation* while those like neo-Reformed thinkers John Piper and Thomas Schreiner believe that God's wrath needs to be assuaged and justice satisfied prefer *propitiation*.

The way out of this dilemma is to follow the logic of Paul's subversion of the sacrificial process. Robert Hamerton-Kelly points out that,

> "The major new element is that Paul inverts the traditional understanding of sacrifice so that God is the offerer, not the receiver, and the scapegoat goes into the sacred precinct rather than out of it. Christ is a divine offering to humankind, not a human offering to God.
>
> In the normal order of sacrifice, humans give and the god receives; here the god gives and humans receive. The usual explanation of this passage is that human sin deserved divine punishment, but in mercy God substituted a propitiatory offering to bear the divine wrath instead

> of humanity. We must insist on the fact that the recipients are human, otherwise we fall into the absurdity of God's giving a propitiatory gift to God. The second point to note is that not only the order of giver and receiver is reversed but also the spatial order. Normally the offerer goes from profane to sacred space to make the offering; here the offerer comes out of sacred space into profane, publically to set forth (*proetheto*) the propitiation (*hilasterion*) there. These inversions of the normal order of sacrifice mean that it is not God who needs to be propitiated, but humanity, and not in the recesses of the Sacred, but in the full light of day."[cci]

The point of this is that if one insists on translating *hilasterion* as propitiation then one must also take into consideration the subversion of the *sacrificial principle*. There is therefore, in this passage no justification for arguing that God's wrath must be propitiated. We humans are the ones who need to be appeased. Whether we translate *hilasterion* as 'propitiation' or 'expiation', in neither case do we need speak of God's wrath being appeased, it is not in the text itself, it can only come from prior assumptions regarding sacrifice in general.[ccii]

If the death of Jesus was not to propitiate the wrath of an angry divinity whose justice had been offended, then what does it actually accomplish? I will highlight three inter-related areas that Paul suggests Christ's death affected: the realm of sin, the rule of law, and the principalities and powers,

Sin, the Law and Jesus' Death

Christ's death affects the realm of sin. Of the sixty-three times Paul uses the word *hamartia* (usually translated as 'sin') fifty-eight of those are in the singular. This bit of linguistic data is important because it suggests that for Paul, sin is to be conceived less as a specific violation of commandments and more as a power or principle of the human condition. It indicates a failure, a breakdown, and a lack of achieving what one sets out to do, recognition that no matter how hard we try we will never be able to achieve what we set out to accomplish. Most often today, sin is conceived in moral terms, but for Paul, it is a description of the Adamic way of existence, a way of being human that may well be seeking God but falls short of its mark, like an arrow shot at a target that doesn't quite make it.

There is a highway by my house where a speed limit sign is posted: 55 miles per hour is the maximum one can drive. Yet regularly people do 60, 65 or even 70 miles per hour. These same people would not think of committing murder, yet they violate the law when they drive. Why is this? Because the consequence of speeding is only a traffic ticket whereas the consequence for murder can be life in prison or the death sentence. We pick and chose which laws we are willing to break. We talk on our cell phones or text message while we drive but we would not rob a store for the same reason. What we don't seem to realize is that bad driving habits also put people's lives in jeopardy but as long as a cop is not around to see it we go with the motto "where there is no law, there is no sin."

We have already seen (5.1, 5.2, 7.1) that there is a direct connection between primal prohibitions and victimage and that law is unable to stop us from sinning and thus make us better "archers" (able to hit the mark). We shall return shortly to this. What we need is a better definition of sin that captures our failure yet also transcends mere moral transgression. Pastor Denny Moon has come up with one of the most realistic definitions I have ever heard: "sin is the destructive way we handle our pain." The root of sin is thus a destructuring of the self and its relationships. This definition is an admirable fit with our understanding of being human. To sin is to break apart our relationships. Sin against God is then not just a violation of taboos, but a propensity to demonstrate a lack of care and concern for our relation to divinity and one another.

How then does law relate to sin? Take a young child for example. The parent lays down a law "do not touch the stove." The parent is aware that the consequence of touching the hot stove is pain. The child learns this the first time they violate the law and touch the stove. In the same way we adults fear certain consequences of breaking social laws and ordinances. It is fear that keeps us in line, fear, not of ruining our relationships, but fear of getting caught.

Take the same parent and child. The parent says the child may not listen to a certain type of music. When I was growing up my mother didn't like many of the rock and roll records I bought. Now they are considered classic rock but to her they were horrid screeching, loud and abrasive. I was not allowed to have albums whose cover art offended her (I bought them anyway). Is a taboo to avoid a hot stove on the same level as one's personal taste in music? When I became a 'born again Christian' in 1975 the church I attended said that rock and roll was the devil's music and I should destroy all my records. What? I could not believe that, so I boxed them up, now they have become collector's items. This may seem to be a trite example but it suffices to demonstrate that so many laws we have are little more than the legislation of personal or cultural taste. Yet we all too frequently make our own personal convictions into universal law. And so any time anyone violates our laws, we get offended.

Here in Lancaster County, PA, I live among various Old Order sects whose women wear head coverings. Many of these groups tie their salvation into the fact that they obey Paul's commands in I Cor. 11 for women to wear head coverings. They look askance at the liberalism of modern Christians who will not obey God's command to wear them and privately muse that we are all going to hell in a hand basket. Is it a sin not to wear a head covering if you are a Christian woman?[cciii] This is just another example of the way in which we define what is sinful based upon ethnic and cultural ideologies.

If sin is 'the destructive way we handle our pain' and is more than just violation of taboos, if sin is a principle at work amongst us that moves us to do things we know have the possibility of breaking us apart and we do them anyway, what does this say about sin? It says that sin is more than breaking a law, for we all pick and chose which laws we will obey and which we will transgress. Christ's death brings an end to all of the nit-picking about what is right and what is wrong because it brings all law under the same judgment as sin. Laws change, so therefore what is sin changes. Many things that are legal now were not legal fifty or five hundred years ago. In some Jewish Scriptures parents are enjoined to stone to death rebellious children; such an act today would get one arrested! It is folly for us to go around accusing each other of sin, and damning each other to hell, when years from now what is immoral or illegal may become moral or legal.

This discussion of sin and its intimate connection with law, prohibition or taboo should by now indicate that the term sin is relative to the cultural prohibitions that seek to stem mimetically originated community crises.[cciv] The cross brings an end to the old way of relating (Rom. 6:6), it renders this way powerless; it also ends the lies by which we distort what we think are our autonomous desires (Eph. 4:22, Col. 3:9). When we realize that we have died with Christ, that we are both victimizers and victims, we can then move beyond our Adamic existence grounded in violence. To die to sin is to recognize that the way we interpret the Law (or God's Instruction = Torah) also dies. This is why Paul can say, "Christ is the end (*telos*) of the law" (Rom. 10:4). He is the end of the Law inasmuch as he fulfills its destiny and its destiny is that of correct interpretation; that is, Jesus lives out the authentic intention of the Law and this means that Jesus is the Law's destiny, at the same time, he is the focus of its misappropriation (Gal 3:13). His death ends once for all any relationship we have to texts that authorize violent retribution.

"He is our peace" (Eph. 2:14) because he has "abolished the law with its commandments and regulations" (Eph 2:15). He has abolished the hostility in all human relationships that are broken because one side is able to accuse the other (Eph. 2:16). Paul reckons that what gets nailed to the cross is not our sins (he never says this), but the law which accuses us of our sin (Col 2:13-15) thus forever ending its accusatory power and ability to judge who can be part of the community and who can be cast out.

There is an important consequence of all this that has been missed in a good deal of Protestant Christianity. Many Protestants readily acknowledge that they are justified by faith and not by "keeping the law" (Gal 3:11), yet they turn around and define sanctification, holiness or the Christian life in terms of keeping the law (usually delineated as a set of cultural taboos). If Christ is the end of the law it means he is the end, there is no turning back to the law in order to establish either our own personal holiness or as a basis for what constitutes authentic Christian community. The only law left is the law of love.

Jesus' Death Is the Death of The Satan

Not only does Christ's death end the reign of sin, the way we destroy ourselves and our relationships through destructive means and not only does Christ's death end the role of law, of prohibitions and commandments as the means by which we determine who is in and who is out, his death also puts an end to the cultural manifestations of sinfully appropriated law, or what Paul calls "the principalities and powers." The recent study of Walter Wink on *The Powers* is the most useful and comprehensive guide to help us understand how Jesus conquered them.[ccv]

Paul uses several terms to describe a reality that is both phenomenal (that which we can observe) and spiritual (that which we cannot observe). These terms include *arke* (Rom 8:28), *exousia* (Rom 13:1) and their combination (Eph. 1:21, 3:10, Col. 1:16). Wink was the first to show that these 'powers' had both a physical manifestation as social institutions and a spiritual dimension. Most discussion of the Powers previous to Wink had focused on one side or the other with spiritualists denying the material manifestation and materialists denying the spirituality of the Powers.[ccvi]

Take the current debate about health care as an example. Health care is deemed a universal human right. Yet the system of health care in America is dominated by insurance companies whose premiums and practices leave a good deal of impoverished folks without any real access to health care. When profit is the basis for medical care the poor will always lack it. There are plenty of horror stories about people needing surgeries that insurance companies deem unnecessary or experimental. Take the story of Natalie Sarkisyan who was denied a liver transplant by insurance giant Cigna. Her family held a rally outside its Los Angeles office and Cigna relented but it was too late, Natalie died a few hours later. Who is to blame here is a question lawyers might ask, but the question Paul might ask is "What is the spirituality of such an institution that denies medical care to the desperate?" Is it not the same as that which shuttles lepers to the margins of society? Are we not dealing with a Power for whom profits dominate and where people are commodities?

All institutions have a spirituality whether it is a political party, a school, a church, synagogue or mosque, a civic association, a business or even a family. One can gauge the spirituality of the institution by the way it treats people. If people are numbers to be crunched or are disposable then that institution continues the negative effects of the scapegoating mechanism.

Jesus' death is the result of several institutions gone to seed in collusion with one another (Roman and Jewish political power, Jewish religious institutions, and the mob). His death exposes the dark side of institutional power that prefers its own survival; "It is better for one man to die than for the nation to perish" (John 11:50). Even so when governments authorize torture or death in the interests of national security they are living as if persons are secondary to the survival and success of the institutional power.

Jesus' death exposes the institutional powers wrong judgment on this score (Colossians 2:13-15, cf. I Cor. 2:6-10)):

> "[13]When you were dead in your sins and in the uncircumcision of your sinful nature, God made you alive with Christ. He forgave us all our sins, [14]having canceled the written code, with its regulations, that was against us and that stood opposed to us; he took it away, nailing it to the cross. [15]And having disarmed the powers and authorities, he made a public spectacle of them, triumphing over them by the cross."

Jesus death is God's "No" to our judgments and to our ability to discern evil from good. Even with the Law, we are incapable of rendering right judgment. As I said earlier, this is a facet of what we might call 'original sin' (5.1). Our inability to make right judgments stems from the fact that we all tend to go along with the judgments of our institutions, our legal systems and our cultures. So, in addition to the principle of sin and the accusatory power of sin (the misrepresentation of Torah), it was necessary for human institutional structures to also come under the judgment of the cross.

Behind both Wink's and Girard's understanding of the Powers lies the hope for social transformation as a result of the proclamation of the Gospel. Using Rene Girard's mimetic realism, Wink observes that the institutions spawned from the violence of scapegoating are used by God to keep social order. These institutions can be social, or political. They include what the Lutherans call the 'orders of creation": family, state, religion and work. Girard has maintained that these structures, grounded in violence, are the means by which humanity tries to keep violence at bay. This suggests that social/political institutions are a sort of *katechon*, "that which holds back anarchy" (II Thess. 2:7). If it were not for these institutions humanity would descend into chaos. On this logic, Wink argues for a three-fold hypothesis:

- The Powers are created
- The Powers are fallen
- The Powers must be redeemed

In light of Walter Wink's work on *The Powers* we might ask: Are our institutions capable of being transformed? For Wink, as for many others, the Powers (our institutions) were created by God. I am not so certain of this inasmuch as I think that mimetic realism has shown us that humans generated them in order to control the problem of retributive vengeance. I am not as socially optimistic as many of my friends who think that they can change the dark spirituality of the Powers. This is also the case, I think, for the apostle Paul who says, "Then comes the end, when he hands over the kingdom to God the Father after he has destroyed all dominion, authority and power" (I Cor. 15:24). These Powers are "the enemy" and are all grounded in the last enemy to be destroyed, "death" (I Cor. 15:26). This does not mean that Wink's insights on the Powers are to be thrown out; on the contrary, it demonstrates that we must challenge the Powers at their very heart and call them to repentance. But I wonder if it is really possible for institutions to change their stripes or their spirituality. I suspect that this important issue will be debated for some time as we seek ways to make our world more humane.

Let's summarize what Jesus' death affects. The death of Jesus is:

- The end of sacred violence
- The end of violent Biblical interpretation
- The end of relationships based upon law
- The reconciliation of enemies
- The turning of the ages, the Eschaton

The last effect of Jesus' death, that it begins a turning of the ages, is what Paul means when he refers to Jesus' death as a new wisdom (I Cor. 2:6-10). This wisdom comes as a revelation of God's Spirit. It is not like the wisdom of this world, a wisdom that lies and kills in the name of God; it is the wisdom that God has died at the hands of our human wisdom. It is the end of our proud human knowledge and of our determinations of right and wrong. In short, it is the end of sin. Karl Barth says,

> "Sin is the obstacle which has to be removed and overcome in the reconciliation of the world with God as its conversion to Him. But it is also the source, which has to be blocked in the atonement, of the destruction which threatens humanity and drags them down. Its wages is death (Rom. 6:23). It is the sting of death (I Cor. 15:56). By it death came into the world (Rom. 5:12)...the very heart of the atonement is the overcoming of sin: sin in its character as

> rebellion against God, and in its character as the ground of humanity's hopeless destiny in death.
>
> The decisive thing is not that He [Jesus] has suffered what we ought to have suffered so that we do not have to suffer it, the destruction to which we have fallen victim by our guilt, and therefore the punishment which we deserve. This is true of course. But it is true only as it derives from the decisive thing that in the suffering and death of Jesus Christ it has come to pass that in his own person he has made an end of us as sinners and therefore of sin itself by going to death as the One who took our place as sinners. In his person he has delivered up us sinners and sin itself to destruction. He has removed us sinners and sin, negated us, cancelled us out: ourselves, our sin, and the accusation, condemnation and perdition which had overtaken us...The man of sin, the first Adam, the cosmos alienated from God, the 'present evil world' (Gal. 1:4) was taken and killed and buried with him on the cross...The passion of Jesus Christ is the judgment of God in which the Judge himself was the judged. And as such it is at its heart and center the victory that has been won for us, in our place, in the battle against sin."[ccvii]

Barth is following the apostle Paul at this point when he connects sin with death. We might automatically think here of our own existential deaths, but since we all still die it is not our existential death that is primarily meant here. Our personal death is only background; it is there only as a sign, a deeper witness to our tendencies as a species toward transferring our sin to an innocent victim and killing them! It is this 'old man', this 'mimetic and rivalrous Adam', who kills that dies.

For Barth, Jesus is the only one who could rightfully judge us and he became subject to our human judgment, 'The Judge Judged in Our Place.' Our false judgment is grounded in our belief that our violence is good and God's will is done when we kill 'the other.' This is why we killed Jesus, the revealer of the nonviolent God. But even this is not held against us. By not counting this against us, God negated sin so that it could not be an issue between God and us.

It is this turning of sin into reconciliation by its negation, by "not reckoning sin to us" (2 Cor. 5:19) that is the turning of the ages. This is accomplished by the negation of our sin, in our condemnation of Jesus, when God raised Jesus from the dead. In the resurrection the lies and false guilt attributed to Jesus were exposed as false, else God would not have raised him from the grave. Our killing of Jesus is the end of our old self (for in judging him we judge ourselves) and in the resurrection of Jesus, the beginning of our new self (for in raising Jesus God negated our judgment as false).

The resurrection of Jesus is God's way of telling us that we have gotten the concepts of justice and judgment all wrong, that we do not know what constitutes true justice and judgment. It is also God's way of removing us from all that lies in the realm of death: sin, the law and the principalities and powers and translating us to a new way of thinking and existing in relationships not grounded in sacred violence but in love.

The resurrection is the promise that we shall not remain forever in the bondage of mimetic desire but can and will be transformed. As the sign of the new age, the future promise in the present, Jesus' resurrection is the basis for all of our hope (I Cor. 15:12-18). More than that, as we shall see in the next section, it is the promise of new life, for it is the Risen Lord whom we know, imitate and follow in the power of His Spirit.

7.4 Life in the Spirit

There are, as Paul Minear has taught us, a lot of different images of the church in the New Testament.[ccviii] In fact, Minear lists over ninety different types of metaphors and symbols used for the church. However the form of the church may be conceived, the one thing common to all discussion of the church in the New Testament is that the church is the community gathered in the Life of the Spirit.

All that we have spoken of Paul in this chapter forms the basis of the new community, a community that no longer engages the scapegoating mechanism for its survival but recognizes that it is gathered around the Last Scapegoat. If the death of Jesus brings an end to our negative imitation of each other's desires, which leads to rivalry and scapegoating, then it is the resurrection of Jesus that offers us a new way of being in the world. Yet the resurrection was not a stand-alone event, for the early Christians believed that Jesus had been set at God's right hand. It was the elevation of the True Human to the right hand of God that formed the basis for their conviction that the death and resurrection of Jesus was to be given ultimate significance as God's work.

Paul follows this logic in 2 Cor. 3:17-18 where he contends that the Spirit of God which had been poured out upon believers was identical to the presence of the Risen Lord (the *Christus praesens* or Present Christ). Talk about the Spirit in today's church is usually amorphous or without form, as though the Spirit was spooky. On the contrary, the Spirit is not without character; the Spirit is God in Christ present with us. The early Christians may not have had the kind of Trinitarian relations developed following Nicaea (325 C.E.) but they were emphatic that the Spirit was the Spirit of Jesus.

The Spirit was the gift of God; God gave God's self to be present *with* us, just as God was in Christ *for* us. Relationality is essential to understanding the work of God in the world and so it is with the Spirit. We observe that the language of the New Testament regarding the Spirit is always done in prepositional form. Prepositions are parts of speech that denote relationship. In, with, at, near, under, above, for, by, to, all denote the way two things are in relationship. So it is with the Spirit.

The church may live in this world but its existence is determined by the world to come, living between the times. The church is more than just a gathering of people who think alike or have an agreed upon social purpose. Living between the times means that while the church receives the promise of redemption, it still awaits finality or ultimacy. For this reason it is impossible to identify the church with the reign of God in Jesus' teaching which always carries with it the prospect of futurity.

In the present and possessed by the Spirit, the church between the times is not guaranteed health, wealth and success. This is the pseudo-promise of those who have what scholars call an over-realized eschatology, where all the blessings of the kingdom can be had in the present. Much like the Corinthians, some Christians think we can have it all now. We can't and don't.

Those possessed by God's Spirit are faced with the same battle against the principalities and powers that also faced Jesus during his ministry. The coming of God's Spirit creates a War of the Worlds. This war is the challenge of the Spirit to the ideologies, bent desires and the death affirming violence of the 'flesh' (*sarx*).

Living between the times is to live with constant struggle; both internal to our personal psyches and external in our relationships manifested as love vs. hate, joy vs. despair, peace vs. retribution. In Galatians 2:19-26 Paul spells out some of the distinctive characteristics of this struggle. The struggle between flesh-Spirit can be recognized as the difference in perspectives between the persecutor and the forgiving victim. The former is dominated by desire out of control, envy, jealousy, rivalry and violence, the latter by peace, patience, self-control, kindness, love, etc.

Living between the times means that we learn to wait patiently and do not force the future. This is something many Christian activists have yet to learn. We cannot bring in the kingdom. There is nothing we can do to hasten God's reign. We can pray for it ("Thy kin(g)dom come") but we cannot force it upon our societies. Neither Paul nor Jesus was a cultural Darwinist; neither believed that the world was getting better. The proof of this is their use of apocalyptic categories when referring to the Spirit. The Spirit was in the process of both revealing the way of God's reign by exposing the violent sinful ways of humanity and also bringing about transformation to those persons who trusted that God's new way was totally different than the ways of human culture. There seems to be no instance in either Jesus or Paul concerning the conversion of social institutions.[ccix]

In North America it seems that Christians, both conservative and liberal, seek to implement the vision that next to the "kingdom of God, America is the last best hope of humanity on earth." It strikes me as odd how these two sides spend so much time warring against each other as they do; and war it is. American Christianity is caught up in a battle, a mimetic conflict, a rivalry that appears to have little in common with the way Jesus or Paul approached society in their times. Paul says, "though we live in the world, we do not wage war as the world does" (2 Cor. 10:3). Both sides claim to be following Jesus and to be "walking in the Spirit", yet one wonders, can such animosity, hatred and belligerence really be manifestations of the Spirit of Peace? Have not both sides sought to implement a vision that is more ideological and less Christ-centered than they might think? Can this not be seen in the kind of tit-for-tat sacrificial scapegoating that goes on in both types of Christendom?

Life in the Spirit for the apostle Paul is nothing other than being yoked with Jesus or the imitation of Christ. His language however is participatory as he speaks of "Christ in us." It is Jesus living his Risen life in us that is the "hope of glory" (Col. 1:27). Not only does Jesus live in us but we also find our life in him, we are "raised with Christ and seated with him at the right hand of God" (Col 3:1). Our life is "hidden with Christ in God" (Col 3:3). What might all this mysterious language mean?

Into the Mystic

Those of us raised in the late twentieth century have learned to be rational and logical. Our left-brains work overtime during the day and, unless we are artisans, it is only at night that our right brains get a chance to exercise when we dream. To be whole persons is to experience both sides of our brains, the right and the left, the logical and the imaginative working together all the time. This occurs when we use our imagination. For some people, using their imagination seems foolish and childish. However, imagination is not the same as fantasy, daydreaming or wishing. Imagination is the ability to see the way things are to the senses and to construct an alternate reality that is just as real.[ccx] For the Christian, this alternate reality has already been constructed; it is the way of God in the world (in the Gospels this goes under the rubric 'the reign of God').

Christianity has a rich tradition of mysticism, as do other world religions. Mysticism is frequently criticized. Soren Kierkegaard said, "Mysticism does not have the patience to wait for God's revelation." Sometimes Christians seek mystical experience hoping that its powerful and overwhelming nature will deliver them from the dismal nature of their mundane lives. Truly experienced, however, the "mystic sweet communion" is the awareness of God's presence in the mundane, the simple and the ordinary. Even while washing dishes, as Brother Lawrence reminds us in *Practicing the Presence of God.*

For Paul, high and lofty mystical experiences were not something upon which he based his sense of God. Rather, it was in the breakdown of life, in its gutters and sewers, in its crosses and insults that Paul knew the extraordinary grace of God (2 Cor. 12:1-10). This comes back to recognizing that the cross of Christ, the abyss of death, is the place where God does God's best work (1.3). Our current American scene is dominated by what Martin Luther called a *theology of glory.* This kind of theology finds God in success, power, triumph, fame and fortune. When things go well with us we say God is blessing us, when things go bad we surmise that God is not pleased with us. We try to do better so we can once again find ourselves in God's blessing. This type of Christianity is nothing more than a subtle form of self-justification since it begins with our best efforts. It is the spirituality of an *economy of exchange* whereby we think that our obedience merits us divine favor.

This is exactly the opposite of an authentic Christian existence that is utterly dependent upon God's grace and knows that even in the deepest darkness God is there (cf. Psalm 139:7-10). Christian mysticism is not about us trying to find a way to God, but about recognizing that God is wherever we are, especially in times of crisis and our dark nights of the soul.

Paul is often maligned because he does not appear to talk about the "historical" Jesus all that much. Yet it is clear from his letters that he was acquainted with (at least some of) the teaching of Jesus as we find it in the Synoptic Gospels. I find the historical skepticism of some scholars unwarranted in this regard. They miss Paul's having had the emerging catechetical tradition at his disposal: the stories and teaching of Jesus that would form the basis for how one lived in relationships. To be sure, that tradition may not have been as developed as we find it in the Gospels, but if one allows an early dating for oral tradition behind *The Didache* (1.4, 4.3) then there is already evidence that Christian formation used Jesus as a model for how to live the Christian life.

Pauline mysticism would then not be seeking to get to know a Jesus he did not know or was unfamiliar with, but learning how to follow Jesus in one's world as Jesus had lived in his own world. For this, Paul used the language of *mimesis* (imitation). The term *mimesis* is found in I Thessalonians (1:6) where the believers became imitators of the apostolic messengers "and of the Lord" and in 2:14 where the Thessalonian Christians became imitators of Jesus in being persecuted for their faith. It is also found in II Thessalonians (3:7, 9) where Paul's tent-making work was a model for the Thessalonian Christians not to become a welfare burden to the Christian community. In I Corinthians 4:16, after laying out his catalogue of hardships, Paul encourages the Corinthians to "imitate me."

Mimesis in Paul is not limited solely to the use of the term itself: in Philippians 2, for example, Paul encourages the Philippian church to "have the same attitude which was in Christ Jesus" and then goes on to quote the hymn found in 2:5-11 where Jesus' self-giving is a model for Christians. It is this self-giving mimesis which lies behind such sayings as Romans 12:1-2 where, like Jesus, Christians are to offer themselves "as living sacrifices." In short, the imitation of Christ pertains to a pattern of life that endures hardship and persecution for the sake of the gospel and those to whom the gospel is proclaimed.

This is identical to the pattern found in the Gospel sayings on persecution. Matthew 5:10-12 and Mark 8:34-35 are materially saying the same thing. The apostolic pattern is the Jesus pattern.

Life in the power of the Spirit for Paul is lived out first in the Christian community where believers are to prefer one another (Phil 2:1-4) and to have "equal concern for one another" (I Cor. 12:24-26). The community is the place where *The Jesus Driven Life* is practiced so that when the community is dispersed in the world it knows how to forgive, how to love, how to be peacemaking. The believer fulfills their obligation to Jesus when, like Jesus, they bears the burden of their fellow believers (Gal. 6:2). The believer does not live with a list of moral obligations or a Christian rulebook. There is only one rule: love. This love is described relationally in I Corinthians 13:

> "1If I speak in the tongues of men and of angels, but have not love, I am only a resounding gong or a clanging cymbal. 2If I have the gift of prophecy and can fathom all mysteries and all knowledge, and if I have a faith that can move mountains, but have not love, I am nothing. 3If I give all I possess to the poor and surrender my body to the flames, but have not love, I gain nothing.
>
> 4Love is patient, love is kind. It does not envy, it does not boast, it is not proud. 5It is not rude, it is not self-seeking, it is not easily angered, it keeps no record of wrongs. 6Love does not delight in evil but rejoices with the truth. 7It always protects, always trusts, always hopes, always perseveres. 8Love never fails."

Living in the Spirit is to live in relationships as Jesus did. Sometimes when I read this passage I notice how easy it is to substitute 'Jesus' for the word 'love.'

The mystical experience of the Risen Christ in the community is the experience of the Holy Spirit (2 Cor. 3:18). The Spirit is not some amorphous entity that brings ecstatic experience in order to ground faith. Rather, the experience of the Spirit is given for the benefit of the community. Thus one's experiences of the Risen Christ are not to be seen as ego boosts, as though those who have them are better than those who don't. The work of the Spirit creates conformation to Christ where experience of the divine, in ecstatic praise, harsh persecution or the mundane task of labor all contribute to the formation of the believer into Christ's image, who is the Image of God. How does this occur?

Imitating Jesus

Earlier (2.4) I referred to the principle of surrender or trust. This trust is beautifully seen in Philippians 2:5-11.

> "Your attitude should be the same as that of Christ Jesus:
> Who, being in very nature God,
> Did not consider equality with God something to be grasped,
> But made himself nothing,
> Taking the very nature of a servant,
> Being made in human likeness.
> And being found in appearance as a man,
> He humbled himself
> And became obedient to death—
> Even death on a cross!
> Therefore God exalted him to the highest place
> And gave him the name that is above every name,
> That at the name of Jesus every knee should bow,
> In heaven and on earth and under the earth,
> And every tongue confess that Jesus Christ is Lord,
> To the glory of God the Father."

Phil 2:5-11 is an early Christian hymn (1.1). This may seem a trite observation being well recognized but it is very significant. The early church, in its hymnology, was already reflecting on the character of this Jesus whom they worshipped. More than simply a piece of tradition, the use of a hymn indicates the liturgical character of the passage. It is the gathered community singing this song of praise. We are reminded that 'the one who sings prays twice'; it is to the context of Christian worship and community life to which this hymn belongs. To limit our observations to dry and dusty exegetical minutiae deprives the text of its power. Certainly the Philippian Church did not spend hours and days debating Christological formulae, as do modern scholars. They sang this hymn as a gathered community. It had the emotional and spiritual component of worship to the living person of Jesus that is often lacking in modern commentaries.

Furthermore, this is a hymn sung in the context of the small Christian community in Philippi, a community undergoing some sort of persecution. This fact is also of significance, for it underscores the perspective of the victim, the hermeneutic from below. To sing this hymn was an act of courage, an act of resistance. Ivo Lesbaupin states 'persecution forms the backdrop of early Christianity' (4.1). We would do well to remember this as we read the apostolic literature.

Paul, or his tradition, uses the rare word (a word found only once in the New Testament) *harpagmos*, which some translate as 'the object to be grasped' and others as 'the act of grasping.' When put this way, the question asks if Jesus were equal with God. Was equality with God something inherent in Jesus or something he lacked? However, from the perspective of mimetic realism we know that there is no desire without an external object ('equality with God') and that the acquisitive character of mimesis stems from a previously desired valuation (what equality with God consists of).

We might inquire as to what significance this makes for our interpretation of Phil. 2:1-11. We suggest that the text is making an anthropological statement. The introduction to the hymn is very strongly anthropocentric but the hymn (2:5-11) reflects something of the originary human story in the book of Genesis (6.1). In other words, we cannot help but think of the original Adam who 'grasped' in comparison to Paul's statement that the Christ of God renounced 'grasping'. Ralph Martin's explains, with relation to the Philippian hymn and the creation account in Genesis 1-2, that "the linguistic agreements between the Septuagint (the Greek translation of the Jewish Scriptures) and the Greek text of Philippians 2 are impressive." He tabulates the parallels:

<u>Adam</u> (Genesis 1-3)	**<u>Christ</u>** (Philippians 2:5-11)
Made in divine image thought it a prize to be grasped at to be as God; and aspired to a reputation	Being the image of God thought it not a prize to be grasped at to be as God; and made himself of no reputation
And spurned being God's servant seeking to be in the likeness of God; and being found in fashion as	And took upon himself the form of a servant and was made in the likeness of humanity and being found in fashion as

a man (of dust, now doomed)	a human
He exalted himself	He humbled himself
and became disobedient	and became obedient
unto death.	unto death
He was condemned & disgraced	God highly exalted Him & gave him the name and rank of Lord

These parallels are impressive. Whether one seeks the background of the hymn in some Primal Man myth, a Heavenly Man myth or Adam speculation in Judaism, the fact remains that we are first of all dealing with something anthropological, the assertion of that which true humanness consists. In particular, we might observe that we are given virtual mirror doubles in Adam (Humanity) and Jesus (The True Human), the one distinction being that Jesus disengages the process of negative mimesis and chooses the will of God engaging a new process, a process of positive mimesis.

This leads us to the difficult problem of 'he emptied himself.' 'Emptying himself' is the obverse of *harpagmos*. They are connected by the adversative *alla*, "but." The act of emptying oneself is an act of 'not-grasping.' They are, therefore, one and the same. It is the self-giving element highlighted here. Grasping leads to rivalrous violence and sacrifice, non-grasping generates self-emptying which is self-giving. One recalls the Johannine words of Jesus, "No one takes my life from me, I lay it down on my own" (John 10:18) or the use of verbs in Hebrews (*fero, anaphero, diaphero*), where Jesus 'offers' himself (rather than verbs of sacrifice, e.g., *thuo*). There is no sacrificial language in the Philippian hymn itself. Yet its logic leads to the cross, which is the end of all sacrifice.

Some scholars have noted "even death on a cross" does not fit the alleged structure of the hymn, that these words are a Pauline addition. Even so, if this is the case, Paul ties in more closely the sacrificial elements of the negative mimetic consequences, recalling the Passion of Jesus, the mob, the unjust verdict and the execution in this brief phrase. It would be Paul's contention that something other than negative mimesis was occurring throughout the Passion. Death is penultimate in the hymn. Life and vindication have the last word. The '*act of grasping*' and the '*self-emptying*' thus describe for us the double-sided character of mimesis, negative and positive. While the former is the background presupposed in the hymn, it is the latter that is highlighted and emphasized.

The story of the Creation and the subsequent spiral into violence of the first Human (the grasping Adam/Eve) is not the only potential Jewish background that has been referenced for our hymn. Some have seen in the hymn language reflected from Isaiah and Deutero-Isaiah, particularly that of the suffering servant (6.3). There have been those who see the cosmic battle of Lucifer in Isaiah reflected in the *harpagmos* of the hymn. Christ vs. Satan.

It is difficult for a mimetic realist to retain composure and not jump for joy, for Rene Girard has spelled out for us the demystification of the devil. The 'satan' is in the Adam and derives from Adam. The 'satan' is humanity's dark side. The downfall of the devil, the defeat of the 'satan,' or the liberation of humankind, whatever is stressed, was a key component in early Christian atonement theory. Can this simply be ignored or can it, in fact, enhance our broader interpretive strategy (see 8.3)?

Some have turned to Isaiah 53, the Song of the Suffering Servant. This servant is 'figural' and representational. It is the Suffering Servant, the people of God, the figure of desolation that inherits the new creation and is thus recapitulated humanity; first Adam becomes last Adam in the Isaianic songs.

Again this is not an either/or. The early Christian community was as creative in their songwriting and literature as a Bob Dylan or a William Shakespeare. Both the Adamic/First Human background and the Suffering Servant could lie behind this hymn, for both are the significant corporate figures not only for the early Christians but also for Jesus himself. Son of Man is not only an eschatological figure but a protological one as well, as F.H. Borsch has shown; there is a first Adam and a last Adam, or Adamic doubles.[ccxi] Both function as corporate figures.

This is important. Corporate figures underscore the insight that we are *interdividual*, interconnected on many levels: social, psychological, spiritual, economic, political, ethnic etc.. In corporate personality (2.2, 6.4), the one can stand for the many (all). James Williams has shown us the mimetic value of this phenomenon particularly with reference to the kings of the Hebrew people. If the king was good, the people were blessed, if the king was bad the people were cursed. The one stood for the many. Corporate personality exhibits a mediating function or role. The high priest is certainly a figure of corporate personality.

Figures of corporate personality highlight the sacrificial mechanism in that they can be substitutionary figures. They stand in on behalf of all the people. They are representative and representation plays a strategic role in mimetic theory (inasmuch as we all model desire). Our modern blindness to this is proportionate to the degree that we have succumbed or been seduced by the romantic lie, the myth of the autonomous self, the deception of the undifferentiated individual (5.1).

Jesus represents the True Adam as the Suffering Servant. The One stands in the place of the Many/All. This is the point about positive mimesis being made in the Philippians hymn.

Yet a further background has been argued for this hymn. David Seeley has proposed, "These verses are based on Isaiah 45, but they resonate with ruler worship as well, and deserve analysis from that perspective." I think Seeley makes a good case that early Christians would naturally think of their current political 'representatives.' Since I posit that the early church thought in terms of what we now call mimetic realism, reflecting on both positive as well as negative mimesis and that they did this in the context of corporate personality (*interdividuality*) then Seeley's proposed background highlights aspects of both Genesis and Isaiah. Jesus is as much an anti-model to Greco-Roman kings as he is to the Hebrew Kings. For the early church there was no distinction between spiritual powers and political ones (3.3, 8.3). Jesus is "the name above all names" no matter where they reside.

What then can be said about the incarnation of Jesus in the life of the church? Does Paul not call the church 'the body of Christ' (I Cor 12)? Also, does he not say to these same Corinthians that the Spirit dwelling in the believers is the Spirit of Jesus (2 Cor 3)? Is not Jesus in some fashion en-fleshed in the life, indeed, the flesh of the believing church? Does Paul not depend on this logic when dealing with the problem of *porneia* in I Cor 6?

I concur with Robert Hamerton-Kelly who sees the Philippians hymn as an example of 'the moral significance of the cross for the life of the community'.[ccxii] Does this mean that Jesus' life (that is, the stories of Jesus passed on orally and textually) is somehow to be slavishly imitated? No, rather as Hamerton-Kelly puts it, "the summary act of the crucifixion, the crucified Christ in his act of self-sacrifice rather than any specific pattern of ethics drawn from the memory of his life" is the point of imitation.[ccxiii]

Both trust and obedience are the keys here (2.4; cf. John 14:1 ff). They are two sides of a coin. I do not separate ethics from salvation, stripping the hymn of its true salvific importance, namely, the realized promise of a transformed humanity, a humanity grounded in Jesus, the True Human who desires only the will of the heavenly *Abba*. An interpretation that is purely about other worldly salvation in the hymn might satisfy those who are happy living in the abstract but it provides no real enfleshment of that salvation. There is no subjective correlation to the objective process with those who divide ethics from salvation. However, as we saw with *harpagmos* and '*self-emptying*,' the hymn itself is descriptive of the incarnational process. This is the '*type*' of Phil. 3:17, "the pattern, the example" given by Paul to his converts. He exhorts us to become "fellow imitators" of this type of no grasping/self-emptying. This choice, this spirituality is reflected autobiographically when Paul says, "I want to know

Christ and the power of His resurrection and the fellowship of sharing in his sufferings, becoming like him in his death, and so, somehow, attaining to the Resurrection from the dead" (3:10).[ccxiv]

So, I must part company with those who assert that an ethical interpretation of the text, and thus the church's living in this mindset with her Lord, is not a real possibility. Per Grande summarizes their conjunction beautifully:

> "The imitation of Christ is each individual's response to the process of dissolving violence and sacrifice. In this respect imitating Christ is the individual's continuation of Christ's work. While the Passion was clearly a sacrificial phenomenon, imitating Christ can be seen as the ethical implication of the Passion. This also means that imitating Christ is the practical step forward, derived from a reflection on Christ. In this sense imitation is a response to Christology and, at the same time, ethically speaking, perhaps the most important part of Christology."[ccxv]

Tom Wright finishes his extensive survey of the Philippians hymn summing up it's meaning by saying,

> "The thrust of the passage in itself is that the one who, before becoming human, possessed divine equality did not regard that status as something to take advantage of, something to exploit, but instead interpreted it as a vocation to obedient humiliation and death; and that God the Father acknowledged the truth of this interpretation by exalting him to share his own divine glory. This means that the passage is well able to fulfill the role, which it has in Paul's developing argument, namely, that of the example which Christians are to imitate. God acknowledged Christ's self-emptying as the true expression of divine equality; he will acknowledge Christian self-emptying in the same way."[ccxvi]

Paul writes to the Roman Christians that this self-giving is the only way to discover the will of God and know what is good, what God wants, what is the perfect thing to do (Romans 12:2). It is with the new mind; that of positive mimesis where we can be compassionate, open to another's pain, able to enter into the experience of the other who is not a rival but a fellow human being because we have a model we can legitimately follow, Jesus. Paul is offering a profound expression of the truth that our real self is "hid with Christ in God" (Col. 3:3). Our truest identity is not measured against anyone else. It is not attained, not taken forcibly, acquired or grasped – it is given. This is Life in the Spirit, life in Christ.

Chapter 8 The Gospel of John

8.1 The Nonviolent Logos

We turn last to my favorite book of the New Testament, the Gospel of John. I prefer to call it the Fourth Gospel. It is the easiest Gospel to read and yet of all the Gospels, it is the most subtle. The writer's use of puns, irony, words with double meanings, allusions to the Jewish Bible and other Jewish traditions all contribute to an incredible tapestry, a way of telling the Jesus story that has nurtured Christian faith since the day it was published (John 20:31). For over two hundred years the Fourth Gospel has been excluded from research into the life of Jesus. I confess that I do not share the opinion of the majority of New Testament scholars in this regard. The work of C.H. Dodd and J.A.T. Robinson has convinced me that there is historical substance to the Fourth Gospel even though the writer has obviously adapted the stories and teaching of Jesus to meet the needs of his own community (as do the writers of the Synoptic Gospels).

My goal is not to mine the Fourth Gospel for the 'historical Jesus.' Rather I want to show, by reading it in the light of mimetic realism, that we are breathing the same Jesus oriented air as Paul and the Synoptic Gospels. Sure, the language, the emphases and the style of the Fourth Gospel are very different from those of the Synoptics. Nevertheless, there is a Christological continuity, a way of seeing Jesus that is common to all four Gospels.

This section will look at the Prologue (John 1:1-18). Many scholars over the years have suggested that the Prologue is based upon a hymn. It seems the early church could not sing enough about Jesus (1.1)! You can get a feel for the possible original song if you take out verses 6-9 and verse 15 (these verses when read together with verse 19 would form a kind of narrative introduction beginning with John the Baptizer, as do the other Gospels). The hymn, like those of Philippians 2:5-11 or Colossians 1:15-20 goes back to the Genesis story, to the creation of the world and humanity. The early church understood that whatever Jesus did was a retelling of the old story *in a new key*. Their singing was a reflection that with Jesus, the new creation, the new humanity, the new way of living had come to expression in their life together.

The *Logos*

In the beginning of the Gospel (1:1-18) we are immediately transported to a strange world as the author begins by speaking of the *Logos*. This term is familiar to us as "Word." Yet it means more than speech. *Logos* is a term used in both Jewish and Greek thought and we will consider it with both worlds in mind. While many things could be said and have been said about the *Logos*, we will stick to those aspects that continue to reveal what I have been saying throughout this book.

Let's start with the Greek background. In philosophy before Socrates, the *Logos* first appears in Heraclitus (c.535-475 B.C.E.) When Heraclitus looked at the world about him and sought to make sense of it, he looked for what we might call 'the structuring principle of reality.' What was it that held the world together? Heraclitus called this principle the *Logos*. But what was the *Logos*? The *Logos* was the principle by which, "Things which are put together are both whole and not whole, brought together and taken apart, in harmony and out of harmony; one thing arises from all things, and all things arise from one thing (Frag. 10)." Humanity is unaware of this structuring principle:

> "Men have no comprehension of the Logos, as I've described it, just as much after they hear about it as they did before they heard about it. Even though all things occur according to the Logos, men seem to have no experience whatsoever, even when they experience the words and deeds which I use to explain *physis* (nature), of how the Logos applies to each thing, and what it is. The rest of mankind are just as unconscious of what they do while awake as they are of what they do while they sleep (Frag 1)."

The structuring principle according to Heraclitus was conflict or war:

> "On the one hand war is the father of all, on the other, the king of everything. On the one hand it designates Gods, on the other, it shows who is human. On the one hand it makes men slaves, on the other, it makes them free" (Frag 53).[ccxvii]

And again from Fragment 80:

> "It is necessary to understand that war is common, strife is customary, and all things happen because of strife and necessity."

These quotes clearly demonstrate that the structuring principle, the *Logos* (or in later Aristotelian philosophy the *Arche*), is violence (*polemos* or *eris*). What might it mean to say that violence, war or conflict is at the heart of all reality?

First, it lends credence to a dualistic view of the universe. This means both good and evil are seen as principles struggling constantly, a yin-yang relationship going back and forth that is necessary to existence. This dualism was not only found in the West in Greek thought but also made its influence felt in Judaism through the influence of Persian Zoroastrianism during the post Exilic period.[ccxviii]

Second, by making *polemos* or war the principle that holds reality together, war is inevitably accepted and justified as morally or ethically acceptable. If conflict is built into the universe, or into a doctrine of God, then it becomes both the problem and the solution. The *pharmakon* (poison, bane) and the *pharmakos* (remedy, blessing) are one and the same thing, two sides of a coin. Conflict, retribution, retaliation, rejection are all *necessary* to this kind of existence, as Heraclitus observed so long ago.

Third, if conflict is natural to the gods, then the god who is the biggest, the best, the strongest, the mightiest is the god of all gods. Whether that god is called Zeus or Chronos, El, Ba'al, Allah, The Unpronounceable Name, or even certain contemporary Jesuses, matters little. What does matter is that the divine is conceived of in categories making conflict necessary and military prowess inevitable.

Fourth, if conflict is 'of the nature of things', it should come as no surprise that the way in which humans conceive divinity is conflicted. Not only are we with our different gods at war with one another, but also our gods are at war with themselves. In polytheism this takes the form of strife amongst the gods themselves. In monotheism, however, all of these battles are internalized so that now justice and mercy, love and wrath, forgiveness and retribution strive together in the heart of god. We called this the problem of the Janus-faced god earlier in the book (1.2, 2.1, 3.2).

Is this the background for the *Logos* of the Fourth Gospel? The answer is both yes and no. Yes, in the sense that both Greek philosophy and the Johannine author recognize there is a structuring principle to the universe. No, in the sense that they have different understandings of the principle. Rene Girard was the first to show this:

> "The Johannine Logos is foreign to any kind of violence; it is therefore forever expelled, an absent Logos that never has had any direct, determining influence over human cultures. These cultures are based on the Heraclitean Logos, the Logos of expulsion, the Logos of violence, which, if it is not recognized, can provide the foundation of a culture. The Johannine Logos discloses the truth of violence by having itself expelled.

> First and foremost, John's Prologue undoubtedly refers to the Passion. But in a more general way, the misrecognition of the Logos and mankind's expulsion of it disclose one of the fundamental principles of human culture."[ccxix]

Girard is saying that when the principle of nonviolence entered the world of violence it could not be tolerated. The true *Logos* comes from God, not the *logic* of our religion. Human culture, founded and maintained by conflict will have nothing to do with a principle that is forgiving, reconciliatory and compassionate. Jesus is the rejected revealer of the reality that his *Abba* is nonviolent, non-retaliatory, non-scapegoating. He "came unto his own and his own would not receive him" (John 1:9). In human culture, the *Logos* of war and death is preferred to the true *Logos* who is life and light.

The concept of the *Logos* began to figure prominently in Christian discussions about Jesus beginning in the mid second century with Justin Martyr (4.4). Justin sought to show the congruence between the biblical revelation and Greek philosophy, following in the footsteps of some very famous Jewish interpreters who also sought to do the same (e.g., Philo of Alexandria). The simple 'mistake' Justin made was to assimilate the violent *Logos* of Greek philosophy with the nonviolent *Logos* of the Johannine tradition (whether Justin was aware of the Fourth Gospel is a matter of debate). By merging the two and arguing for their compatibility, Justin opened the door for *polemos* (conflict) to infect the radical nonviolent character of the Christian revelation, leading to the possibility that god can be retributively violent, therefore Janus-faced.

The *Logos* in Judaism

The other background we will explore for the Johannine *Logos* is the Jewish tradition. Within this tradition Raymond Brown[ccxx] identifies four possible areas in understanding "the Word" that may have influenced the author of the Prologue:

- "The Word of the Lord"
- Personified Wisdom
- Jewish Speculation on the Torah
- The Use of *Memra* in the Targums

First, Brown notes the "word of the Lord" which is a term frequently found in the prophets (Hosea 1:1, Joel 1:1). God's word is active, dynamic and life giving (Deut. 32:46-47). It is God communicating to the people through the medium of human beings.

Second, is personified Wisdom, the living and creative *Sophia*. We have already had occasion (6.4) to note that Wisdom can be seen as a personification, an agent of God. Wisdom participates with God in the creation of the cosmos, is at God's right hand, and is the master crafter at God's side, and the one whom God used to bring about his mighty saving acts from Adam to Moses (Prov. 8:22-31, Wis. of Sol. 7:22, 8:4, 10:1-8).

Third, the *Logos* of John 1 may hearken back to the role of the Torah, personified in latter rabbinic literature much the same way Wisdom was personified in the centuries before Jesus. Indeed, in Proverbs 8, Wisdom = Torah (also in 4 Maccabees 1:16). In a commentary on Deuteronomy 11:10 several centuries after Jesus, the rabbis would use Proverbs 8:22 to identify Torah with Wisdom: "The Law, because it is more highly prized than anything, was created before everything, as it is said, 'The Lord created me as the beginning of His ways.'"[ccxxi]

Fourth, Brown notes the possible influence of the *Memra* (word, speech) of the Lord. In post-exilic Judaism there was a tendency to remove or qualify those biblical texts that made God sound human (as though God had a mouth or arms, legs, eyes, etc). Thus instead of saying "God said, "Let there be light'", the Aramaic paraphrases of the Jewish Scriptures (*Targums*, 2.1) read "And the *Memra* of the Lord said 'Let there be light.'" Like Wisdom (and Torah), the *Memra* of the Lord could also save. Brown cites Exodus 3:12 as an example.

> If in Exodus 3:12 God says, 'I will be with you,' in the Targum Onkelos God says 'My *Memra* will be your support.' If in Exodus 19:17 we are told Moses brought the people out of the camp to meet God, in Targum Onkelos we are told that they were brought to the *Memra* of God."[ccxxii]

Rather than seeing these four alternatives as mutually exclusive, we might see them as intersecting one another: Torah/Wisdom/Word is the structuring principle of the universe. Indeed, the world was created for the sake of Torah according to some rabbis citing Proverbs 3:19. Torah was the final, ultimate revelation because it was the meta-map upon which all was created and by which all things exist.[ccxxiii]

The various characteristics attributed to the *Logos* of the Fourth Gospel could all have been attributed to Torah: presence with God in the beginning, agent of creation, life and light. C.H. Dodd confirms this when he says, "It is instructive to observe that many of the propositions referring to the Logos in the Prologue are the counterparts of rabbinic statements referring to Torah."[ccxxiv] Yet this one attribute could not: "The *Logos* became flesh" (1:14). This would have been an intolerable statement not only for Greek philosophy for which the material world was inferior to the world of eternal ideas. It would also have been problematic for Judaism because Torah was divine, not human in its origin and nature.

What then shall we make of all this? I tend to think the writer of the Fourth Gospel would have been aware of both backgrounds, but was particularly concerned to deal with the Jewish background *inasmuch as the same problem existed for Torah in Judaism as the Logos in Greek philosophy, namely, the problem of violence.* We have already seen this in the writings of the apostle Paul. There the fact that Torah could be interpreted within the framework of a zealous nationalistic (violent) hermeneutic was its Achilles heel. The Torah was "weakened through sinful flesh" (Romans 8:3) that is, it was susceptible to an interpretation that was not true to the revelation coming through it. This same critique of a violent interpretation of Torah occurs in the Fourth Gospel in a different manner, but it amounts to the same thing. "We have a divine Instruction (or Torah), and according to that Instruction he must die" (John 19:7). This is the problem.

The Prologue states, "The Torah was given by Moses, grace and truth came through Jesus Christ (1:17)." We have already explored Jesus' relation to the revelation given in the Jewish Bible in the Synoptic Gospels and in Paul. We found in all cases the issue was the way in which the Torah was interpreted. When we turn to the Fourth Gospel we find the same thing. In order to understand this, we shall first look at texts that mention Torah in the Fourth Gospel.

When the Law is Not Legal

There are fourteen occurrences of the term "law" (*nomos*) in the Fourth Gospel (1:17, 45, 7:19, 23, 49, 51, 8:17, 10:34, 12:34, 15:25, 18:31 and 19:7). Chapter 7 has a third of those references. They are part of a controversial dialogue Jesus has with the religious authorities regarding his healing of a man on the Sabbath (John 5:9). The Sabbath command was part of the central text of Judaism, the Decalogue or Ten Commandments (Exodus 20:8) and is the longest commandment in the Decalogue and the only commandment that is tied to the creation story. As God rested on the seventh day of creation so also must the people rest.

It would appear that Jesus contravened the Sabbath when he 'worked', when he healed the man at the pool of Bethesda. His counter argument runs, if it is acceptable to circumcise a young boy on the Sabbath (and thus cause pain and suffering), it should be more acceptable to heal. The Pharisees, seeing that the crowds in the Temple were turning to Jesus, scorn them and retort, "This mob knows nothing of the Law – there is a curse on them." Finally, Nicodemus, who had come to Jesus by night in John 3;2, says, "Does our Law condemn a man without first hearing him to find out what he is doing?"

The Law authorizes the process of scapegoating vividly in this passage (cf. also John 5:16). The authorities would seek to kill Jesus because he has interpreted the text outside of the framework they are committed to, which is a way of interpretation that depends on forms of social exclusion. This is demonstrated by their retort that there is a curse on the mob since they obviously do not follow the Law as faithfully as the Pharisees. This "curse" hearkens back to the blessings and curses of the book of Deuteronomy, where the people are promised God's blessing if they keep all his commandments but are cursed if they don't. From the perspective of the religious authorities, the unlearned folk who didn't take time to study Torah could not obey it correctly and thus, lie under a curse from God.

In John 5:39, after the healing of the man at the Sheep Gate, Jesus had already berated his interrogators and observed that though they faithfully studied the Scriptures they missed what the Scriptures were saying. The verb used (Greek: *eraunao*) translates the Aramaic term *deresh*, from which derives the word *midrash*. Jesus critiques the intensive study of the Scriptures by the Pharisees, a laudable effort by any standard, as missing the point.

This same indictment can be brought against North American Christianity. We are encouraged to do daily devotions, to join Bible Study groups, we listen to teachers in Sunday School and sermons, attend Bible Conferences at Bible camps, buy study books at Bible Book Stores. Yet, for all of our intensive Bible work, how is it that we Christians can still engage in social ostracism, justification of violence, war and public execution as well as criticism of those whose work is oriented toward healing? Are we not the modern equivalents of the religious authorities of Jesus' day?

At stake in this discussion is whether God's Instruction (Torah) is to be interpreted as a healing Instruction or whether it is to be used to perpetuate our familiar sacrificial religious and societal violence. It is not the Torah itself that is the problem, but the way it gets interpreted by the religious community, Jewish and Christian. Even today, contemporary Judaism experiences this as much as Christianity. Yet many of the rabbis who helped shape Judaism following the destruction of the Temple tended toward a healing interpretation of Torah, a more (shall I say it?) liberal and liberating perspective. Fortunately, this line of interpretation can be found in synagogues and churches across North America today.

Continuing on, a violent interpretation of Torah is also the issue in the story of the woman taken in adultery in John 7:53-8:11.[ccxxv] There the Pharisees and scribes seek to trap Jesus into acknowledging that the Torah justifies social violence, "Teacher, this woman was caught in the act of adultery. In the Law Moses commanded us to stone such a woman. Now what do you say?" Jesus can either affirm the validity of the commandment or he can deny it. He does neither. What he does it to point out that the one who cannot be judged by the Law has the right to throw the first stone. As each one looked to his life, they realized that at some point large or small, neither had they kept the commandments. So, they dropped their stones.

In 8:17 the Law is given a possessive: when Jesus speaks he refers to "your Law"; when the religious authorities speak they refer to "our Law" (10:34, 15:25, 19:7). The exceptions are the crowds in 12:34 who refer to "the Law" and Pilate in 18:31 who, like Jesus, refers to "your law." What is the significance of this possessive? It would appear that in 8:17, 10:34 and 15:25 the issue once again has to do with using the Law as a tool of justification of social violence. In 8:17 it is whether or not Jesus' testimony was to be accepted, in 10:34 it has to do with the charge of blasphemy and in 15:25 Jesus states that even the Law (in this case Psalm 35:19, 69:4) recognizes "They hated me without a cause." In every case where the word *nomos* (Law) appears in the Fourth Gospel it is strategically tied to the problem of violence. The Fourth Gospel, like the Synoptics, Jesus and Paul, all have as their major central concern what occurs when the sacred biblical text is used to justify violence.

John 7:19 echoes 1:17, "Has not Moses given you the Law? Yet not one of you keeps the Law. Why are you trying to kill me?" The problem with the Law is not its software, but its operating system. It is not a matter of simply liking some texts and not liking others, of accepting some texts and rejecting others. It is the recognition that the Law contains two very clear ways of interpreting itself (see 5.4, 7.1), one oriented to continued justification of sacred violence, the other oriented to revelation of God's rejection of all sacrificial logic. The 'problem' with the legislation of Torah lies in this double aspect *when it is seen as a single aspect.* To make this mistake, as did so many of Jesus' contemporaries (and our own), is to miss the actual salvific work that God has been doing from the beginning with both Jew and Gentile.

So back to our initial question: Is the background of the Prologue to be seen in the light of Greek philosophy or Judaism? I would suggest both but focused on Judaism, for pagan cultures and the Judaisms of Jesus' day were embedded in violence, justifying that violence by the use of *the sacrificial principle* in an *economy of exchange*. All culture depends upon victims; the biblical revelation, both Older and Newer Testaments seek to move the people of God out of that framework into a new way of thinking and living.

I want to state again clearly that the issue is not Christianity vs. Judaism.[ccxxvi] The divide, either Jewish or Christian, is between those who, interpret the Scriptures as justification for violence or whether like Jesus, many rabbis, the Gospel writers and Paul, interpret the Scriptures as the in-breaking revelation of God's non-retributive character. It is this revelation that forms the key to the relationship between God and Jesus, as we shall see in the next section.

8.2 The Life-Giving Imitation of the Son

For almost two thousand years, Christians have done their theology within the framework of Greek philosophical categories (4.3). From Justin Martyr to the present, we have understood terms like 'God', 'creation', 'time and eternity' and 'existence' not by biblical self-definition but by prevailing cultural understandings and their Gnostic underpinnings.[ccxxvii] All of this came crashing down when Karl Barth rocked the theological world by insisting that theology begins and ends and takes its definitions from the Biblical story apart from dependence on any philosophical system. At the end of the twentieth century philosophy itself imploded under the hammer of Jacques Derrida and Deconstruction.

This experience has been disconcerting to many who still labor under the illusion that we know what we mean by terms like 'God.' Indeed so far and so fast has this deconstructive phenomenon spread that many say we are in a post-Christian postmodern world. It would seem Christian theology has been left in a shambles. In our time, there is virtually little or no agreement left on anything regarding the Christian faith.

The Fourth Gospel has been a prime target in the battle of the deconstruction of philosophy and Christianity. The Jesus of the Fourth Gospel is quite different from the Jesus portrayed in the Synoptic Gospels. This especially comes to the fore in discussions of Jesus' divinity. Whereas, in the Synoptics, Jesus makes no 'divine' claims for himself, in the Fourth Gospel he is constantly accused of such. Modern liberal Christianity long ago threw out the Fourth Gospel precisely because it could not see how Jesus was divine. The older creedal affirmations that Jesus was "God of God, light of light, true God of true God" made no sense to their enlightened ways of thinking.

How then are we supposed to make sense of the Fourth Gospel's claim that "the *Logos* was God?" If metaphysics is no longer viable, if we cannot speak in terms of Greek philosophy shall we just jettison the Fourth Gospel from our understanding of Jesus' message and mission? What does this mean for a doctrine of the Trinity? Many have left all this creedal talk behind, preferring a Jesus who is "truly human" but bears no relation to divinity itself. They argue that there are too many problems with a metaphysical approach, an approach that depends upon contested and false thinking about God. They throw the linguistic baby out with the conceptual bathwater! I agree with the former problem but not with the latter solution. I want to suggest rather than talking about Jesus' nature (being, substance) we talk about his character. This is not a move to detract from the question about the divinity of Jesus, but to frame it in a way that captures the heart of the kind of revelation Jesus brings in his full humanity and is not dependent on metaphysics.

In order to do this let us take a cue from a remark I heard Robert Hamerton-Kelly recently make: Metaphysics, as a way of understanding "what is", is being replaced by cognitive science, the study of the human brain. This allows us to move from abstract discussions of what constitutes words like "being" and "nature" to what we can observe (or the phenomenological) by scientific experimentation. Our brains and our capacity to think, organize and imagine are what allow us as a species to be at the top of the evolutionary chain. The science of *how* our brains work is far more real than any philosophical definition.

I mentioned earlier (5.1) that recent discoveries in the neurosciences have opened new doors for us to understand how we humans are imitatively hard-wired. We copy one another on a nonconscious level constantly. Note that the Fourth Gospel does not use the term imitation (*mimesis*). Yet, all through the Christology of the Fourth Gospel imitation is the key to understanding Jesus' relation to his *Abba*. It is the identity of the heavenly *Abba* with that of the Son, Jesus, that brings to the fore the true character of what is being revealed and how that revelation saves us.

Just as in Paul (7.2), so also in the Fourth Gospel, it is God who initiates our salvation. Our religious giving in order to receive, *do ut des, the sacrificial principle* (3.2) is discounted for it is God who "gives the Son" freely and without condition or request (3:16). The *Abba* sends the Son (3:34, 4:34, 5:36, 7:28-29), the Son is "bread from heaven" sent by God (6:32, 57). The content of the Son's message comes from God (7:16). The actions of the Son please the One who sent him (8:29). The *Abba* hears the prayers of the Son whom He sent (11:41). Faith in the Son is also faith in the sending *Abba* (12:44). Jesus, in the Fourth Gospel understands that his is a divine sending, he is acting as an agent of the Father (13:3) but he will also be mistreated as God's agent because his persecutors do not see *that his character and God's character and behavior are one and the same* (15:21).

The Gospel Changes Our View of God

If the Son is God's agent, God's ambassador, sent by God on a mission to God's people what happens when the people's view of God is different than that announced by Jesus? What happens when Jesus' behavior, which he claims amounts to God's behavior, is different from that which is expected? This is what is at stake here. Then, even as now, Christians, like the Jewish religious leadership of Jesus' era, have made assumptions about the character of God. When Jesus shatters these assumptions, which are nothing more than idolatrous presuppositions, he will be rejected (1:9).

It is the Son, not the religious authorities or theologians who does the will of the *Abba* (4:34, 6:38, 10:25, 37). The Father bears witness to the acts and character of the Son (5:31, 37). Those who really listen to God come to Jesus (6:45), for as God's agent, his message is the message of God. How does Jesus know his message is God's message? He imitates God; he testifies to the God he has known, bearing witness to the kind of God who has broken into our depraved violent world (3:32), even though his God is rejected and people around him reject his message.

In 5:19 this imitative aspect of Jesus' relation to God is blatant: The Son "Can do nothing by himself; he can only do what he sees his Father doing, because whatever the Father does, the Son also does." How can this be? "The Father loves the Son and shows him all that he does." Like a child who learns by imitating their parents, so too Jesus is claiming that his behavior and teaching comes as a result of copying God. As a human child is not metaphysically the same as her parent, so too, there is no need to interpret these texts in the abstract ways of Greek philosophy. They can be understood now in the same way we understand all character formation, in terms of imitation.

One of the claims of the Son is that his hearers "do not know God" (8:28-29). This is astonishing because, after all, these teachers and 'theologians' were people steeped in their Scriptures. Surely they knew God, from his words and works in the Jewish Bible. Surely they could exegete their texts, read all of the various names of God and discern God's character. Yet, when all is said and done they failed. Why? Because, unlike Jesus, they missed the double trajectory, the internal self-critique, found within the Scriptures themselves. They were still entrenched in their belief in a Janus-faced god. They could not hear Jesus because they preferred their idolatry to God's voice (8:47). The Fourth Gospel is replete with a critique of false conceptions of God (1:17-18, 5:37ff, 6:44, 8:31-58, 10:31-39, cf. I John 5:20).

The Son, though, does not say or teach anything that he has not already seen and heard from God. He has "been commanded by God on what to say and how to say it" (12:49). Both the medium and the message are tied together. How Jesus acts and what he says are all of one piece. The conclusion we must draw from this is that whatever we may think we know about God or say about God cannot be different from what we know and say about Jesus. We cannot play them off against one another as though one is a get-tough lawgiver while the other is a submissive participant in a tragic play. No, just as God "judges no one" (5:22) so also the Son does not judge (12:47). It is wrong to begin our understanding of God as Judge, Jury and Executioner. For the Son was sent that we might have life (10:10), and even as God gives life, so also the Son gives life (5:21). It is as Lifegiver, not Lifetaker that Creator of all wishes to be known!

If, as has been suggested all through this book, it is the nonviolent, non-retributive Jesus who reveals that God is like him, nonviolent and non-retributive, then it is time for us to change our doctrine of God. I find it strange when someone murders someone else claiming that God or Jesus told him or her to do so, we lock him or her up in a prison or a mental institution. We reject a God who would tell anyone to kill someone else. We somehow instinctively know the Divine is separate from this kind of death dealing enterprise.

Yet when a world leader takes a country to war and claims divine authorization for it, we are willing to accept that as warrant or justification for retaliation. This is exactly what a recent head of state did when he claimed before going to war in Iraq, he did not inquire of his earthly father, a former President, but instead sought his "heavenly Father's" advice. Evidently, God had changed his mind from his revelation in Jesus and encouraged this man to attack his enemies. Why then didn't we commit him to years of intensive therapy? Is it because we really think that God is different from Jesus? This leader of the free world and his administration sought their warrant for war from the kind of zealous reading of the biblical narrative rejected by Jesus and the apostolic church. In this sense, the Christians who participated in that administration's justification for war were not listening to the *Abba* of Jesus but to their real 'Father', the one who from the beginning was a liar and a murderer (8:42-47).

The consequences of seeing the identity of the Son, Jesus, with God are immense and paradigm altering. The character of the one is the character of the other. It is the doctrine of God that is being changed before our eyes in the witness of the Scriptures, both Jewish and Christian. Our failure to see this is due to our allegiance to our pagan sacrificial ways of thinking and our willingness to keep trying to prop up our religious and social systems with scapegoats.

I have little doubt that *that* President and the other Christians in his administration were sincere in their deliberations. I also have no doubt they subscribed to the kinds of thinking that have always undergirded human culture. They read their Bibles, not from Jesus' perspective, but from the perspective of a Christianity that has separated the Father from the Son. They took their definition of God from the Greek philosophical tradition and from the names of God in the Old Testament. They would not or could not allow themselves to see the light Jesus was bringing into their darkness. They would not or could not see that by rejecting the option of restorative justice, of a transformative spirituality, of forgiveness, they were rejecting God's nonviolent *Logos*. So, here we are, nine years down the line, still mired in a war it is doubtful we can win, claim victory and come home to glory and honor. American young men and women, and many tens of thousands of innocents continue to die because one man consulted his

"God" who gave him permission to kill others. This is the real tragedy of this kind of faith. This kind of faith can only lead to death and destruction. It is not the faith of Jesus, nor is it Christian faith; it is idolatry.

On December 10, 2009 our current President took a similar approach in his Nobel Prize acceptance speech. While less 'Evangelical' (and Manichean) than his predecessor, he still thinks within the same dualistic framework (or two kingdom theory). He said,

> "I make this statement mindful of what Martin Luther King said in this same ceremony years ago -- "Violence never brings permanent peace. It solves no social problem: it merely creates new and more complicated ones." As someone who stands here as a direct consequence of Dr. King's life's work, I am living testimony to the moral force of nonviolence. I know there is nothing weak -- nothing passive -- nothing naive -- in the creed and lives of Gandhi and King.
>
> But as a head of state sworn to protect and defend my nation, I cannot be guided by their examples alone. I face the world as it is, and cannot stand idle in the face of threats to the American people. For make no mistake: Evil does exist in the world. A nonviolent movement could not have halted Hitler's armies. Negotiations cannot convince al Qaeda's leaders to lay down their arms. To say that force is sometimes necessary is not a call to cynicism -- it is a recognition of history; the imperfections of man and the limits of reason.
>
> So yes, the instruments of war do have a role to play in preserving the peace. And yet this truth must coexist with another -- that no matter how justified, war promises human tragedy."[ccxxviii]

I do not say this to scapegoat the Presidents; it runs deeper than that. They believed what they had been told (whether by Dobson or Niebuhr). Nor do I blame the religious right in this country, it runs deeper than that; they believe what they have been told. Nor can I blame Protestant or Catholic Christianity; it runs deeper than that. Nor can I blame Judaism, the parent of Christianity; it runs deeper than that. The fault lies deep in our social genes, it lies in our religiousness. It goes back to our origins as a species, back to our mythic past, when we first discovered that violence was both poison and balm (5.3, 6.1). It lies in the deception we as a species have embraced. We are all "of our father the devil." All of us have participated in victimizing others.

The boundaries between individuals killing in the name of Jesus and leaders killing in the name of God are blurred in our culture. The one we abhor, the other we acknowledge, yet they are one and the same thing. If we confess the Holy Spirit to be 'The Lord and Giver of Life' we could never authorize violence in any fashion, no matter how great or worthy the cause. The God of the Bible is the God of life, not death. Scapegoating sacrifice is what we humans contribute to history's cause. This is why it is crucial for us to see that the Holy Spirit brings to our memory everything Jesus teaches. The Spirit does not bring to our memory every bit of what 'the Bible' teaches without discernment. That is too ambiguous and it leaves the door wide open for all kinds of sick theology, theology generated not from the Cross of Jesus, but theology generated from the perspective of the persecutor, the perspective of the ones in power. The Holy Spirit teaches us and reminds us of Jesus, only Jesus, because the *Abba* in Jesus' name gives the Holy Spirit. If what we believe is not congruent with Jesus, then we will have learned from another spirit, the devil, the Satan.

To Love One Must Renounce Violence

The alternative to our religious violence is to recognize, once for all, that we must renounce violence, as did our Lord. To do so is to bring us to a new way of life, of living in relationship. This is the way of *agape*, the way of love. *Agape* suffuses the New Testament. The apostolic church breathed the air of love, God's love for the world, lived in Jesus' life, shown in Jesus' death, vindicated in Jesus' resurrection, established in Jesus' ascension to the right hand of God.

Like most of his vocabulary, John prefers verbs to nouns, so the word 'love' is found much less than the verb 'to love.' Love is not a thing but an action of one party for another, a way of existing in relationships. Love for the other, no matter how they treat you, is of the essence of the Christian life (1.2). The way of love is radical and new:

> "A new commandment I give you: Love one another. As I have loved you, so you must love one another. All will know you are my apprentices if you love one another." (John 13:34-35)

We have already covered aspects of the breadth of this love, even for the enemy other. What the Fourth Gospel gives us is not a list of characteristics of love, as Paul did in I Corinthians 13; we are given a model of love. We are to love each other as Jesus has loved us. He is the model we imitate. He is the one we follow and so learn how to love. It is a difficult path. Even Peter misunderstood. Immediately after Jesus gave the new commandment to love Peter insists he is willing to go to holy war with Jesus. Just like we saw in Mark 8 (2.2), Peter still doesn't get "the full extent of Jesus' love" (13:1).

Peter, who is named as the one who draws the sword in Gethsemane (18:10), doesn't get it. Even on the last night of Jesus' life, having followed Jesus for three years, Peter was still locked into the way of thinking that has bound all religious people from time immemorial; he still had a god who could justify violence.

There may be some who feel I am arguing that Jesus truly and fully reveals God and I suppose I am. Whether from politeness or political correctness or a genuine desire to be ecumenical in things religious it is difficult for some to accept the claim of the New Testament that Jesus was the distinctive (although not unique) human revelation of God. Neither Moses nor Mahomet claimed to be the personal incarnation of deity, nor did their followers claim such for them, although the claim has been made in other religions ancient and modern.

The Gospels make this claim only in the light of one fact above all: God raised Jesus from the dead.[ccxxix] However we think they may have understood the resurrection, it was the seminal event that changed all of their thinking. The resurrection is not 'proof' of Jesus' divinity, contrary to what some Christian apologists have asserted. The resurrection is proof that God recognizes Jesus' human life as what a human life lived in God's Spirit looks like. This is the logic of the hymn in Philippians 2:5-11 (7.4), where the "for this reason" hearkens back to Jesus posture of humility, offering himself in non-retributive service. This is why God gave to Jesus the Name, the Unpronounceable Name, the Name above all Names. It explains how the early church and then the whole church following Nicaea, could call Jesus 'God.' The Father-Son identity hinges not upon metaphysical speculation but upon agency and Jesus' faithfulness to the will of his *Abba*. If such is the case, then it is also possible for us to follow him, to live as he lived and thus to also be children of the heavenly *Abba* (1:12).

The Fourth Gospel presents Jesus as the true witness or agent of God, the authoritative revelation of God *in human form*. As Christians we are called to use him as our model when we follow him, hear his word to us and obey. We can discern his intentions as we read the Gospel stories about him, since we know his intentionality is that of God. This can only be so when we have made Jesus the intentional object of our desire. The Anabaptist maxim "to know Christ is to follow him, to follow Christ is to know him" is our valid starting point. To follow Jesus is to be like God, for God and Jesus have one and the same character (8:58, 10:15, 30, 38, 14:6, 9-11, 20, 16:15, 17:10, 21-23, cf. 20:28).

If we let go of our prejudices surrounding the Gospels and take the risk of actually choosing to follow Jesus, to be yoked with him, we too, like him, can know and do the will of God. Discerning intentionality has already been put to the test in experiments with the human brain. I am suggesting that real transformation is the case for those who chose an intentional relationship with Jesus.

> "Understanding the intentions of others while watching their actions is a fundamental building block of social behavior. The neural and functional mechanisms underlying this ability are still poorly understood. To investigate these mechanisms we used functional magnetic resonance imaging. Twenty-three subjects watched three kinds of stimuli: grasping hand actions without a context, context only (scenes containing objects), and grasping hand actions performed in two different contexts. In the latter condition the context suggested the intention associated with the grasping action (either drinking or cleaning). Actions embedded in contexts, compared with the other two conditions, yielded a significant signal increase in the posterior part of the inferior frontal gyrus and the adjacent sector of the ventral premotor cortex where hand actions are represented. Thus, premotor mirror neuron areas—areas active during the execution and the observation of an action—previously thought to be involved only in action recognition are actually also involved in understanding the intentions of others. To ascribe an intention is to infer a forthcoming new goal, and this is an operation that the motor system does automatically." Vittori Gallese[ccxxx]

This astonishing capacity of the human brain to be able to not only imitate others but also to discern their intentionality is what lies behind the statement found in the Upper Room discourse (John 13-16) "Anyone who has faith in me will do what I have been doing. He/She will do even greater things than these because I am going to the Father" (14:12). Faith in Jesus is the trust or surrender we have already mentioned many times. It is to be able to discern the intention of God (Romans 12:1-2). It is to acknowledge that the Jesus who died is the same Jesus who has been raised from the dead by God and now lives among his followers. It is to believe that we not only know him but can "hear his voice" (10:16), the authentic voice of God. As we make our choice to listen to Jesus and follow him our own lives are transformed into his image and "On that day you will realize that I am in my Father, and you are in me, and I am in you" (14:20-21). Jesus promises to show himself to us!

How does the Fourth Gospel express Jesus present relationship to believers? In 5.1 we observed the need for contemporary Christianity to recover what is called "the present Christ" (*Christus praesens*). This entails that we now think through our understanding of the Holy Spirit, for the Spirit is the Lord.

8.3 The Spirit-Paraclete

Luke, Paul and the author of the Fourth Gospel are the canonical theologians of the Holy Spirit. Each in their own way speaks of the Holy Spirit, yet they all have at least one thing in common. For each writer, the Holy Spirit is intimately connected to Jesus. In Luke's Gospel, Jesus is filled with the Spirit and his ministry is in the power of the Spirit (Luke 3:21-22, 4:18-19, 10:21); in Acts the Spirit comes to the Christian community in Jesus' name. In Paul, the Spirit is the Spirit of God poured out through Jesus, so much so, that it can be said, "The Lord is the Spirit" (2 Cor. 3:17-18).

In the Fourth Gospel, the Spirit is also deeply connected to Jesus. This, observation is a crucial one in our so-called postmodern world inasmuch as there are forms of Christianity where experiences of the Spirit abound yet where Jesus is little to be seen. It doesn't matter whether these 'Spirit-filled' congregations are conservative or liberal. In some churches experience of the Spirit equals a sort of Christian triumphalism. In other churches experience of the Spirit is a mystical, fuzzy, warm, pea-soup-on-a-cold-day kind of thing. In still other churches, the manifestation of the Spirit is found in a loud, pompous, miraculous hysteria. But where is Jesus?

There is another spirit that haunts North American Christianity today and it is not the Spirit of Jesus. It does not have its origin in the God of Love, but in something else. It is the spirit one sees at a high school football game or a political rally. One can find it at a concert or a rave. It manifests itself in cathedrals, mega-churches and in small Christian (so-called) sects. It is the spirit of the mob, often manifesting as the spirit of fear.

Fear is a great motivator. Sales people understand this well. Fear of loss is greater than hope of gain. That's why sales people do a 'take away': "This is for a limited time only", "there are only a few models left" or "once these are gone at this price that's it." Churches can be dominated by this fear as well. It can be fear of others who are socially different, whether race, gender orientation or political affiliation. Fear of those whose doctrine is different then one's own. Fear grounded in national or ethnic pride. There is fear of losing the status quo or one's understanding of morality. This fear does not come from God, for in God, "Perfect love casts out fear" (I John 4:18). This is especially true when it comes to Christian preaching that uses "the fear of the Lord" to inculcate morality or to 'save souls' from an eternal Abu Ghraib. Fear has to do with punishment, therefore preaching which is oriented to speaking of a punishing God is preaching that has lost its focus on the gracious self-giving character of God.

The spirit of fear comes from the *sacrificial principle*. This occurs when a community perceives themselves as an in-group over against an out-group. The out-group functions as a scapegoat to keep the in-group together.

Those inside the in-group live in fear of being part of the out-group. To be part of the out-group is to be outside the redeemed community. Cyprian said in the third century "outside the church there is no salvation." Sadly today, this maxim has come to be used to defend Christian thinking that it is *my* group, *my* church, *and my* tradition that saves. Those outside of this are damned.

No one wants to be a scapegoat; it is not exactly an office for which one runs. Yet, as I have argued all through this book, human culture, whether religious or 'secular', needs its scapegoats in order to function as a community. There is no human community without victims. We define ourselves less by who we are than by who we are not. It is this spirit that is created in so many churches across North America Sunday by Sunday.

Who Or What is the Devil?

Jesus was acquainted with this spirit and he cast it out at every turn in his ministry.[ccxxxi] The spirit of fear is the satanic spirit. The term 'satan' means prosecuting attorney. The satan plays this role in the Prologue to Job as we have seen (6.2). This is also the satan's function in Zechariah 3:1 where it accuses the high priest Joshua. In Revelation "that ancient serpent called the devil or Satan" is called "the accuser of the brethren" (Rev 12:9-10). The satanic is the accusatory, the finger pointing at someone, the blamer. The 'satan' is humanity sickly twisted on itself, assuring its own survival by transferring its hatred and hostility onto another (6.1).

A very brief overview of the satan is in order here.[ccxxxii] Far too much of what Christians believe about the satan owes more to medieval legend and Hollywood speculation than it does to Scripture. There is probably more misunderstanding about the devil in Christian thought than anything else and wrongly informs more topics than anything else. It is not possible to go into detail on all these topics. Therefore the focus of this brief discussion will concern the prosecutorial role of the satan.

In the earliest Jewish tradition, as mentioned, the satan is part of the 'heavenly council' (Job 1-2). He is the heavenly Attorney General going about to make sure that those who do not do the will of God are exposed. After the Exile, and under the influence of Persian dualism, the satan will be split off from God and become the independent principle of evil. In later Jewish literature like I Enoch, the satanic legend is developed. Here, the satan (who goes by many names), leads a rebellion in heaven and, along with his army, is cast out of heaven. It is only at this point that the satan takes on, as it were, a personality of it's own. The satan then becomes the highest being who turned to evil. The Genesis story of the human's seduction in the Garden of Eden, which does not mention the satan (only a 'shrewd serpent'), is then interpreted in the light of this later development. The quote from Revelation 12 above reflects this ancient tradition.

The problem is not the concept of the satan, for evil is very real. The primary problem occurs when the satan is made otherworldly, made into some kind of power almost, but not quite, as powerful as God. Evil then is something that originates outside human history. This creates all sorts of theological problems (the technical term is '*theodicy*'). We can already see this in Isaiah where God says, "I form the light and create darkness, I bring prosperity and create disaster; I the Lord, do these things" (Isaiah 45:7). In this view 'God' is ultimately responsible for evil. The two sides that have been created in heaven, good and evil, have their counterparts on earth, in good people and bad people. Just as God goes to war against the satan, so also below, good people go to war against bad people. It is this logic that informed ancient Jewish sectarianism and zealous interpretation of their Scriptures, medieval Christian superstition and the Crusades, and modern use of the Bible to justify violence and war against ethnic or national enemies.

When I reject this otherworldly personalizing of the satan (inasmuch as I reject the dualism that informs it), I nevertheless affirm that for the biblical writers evil is very real. The Jewish rabbinic tradition also acknowledged the reality of evil and not all Jewish teachers made the devil otherworldly. With great insight, some rabbis understood that evil arises from within the human being. So it was that they formulated the dualism of good and evil not in terms of a heavenly conflict between God and Satan, but as the two principles that war within the human soul. These two principles are *yetzer-ha-ra* and the *yetzer-ha-tov*, the impulse toward evil and the impulse toward good. The apostle Paul reflects this two *yetzer* thinking in Romans 7 and Galatians 5. It is also possible that it lies behind James 1:13-15.[ccxxxiii]

The anthropologizing of evil, or understanding evil as a human rather than a divine phenomenon, is an important contribution made by the rabbis. Rene Girard has exploited this insight in our own time for the way we read the Bible, particularly the New Testament. Some may feel that I am taking the "oomph" out of evil by demystifying it; I would contend however, that with the rabbis, Jesus, Paul, James and now mimetic realism, the radical character of evil is to be placed squarely on human shoulders.

God, Defender for the Accused

If the satan is the accuser, the Prosecuting attorney, are we then left without defense? Not at all for Jesus promised he would send to us a Defense Attorney, the *Paraclete*. John 14:15-18 says,

> "15If you love me, you will obey what I command. 16And I will ask the Father, and he will give you another Counselor to be with you forever— 17the Spirit of truth. The world cannot accept him, because it neither sees him nor knows him. But you know him, for he lives with you and will be in you. 18I will not leave you as orphans; I will come to you."

And in John 16:7-15 it says,

> "7Unless I go away, the Counselor will not come to you; but if I go, I will send him to you. 8When he comes, he will convict the world of guilt in regard to sin and righteousness and judgment: 9in regard to sin, because men do not believe in me; 10in regard to righteousness, because I am going to the Father, where you can see me no longer; 11and in regard to judgment, because the prince of this world now stands condemned. 12I have much more to say to you, more than you can now bear. 13But when he, the Spirit of truth, comes, he will guide you into all truth. He will not speak on his own; he will speak only what he hears, and he will tell you what is yet to come. 14He will bring glory to me by taking from what is mine and making it known to you. 15All that belongs to the Father is mine. That is why I said the Spirit will take from what is mine and make it known to you."

The King James translated *Paraclete* as 'Comforter' but notice in the NIV this has become 'Counselor.' True it is a comfort to have a defender, but 'counselor' is a more appropriate translation as the term reflects the advocacy or legal role of the Spirit. In contrast to the satanic spirit that accuses, God's Spirit defends us.

If, as explained in chapter 5, the satanic is the human religious impulse toward scapegoating, using violence to cast out violence, then the work of the Spirit is to defend the victim of unjust persecution, expose the victimizer's lies and vindicate the victim. It is no mistake that the *Paraclete* sayings in the Fourth Gospel are closely tied in with persecution of the followers of Jesus.

The Spirit, as advocate, intercedes for us (cf. Romans 8:26-27). Israel was not unacquainted with intercessors. Gary Burge helpfully summarizes the developing role of intercessor in Israel's history. In the Torah Abraham (Gen. 18:22-23) and Moses (Exodus 32:11-14) are intercessors. Later, there is "Samuel (I Sam. 7:8-9) and prophets such as Amos (Amos 7:2, 5-6) and Jeremiah (Jer. 14:7-9, 19-22) [who] can be noted as characteristic advocates for Israel."[ccxxxiv] Burge also notes that in the Jewish Scriptures Israel's intercessors could also function as accusers. This would make sense inasmuch as those who are agents of a Janus-faced god would also themselves take on opposing roles. The Holy Spirit in the Fourth Gospel does not have this double character.

The Spirit is like Jesus. Jesus' saying about sending "another Counselor" used a Greek word (*allos*) meaning another *of the same kind as himself.* James Alison makes the point that just as an Accuser sat before the ancient city gate ready to mete out justice, so also another *go'el*, a Redeemer, intercessor or defense attorney was also present. If the satan is the former, the Holy Spirit is the latter *just like Jesus.*

Burge explains this best:

> "The person of Christ and his work inform both the image of the Paraclete and all that he does. As Christ was to his disciples, so the Paraclete will be to them. Indeed, the Paraclete has no autonomy from Christ. The Paraclete is not a replacement figure for Christ because Christ is in effect still present. It is *Christus Praesens* that speaks through the Paraclete and directs his revealing activity. When one encountered the Spirit Paraclete in the Johannine community, one encountered the Risen Christ. *Therefore we can conclude that the single most important feature of the Johannine Paraclete is its Christological concentration. Christ is the template within the Fourth Evangelist's thinking that has given shape and meaning to the Spirit.*"[ccxxxv]

It is important to note since neither the *Abba* nor the Son judges so the Spirit is not a spirit of judgment. The Spirit will "convict" (*elegko*) the world but conviction is different than judgment (*krino*). To convict is to show someone their fault or error, this being what the Spirit has done through the pages of Scripture from the beginning. We have frequently understood this conviction to be in terms of morality or personal guilt in relation to laws and taboos, but the work of the Spirit is to expose the lies surrounding our propensity toward victimage. "God did not send his Son into the world to judge the world but to save the world through him" (John 3:17).

The Holy Spirit and Jesus' Death

Paraclete sayings are connected with persecution, which have been discussed as the violence of all against one, or the scapegoat mechanism. The Fourth Gospel also makes the connection between the Spirit and Jesus' death in 7:37-39 although it may be easily missed.

> 37On the last and greatest day of the Feast, Jesus stood and said in a loud voice, "If anyone is thirsty, let him come to me and drink.
> 38Whoever believes in me, as the Scripture has said, streams of living water will flow from within him." 39By this he meant the

> Spirit, whom those who believed in him were later to receive. Up to that time the Spirit had not been given, since Jesus had not yet been glorified.

The context of this passage is the Temple, specifically a ceremony of the Feast of Sukkoth or Booths. More specifically it refers to the water offering of the first seven days that was not offered on the eighth day ('the last, great day').[ccxxxvi] It would be like someone announcing real freedom at the Lincoln Memorial on the Fourth of July at fireworks time, if there were no fireworks after there had been at that time for the previous week.

Jesus' offer of water is reminiscent of Moses in the wilderness where Moses brings forth water from a rock. That story is told twice in Torah, in Exodus 17:1-7 and Numbers 20:1-13.[ccxxxvii] There are differences in the two stories that the rabbis recognized. In Exodus, Moses is commanded to strike the rock, in Numbers to speak to the rock. Now the Numbers text is interesting for when God commands Moses to strike the rock, Moses strikes the rock twice. Why? The rabbis explained this in their commentary by saying ""Moses struck the rock twice, and first it gushed out blood and then water" (commenting on Psalm 78:20).[ccxxxviii] How did they figure that the rock gushed out blood? Because the words "gushed out" in Hebrew are found in Psalm 78:20 with reference to the water from the rock and also in Leviticus 15:19-20 with reference to a woman's menstrual blood. Therefore, they concluded, the first time it gushed out blood, the second time water. The *Palestinian Targum to Numbers* 20:11 also reflects this tradition when it says "and Moses lifted up his hand, and with his rod and struck the rock twice: at the first time it dropped blood; but at the second time there came forth a multitude of waters."

We might immediately think of Jesus being struck with the lance of the Roman soldier in John 19:34: "Instead [of breaking Jesus' legs], one of the soldiers pierced Jesus' side with a spear, bringing a sudden flow of blood and water." How does the story in John 7:37-39 relate to John 19:34? The connection is to be found in the rabbinic interpretation of the rock story found in Numbers 20. Yet John 7:37-39 does not speak of blood or Jesus death or does it?

We must first ask: does the text say it is the believer or Jesus from whom living waters flow? The NIV translation would seem to indicate that it is from the believer. Recognizing that the early manuscripts of the Greek New Testament did not have punctuation, some ancient church authorities and some modern scholars suggest punctuating the text differently so it reads:

> "'If any person is thirsty, let them come to me.
> Whoever believes in me, let them drink.'"

> As the Scripture has said, 'streams of living water will flow from within him.'"

This makes Jesus the source of living water. This is congruent with what Jesus said to the woman at the Samaritan well in John 4:13-14:

> "[13]Jesus answered, "Everyone who drinks this water will be thirsty again, [14]but whoever drinks the water I give him will never thirst. Indeed, the water I give him will become in him a spring of water welling up to eternal life."

Jesus is the source of living water, not the believer, just as he is the source of living bread in John 6. This Christological focus is entirely consistent with the emphasis of the Fourth Gospel on Jesus as the revelation of God and the true source of the life of God. Jesus is thus the fount of the Spirit, the one from whom the Spirit is given. But we still have to ask, where is the blood mentioned? How do we get from John 7:37-39 to John 19:34?

The answer lies in the term 'glorified.' The author notes that the "Spirit was not yet given because Jesus was not yet glorified." We tend to think of glorification as something lofty, the achievement of celebrity status. Some will say that Jesus had not yet ascended to heaven, as in Acts 1:9 so of course the Spirit could not yet be given. Glory is a term reserved for the best, the highest of achievements. Should we understand the Fourth Gospel to say that Jesus will be the source of living water, the Holy Spirit after he has ascended to heaven? Not quite.

The term 'glory' holds the key. It is one of the words the Fourth Gospel uses that has a double meaning. Double meaning words abound in this Gospel. John 3:1-15 has a number of examples *Nuktos* (night), *Semeia* (signs), *Anothen* (again/above), *Pneuma* (spirit/wind/breath), *Hupsao* (exalt/lift up). '*Nuktos*' can mean when the moon is out or when spiritual darkness is present (cf. 13:30). *Pneuma* is used both of human breath and God's breath, earthly wind and God's moving through the world. Nicodemus understands Jesus to say he must be born 'again' chronologically; Jesus refers to being born 'from above', from heaven. *Hupsao* in most of the New Testament means exalted as in I Peter 4:6 "Humble yourself, therefore under God's mighty hand that he may lift you up (*hupsao*) in good time." In the Fourth Gospel the verb is used of Jesus being exalted all right, exalted six feet off the ground in the abject humiliation of crucifixion! The same with *doksazo*, 'to glorify.' Glorification in the Fourth Gospel, like exaltation, takes place in deepest humiliation. This use of double meaning words is the way the author turns upside down our normal thinking about things and reveals that we have not understood Jesus' death until we understand it as his moment of greatest glory, as the moment when God glorified Jesus.[ccxxxix]

Jesus makes this connection between death and glorification in John 12:23-25.

As we come back to our interpretation of the Spirit in John 7:37-39 we see it is the reference to 'glory' which indicates Jesus' death and thus the blood that will come forth from his side, along with the water. It is in Jesus' death where God pours out the Spirit. It is the innocent victim who is the source of God's revelation, the font of the Spirit! This is the new logic or *Logos*, which James Alison has rightly termed 'the intelligence of the victim.' It literally creates a new way to think (it generates its own epistemology). Whereas the community thinks it is doing God a favor by getting rid of the 'blasphemer', God pours out God's very inner life in the Crucified. It is not in transcendent glory that the Spirit comes to us but in the abject humiliation of victimage. We might begin to reconsider then, how we understand those persons whom our church communities have marginalized, judged or condemned.

The Spirit can "convict the world in regard to sin, righteousness and judgment' because the Spirit is given in the dying victim who was sinned against and unrighteously judged. Even so, the Spirit is convicting our modern church of false judgments regarding those who have been excluded and scapegoated as the result of our righteous (sic) law keeping. We were never meant to be a community whose spirit came from violence or retribution, from in-group/out-group demarcation. What kind of community were we meant to be? This is the question for our next section.

8.4 The Beloved Community

The Fourth Gospel has proven no different from the Synoptics or Paul when read through the lens of mimetic realism. The issue of violence is still prominent in the *Logos* of the Prologue. The imitation of the Father by the Son provides a key place by which we can profitably explore the value of imitation and intention. The *Spirit-Paraclete* sayings and the connection of the Spirit with Jesus death allows us to see the defense and vindication of the victim as a theme taken up by the Johannine author; a theme found from Genesis to Revelation.

If, as the Fourth Gospel claims, we can speak of Jesus as the human imitator of God *par excellence* ('the Word enfleshed' 1:14), then it is also possible to speak of the Father 'living' in and through the life of the Son and hence, of the divinity of Jesus. This is the claim ultimately vindicated in the resurrection of Jesus. In John 20:20 he appears not as one unaffected by the violence against him; he comes to the disciples and to us as One wounded. "See the scars on my hands and feet. Place your hand in the hole between my ribs." He comes back from the dead as the wounded victim but unlike the many victims of historical and mythic record, he brings a word of peace (*shalom*).

In his prayer in the garden (John 17) Jesus anticipates that his disciples will share in the divine life. "That they may be in us, just as you are in me and I am in you, Father." This subjectivity is the appropriation of the life we know from the Gospel tradition, now enfleshed in our very own existence. If in the Gospels we may speak of the objective Life of Jesus (the 'so-called' historical Jesus), so also by the gift of the Spirit we may also speak of the subjective life of Jesus in us (the Present Christ or the *Christus Praesens*). The life we now live is lived in Jesus. He is the vine and we are the branches (John 15:1-9). Where the vine ends and the branches begin is not possible to tell. So it is with us. This is the secret of Christian existence. We are not merged with Jesus so that we may confuse our identity with him, anymore than he is merged with the Father and so loses his identity. To suggest such is to end in a metaphysical miasma and psychological grandiosity. Rather, inasmuch as we imitate Jesus by living in love, as he imitated his *Abba* and lived in love, we become like him.

As we live together in love, we become a community of faith. The Fourth Gospel never uses the word church (*ekklesia* or assembly) but that does not mean it has no concept of Christian community. Unlike Paul who took the word *ekklesia* over from the urban cultural world (as a group that assembled for a specific purpose like a guild or a burial society), the Fourth Gospel does not use a specific term for when the church gathers. However it is clear that the community gathers (cf. John 20:19).

For the moment let us recall how human community is formed in mimetic realism. Community takes place in the all against one mechanism of selectively transferring hostility to a (random) innocent victim. The unity of the community is the unity of violence. Girard has said that only two things have the power to create reconciliation and unity: violence and love. It is the former we use in our group formation when we unite around our victims. This is the incredible power of violence and why it is so difficult for us to give it up. If we give up violence or the threat of violence (whether divine or human) we fear that our world will come apart. As scary as it may sound, this is the whole purpose of Christ's coming into the world. Jesus has come to save us from the deadly infection of community building and maintenance dependent upon victims, *in other words, he has come to save us from the world we humans have created.*

The only alternative is for us to live in love. We would not know this love had God not first shown us. "This is love, not that we loved God but that God first loved us" (I John 4:10). A community that originates and maintains itself in love does not need scapegoats for it is centered on the ultimate marginalized victim, God in Christ. It is no longer an in-group that needs an out-group. As the followers of Jesus we gather around the Vindicated Victim and thus are repentantly aware how our propensity to create victims and to make those victims sacred (as though God wanted them) is real.

This existence as 'gathered group around the Risen Vindicated Victim, Jesus Christ' we call church. However, as I noted in the Introduction, the Jesus of so much contemporary Christianity is a cipher or symbol of our own projected version of what constitutes success, power, glory, and fame. In this way of thinking, The Wounded Christ is only seen as a sacrificial offering to assuage God's anger toward us. Otherwise, so they assert, his wounds hold no meaning for us. Yet Jesus' wounds can hold the deepest significance for us when in him we see our own woundedness as those who have been hurt by others and we see those whom we have wounded.

The gathered community of the faithful around Jesus thus cares for one another as the fulfillment of 'the law of love.' In a sense, 'being church' or gathered as any group in the name of Jesus, is where we practice our discipleship skills. We should not expect to be perfect nor should we expect others to be perfect. This is where forgiveness becomes such an important discipline among sisters and brothers. We *practice* forgiveness (3.2). Like any skill it is difficult at first. But the more you do it, the better you get at it and the easier it becomes.

The church can feel like a wonderful hospital, in imitation of the hospitality of Jesus. The wounded, both those who have been hurt and those who have hurt others are no longer judged and condemned. Unlike our culture, we apply 'the law of love' to organize ourselves, thus creating one overarching model of mercy (3.2). Those who have violated themselves and others (because they have violated social taboos) are forgiven and invited to a life of transformation; those who have been hurt are not viewed as problems to be solved but as persons to be embraced. Instead of passing judgment we remember that our God has come to save, redeem and transform us. We realize we have no final word on all kinds of issues, moral and doctrinal and we make no rules to keep the wounded away from ourselves. Instead with open arms like those of the Wounded Healer (Henri Nouwen), we welcome the hurt, the sinner, and the lost to come change with us receiving our love and experiencing God's love in community. We do not take up crusades for our friends or ourselves when we are harmed remembering that it was God's word of forgiveness that brought us into the community of Jesus. All of this happens when we replace Morality or 'the rule of law' as our center with 'Jesus.'

The Johannine writer recognizes (as Jesus and Paul also saw) that law is not the part of the solution but part of the problem. It is a problem because laws, rules, taboos and mores exacerbate our tendency to be destructive and self-destructive. Structuring a community around law inevitably leads to creating boundaries by which we define ourselves over against others. I repeat what I said earlier: law (prohibitions) arises from our sinful tendency to make victims of those who are different from us. Laws stop us from demonstrating mercy to those we think God has abandoned or judged. If the only law that we are to follow is the law of love, what results is the calling of the church not to create barriers but to tear them down.

Does this mean there is no room for discussions of morality or ethics within the Christian community? Not at all. But all of these conversations that name certain behaviors as 'sinful' must stem from whether or not said behavior is harmful to others, not whether the Bible has certain verses that condemn the behavior. Certain behaviors are both condoned and condemned in Scripture.

For example, the current discussion of same sex relations in the church is too frequently focused on a few verses (only five really) that 'condemn' such relations. I find it interesting that the type of Christianity which condemns same sex relations based upon half a dozen verses ignores the literally thousands of references to poverty. I also find it strange that the type of Christian community claiming to be tolerant and egalitarian excoriates those who tend to be more conservative than they would prefer. None of us has an exclusive claim on God, except Jesus. He alone must be our starting point if we are going to find a way out of the maze created by our Christian tradition where obedience is moral not filial (or relational).

Following Jesus is to discover that obedience is love and love is obedience. We no longer differentiate our love of God from our love of each other. I John 4:7-12 brings together our love for God and the concrete ways we are called to love one another. "Beloved, since God has loved us, we also ought to love each other." This is also a key argument of the epistle of James (James 2:1-13 where "mercy triumphs over judgment."). There is no separation of piety and behavior, of theology from ethics; they are two sides of a coin, the one cannot exist without the other (1.2, 3.4).

To love as God loves is to exist within God, to be suffused with God and to participate in the divine life itself. The early church understood this when they formulated the great creed of Nicaea. The three articles on the Trinity, Father, Son and Holy Spirit are followed by an article on the church. The four articles belong together for the church is the community gathered together in the name of this One God who is seen as relational and self-giving. The early church had a word for this Trinitarian self-giving, *perichoresis*, which has the connotation of dancing together. It is the character of God to be self-giving: this is the emphasis of the New Testament writers. The *Abba* gives the Son and sends the Spirit, the Son bears witness to the *Abba*, imitates the *Abba* and is the human life through whom God gives the Spirit, the Spirit bears witness to the Son and thus brings glory to the *Abba*. God is a beautiful dancer!

Making Personal Connections

I would like to close this book with a personal story that captures, for me, all that I have been saying. I am sitting here in Kansas having concluded two days of meetings. Almost everyone has gone to the airport. I want to finish writing this manuscript by Tuesday, it is now Saturday, and I am struggling with how to end it. The meetings went well, and I have had some extraordinary AHA! moments that brought together a number of important personal issues with which I have been wrestling. I offer this story about how this meeting helped me to realize crucial connections even as I am writing this book. As stated at the end of the Introduction, I have a gut feeling I am writing this book to myself and that you are welcome to the conversation. Sitting here in the quiet of the dining hall I turned to the leader of our meeting, Bill Hartnett and asked him if I could run by him my experience of the last several days. As I laid it all out, it dawned on me that this weekend had been a life changing time, a time where many pieces of the puzzle came together in a very concrete personal way.

Three things in particular came together for me: a new understanding of my relationship with my wife, an understanding of my experience during this weekend gathering and some of the theological thought of this book. They serendipitously merged at the right time. But that is the way God works, isn't it?

My marriage has been a journey. It has been a rocky journey because I have had to grow up. I hate growing up. I much prefer to do my own thing. I am basically a selfish person who thinks the world revolves around me. My marriage has been rocky not because I have a spouse who is difficult to live with but because I have been the difficult spouse. Over the years I have had to learn to let go of my temper and my need to always be fighting with someone. I think I have been more or less successful with this, as I do not relish arguments like I used to, although I really do enjoy cutting edge dialogue and debating in a friendly context.

Growing up I learned to cope with pain by engaging in addictive behaviors; it was the pattern of my family system. Learning to deal with these behaviors and finding new ways to cope with pain has been a real challenge for me during my adulthood. My wife has been very patient over the years and her willingness to struggle through things with me has earned her my admiration and respect. For some time now she has been wanting me to take additional positive steps of doing things like eating healthy, exercising and learning how to live a holistic lifestyle. These things are also important to her wholeness and our wholeness together yet I often experience her encouragement as law. 'Do this, don't do that.' I am a bit of a rebel and when "told" to do something I tend to do otherwise. Romans 7 has been my existential experience more than Romans 8.

These past few days (back to my story) I participated with a group of about twenty people in planning a festival on the 'arts, faith and justice.' There was a consensus that it was not to be called a Christian festival but rather a festival whose hospitality was such that Jesus could be experienced by any and all who chose to attend (Anonymous Christianity meets Woodstock). Having read this book, you can tell how important Jesus is for me. As far as I am concerned, in Christianity, it is all about Jesus or it is about nothing. So I did my best to listen carefully as to why Jesus would not be front and center of this festival. I pointed out to the group that during our worship times this weekend Jesus was central to us, yet during our festival planning there seemed to be a shying away from naming Him.

My normal tendency would have been to just label the group as 'liberal' and be done with it. But I sensed that the conversation was not disparaging of being Jesus focused; it was more about coming to a sense of how we can live out the life of Christ, rather than just talk about him. From this I began to let go of my agenda and to listen even more deeply. A new acquaintance from England, Steve Foster, pointed out that the festival we were planning was to be a space where real dialogue, conversation and honest debate could take place, where people could come and experience Jesus as He wished. What I began to discern as the planning progressed was that we were becoming a community of sorts. Conversations, meals and worship together tend to form community. I knew I was heard but more importantly I knew I was listening, I was trusting.

Throughout this book I have discussed the principle of 'trust in' (or surrender to) Jesus as the key to positive imitation. I wanted this last chapter to be the place to discuss our participation in the divine life, the dance of the wonderful Trinitarian God we name as Abba, Son and Holy Spirit. After all of the deconstructing and reconstructing that has gone on these past several hundred pages it seemed the book should end on a note of great hopefulness. Then it hit me like a ton of bricks: the insight I have been seeking and praying for is, namely, that there is a reason our experience of God in Christ as church is compared in Ephesians 5 to a committed relationship. It has to do with what desiring the desire of the other means. Desire is inevitable; *what*, *who*, and *how* we desire is everything.

I have known for a long time that desire is a problem from my work in mimetic realism. As we saw earlier (5.2), all of our desire is imitated leading us to rivalry and scapegoating. But as James Alison, Rebecca Adams, Tony Bartlett and others have pointed out desire can be transformed. Jesus brought about this transformation when he broke free of mimetic desire as bondage to the other and instead desired God only. Yet the New Testament does not limit Jesus' desire to God alone. Particularly in Paul and the Fourth Gospel, Jesus' desire is *for us*. This *for us* character of his desire, that is, Jesus' life of good, beneficial, salvific and redemptive acts, is at the heart of God's action in our celebration of the Eucharist. Christ gives himself as bread *for us*; Christ offers his blood *for us, for our forgiveness.*

In our relationship with Jesus we not only learn to desire God as he desired God, we also learn the secret of Trinitarian existence: to desire the desire of the other *for us*. This parallels what we learn in a committed relationship where both partners have as their focus a desire to imitate Jesus' desire. We desire the desire of the other *that is for us*. We need not experience that desire as law. We do not desire the other, nor do we desire the abstract desire of the other (as an object oriented desire). In an authentic relationship of love both parties desire whatever is healing and beneficial for the other. In words more familiar to us, they learn to give up their own desires and serve the other.

This service is not the passive, "I am your slave and exist to do your will," kind of existence. It only occurs when there is a mutual self-giving, when both parties in the relationship desire to be *for the other*. Object oriented desire creates a triangle, there is you, me, and what one of us wants and thus models desire for the object. Love is the self-giving that occurs when two persons mutually inter-penetrate one another's desire *for the other*. The only thing desired is whatever is beneficial for the other.

When I desire what is best for my wife, it is not my desire that is fulfilled but her best desire for herself given in her desire to follow God, as Jesus desired God. When my wife desires what is best for me, not as something she wants but as that which is my desire as I follow Jesus, I experience her desire as not an obstacle, or law, rather I trust that her love for me is her motivation. Thus when I desire her desire *for me*, I am not imitating her desire as much as I am learning to let go of my desire for myself and allow her to "dwell in me." This experience is analogous to that of Jesus and the church.

As gathered community we can come with our agendas, plans, dreams and hopes, that is, we can come with all our objects of desire. When we confuse our 'objects of desire' with God's desires and assume that they are one and the same we miss out on discerning and experiencing God's desire. We confuse our illusions of success, growth, fame and fortune with God's desire for mercy, peace, justice and love. God's desire is known in the letting go of all our agendas and learning to live as Jesus lived. With open hands we can let our desire be transformed and come to experience that the desire of God is always *for us*. This is why we constantly take our place around the

Vindicated Victim, cognizant of his wounds and proclaim that this is "his body *broken for us*" and "his blood *shed for us*." His body broken *by* us and his blood, shed *by* us, is given *for us*.

From one perspective it can be said that we killed Jesus, we are his murderers. But there is also another perspective on the death of Christ little noticed in studies on the atonement. It provides us with the final piece of *how* it is that we can truly live in forgiveness as a new community grounded in love. In John 10:18 Jesus says, "No one takes my life from me, but I lay it down of my own accord. I have authority to lay it down and authority to take it up again." In the light of this saying we are not led to understand Jesus' death as a murder. Yes, Jesus will die and yes it is we who will kill him. Nor is Jesus' death to be understood as a sacrifice. Nowhere are we led to understand Jesus' death as something desired by God.[ccxl] It is true that Jesus can be referred to as "The Lamb of God who takes away the sins of the world" (1:29, cf 1:36). But even here there is a conflation of the Passover lamb with the goat of the Day of Atonement. Jesus takes away the sins of the world by effectively not allowing death to have the last word.

Jesus' death must be of another order if it is neither a murder nor a sacrifice. It is this new category, this new way of thinking that the apostolic witness seeks to open up. This new way is that of Jesus' self-offering. Like a black hole sucking in everything, so Jesus' death absorbs all of our violence and our death dealing paradigms. But more than that Jesus' death completes the creation. The "It is finished" (*tetelestai*) of John 19:30 alludes to the work which has been ongoing since the beginning of the creation; "my Father is always at work to this very day and I, too, am working" (5:17). The work of God ceases, not on the seventh day of the Genesis account, but on the cross of Christ. Jesus' death is the final moment, the pinnacle, the Omega Point, of this world's creation. The world is over and a new creation will soon be revealed "in three days." The True Human is now complete. The possibility of humanity's transformation is now a reality.

This is the kind of life we are called to experience as the gathered beloved community, this mutual interpenetration of love. God in God's inner Trinitarian self is the originary beloved community, but flowing out from God's own inter-personal love is God's love for us meant to be experienced by us, in and through one another. This then is the fulfillment of the commandment to "love one another as I have loved you." It is to be moved by the same Spirit that animated Jesus both in his earthly life and in his Resurrected life, the Spirit of God's love. This is what I hope to have communicated in *The Jesus Driven Life*. To know that there is substantively no difference between Jesus' relationship with God and ours, and that in him and through him we too may find ourselves transformed 'from glory to glory', becoming more authentically human and thus, more authentically related to God. It is to be mutually penetrated, we in Him and He in us. In so doing we are not destroyed but enhanced, for it is ourselves that we see in Him, ourselves remade in God's authentic and true image, ourselves in the fullness of human existence.

Let us therefore come together with open hearts, open minds and open hands to repent, putting away whatever hinders us, and turn to Jesus. Let us ask for his Spirit to fill us (Luke 11:13) and to transform our desires so that, as imitators of Jesus, we may be daily moved to give ourselves in love as he has given himself for us and for our world.

We cannot achieve this by our efforts; it comes to us as redemptive grace, as loving gift. We cannot demand it or oblige God to give it. We can only ask. This can only be described as the audacious self-giving of a loving Creator for the creation. This *is* the gospel, the good news that the world longs to hear and needs if it is ever going to renounce violence, scapegoating hatred, vengeance and discrimination. This *is* the message that transforms us from death oriented scapegoating to life giving self-sharing people. This *is* our hope, for "now we are the children of God, and what we will be has not yet been made known. But we know that when he appears, we shall be like him, for we shall see him as he is. Everyone who has this hope in Jesus purifies themselves, just as Jesus is pure" (I John 3: 2-3).

"Hold the Light, Hold the Light

After all, we've come a long, long glorious way

And at the start of every day

A child begins to play

And all we need to know

Is that the future is a friend of yours and mine."[ccxli]

Afterword by Walter Wink

I scarcely know how to find words to do justice to this brilliant study. *The Jesus Driven Life* is nothing less than a magisterial synthesis of much that can be known about Jesus and the early centuries of Christianity and their continuing relevance for today. I have long been convinced that Jesus has been replaced as the center of Christianity. This has had negative effects on the way the Bible has been interpreted throughout the history of the Christian tradition. At times hard and fast dogmas have held sway, dogmas that have little to do with the person and teaching of Jesus. My first book *The Bible in Human Transformation* was my attempt to reckon with the way Jesus had been displaced as the interpretive center of the Bible in post-Enlightenment critical approaches to Scripture.

Christians have become accustomed to reading the Bible from 'inside the box.' This box, as Michael points out, begins already in the early church and the questions put by significant church leaders of that time have dominated our answers whether they are ancient, medieval or modern, Catholic, Protestant or Anabaptist, pre- or post critical. Michael argues that so many ways of reading Scripture, from both conservative and progressive perspectives stem from a common set of shared presuppositions that have little to do with Jesus. This way of reading Scripture and the time for change is long overdue.

By putting Jesus front and center of the interpretive task, *The Jesus Driven Life* offers bold, innovative and challenging ways of interpreting the Bible. More so, Michael understands the importance of contexting Jesus within his Jewish culture and how that helps to see the creative ways Jesus engaged his sacred writings.

The Bible is a book of power. From the time its stories began to be gathered and written down, it has been a source of liberating wisdom for those with ears to hear. Yet even within its own pages there are those who would tell the story of God's redemptive activity from the perspective of the elite and powerful. This way of narrating God's work in the world is already powerfully critiqued in the ancient prophets of Judaism.

My work on *The Powers* sought to follow in the footsteps of this ancient prophetic tradition, carried on in both Christianity and Judaism in spite of all the attempts of these Powers to turn the Bible to their own advantage. As a life-long adherent of peace and nonviolence I am always concerned when the Bible is used to oppress the already downtrodden. Sometimes I am downright angry. Nevertheless, I am compelled to recognize that the darkness that seems to cover the world also resides in my own soul. So I have often found myself repenting of the ways the tricky tendrils of the Powers have also influenced my own reading of the biblical text.

Reading the Bible from the perspective of nonviolence and peacemaking may seem to be an impossible task. There seem to be so many stories of the violence of God and of God's people. Yet as I mentioned, there is also another way of reading Scripture that places love, peace and reconciliation at its center. *The Jesus Driven Life* follows along this path.

I have followed the intellectual development of Michael Hardin for almost twenty years. I can still recall a meeting in New Orleans where we presented papers together in an academic forum. Here at last is the fruit of those tentative beginnings. When I met Michael he was already an aficionado of the work of Rene Girard. I too have found Girard's mimetic theory compelling. It helped me frame what I call 'the myth of redemptive violence.' Like me, Michael has also been influenced by the work of Paul Ricoeur, particularly the way Ricoeur interprets the Bible. Both Girard and Ricoeur, like the biblical prophets, recognize the multivalent ways Scripture speaks.

This plurality of voices does not hinder the revelatory liberating word from going forth, rather it enables us to see ways we can and have misread the Bible. We are turned to new paths where reading the Bible is once again cause for repentance, release from the bondage of our tendency to violence, and brings hope in relation to both our friends and our enemies.

The Jesus Driven Life goes beyond the findings of historical-critical scholarship to deal with the Living Christ, the Lord of church and world, the "light that shines in our darkness." Following on the research I began in *The Human Being* Michael has shown that, like Jesus, we too can be channels of revelation, love and forgiveness. He demonstrates how Jesus, the True Human (which is how I translate 'son of man') models for us what an authentic relationship with God looks like. Like Jesus we too can announce God's good reign, healing the sick and casting out evil from those structures that turn us away from peace and reconciliation. This missional authority given to the disciples in the Gospels is also given to us as we follow Jesus.

Finally, Michael underscores that when we consider Jesus it is essential that we follow him if we are to know him. Pure objective knowledge of Jesus is just not possible; we humans are a mix of both objective and subjective dimensions. The one without the other leads to either historical sterility or privatized speculation. Both are necessary in the interpretive task. If Christians do not take the risk of following Jesus how will they ever speak authentically about him?

I hope that *The Jesus Driven Life* has a wide audience. I pray that its peaceful vision of God and the world would take hold of Christianity. I know that if Christians were to follow *just Jesus* the church would look different and the future would be more hopeful. It is time for us to read the Bible as Jesus read the Bible. As I say in the Introduction to *Unmasking the Powers*, "The real test of the canon of Scripture is whether it has the power, in each new age, to evoke life, to strike fire, to convey the stark reality of God's hunger to be known." Michael's *The Jesus Driven Life* moves us in this direction. Can we imagine the world differently? Yes we can!

Sandisfield MA
January 2010

Old Testament

John

John

Acts

Romans

I Corinthians

Book List

Complete bibliographical information can be found by entering the book title into www.amazon.com. It is not exhaustive but suggestive; it is meant as a resource for those who wish to pursue further study.

Primary Sources:

The Holy Bible (New International Version)

The Apocrypha (Revised Standard Version)

Josephus (Loeb Classical Library)

James A. Charlesworth The Old Testament Pseudepigrapha (2 vol)

Herbert Danby The Mishnah

Jacob Neusner The Tosefta

Jacob Lauterbach Mekilta de-Rabbi Ishmael (3 vol)

C.D. Yonge The Works of Philo

Wise, Abegg & Cook ed., The Dead Sea Scrolls

Cathcart, Maher, McNamara Eds. The Aramaic Bible: The Targums

Reference Works:

Emil Shurer The History of the Jewish People in the Age of Jesus Christ (rev. ed. Matthew Black, Geza Vermes, & Fergus Millar 4 vol)

S. Safrai & M. Stern ed. The Jewish People in the First Century (2 vol)

S. Safrai, et al, The Literature of the Sages (2 vol)

Claude Montefiore and Hebert Lowe A Rabbinic Anthology

Martin Jan Mulder Mikra

E.P. Sanders Judaism: Practice and Belief

G.F. Moore Judaism (2 vol)

Martin Hengel Judaism and Hellenism (2 vol)

Reference Works

James A. Charlesworth Jesus and the Dead Sea Scrolls

Jacob Neusner Understanding Rabbinic Judaism

Solomon Schecter Aspects of Rabbinic Theology

Gabriele Boccaccini Roots of Rabbinic Judaism

Joachim Jeremias Jerusalem in the Time of Jesus

David Flusser Judaism of the Second Temple Period (2 vol)

Ephraim E. Urbach The Sages: The World and Wisdom of the Rabbis of the Talmud

Gustaf Dalman Jesus-Jeshua & The Words of Jesus

Matthew Black An Aramaic Approach to the Gospels and Acts

Endnotes

---

[i] The best introduction to the 'zealot Jesus' hypothesis is Ernst Bammel "*The Revolution Theory from Reimarus to Brandon*" in Jesus and the Politics of His Day (Cambridge: Cambridge University Press, 1984), 11-68.
[ii] (San Francisco: Harper & Row, 1987). His later work in Systematics and his program to integrate biblical studies and theology is just as foundational for me. His major works in chronological order include Must There Be Scapegoats? (German edition 1978); Der wunderbare Tausch (Munchen: Kosel, 1986); Jesus in the Drama of Salvation (New York: Crossroad, 1999) [German edition 1990]; Jesus of Nazareth: How He Understood His Life (New York: Crossroad, 1998) [German edition 1991); Banished from Eden (Herefordshire: Gracewing, 2006) [German edition 1997).
[iii] Another very influential book for me has been Dietrich Ritschl Memory and Hope: An Inquiry Concerning the Presence of Christ (New York: Macmillan, 1967).
[iv] Richard A. Burridge, Imitating Jesus: An Inclusive Approach to New Testament Ethics (Grand Rapids: Eerdmans, 2007), 25.
[v] I understand this to be the burden of Dale Allison Jr's The Historical Christ and the Theological Jesus (Grand Rapids: Eerdmans, 2009). See also Luke Timothy Johnson's The Real Jesus (San Francisco: Harper, 1996). In saying this I am not discounting attempts to discern the historical Jesus. I am, however, aware that "There is no historical task which so reveals a man's [sic] true self as the writing of a Life of Jesus…Each individual creates him in accordance with his own character", Albert Schweitzer The Quest of the Historical Jesus (New York: Macmillan, 1968), 4. See also Robert Hamerton-Kelly, The Gospel and the Sacred (Minneapolis: Fortress, 1994), 14 "The [Gospel] text has been structured by the impact of Jesus on the deep structure of human existence, and this can be discerned without certifying any single event or saying as from the historical Jesus himself." Nevertheless, "The historical Jesus is the gospel in the Gospel." I also affirm the theses of Dietrich Ritschl that "*the post-Easter biblical books are not a commentary on the historical Jesus but on Easter*, and that *the resurrected Christ can be recognized only in the church*. These affirmations represent nothing new, but we have seen that Western theology has had difficulties in combining these two", Memory and Hope, op. cit., 202-203. I would like to suggest that these two theses form the backbone of Christian praxis or discipleship. The Lord of the Church, the crucified and risen Jesus walks with her every step of the way, even when she is not on his way. Theologically this is the importance of the *Christus praesens*.
[vi] On the oxymoronic character of this phrase see the important essay by Marcus Bockmuehl "*God's Life as a Jew: Remembering the Son of God as Son of David*" in Beverly Roberts Gaventa and Richard B. Hays eds., Seeking the Identity of Jesus (Grand Rapids: Eerdmans, 2008), 60-78.
[vii] "Girard has proffered not simply *research*, that is, but a research *programme*…It would be extremely difficult to name another twentieth century

thinker in the humanities who has so drawn thinkers both in the humanities and in the sciences", Chris Fleming, Rene Girard: Violence and Mimesis (Malden: Polity Press, 2004), 153.
[viii] Memory and Hope, op. cit., 61.
[ix] James Alison observes that "we are set free to begin to re-imagine creation" and that part of this reimagining is an "invitation to rescue a part of the Good News that has fallen prisoner to Babylon" *in "Spluttering Up the Beach to Nineveh"* Contagion Volume 7 (Spring) 2000, 120. I suspect Alison is making a play on Luther's *Babylonian Captivity of the Church*. Even so today the good news is held hostage by an alien epistemology.
[x] "The proclamation to return unconditionally to the laws of Jesus might be a fundamental theology of liberation for Western people today." Ulrich Luz Matthew in History: Interpretation, Influence, and Effects (Minneapolis: Fortress, 1994), 32.
[xi] Tony is one of the most perceptive and critically literate interpreters of contemporary American Christian culture. I have learned much from Tony over the years. His new book, *Virtually Christian* (forthcoming), is a powerful discerning of 'the signs of the times.' Tony's website: www.woodhathhope.com
[xii] Ulrich Luz points to the three main hermeneutical problems of historical-criticism: "The barrier between past and present, the barrier between objective meaning of a text and personal interpretation, and the problem of plurality in the Bible itself" Matthew In History, op. cit., 37.
[xiii] This is "*Story Shaping Story*" to quote the subtitle of Willard Swartley's Israel's Scripture Traditions and the Synoptic Gospels (Peabody: Hendrickson Publishers, 1994). The charge of Marcionism cannot be righteously laid against my view of the relation of the Testaments. I am stating here in no unequivocal terms, the Jewish Scriptures are a crucial component of an authentic Christian theology.
[xiv] I am not a believer in 'scholarly consensus.' The majority is often not in the right. I have never been convinced that a document 'Q' existed or that Secret Mark was real. I do however, look for certain patterns as I read the work of scholars. The changes in a pattern of thought usually indicate a barrier that is being broken through. One could trace the question of whether or not Jesus utilized apocalyptic as a category in this way and observe the many and significant shifts over the last 150 years while at the same time noting the exponential growth of violence. These are not unrelated. The rise (and fall, and rise) of apocalyptic thought is the Western Christian non-conscious' way of speaking about the incredible moral atrocity that was the twentieth century and may be the legacy of the twenty-first century unless we change our thinking.
[xv] David Dungan captures the problem for these folks: "The Enlightenment principle of autonomous reason and the scientist's unquestioned right to universal skepticism has crashed head-on into the Protestant principle of *sola scriptura* and destroyed it." A History of the Synoptic Problem (New York: Doubleday, 1999), 364. Luz, Matthew in History, op. cit., 76 argues that *sola*

scriptura is a theological fiction. "Scripture is never 'alone' it belongs to its rich history of effects, as the stem of a tree belongs to its branches."

[xvi] Doxology is an epistemological category. "The Western neglect of the Eastern doxological approach to Christology resulted in the medieval type of theology which was concerned primarily with God rather than with God in Christ." Ritschl, Memory and Hope, op. cit., 115; on the subordination of Jesus in Christian worship see Joseph Jungmann The Place of Christ in Liturgical Prayer (Staten Island: Alba House, 1965). On the other hand, a good example of Protestant theology beginning with doxology is Geoffrey Wainwright's Doxology (Oxford: Oxford University Press, 1984).

[xvii] See Walter Wink's astute observation on early Christian singing: "This hymn [Col. 1:15-20] was sung. It was not composed primarily to inform, but to arm the faithful to carry their message to the very citadel of the Powers themselves. The early church sang its way through the Roman Empire, through persecution and estrangement and violent death. Theirs was a world no less derelict to its Center than ours, the evils they faced no less daunting. But they had songs that recalled them to a transcendent perspective so vast, so real, and so ultimate that not even the power of death could still their singing" *"The Hymn of the Cosmic Christ"* in The Conversation Continues: Studies in Paul and John, ed., Robert T. Fortna and Beverly R. Gaventa (Nashville: Abingdon, 1990), 242-243.

[xviii] The Table Talk of Martin Luther, edited and with an Introduction by Thomas S. Kepler (Grand Rapids: Baker, 1979 reprint) # 164, page 106.

[xix] See George Hunsinger, How To Read Karl Barth (New York: Oxford, 1991), 32ff; also James Wm. McClendon, Jr., Doctrine: Systematic Theology Vol 2 (Nashville: Abingdon, 1994), 280ff, whose strategy is to begin with the particular revelation of God's rule in Christ. "God…is no Absolute abstract in the heavens, no first principle posited by someone's philosophy, far less is God the Nobodaddy of popular culture, or the nonexistent *theos* of post-Enlightenment atheism. Rather, 'God' here is God known in the story Christians call gospel – the Jesus story in its full depth and length and height."

[xx] (Grand Rapids: Zondervan, 2002). I have a review of The Purpose Driven Life on my website at http://preachingpeace.org/documents/Analysis_of_Rick_Warren.pdf.

[xxi] Craig Carter suggests that "Liberalism is the new Constantinianism" in Peace Be With You: Christ's Benediction amid Violent Empires (Telford: Cascadia 2010), edited by Sharon Baker and Michael Hardin, 30. Liberal or Progressive Christians would profit from being aware of the subtle ways that they too, like Conservative Christians, have bought into Empire-theology without realizing it. I cannot, however, accept Carter's conclusion that "If there is to be any real hope for Western culture—any future for our civilization—it can only come from a return to, and embrace of, law. It is, perhaps, somewhat ironic that, for a liberal culture, it turns out that the good news is the message of God's law embedded in creation and written in Scripture. For an age like ours, law is gospel (52)." Contrast this with E.P. Sander's observation that "While looking for the restoration of Israel, he [Jesus] did not follow the majority and urge the

traditional means towards that end: repentance and a return to observance of the law" in Jesus and Judaism (Philadelphia: Fortress, 1985), 119. Carter's solution is the exact opposite of Jesus, Paul or the Fourth Gospel.

[xxii] Jacob Neusner, First Century Judaism in Exile (Nashville: Abingdon, 1975), 67 commenting on Rabbi Yohanan ben Zakkai's time in Galilee (circa 20-40 C.E.) says that Galileans "eagerly asked one another as well as itinerant preachers what they must do to keep the faith, because they could not look back upon their forefathers who for many generations had done things thus and so." The reason for this was that Galilee was an area of forced conversions about 150 years previously. They did not have the lengthy history that southerners (Judeans) had.

[xxiii] Note to the reader: Bringing in the metaphor of the Janus-Faced god is important. I will elaborate on this metaphor of the two-sided god, whether it is the dualistic god of Babylon, Persia, Greece, Egypt, Rome, Israel or America. Janus is only a metaphor, but it expresses a way of understanding how and why some theologians insist on holding God's quite varied attributes 'in tension.' Dietrich Ritschl The Logic of Theology (Philadelphia: Fortress, 1987), 63 speaks of 'The Janus-face of church history.' It is not possible to tell the story of Christianity from only its good side; there is also a dark side, a very dark side. This is due to the fact that Christians have accepted the Janus-faced God as the God of Jesus Christ. Ritschl argues, "The tragedy and depth of the ambivalence of church history cannot be plumbed with the means of secular scientific historiography. The contrast between the consequences of the three decisive false steps – the detachment of the Christian church from Judaism, the assimilation of the church to political power structures and the intellectual capacity of the minds of the economically and educationally poor – and the countless acts of mercy, forgiveness and therapeutic help can only be seen by those who 'stand in' the story of Israel and the church as the double countenance of a single history and the relevant consequences drawn.."

[xxiv] There is some debate on whether Jesus criticized the Torah or the interpretation of the Torah. I am arguing that in doing the latter, he does the former and that that critique is already embedded not only in the prophetic critique of the Law but within the Torah itself as Jesus himself reflects in Mark 10:2-12. On this see the very important work by Sandor Goodhart, Sacrificing Commentary (Baltimore: Johns Hopkins University Press, 1996), especially his thesis concerning the textual character of the 'law of anti-idolatry.' See his essays on biblical interpretation 99-212. Ben. F. Meyer, The Aims of Jesus (London: SCM Press, 1979), 142, notes that the realized eschatology of Jesus had as its implication the revision of the Torah and that "the authority of the teacher, Jesus, would at once shape and respond to the eschatological state of affairs brought about by his proclamation." Ernst Bammel shares this opinion, "It was an abiding axiom for all Jews that the Torah was the final dispensation of God, although differences might appear in the interpretation of this divine precept. It is widely assumed that Jesus shared this view, but several texts can be adduced in which a conflict of Jesus with the Torah can be denied only by

forced exegesis" and "for Jesus the Torah formed 'no longer the focus and ultimate standard…Jesus – unlike the whole body of his Jewish contemporaries – stood not *under*, but *above* the Torah received by Moses at Sinai.'…The attack of Jesus on the Torah confronts us finally with the unprecedented claim of Jesus to authority, a fact which is being increasingly recognized by scholars" in Ernst Bammel and C.F.D. Moule ed., Jesus and the Politics of His Day (Cambridge: Cambridge University Press, 1984), 138, 142. The interior quote is from Martin Hengel, The Charismatic Leader and His Followers (New York: Crossroads, 1981), 70. Hengel goes on to observe "Deeply conscious of the inbreaking of God's rule, Jesus for the first time in Judaism looks behind the Law of Moses toward the original will of God."

[xxv] We do well to heed the advice of Tom Smail, Like Father, Like Son (Grand Rapids: Eerdmans, 2005), 35-36 who argues that "instead of imposing our experiences of fatherhood on God, we look at the kind of fatherhood that is revealed in God's relationship to Jesus and let ourselves be told that that is the kind of relationship he wants to have with us, his children, and that we are to have with one another, a relationship that has at its heart not patriarchal domination but liberating love."

[xxvi] The best treatment is Alister E. McGrath Luther's Theology of the Cross (Oxford: Blackwell, 1985); see also Walther von Loewenich Luther's Theology of the Cross (Minneapolis: Augsburg, 1976) and Regin Prenter Luther's Theology of the Cross (Philadelphia: Fortress, 1971).

[xxvii] Here I must part company with Martin Hengel, The Atonement (Philadelphia: Fortress, 1981), 41, who finds that the use of Psalm 22 does not reflect "the pattern of humiliation and exaltation [which] is far too general and imprecise to interpret the event which Mark so skillfully and with such deep theological precision narrates. He [Mark] is concerned with the utterly unique event of the passion and crucifixion." As I hope to show in 6.4, Jesus' death is precisely to be interpreted as an example of the general human tendency to scapegoat the 'righteous.'

[xxviii] On crucifixion and its physical limitation see Martin Hengel Crucifixion (Philadelphia: Fortress, 1977), 22ff.

[xxix] This is how Raymund Schwager interprets the parable of the talents (Matt. 25:14-30), Jesus of Nazareth, op. cit., 94. In this novella, Jesus says "You find it hard to understand the lord in the parable. Yet how will you grasp the good news and judgment of God? Why do you focus only on the money and not the hearts in which everything is decided and in which the countenance of God is reflected…Because of their faithfulness and trust the first two servants found a kindly lord. Because of his anxiety and distrust the third servant confronted a severe judge. Their hearts decided how the lord could present himself to them. Whoever has and believes will be ready to receive without limits. Whoever bears suspicion in his heart, his distrust undermines what he already has."

[xxx] See Raymund Schwager *"Suffering, Victims and Poetic Inspiration"* Contagion Volume 1 (Spring) 1994, 66 note 3 who notes, "In the religious tradition of Israel there was a conception of hell even before Jesus. This hell,

however, was only destined for the heathens and apostates and, therefore, did not turn into a vital problem within the religious community as it only concerned those who were 'out.' In contrast to that, Jesus' preaching about hell was particularly directed at the leaders of Israel, which gave rise to deep problems in the center of faith."

[xxxi] N.T. Wright places this judgment on the scribes and Pharisees, Jesus and the Victory of God, op. cit., 330 and interprets this phrase to mean "it would be better to abandon that which was most cherished than go straight ahead into the conflagration." This is possible, but if this saying was, whether originally or also, directed to priests, it suggests the need to re-interpret Jesus' relation to the sacrificial system.

[xxxii] Evangelicals who question 'hell' and its place in Christian doctrine can now profitably turn to two recent publications: Brad Jersak Her Gates Will Never Be Shut (Eugene: Wipf & Stock, 2009) and Sharon Baker, Razing Hell (Louisville: WJKP, 2010).

[xxxiii] This is the title of the hymn by Lena Sandell.

[xxxiv] Luz, Matthew in History, 52-53, "The Reformation understanding of the church has a dangerous tendency toward idealism and is not really able to define the reality of the church. Such a church has no urgent need to change and reform its praxis, because praxis is not so important and every church is a church of sinners…Matthew's concept of the church is very different. His basic idea is that of the disciples who follow Jesus."

[xxxv] *The Didache* and other important early Christian writings can be found in The Apostolic Fathers translated by Michael W. Holmes (Grand Rapids: Baker, 2007), which is based upon the work of J.B. Lightfoot and J.R. Harmer. Kirsopp Lake has also translated them in the Loeb Classical Library, The Apostolic Fathers 2 volumes (Cambridge: Harvard University Press, 1919); see also Early Christian Fathers, Cyril C. Richardson ed. (Philadelphia: Westminster, 1958) for a selection of the Apostolic Fathers, Justin Martyr, Athenogoras and Irenaeus. I am in substantial agreement with the work of Aaron Milevec, The Didache (Mahwah: The Newman Press, 2003). My only criticism is that Milavec misunderstands the role of nonviolence in Christian formation.

[xxxvi] William V. Harris, Ancient Literacy (Cambridge: Harvard University Press, 1989).

[xxxvii] Martin Hengel, The Four Gospels and the One Gospel of Jesus Christ (Harrisburg: Trinity International, 2000), underscores the role of early Christian catechesis in the church's use of the Septuagint and the formation of, at least, Mark and Matthew. "Just like Mark, his [Matthew's] Gospel too aimed at reading in worship, but at least as much also intensive use in catechetical and ethical instruction in the early Christian communities. (99)" "Had the writings of the Old Testament been unimportant for early Christian worship, it would not have been possible to use them so intensively in arguments. The same is true of catechetical instruction. (117)" Speaking of the collections of books in the early church Hengel comments "Probably the Roman community also had a collection (or several collections) of sayings of the Lord with a catechetical orientation in

its book cupboard, which it could later dispense with because of the major Gospels. (128)" Michelle Slee, The Church at Antioch in the First Century C.E.: Communion and Conflict (London: Sheffield Academic Press, 2003) 60, also argues that *The Didache* "chapters 1-6 function as pre-baptismal catechetical instructions for Gentiles entering the church."

[xxxviii] Huub Van de Sandt ed., Matthew and the Didache (Philadelphia: Fortress, 2005). Slee, The Church at Antioch, op. cit., argues that both *The Didache* and the Gospel of Matthew came from the Antiochene church, perhaps a generation apart.

[xxxix] Much could and should be said about the sociological implications of Jesus' views on divorce and his concern for women. In cultures where women are chattel, reduced to no more than property, Jesus' teaching on divorce has significant meaning. It also has profound meaning for patriarchal Christian cultures.

[xl] Self Deception and Wholeness in Paul and Matthew (Minneapolis: Fortress, 1990), 94.

[xli] Like many of Jesus' sayings, there are rabbinic parallels. Gustaf Dalman Jesus-Jeshua (London: SPCK, 1929), 224 lists six, e.g., "With the measure with which one measures, it will be measured unto him" (M. Sotah i.7; Tos. Sot. Iii. 1,2, Sifre 28b). It is not whether Jesus used ideas he learned from his tradition, he did; the real question is whence and why did he also reflect certain elements of his religious environment. That is, does Jesus' 'cherry-picking' of his environment follow the same hermeneutic he has when reading Scripture? I think it does.

[xlii] A description of the 'kingdom' that seems to capture both it's deconstructive dimension and it's reconstructive aspect comes from Robert Hamerton-Kelly, The Gospel and the Sacred, op. cit., 12 "The kingdom is the power of compassion for victims, structured by the imitation of Christ, especially in his self-sacrifice on the cross." Both of these stem from the new perspective Jesus brings.

[xliii] David H. Kelsey The Uses of Scripture in Recent Theology (Philadelphia: Fortress, 1975).

[xliv] James R. Edwards, however, notes the number of Hebraisms found in this text, The Hebrew Gospel & the Development of the Synoptic Tradition (Grand Rapids: Eerdmans, 2009), 300-301. Luke's introduction to his work (Luke 1:1-4) indicates his use of sources, one of which may have been a Hebrew Gospel. On Luke 1:1-4 see also Richard Bauckham, Jesus and the Eyewitnesses (Grand Rapids: Eerdmans, 2006), 114-124.

[xlv] Martin Hengel The Charismatic Leader and His Followers (New York: Crossroad, 1981), 45 n.19 quotes Strack-Billerbeck (4.156) "Reading the Scriptures in the synagogue was something which, apart from some exceptions, everyone could in principle do.'" Hengel goes on to observe that this was also true of targumists.

[xlvi] Some scholars work with the assumption that Hebrew was a dead language in Jesus' day. However, recent evidence indicates that there was a renaissance of

Hebrew following the Maccabean revolt and that it is likely that Hebrew in addition to being the language used for sacred texts was also spoken, at least in Judea. Galilean peasantry would not (I suspect) have had acquaintance with Hebrew as a spoken tongue, hence the need for a Targum (translation into Aramaic) when reading Jewish Scriptures in worship.

[xlvii] Bruce Chilton has shown the influence of the Isaiah Targum on Jesus' teaching on the 'kingdom of God' A Galilean Rabbi and His Bible (Wilmington: Michael Glazier, 1984); Isabel Ann Massey details the parallels between the Sermon on the Mount and the Aramaic Targums, Interpreting the Sermon on the Mount in the Light of Jewish Tradition as Evidenced in the Palestinian Targums of the Pentateuch (Lewiston: Edwin Mellen, 1991).

[xlviii] Joachim Jeremias, New Testament Theology (New York: Scribner's, 1971), 206 who also notes "In Matt. 11:15 he [Jesus] passes over the eschatological vengeance on the Gentiles, although it is announced in all three Old Testament passages which he takes up (Isa. 35:5, 29:18f; 61:1). This omission of the vengeance is part of the offense of the message against which Jesus issues a warning." See also Matt. 23:31 for another example of *marturein* as a dative of disadvantage.

[xlix] Robert Daly says "The pervasiveness of violence in the Bible is a major problem and challenge for Christians and Jews alike. No major Christian biblical theology has yet made sense of this", in *"Violence and Institution in Christianity"* Contagion Volume 9 (Spring) 2002, 6. I hope *The Jesus Driven Life* will fill that hole. In a similar vein Walter Wink said "Few Christians have risen to Marcion's challenge to critique the image of God thoroughly in the light of the cross" Cracking the Gnostic Code: The Powers in Gnosticism (Atlanta: Scholars Press, 1993), 29. I accept Marcion's challenge.

[l] Cf e.g., Honi the Circle Drawer in Geza Vermes, Jesus the Jew (London: Collins, 1973), 69; David Flusser, The Sage from Galilee, op. cit., 98. A more negative assessment is given by John P. Meier, A Marginal Jew, Vol 2 (New York: Doubleday, 1994), 581ff.

[li] There is an interesting parallel here in the use of the Isaiah text in the Dead Sea Scrolls (4Q521, Redemption and Resurrection). The fragment's use of the term 'Messiah' and the catena of Isaiah texts without the 'judgment sayings' are brought together, as in Luke. If, as some suspect, John the Baptist had some connection with Qumran might it be possible to suggest that Jesus may well have known a teaching such as this and quotes it back to John in almost ironic fashion?

[lii] Richard Bauckham has shown that the category of divine salvific figures or mediators was present in Second Temple Judaism, Jesus and the God of Israel (Grand Rapids: Eerdmans, 2008). Enoch scholars have also recognized that the heavenly son of man in I Enoch predates the Christian tradition and (in their view) most likely influenced early Christian Christology. See Gabriele Boccaccini ed., Enoch and the Messiah Son of Man (Grand Rapids: Eerdmans, 2007). The Epistle of Jude (vss. 14-15) even quotes I Enoch 1:9.

[liii] This literature can be found in the Old Testament Pseudepigrapha.

[liv] David McCracken *"Scandal and Imitation in Matthew, Kierkegaard and Girard"* Contagion Volume 4 (Spring) 1997, 149ff, makes the very important connection to *scandal*, and Jesus as a different type of model when discussing this text. *Scandal* is a key concept in mimetic realism that explores misunderstanding. Why do people get it wrong (become scandalized)? I refer the reader to Girard and his interpreters for a nuanced discussion of this very important point.
[lv] James H. Charlesworth "*From Messianology to Christology: Problems and Prospects*" in James H. Charlesworth ed., The Messiah (Minneapolis: Fortress, 1992), 5.
[lvi] So Ben Witherington The Christology of Jesus (Minneapolis: Fortress, 1990), 246. The multi-faceted background of the phrase 'son of man' and Jesus' familiarity with them all may have made it the optimal self-reference tool. David Flusser, The Sage from Galilee, op. cit. in a similar way, understands the phrase 'son of man' to go through an emerging mode of connections, first anthropological, then eschatological and representative. Flusser has three ways Jesus understood 'son of man': 'Son of man' means 1) simply a term for man, 2) self-referential 'euphemistic circumlocution' and 3) the eschatological advent of the S/son of Man.' Even so Flusser avers, "If I am right, then the threefold meaning of the designation 'son of man' in the mouth of Jesus betrays his manner of sometimes creating a kind of fourth dimension behind his utterances. (110-111)" Christian scholars would do well to heed this sage Jewish advice, others might too.
[lvii] The Human Being (Minneapolis: Fortress, 2002).
[lviii] The Sage of Galilee, op. cit. 79.
[lix] I am taking this notion of 'holiness codes' and Jesus' 'mercy code' from Marcus Borg Conflict, Holiness and Politics in the Teaching of Jesus (Lewiston: Edwin Mellen Press, 1984). See also John Bowker, Jesus and the Pharisees (Cambridge: Cambridge University Press, 1973), 15-16 who observes that "fundamental in the Hakamic [the Sages] movement was a vision of holiness – a vision of implementing what God required of his people if they were to *be* his people. There is nothing surprising in the vision itself; it was shared by many other Jews. The real issue was how to achieve it: how is it possible for the command, 'Be holy as I am holy, to be implemented'? Many of the divisions among Jews during the period of the second commonwealth were in fact a consequence of different answers being given to that deeply basic question." Jesus' reframing of the holiness issue was thus not *sui generis* among his contemporaries.
[lx] See Josephus' writings.
[lxi] On Jesus' *mamzer* status see Andries van Aarde, Fatherless in Galilee: Jesus as a Child of God (Harrisburg: Trinity Press, 2001); Bruce Chilton, Rabbi Jesus: An Intimate Biography (New York: Doubleday, 2000); Jane Schaberg, The Illegitimacy of Jesus (New York: Harper and Row, 1987); Joachim Jeremias, Jerusalem in the Time of Jesus (London: SCM, 1969), 337-341

---

lxii Bruce Dickson interprets the religion of the Paleolithic period as manifested in southwestern Europe, The Dawn of Belief (Tucson: University of Arizona Press, 1990). I would particularly note his observation on 42ff regarding human use of skin pigmentation as a differentiating marker. The community self-mutilates. Juxtaposed with Girard's understanding of the originary murder, it cries out for an interpretation in terms of the generative mimetic scapegoating mechanism.

lxiii The following paragraphs are broad generalizations rather than descriptions. Precise historical descriptions of each of these groups and their sub groups (and other related groups), as well as their development, would be a book in itself.

lxiv First Century Judaism in Crisis, op. cit., 36.

lxv James C. VanderKam The Dead Sea Scrolls Today (Eerdmans: Grand Rapids, 1994); James H. Charlesworth, ed. Jesus and the Dead Sea Scrolls (New York: Doubleday, 1992); Gabriele Boccaccini, ed. Enoch and Qumran Origins (Grand Rapids: Eerdmans, 2005).

lxvi "To the Jew the Law was not merely a set of rules of conduct such as might have been evolved of human wisdom considering the pros and cons of different lines of action and carefully working out the greatest happiness of the greatest number. It was the revelation of God's will and therefore of God himself. Jesus stands in this tradition, and where he criticizes or amends the existing Law it is in order to express more adequately what is for him the will of God." T.W. Manson, The Sayings of Jesus (London: SCM, 1949), 36. The necessary conclusion is that Jesus was expressing God's self, and that Jesus' orientation to the Law is God's orientation to it.

lxvii David Flusser, The Sage from Galilee (Grand Rapids: Eerdmans, 2007), 57 says that this "is also an old rabbinical saying." He cites Mekhilta de-Rabbi Ishmael on Exodus 15:2. There the rabbis exegeted the double phrase 'My God' from Psalm 22:1. "My God. With me he dealt according to the rule of mercy, while with my fathers He dealt according to the rule of justice. And how do we know that 'My God' (*Eli*) signifies the rule of mercy? It is said: 'My God, my God (*Eli Eli*) why hast Thou forsaken me?' (Ps. 22:2). And it also says: 'Heal her now, O God (*El*) I Beseech Thee' (Num.12:13). And it also says: 'The Lord is God (*El*) and hath given us light.' (Psalm 118:27)." The rabbi is arguing that when the word *El* appears for God one should interpret *El* as merciful. Indeed such may be the case, but Jesus takes this further by explicitly making God a model of sociological behavior. Mekhilta de-Rabbi Ishmael, (Philadelphia: Jewish Publication Society, 1933), Vol. 2, 28. The Targum Pseudo-Jonathan on Leviticus at 22:28 reads "as our father is merciful in heaven, so you must be merciful on earth."

lxviii David Oakman, Jesus and the Economic Questions of His Day, op. cit (xiii) queries "If Jesus spoke primarily to peasants, why did that audience not decisively respond to his message? Why did they ultimately reject his way? And why were the majority of post-Easter followers of Jesus artisans like himself? I think an explanation must be found through sociological considerations. Jesus attacked the Temple and the first-century ethos of self-sufficiency. These were at least two of the basic 'props' of the ancient Jewish peasantry value system." See also Sean Freyne, Galilee, Jesus and the Gospels (Philadelphia: Fortress, 1988), 251 who says "Jesus' attitude towards temple and land…would inevitably have clashed not just on details but in terms of a basic perspective, with several of the known groups." A very good book on the social world of Jesus is K.C. Hanson and Douglas Oakman, Palestine in the Time of Jesus (Minneapolis: Fortress, 1998).

[lxix] Sean Freyne, Galilee, Jesus and the Gospels op. cit., 225 who follows E.P. Sanders Jesus and Judaism (Philadelphia: Fortress, 1985), 63ff, points to the problem of anachronism among those who argue for a 'cleansing of the Temple' whereby they intend "to distinguish the temple ordained by God – which Jesus did not attack – from the Jewish 'abuse of the divine institution – which Jesus did attack…This seems to owe more to the nineteenth century view that what is external is bad than to a first century Jewish view."

[lxx] "Jesus seems to have had an ambivalent, though predominantly critical, view of the Temple" William Herzog, Prophet and Teacher (Nashville: Westminster John Knox, 2005), 158. See also C.F.D. Moule, The Birth of the New Testament (London: A&C Black, 1966) 15, who notes "It is impossible to doubt that Jesus worshipped in the Temple…What is not expressly evidenced is that Jesus himself ever offered an animal sacrifice."

[lxxi] In a dispute about cleanness/uncleanness (regarding the *tevel-yom*), Yohanan ben Zakkai and the Pharisees ruled against the stringent regulations of the Sadducees. But what appears as a minor dispute had great implications. Jacob Neusner, First Century Judaism in Crisis, op cit., 86-87 says, "The Pharisees, led by Yohanan ben Zakkai, were attempting not merely to rule the sanctuary, but to exclude from the Temple all who did not accept their rulings. To appreciate the effrontery of the rabbis, we must recall that the Sadducees probably regarded themselves as direct heirs of the line of Zaddoq." The Pharisees thus "would have rendered unclean and profane not merely the Sadducees of the first century, but *all* that had been said and done in the Temple for nearly a thousand years." Those who controlled the priesthood would not listen to the Pharisees, the Essenes, Yohanan the Baptizer or Jesus.

[lxxii] Jeremiah 7:21-23 is translated in the New International Version: "this is what the LORD Almighty, the God of Israel, says: Go ahead, add your burnt offerings to your other sacrifices and eat the meat yourselves! [22] *For when I brought your forefathers out of Egypt and spoke to them, I did not just give them commands about burnt offerings and sacrifices*, [23] but I gave them this command: Obey me, and I will be your God and you will be my people." According to this translation, God gave many commands following the Exodus from Egypt; among them were commands about the sacrificial system. Now contrast the NIV translation of 7:22 with the translation of the Revised Standard Version: "For in the day that I brought your ancestors out of the land of Egypt, I did not speak to them or command them concerning burnt offerings and sacrifices."

There is in the NIV the addition of the little word '*just.*' The addition of this word indicates that among all the commandments given on Sinai were those of the sacrificial system, something that is certainly the case in Torah. Yet the RSV and almost all other translations do not have this addition. Jeremiah is saying that the sacrificial system was not part of the original Torah. The NIV translators (primarily conservative Evangelicals) could not handle the possibility that Jeremiah could be in contradiction to Torah and so brought his speech in line with what was in Torah. Yet, it is clear from the context that Jeremiah is a trenchant critic of the sacrificial system and the Temple.

[lxxiii] Discipleship (Minneapolis: Fortress, 2001) 43.

[lxxiv] This is certainly the way Ulrich Luz sees the Matthean tradition and community. Luz notes "the core of Matthean ecclesiology: *Discipleship means life in Christ's pattern*" in Matthew in History, op. cit., 48.

[lxxv] T.W. Manson, The Teaching of Jesus (Cambridge: Cambridge University Press, 1935), 239-240; so also Witherington The Christology of Jesus, op. cit., 16.

[lxxvi] There is a very helpful section on this in Ephraim E. Urbach The Sages: The World and Wisdom of the Rabbis of the Talmud (Cambridge: Harvard University Press, 1975), 400-419.

[lxxvii] The Sage of Galilee (Grand Rapids: Eerdmans, 2007), 75.

[lxxviii] This does not mean that Jesus did not care about God's creation. When we use sacred places, implicitly we are using space reserved for sacrifice. True worship is not about sacrifice but about the end of sacrifice. When Jesus speaks of the land, he does so outside the perspective of the Powers, those who control 'the sacred' (in the sense of Girard and Wink, 7.3). Jesus speaks from a more gracious relationship to the lilies and the sparrows than that experienced by the masses. This 'other' kind of thinking requires the ability to make one's way comfortably in the creation. In another place I wrote, "Jesus is walking alone one night in the wilderness. It is getting cooler. Does he know how to make a fire? Shall he just he just pull out his Bic or a book of matches? How did he make fire? If he was thirsty do you think he knew how to find water? Wild edibles? When scholars imagine Jesus alone in the wilderness they have a tendency to imagine themselves as civilized humans in the wilderness and so project their own insecurities or else they jump on the 'Jesus was divine' bandwagon and single Jesus out as one with special privilege. Both of these are understandable but incorrect. They fail to take into account Jesus' potential 'shamanistic' (wilderness) background." While some scholars speculate about where Jesus might have been prior to his public ministry, I think that he learned from, possibly Essenes, how to live with the bounty of the earth. So had the Baptist, his mentor.

> On a personal note, for me the only way to do this was to learn a completely new perspective, that of the First World, the aboriginal traditions. Getting outside the perspective of civilization through wilderness survival training has been very beneficial to me. I am grateful to Tom Brown Jr. for sharing his story and the teachings of

Grandfather. See Grandfather (New York; Berkley, 2001). It was Grandfather who helped me understand the relationship between Jesus and God's good creation, including humanity. I would urge everyone to read George E. Tinker Spirit and Resistance (Philadelphia: Fortress, 2004) and heed his admonitions about how to respectfully engage Native American life and thought.

[lxxix] See W.D. Davies The Gospel and the Land: Early Christianity and Jewish Territorial Doctrine (Berkeley: University of California Press, 1974) for an exhaustive survey of this topic.

[lxxx] Kin(g)dom is the expression of the phrase 'kingdom' which feminist biblical scholars have coined to remind us that the kingdom is neither a place nor patriarchal but refers primarily to the quality and kind of relationships we have as children of God. I think that this is a crucial and important insight and so will use it to speak of God's reign.

[lxxxi] Op. cit., 104, "…Make a list of the different names of God and focus on them. God's names are not arbitrary; they tell us about different aspects of his (sic) character. In the Old Testament, God gradually revealed himself to Israel by introducing new names for himself…"

[lxxxii] See the important discussion of theological axioms in Dietrich Ritschl The Logic of Theology (Philadelphia: Fortress, 1986); also Eberhard Jungel God as the Mystery of the World (Grand Rapids: Eerdmans, 1983).

[lxxxiii] (New York: Schocken, 1974), 581-582.

[lxxxiv] G. Kittel in Theological Dictionary of the New Testament (Grand Rapids: Eerdmans, 1964), Vol 1: 213 notes "The distinctive statistical evidence shows that the special use of *akolouthein* is strictly limited to discipleship to Christ; apart from a single reference in Revelation, it is found exclusively in the four Gospels [in this sense]." Parentheses mine. See also Hengel The Charismatic Leader, op. cit., 86, n. 9.

[lxxxv] Some Christians speak of forgiveness without mentioning justice; others emphasize justice and omit talk of forgiveness. The two are inseparable. The separation of forgiveness and justice is but one symptom of the chasm between theology and ethics. The Pauline way of putting this is 'God's Righteousness' (*dikaiosune theou*) which responds to the question: how do you justify a God who freely forgives all and one alike?

[lxxxvi] In his excellent book Beyond Retribution (Grand Rapids: Eerdmans, 2001), 263-275, Christopher Marshall lays out five key components of what forgiveness is and is not. Forgiveness 1) is the response of victims, 2) is something freely given to the perpetrator, 3) is also release for the victim, 4) does not repay in kind and 5) is fulfilled in reconciliation. Forgiveness *is not* 1) weakness, 2) an excusing of wrong, 3) denial, 4) forgetfulness or 5) automatic.

[lxxxvii] Love as forgiveness is the obverse of retaliatory violence. Helmut Merkel argues, "If conduct toward one's fellows is to be so totally determined by love that not only are vindictive acts and thoughts to be eschewed, but even intercession for one's enemy is required, then there can be no justification for Zealot acts of violence against a fellow-man [sic]. All ideals, however great or

sacred they may be, must be subordinated to love for one's neighbor. With this precept Jesus placed himself outside all parties and groups of his time." Bammel and Moule ed., Jesus and the Politics of His Day, op. cit., 144.
[lxxxviii] For the co-ordination of Anselm's Cur Deus Homo? and the Crusade battlefields see Anthony Bartlett, Cross Purposes (Harrisburg: Trinity Press, 2001), 95ff. Bartlett's work is a masterpiece of logic in the deconstruction of the satisfaction theory of the atonement.
[lxxxix] Institutes of the Christian Religion (Philadelphia: Westminster, 1960), 2.XII.4.
[xc] The Promises of God (Grand Rapids: Baker, 2009).
[xci] Tom Wright, Jesus and the Victory of God (Minneapolis: Fortress, 1996), 14: "If the main purpose of Jesus' ministry was to die on the cross, as the outworking of an abstracted atonement-theology, it starts to look as though he simply took on the establishment in order to get himself crucified, so that the abstract sacrificial theology could be put into effect. This makes both ministry and death look like sheer contrivance."
[xcii] Gustaf Dalman Jesus-Jeshua, op. cit., 12, notes that *Boanerges* of Mk. 3:17 "probably goes back to the Aramaic *bene regesh*, 'sons of rage', and does not mean (as it is often understood) 'sons of thunder.'
[xciii] Jesus and His Death: Historiography, the Historical Jesus and Atonement Theory (Waco: Baylor University Press, 2005), 357; also Witherington The Christology of Jesus, op. cit., 255.
[xciv] Covenant of Peace, (Grand Rapids: Eerdmans, 2006), 193.
[xcv] On this see Klaus Wengst, Pax Romana and the Peace of Jesus Christ (Philadelphia: Fortress, 1987).
[xcvi] (Grand Rapids: Eerdmans, 2007), 309.
[xcvii] The consequences of the parables are this worldly. "Parables point not to another, supernatural world but to a new potentiality within this world of ours: to a real possibility of coming to see life and the world, and to experience them, in a way quite different from the one we are accustomed to. Edward Schillebeeckx, Jesus: An Experiment in Christology (New York: Random House, 1979), 157.
[xcviii] The Teaching of Jesus (Cambridge: Cambridge University Press, 1935), 73.
[xcix] James Wm. McClendon Jr., Witness: Systematic Theology Vol. 3 (Nashville: Abingdon, 2000), 60 comes close to my interpretation although he places the emphasis on the preacher as farmer discerning the types of soil/hearers so as to understand success or failure of mission. Nevertheless it is the soils, not the sower that is highlighted in the interpretation. I think we should no longer title this 'The Parable of the Sower' but 'The Parable of the Soils.' Parables are about how and why people accept or reject the message of the kingdom of God.
[c] The Teaching of Jesus, op. cit., 66ff.
[ci] So, e.g., Charles E. Carlston, The Parables of the Triple Tradition (Philadelphia: Fortress, 1975), 3-9. See the discussion in Schwager, Banished from Eden, op. cit., 152, who notes that the text in Mark does not correspond to any known text type (Masoretic, LXX or Targum) and that the "He" of "He

blinded their eyes" cannot refer to God (contrary to some exegetes) but refers to "the fear of other humans, or Satan…as the agent that hardens the heart and [of which] Christ is the healer."

[cii] The end result of a New Testament canon is both a blessing and a bane. The bane consists of Constantinian politics and its influence on accepted books and later, the faulty assumption of the 'No revelation after Ezra' principle. For the former see David L. Dungan Constantine's Bible: Politics and the Making of the New Testament (Minneapolis: Fortress, 2007).

[ciii] Engaging the Powers (Minneapolis: Fortress, 1992), 175-77.

[civ] Hans von Campenhausen, "*Christians and Military Service in the Early Church*," in Tradition and Life in the Church (Philadelphia: Fortress, 1968), 161.

[cv] Lisa Cahill, "*Nonresistance, Defense, Violence, and the Kingdom in Christian Tradition*" Interpretation (October 1984): 382.

[cvi] There is a very important discussion of the role of the merged Church/Empire as the *katechon* ('that which restrains") of II Thess. 2:7 in early Christian thinkers like Hippolytus and Tertullian and down to Hobbes, who secularizes sacrificial Christianity. See Wolfgang Palaver *"Hobbes and the Katechon: The Secularization of Sacrificial Christianity"* Contagion Volume 2 (Spring) 1995.

[cvii] Interestingly, one of the earliest references to being 'post-Constantinian' that I have found is by Massey Shepherd Jr. from an essay written in the mid 1960's! He says "It would be far more accurate, from a historical point of view, to describe the contemporary crisis of Christianity as the emergence of the 'post-Constantinian age'…The broad signs of their dissolution are evident" in "*Before and After Constantine*", The Impact of the Church Upon Its Culture (Chicago: University of Chicago Press, 1968) edited by Jerald C. Brauer. And this was before the death of God movement, feminist theology, liberation theology, the renaissance in Bonhoeffer studies and John Howard Yoder!

[cviii] Robert M Grant Eusebius as Church Historian (Oxford: Clarendon Press, 1980); Glenn F. Chestnut The First Christian Histories (Macon: Mercer University Press, 1986); Timothy Barnes Constantine and Eusebius (Cambridge: Harvard University Press, 1981); G.W. Trompf Early Christian Historiography (London: Equinox, 2000).

[cix] Peter Brown, *Augustine of Hippo* (Berkeley: University of California Press, 1967), 235.

[cx] Ritschl, Memory and Hope, op. cit., 115-121, examines Augustine's theory of election and concludes, "It would be possible to reproduce large parts of Augustine's theology without mentioning Christ at all."

[cxi] Like Ritschl, I critique Augustine not for the great work that he did in his time, but for the way he has been and is being appropriated *as though the foundation laid by Augustine could be traced back to Jesus and Paul.* Concerning Augustine's individualistic anthropology and the piety of the 'blessed vision of God', Ritschl comments "It is high time that this Augustinian creed, despite all its beauty, be replaced today by the humble but nevertheless daring confession that we Christians today have never had such visions of God and we do not desire to have them; we desire a *vision of man because of God not*

a vision of God in spite of man. But such a creed is possible only on the basis of a Christological understanding of the knowledge of God, for Christ 'is the icon of the invisible God' (Col 1:15)", Memory and Hope, op. cit., 129.
[cxii] Augustine of Hippo op. cit., 240. See also Ritschl, Memory and Hope, op. cit., 123, citing Altaner, Patrology (New York: Herder and Herder, 1961) 532: "Augustine paved the way for St. Thomas Aquinas, who attempted to provide the medieval Inquisition with a theological foundation."
[cxiii] Several recent works highlight the importance of this and correct it. Hayim Goren Perelmuter, Siblings: Rabbinic Judaism and Early Christianity at Their Beginnings (New York: Paulist Press, 1989); Tikva Frymer-Kensky et. al., Christianity in Jewish Terms (Boulder: Westview Press, 2000); John Howard Yoder, The Jewish-Christian Schism Revisited (Grand Rapids: Eerdmans, 2003); Adam Becker and Annette Yoshiko Reed, The Ways That Never Parted (Minneapolis: Fortress, 2007); Matt Jackson-McCabe ed., Jewish Christianity Reconsidered (Minneapolis: Fortress, 2007).
[cxiv] Triumphalism depends upon the Deuteronomic hermeneutic that foretells blessings for obedience and curses for disobedience. A debate here in Lancaster, PA, highlights a current manifestation of this line of thinking. Some family owned grocery stores are opening on Sundays in order to keep up with the competition of the large chain stores. Conservative religious folk decry this. In the opinion section of our local paper, the *Intelligencer Journal* (Jan. 5, 2010), one reader writes, "I wish to congratulate Shady Maple for staying closed on Sundays. Our country has been blessed and prospered since many people observe the Sabbath." American prosperity, evidently, has nothing to do with violence and everything to do with keeping one of the Ten Commandments. I suspect Jesus would differ.
[cxv] The most comprehensive documentation on the writing and 'canonization' of the Hebrew Scriptures is Martin Jan Mulder, ed., Mikra (Philadelphia: Fortress, 1988).
[cxvi] Contrary to some, Marcion did not originate a 'canon' of New Testament writings. Martin Hengel has demonstrated that the four canonical Gospels were recognized and antedated Marcion's truncation. The Four Gospels and the One Gospel of Jesus Christ (Harrisburg: Trinity Press International, 2000).
[cxvii] "[The early Christian fathers] chief shortcoming is not in the realm of Christology, but rather in their most unfortunate way of dealing with the Old Testament, i.e., in hermeneutics, where they opened the doors to Stoic concepts, which also negatively influenced Tertullian and through him Western Theology" Dietrich Ritschl, Memory and Hope, op cit., 81.
[cxviii] "*The Biblical Origins and Patristic Development of Typology*" in Essays on Typology (London: SCM, 1957) ed., by G.W.H. Lampe and K.J. Woolcombe, 69.
[cxix] Things Hidden from the Foundation of the World (Stanford: Stanford University Press, 1987), 233.
[cxx] David M. Hay, Glory at the Right Hand: Psalm 110 in Early Christianity (Nashville: Abingdon, 1973), 24.

[cxxi] This is also true in emerging rabbinic Judaism of the second-third centuries in spite of the fact that the Mishnah (compiled c. 200 C.E.) is replete with regulations concerning appropriate priestly activity in the Temple (which no longer existed).
[cxxii] The Hebrew Gospel has not fared well in either New Testament or early church scholarship. But James Edwards has made an interesting case that this Gospel had a significant role to play in the formation of Luke's Gospel. See his The Hebrew Gospel and the Development of the Synoptic Tradition, op. cit.
[cxxiii] Obedience is usually not a category when discussing epistemology. Yet the gospel contains its own epistemology, known through imitation (*akolouthein* or *imitatio*), experienced in doxology. This has always been a problem for Reformation hermeneutics. The Anabaptists were the ones to make the case that discipleship was a radical following of Jesus. Protestantism, following the Reformation was obliged to turn obedience into a moral category since it had been rejected from its epistemology. Mennonite John Howard Yoder was a vigorous exponent of the viewpoint that authentic interpretation of the Bible only occurs in the context of a local Christian community (congregation, house church) who chose to listen carefully to Jesus and implement what they hear. Sadly, Anabaptists lack any connection to the larger liturgical tradition of historic Christianity and are thus compromised doxologically.
[cxxiv] (Grand Rapids: Eerdmans, 1982), viii.
[cxxv] Tom Smail, Like Father, Like Son, op. cit., 78.
[cxxvi] Ritschl has a counter melody to this assertion: "Augustine's theology is the beginning of the Western discovery of the individual personality…and the founding of a Christian anthropology which can only very artificially be brought into harmony with the Old and New Testaments" in Memory and Hope, op. cit. 107.
[cxxvii] *"Rene Girard in Contemporary Philosophy"* in Contagion Volume 10 (Spring) 2003, 99.
[cxxviii] "What Girard suggested that biblical monotheism offered, then, was not simply an 'ethics' or 'morality' – as modern readings of this tradition have been prone to conclude, at least since Kant – but a substantive epistemology, a form of knowledge correlative of one of the deepest (anthropological) senses of what commonly goes under the name 'revelation' – a cognitive insight which offers humanity the possibility of 'redemption' from the violent structures it ceaselessly reiterates", Chris Fleming, Rene Girard: Violence and Mimesis op. cit., 114.
[cxxix] Battling to the End (East Lansing: Michigan State University Press, 2010). Girard says that "The apocalypse has to be taken out of fundamentalist hands" and that "The future of the world is out of our control, and yet it is in our hands" (48-49).
[cxxx] On this question and its impact on the doctrine of God see Regina M. Schwartz, The Curse of Cain: The Violent Legacy of Monotheism (Chicago: University of Chicago Press, 1997).

[cxxxi] Gudmundur Ingi Markusson *"Violent Memes and Suspicious Minds: Girard's Scapegoat Mechanism in the Light of Evolution and Memetics"* in Contagion Volume 11 (Spring) 2004, has a helpful essay that shows how the process of 'natural selection' works in social contexts. A key insight for me was Markusson's correlation of reproducing systems and 'ritualized penalizing.' He says "The (social) system would ensure its reproduction by including instructions for public punishment of victims. Such ritualized processes, in which the members of the group actively participate, would serve to reaffirm the principles and criteria of the system. In a sense, a ritualized penalizing process, along with the instructions for carrying it out, would function as an organism's reproductive system." I have termed this *the sacrificial hermeneutic.*

[cxxxii] http://www.hamertonkelly.com/talks/Theory_of_Religion_and_Violence.html

[cxxxiii] See Gregory Boyd, The Myth of a Christian Nation (Grand Rapids: Zondervan, 2005). Rethinking the triumphal (patriotic) rendering of American history is downright distasteful to many. I understand this. But I believe in the possibility of transformation and still hope for a time when America might be known as truly benevolent. I also believe that we will not find our true selves as Americans unless we repent. A very helpful book in this regard is Jon Pahl, Empire of Sacrifice (New York: New York University Press, 2009). Pahl shows that violence is at the structural heart of what it means to be the American people.

[cxxxiv] Jonathan Sauder sees I John dealing explicitly with this. "The author of 1st John closes his letter with a warning against idolatry. He does not have merely heathen idolatry in mind here. Throughout his preceding arguments it is clear that he is warning against an allegedly Christian theology in which God has a light and a dark side, a theology in which love and lethality are seen as morally compatible. According to this New Testament author, any theology not thoroughly restructured around the earthly Jesus is not about the 'true God' and is thus equivalent to idol-making." "*Must There Be Shunning? Tradition, Mimesis, and Resacralization in Historic Peace Church Orthopraxy*" in Peace Be With You: Christ's Benediction amid Violent Empires edited by Sharon Baker and Michael Hardin, op cit., 288 n45.

[cxxxv] Alister McGrath, A Life of Calvin (Oxford: Blackwell, 1990), 152 (citing the Institutes of the Christian Religion, 1.3.1 and 1.5.1). This is the Christian version of the old Logos-as-sperm theory of Greek Philosophy and Justin Martyr. Calvin says, "There is within the human mind, and indeed by natural instinct, an awareness of divinity. This we take to be beyond controversy." In fact, it is not beyond controversy anymore. It is front and center in the problem of natural theology as well as postfoundationalist thought. Furthermore, the editor of the Institutes, John T. McNeill, notes that Calvin depends upon the Roman orator Cicero for his theory. In all of 1.3.1, there is only one biblical citation, Lev. 26:36. Calvin's doctrine, at this point, has no scriptural backing.

[cxxxvi] I See Satan Fall Like Lightning (Maryknoll: Orbis, 2001) 142-143.

[cxxxvii] See Tony Bartlett, *"The Party's Over (Almost): Terminal Celebration in Contemporary Film"* Contagion Volume 5 (Spring 1998) 1-13.
[cxxxviii] Ibid, 144. Girard refuses to follow Marcion instead seeing the Testamental unity as "real and substantial" in clearing the victim of guilt. Rene Girard, I See Satan op. cit., 123 and 129 where he says, "seeing as 'prophetic' the interrelation of all texts that denounce persecutory illusions is based on a profound intuition of the continuity between the Hebrew Bible and the Gospels."
[cxxxix] In Robert Hamerton-Kelly ed., Violent Origins (Stanford: Stanford University Press, 1987), 141.
[cxl] Ibid, 117.
[cxli] The internal quote is from Rene Girard, I See Satan, op. cit., 28.
[cxlii] Ibid, 106.
[cxliii] "*Rejecting Violent Judgment: Luke 9:52-56 And Its Relatives*" in Journal of Biblical Literature 121 no 3 Fall 2002, 459-478.
[cxliv] Rene Girard, "*The Evangelical Subversion of Myth*" in Politics and Apocalypse (East Lansing: Michigan State University Press, 2007), 36.
[cxlv] Ibid, 116.
[cxlvi] Ibid, 118-119.
[cxlvii] Rene Girard, I See Satan Fall Like Lightning, 130.
[cxlviii] McClendon, Doctrine: Systematic Theology Vol 2 (Nashville: Abingdon, 1994) 240ff also points to the connection between knowing Jesus and interpreting Scripture and the consequent reconstruction of our epistemology in our encounter with the Risen Lord.
[cxlix] The Joy of Being Wrong (New York: Crossroad Publishing, 1998), 67.
[cl] Ibid, 68.
[cli] John Calvin, Institutes of the Christian Religion, op. cit., 35.
[clii] The Joy of Being Wrong, op. cit., 77.
[cliii] Hans Denck, cited by C.J. Dyck in "*Hermeneutics and Discipleship*" in Essays on Biblical Interpretation: Anabaptist-Mennonite Perspectives, ed. Willard Swartley (Elkhart: Institute of Mennonite Studies, 1984), 30. See also Stuart Murray, Biblical Interpretation in the Anabaptist Tradition (Kitchener: Pandora Press, 2000), 186-205, who points out the crucial second half of Denck's statement "and no one can follow him unless he first knows him." I think that this is also true of Kierkegaard's and Bonhoeffer's definition of discipleship.
[cliv] "*The Violence of God and the Hermeneutics of Paul*" in The Work of Jesus Christ in an Anabaptist Perspective (Telford: Cascadia Publishing, 2008), 89.
[clv] The Joy of Being Wrong, op. cit., 79.
[clvi] Ibid, 80.
[clvii] Ibid, 81.
[clviii] Ibid, 83.
[clix] This method of interpretation has strong advocacy in the work Rene Girard, Sandor Goodhart, Paul Ricoeur, John Howard Yoder and Jean-Luc Marion.
[clx] "*Mimetic Theory & Christian Theology in the 21st Century*" in For Rene Girard: Essays in Friendship & Truth (Ann Arbor: University of Michigan Press,

2009), 270-271. The Latin phrase is an allusion to Dietrich Bonhoeffer's letter of July 16, 1944 in Letters and Papers from Prison (New York: Macmillan, 1972), 360.

[clxi] Following contemporary critical theory I will refer to the two writers of Genesis 1-11 as the Priestly and the Yahwist writers.

[clxii] See Jean-Michel Oughourlian The Genesis of Desire (East Lansing: Michigan State University Press, 2010), 43-80 and Paul Duff and Joseph Hallman "*Murder in the Garden? The Envy of the Gods in Genesis 2 and 3*" Contagion Volume 3 (Spring) 1996 for readings of Genesis 2-3 informed by mimetic realism.

[clxiii] See the creative reading of this text by Sandor Goodhart "*The End of Sacrifice: Reading Rene Girard and the Hebrew Bible*" Contagion Volume 14 (Spring) 2007, 59-78.

[clxiv] The Priestly and Yahwist writers' stories are merged into one contiguous narrative. P stands for the Priestly writer and Y for the Yahwist. Genesis 6:9-22 P; *7:1-5 Y*; 7:6 P; *7:7 Y*; 7:8-9 P; *7:10 Y*; 7:11 P; *7:12 Y*; 7:13-21 P; *7:22-23 Y*; 7:24-8:2a P; *8:2b-3a Y*; 8:3b-5 P; *8:6-12 Y*; 8:13a Y; 8:13b-19 P; *8:20-22 Y Conclusion*; 9:1-12 P *Conclusion.*

[clxv] Revelations: Personal Responses to Books of the Bible (Edinburgh: Canongate, 2005), 138, 140.

[clxvi] Walter Brueggemann David's Truth in Israel's Imagination and Memory (Philadelphia: Fortress, 1985).

[clxvii] The Conversion of the Imagination: Paul as Interpreter of Israel's Scripture (Grand Rapids: Eerdmans, 2005), 107.

[clxviii] Robert Hamerton-Kelly notes "The victim surrounded by persecutors is clearly a major category in the Psalms, present in two-thirds of the collection; one hundred out of the one hundred fifty explicitly or implicitly refer to a victim surrounded by enemies" in *"The Mob and the Victim in the Psalms and Job"* Contagion Volume 8 (Spring) 2001, 152.

[clxix] Messianic Exegesis (Philadelphia: Fortress, 1988), 89.

[clxx](Sermon) John Piper, "*Do I Not Hate Those Who Hate You O Lord*" Oct 3, 2000.

[clxxi] Job: The Victim of His People (Stanford: Stanford University Press, 1987), 5.

[clxxii] James G. Williams in his essay on Job astutely says, "I have argued strenuously to save not the text but the Job of the text, the victim who has cried out to God and his friends. This Job now needs defenders, in my estimation. The first obligation of the interpreter who stands in service to the biblical tradition of the disclosure of the innocent victim is not to the text as such but to the victim and to the God of love and justice. As Girard has argued, this obligation is a moral demand requiring a 'transformative reading' which is in effect a deliberate misreading. Faced with certain choices 'one must either do violence to the text or let the text do violence to innocent victims'" in The Bible, Violence and the Sacred (New York: Harper/Collins, 1991), 172 quoting Girard The Scapegoat (Baltimore: Johns Hopkins University Press, 1986), 8.

[clxxiii] Isaiah 40-66. (Interpretation) A Bible Commentary for Teaching and Preaching (Louisville: WJKP, 1995).
[clxxiv] The Isaiah Targum translated and edited by Bruce D. Chilton (Wilmington: Michael Glazier, 1987), 102-105.

[clxxv] Jesus And The Suffering Servant: Isaiah 53 and Christian Origins, (Eugene: Wipf & Stock, 2009) edited by William H. Bellinger and William R. Farmer, 97.
[clxxvi] Jesus the Sage: The Pilgrimage of Wisdom (Minneapolis: Fortress, 1994).
[clxxvii] Jacob Neusner, First Century Judaism in Crisis, op cit., 74 speaks of the various *loci* of authority in first century Judaism. First is the authority of the charismatic sage (or rabbi), like Yohanan ben Zakkai's pupil Hanina ben Dosa (or for that matter Jesus of Nazareth); see also Martin Hengel, The Charismatic Leader and His Followers, (New York: Crossroad, 1981). Second, for Neusner is the sacerdotal authority of the priesthood "by reason of a legitimate place in the [Temple] cult." Finally there was the authority of the sage who could only fall back upon "his teaching and his own embodiment of the burden of his message." David Flusser, The Sage from Galilee shows that Jesus demonstrated aspects of the first and third of Neusner's categories. Little wonder then that the crowds have a hard time also figuring out the source of Jesus' authority (Mark 1:27).
[clxxviii] Jesus the Sage, op. cit., 161.
[clxxix] In Paul Among Jews and Gentiles (Philadelphia: Fortress, 1976) 78-96.
[clxxx] There is also another very important aspect to the story of Paul's conversion in Acts that is easily overlooked according to John Stoner. John points out that Paul was taken as a blind 'captive' (so to speak) to the home of someone who, just yesterday, was perceived as the mortal enemy. What kind of treatment might Paul have expected? The first words out of Ananias mouth are "Brother Saul." With these words kinship is acknowledged, a bond is forged, friendships begun. We should call him Ananias the Peacemaker. Some groups would have just killed Paul and left his carcass to rot in the desert. The Christians were different; they were forgiving!
[clxxxi] Peter J. Tomson Paul and the Jewish Law: Halakah in the Letters of the Apostle to the Gentiles (Minneapolis: Fortress, 1990), 173 (Shammaites killing Hillelites), 175 (anti-Gentile Zealot sentiment).
[clxxxii] The Pre-Christian Paul (London: SCM Press, 1991), 70.
[clxxxiii] Jerome Murphy-O'Connor, Becoming Human Together (Wilmington: Michael Glazier, 1982), 34-35.
[clxxxiv] The commentary on Galatians by J. Louis Martyn, (New York: Doubleday, 1997) is a landmark study on Paul and his understanding of the Law in relation to the event of Jesus Christ.
[clxxxv] Op. cit., 502.
[clxxxvi] Op. cit., 502-512.
[clxxxvii] The Deliverance of God (Grand Rapids: Eerdmans, 2009). This book is a theological *tour de force*. Campbell's reading of Romans and Martyn's reading of Galatians establish a firm foundation for the perspective offered here.

Douglas Harink's Paul among the Postliberals (Grand Rapids: Brazos, 2003) also utilizes a similar reading of Paul.

[clxxxviii] Campbell's reading in not a 'new' thing; it has been present in the church for a long time, back to the early Eastern (Greek) church's reading of Paul. Ritschl notes that the western argument for justification as the heart of Pauline theology is not the only historically viable approach to Paul. "The Eastern tradition has not taken up the Pauline speech of justification, but has, beginning with Irenaeus, interpreted the Pauline epistles in the light of the Spirit passages" in Memory and Hope, op. cit., 98.

[clxxxix] We know that Paul refers to the teaching of the false teachers in Galatians even as he quotes the problems of the Corinthian church from a letter he received. Scholars refer to Paul's use of the literary genre of *diatribe* when they assert that Paul encodes certain opponents in his letters. This simple fact ought to alert us that not everything in Paul's letters represents Pauline thinking.

[cxc] Op. cit., 706, parentheses are mine. Douglas shows that the conventional reading of Paul imports the Teacher's theology back into Paul, thus assimilating Paul to the very so-called gospel he opposed. Thus "we end up with just the theological shortcomings of the Teacher, now writ large in Justification theory and transposed into a slightly more Christian and pagan key. (707)" "It is very important to appreciate that this analysis is consequently not an attack on *the* gospel but an attack on *a version of* the gospel, and *one that I maintain Paul himself would view as false* (934, italics in original)."

[cxci] Richard Hays observes that 2 Cor. 3:13-18 is not about a literal vs. a spiritual reading of the Jewish Scriptures but one that requires an *incarnation* of the reading, that is, the church is the visible community of the text which is interpreted. "According to 2 Cor. 3:7-18, when God's Spirit-inscribed people encounter Scripture, a transformation occurs that is fundamentally hermeneutical in character." Echoes of Scripture in the Letters of Paul (New Haven: Yale, 1989), 131. We will pick up this point further in 7.4.

[cxcii] Michelle Slee makes a strong case that a Torah-less Gospel first came to fruition in the church at Antioch, The Church at Antioch, op. cit. The question that rose from a shared Jewish-Gentile Eucharist was whether Gentiles had to become Jews in order for Jews to eat with them. Did the Jerusalem church bring holiness codes to Antioch? Did they not understand Jesus' critique of these codes? Was James, Jesus' brother behind this misunderstanding? Slee's thesis that the Didache was composed after the Antioch incident could explain why it begins with the great commandment and the mercy code. Paul discusses the Antioch incident in Galatians 2:11-21. And the problem in Galatia? Holiness codes!

[cxciii] The New Perspective on Paul (Grand Rapids: Eerdmans, 2008), 150.

[cxciv] Sacred Violence: Paul's Hermeneutic of the Cross (Minneapolis: Fortress, 1992), 160.

[cxcv] In fact it does otherwise. Altaner, Patrology op. cit., 526 concludes, "From the beginning Augustine's doctrine of grace which is based on a frightening

conception of God has roused opposition within the Church, and subsequently has caused grave errors."

[cxcvi] The Logic of Theology (Philadelphia: Fortress, 1987), 128.

[cxcvii] Ibid, 128-129.

[cxcviii] The Climax of the Covenant (Minneapolis: Fortress, 1992), 261.

[cxcix] Reconciliation: A Study of Paul's Theology (Atlanta: John Knox, 1981), 40.

[cc] As the devil is an anthropological (not a theological) concept so also is 'the wrath' or 'the wrath of God.' At some point in the future I plan to write a study on this. For now I recommend Paul Nuechterlein's comments at www.girardianlectionary.net.

[cci] Sacred Violence, op. cit., 80. See also the (virtually) exhaustive exegesis on this passage by Campbell, op. cit., 601-714.

[ccii] One of the debits of the work of Rita Nakashima Brock and Rebecca Ann Parker, Saving Paradise (New York: Beacon, 2009) is their narrow focus on the cross as a sacrificial event. One is reminded of Wilhelm Bousset's interpretation of early Christian worship. Mark Heim has shown that atonement images in the early church can be found and they relate not to the resurrected Christ on the cross, but to Christ as the scapegoat. Using the carvings on the Brescia casket (circa 350 C.E.). Heim points out that the structure of the narratives on the casket (Jonah, Susanna and Daniel) is related to the structure of the passion narrative. Girard's reading of the atonement is given credence from this bit of archeology. See Heim *"Missing the Cross? Types of the Passion in Early Christian Art"* Contagion Volume 13 (Spring) 2006, 193 who says "The artist of the Brescia casket used a vocabulary of figures that placed the passion narrative in the context of God's action to overcome sacred violence. Christ is all three of the types – subject to false accusation and yet vindicated by God."

[cciii] Some argue that in Paul's day pagan temple prostitutes wore their hair flowing down and uncovered which was a sign of the position and availability of 'cultic sex.' There seems to be little evidence that this was a problem in Corinth and the actual evidence of such a context for I Cor. 11 is disputed. Others see the head covering having to do with the role of the sacrificer (whose head was covered) in ritual practice. Either way I Cor. 11 is a conundrum difficult to interpret.

[cciv] However, lest one think that by this statement I am invalidating the Torah, let me say that I think that Girard I See Satan, op. cit. 7-18, has admirably demonstrated the incredible wisdom of the Ten Commandments, particularly their insight into the problem of rivalrous desire. The Ten Commandments are a key point of enlightenment in our religious development as a species. And they are far more than just legal code.

[ccv] Naming the Powers (1984), Unmasking the Powers (1986), Engaging the Powers (1992), When the Powers Fall (1998) all published by Fortress Press and Cracking the Gnostic Code: The Powers in Gnosticism (Atlanta: Scholar's Press, 1993), and The Powers That Be (New York: Doubleday, 1999). See also an engagement of this series in Transforming the Powers: Peace, Justice and the Domination System edited by Ray Gingerich and Ted Grimsrud (Minneapolis:

Fortress, 2006). The satanic solution, the solution of the Powers, is to use violence to stop violence. In this regard Simon Taylor judiciously observes "The methods of satanic salvation cannot bring salvation from that salvation. Jesus' victory over Satan consists not of expelling Satan but in being expelled by Satan, executed on the cross. In this expulsion, the murderous lie on which satanic salvation rests is exposed. Satan wins the battle, and yet in winning loses as the murderous secret is exposed to the public gaze" in "*Save Us From Being Saved: Girard's Critical Soteriology*" Contagion Volume 12 (Spring), 2006, 26.

[ccvi] Any discussion of the Powers must mention the work of Jacques Ellul, who was Professor of Law at Bordeaux, a contemporary of Wink. Ellul's theological exegesis of Scripture is a corollary of his sociological approach to culture. His descriptions of technological society on the one hand, and theological/biblical critique of them correspond to the dual reality of Wink's Powers. Like Wink, Ellul argued in his early work that institutionalization was a part of the created order. To be sure, like Barth, these concepts come under 'the Lordship of Christ' rather than a doctrine of creation. For Ellul biblical law has three exclusive aspects: institution, human rights and justice. Yet he observes, "In spite of all research, in most cases it is not possible to determine the exact beginning in time and the rational origin of an institution" The Theological Foundation of Law (New York: Seabury, 1960) 76. The former may never be and probably will never be known, it exists as a mythological incident(s); but Girard has in fact given us a rational understanding of the rise of institutions as a result of ritualized successful victimage. If this is so, then there is no need to fallback upon any 'orders of creation' theory. On Ellul see "*Violence, Anarchy and Scripture: Jacques Ellul and René Girard*" by Matthew Pattillo Contagion Volume 11, (Spring) 2004.

[ccvii] Karl Barth, Church Dogmatics IV/1 (London: T&T Clark: 1956), 253-254.

[ccviii] Images of the Church in the New Testament (Philadelphia: Westminster, 1960).

[ccix] Walter Wink and I had a long conversation about this statement. My point was that followers of Jesus address the 'theological/spiritual' side of the Powers. Why? Institutions depend on victimage; what happens to structural powers oriented to sacrifice and victimage when deprived of that mechanism? The closest Jesus comes to public protest is the social, because public, prophetic action in the Temple, but it was just that and not an organized movement. That would have been seen as seditious and started a riot and called down the Roman garrison from Fortress Antonia (cf. Luke 13: 1ff). I see Ched Myer's point in Binding the Strong Man (New York: Orbis, 1990) that Jesus' occupation of the Temple might be called a 'nonviolent civil action' but even that phrase connotes organization that was not present *that* day. Contemporary protest movements, on the other hand, can be highly organized. I do not think Jesus was leading anyone to do anything *that* day; rather he was enacting a parable.

[ccx] Mysticism is a crucial aspect of religious experience. See the excellent Brazos Introduction to Christian Spirituality (Grand Rapids: Brazos, 2008) by Evan B. Howard. Some readers who have a theological paradigm that is

'objectively' oriented, e.g., those who insist on a forensic doctrine of justification by faith should note that neither Luther nor Calvin eschews a 'mystical' aspect to the Christian life. For Luther see Bengt Hoffmann, Luther and the Mystics (Minneapolis: Augsburg, 1976) and for Calvin see Lucien Joseph Richard, The Spirituality of John Calvin (Atlanta: John Knox, 1974). Hoffmann astutely observes "to keep in touch with the times many theological systematizers have adopted verifiability codes from scientific materialism. They fail to bring the gospel's mystical and supernatural components into their theological purview." Fortunately this is not true of all Christian theology.

[ccxi] The Son of Man in Myth and History (Philadelphia: Fortress, 1967).

[ccxii] Sacred Violence, op. cit., 85.

[ccxiii] The "fact of the divine self-emptying is paradigmatic." Ibid, 176.

[ccxiv] I have always been interested in the positive dynamics of imitation, particularly when applied to Jesus as a model. One of my earliest published essays looks at Maximus Confessor in the light of both negative and positive mimesis, "*Mimesis and Dominion: The Dynamics of Violence and the Imitation of Christ in Maximus Confessor*" St. Vladimir's Theological Quarterly Volume 36, No. 4, 1992. Reprinted with permission at http://preachingpeace.org/documents/Mimesis_and_Dominion_Essay.pdf.

[ccxv] "*Girard's Christology*" at http://preachingpeace.org/documents/Girard_Christology.pdf, page 23.

[ccxvi] The Climax of the Covenant (Minneapolis: Fortress, 1992), 97.

[ccxvii] This is the translation of Robert Hamerton-Kelly (unpublished paper).

[ccxviii] Zoroaster was a Persian reformer of religion who lived sometime in the 10th-8th centuries B.C.E. The best introduction to dualism in religion is Yuri Stoyanov The Other God: Dualist Religion from Antiquity to the Cathar Heresy (New Haven: Yale University Press, 2000).

[ccxix] Things Hidden from the Foundation of the World (Stanford: Stanford University Press, 1987), 271.

[ccxx] The Gospel according to John (Garden City: Doubleday and Co., 1966), 520ff.

[ccxxi] Sifre Deut. 37, cited in G.F. Moore, Judaism Vol. 1 (New York: Schocken, 1971), 266.

[ccxxii] Op. cit., 524.

[ccxxiii] Margaret Barker, Temple Theology (London: SPCK, 2004) makes some interesting connections between the Priestly creation narrative, Ezekiel's chariot and the architectural structure of the Jerusalem Temple in this regard.

[ccxxiv] The Interpretation of the Fourth Gospel (Cambridge: Cambridge University Press, 1960), 85.

[ccxxv] This story is textually questionable nevertheless I suspect it is authentic to the Jesus tradition.

[ccxxvi] Girard has an intriguing comment on the *Logos*, Hegel, Heidegger and the unity of the biblical Testaments, Battling to the End, op. cit., 49: "I am especially surprised that Hegel did not see the special relationship that both unites and separates what Christians call the two Testaments. It is essential to

think about. By seeing 'order' and 'commandment' in the Johannine *Logos*, Heidegger joined a tradition of modern thought that dated back to Hegel. Hegel turned the God of the Law into the God who crushes, the God of imperious domination. To do so is to misunderstand the Bible, and that misunderstanding is rooted in the inability of Christians themselves to see that the two Testaments are one, an inability whose roots are too often ascribed to St. Paul's teaching." Because they are one, any theory of the relationship that was supercessionist would be false, *and such are the inspiration theories of much Protestantism.*

[ccxxvii] Philip Lee, Against the Protestant Gnostics (New York: Oxford University Press, 1987) has demonstrated that American Christianity, both conservative and liberal is fundamentally Gnostic. His is an important work that has not received the attention it deserves. Dietrich Ritschl also notes the docetic tendency of modern theology, Memory and Hope, op. cit., 97.

[ccxxviii] Taken from the text of President Obama's Nobel Prize Speech. On January 28, 2010, he was in Tampa addressing the crowds after his first State of the Union Address the previous evening. He reiterated that he told them two weeks before the 2009 election that "change doesn't come without a fight." This is the greatest evidence that he has capitulated not to Jesus but to the Christ of sacrificial liberal American Christianity. Here one can really see the influence of Niebuhr on Obama.

[ccxxix] See N.T. Wright, The Resurrection of the Son of God (Minneapolis: Fortress, 2003) for a virtually exhaustive justification of this claim.

[ccxxx] Gallese is one of the key researchers into mirror neurons. He is Full Professor of Human Physiology at the University of Parma (Italy). A number of his important essays can be found at www.unipr.it/arpa/mirror/english/staff/gallese.htm. See also Marco Iacoboni Mirroring People (New York: Farrar, Strauss, Giroux, 2008); Scott Garrels "*Imitation, Mirror Neurons, and Mimetic Desire*" Contagion Volume 12 Spring 2006.

[ccxxxi] The story of the Gerasene demoniac in Mark 5:1-20 is a classic story of the scapegoat of a community, who, possessed by the spirit of fear accepts the community's judgment and thus also scapegoats himself ("Night and day among the tombs and in the hills he would cry out and cut himself with stones"). Rene Girard brings profound insight to this text in The Scapegoat (Baltimore: Johns Hopkins University Press, 1986), 165-183. The demoniac is possessed by 'Legion', a sure sign he has internalized the multiple unanimous voices of the community that had marginalized him (and perhaps even 'politicized' him; note the use of the Roman military designation 'Legion').

[ccxxxii] Those wishing to explore this further should consult the four-volume work by Jeffrey Burton Russell, The Devil (1977), Satan (1981), Lucifer (1984) and Mephistopheles (1986) as well as a summary of these books in The Prince of Darkness (1988) all published by Cornell University Press. Four other helpful books are Henry Ansgar Kelly, Satan: A Biography (New York: Cambridge University Press, 2006); Elaine Pagels, The Origin of Satan (New York: Random House, 1995); T.J. Wray and Gregory Mobley, The Birth of Satan

(New York: Palgrave Macmillan, 2005) and Gerald Messadie, A History of the Devil (New York: Kodansha International, 1996). Alan E. Bernstein The Formation of Hell: Death and Retribution in the Ancient and Early Christian Worlds (Ithaca: Cornell University Press, 1993) contains helpful information. Raymund Schwager interprets the devil anthropologically but in ways congruent with Wink's and Ellul's analysis of structural sin in Banished from Eden, op. cit., 143-165.

[ccxxxiii] Note that the NIV has "evil desire." The Greek text does not have the word 'evil.'

[ccxxxiv] Gary M. Burge, The Anointed Community: The Holy Spirit in the Johannine Tradition (Grand Rapids: Eerdmans, 1987), 13ff.

[ccxxxv] Ibid, 41.

[ccxxxvi] Mishnah Sukkah 4.9: 'The Water Libation, seven days' – what was the manner of this? They used to fill a golden flagon holding 3 logs (*about one and a half pints*) with water from Siloam. When they reached the Water Gate they blew (on the *shofar*) a sustained, a quavering, and another sustained blast. (The priest whose turn it was) went up the Altar-Ramp and turned to the right where there were two silver bowls. R. Judah says, "They were of plaster, but their appearance was darkened because of the wine. They had each a hole like to a narrow snout, one wide and the other narrow, so that both bowls emptied themselves together. The bowl to the west was for water and that to the east was for wine. But if the flagon of water was emptied into the bowl for wine, or the flagon of wine into the bowl for water, that sufficed.' R. Judah says, 'with one log they could perform the libations throughout eight days. To the priest who performed the libation they used to say, 'Lift up your hand!' for once a certain one poured the libation over his feet, and all the people threw their citrons at him.'" Commenting on the Mishnah, Tosephta Sukkah 3:16 says:

A. At what time do they pour the water libation?
B. Along with the offering up of the limbs of the whole daily offering.
C. For there was already the case of the Boethusian who poured out the water on his feet, and all the people stoned him with their lemons.
D. And the horn of the altar was damaged, so the sacred service was cancelled for that day, until they brought a lump of salt and put it on it, so that the altar should not appear to be damaged.

This story is recorded in Josephus Antiquities XIII.5 "As to Alexander (Jannaeus, 103-76 B.C.E.), his own people were seditious against him; for at a festival which was then celebrated, when he stood upon the altar, and was going to sacrifice, the nation rose against him and pelted him with their citrons (which the law required), that at the feast of tabernacles every one should have branches of palm tree and citron tree. They also reviled him, as derived from a captive, and so unworthy of his dignity and of sacrificing. At this he was in a rage and slew about 6,000. He also built a partition wall of wood round the altar and the temple, as far as that partition within which it was only lawful for the priests to enter; and by this means he obstructed the multitude from coming at him." In the Babylonian Talmud (bSukkah 48b) the story is told of a Sadducee who, on the Feast of Tabernacles, once poured the customary libation of water, not on the altar, but on his feet, whereupon the people pelted him with lemons.

[ccxxxvii] This phenomenon of telling a story twice is known as a doublet. It may look like two different stories, but is the same story told two different ways. Torah is full of doublets. Doublets also occur throughout the Jewish Scriptures and even in the Gospels (e.g., the feeding of the 5,000 and the feeding of the 4,000).

[ccxxxviii] Exodus Rabbah 122a.

[ccxxxix] Jesus' death/resurrection is misunderstood at least eight times in the Fourth Gospel and is a major theme: 2:19-21, 6:51-53, 7:33-36, 8:21-22, 12:32-34, 13:36-38, 14:4-6, 16:16-19. This was not only a problem for first century Christians but is also twenty-first century Christians as well. The hermeneutic of the Johannine 'double-words' is meant to help us read the text on two levels. For the Johannine community, these double words are indicators of a greater dialectic; the *kosmos* structured on the violent *Logos*, and the revelation of God within that *kosmos* with a *Logos* of his own, the non-retributive Jesus Christ.

[ccxl] Sometimes the Gospels use the Greek term *dei* ("it is necessary or inevitable") when referring to Jesus' death. Those who affirm a view of punitive atonement consider the inevitability to lie with God as though God desired Jesus' death or needed it to appease the divine wrath. I would contend that the inevitability lies with our human propensity to extrude victims. This choice is not an exegetical decision but one made by an *a priori* assumption of the relationship between violence/sacrifice and the sacred/God.

[ccxli] From the song "*Holy Lamb*", written by Jon Anderson, performed by Yes (from *Big Generator*).